CHINESE THEORIES OF FICTION

SUNY series in Chinese Philosophy and Culture

____

Roger T. Ames, *editor*

CHINESE THEORIES OF FICTION

A Non Western Narrative System

Ming Dong Gu

STATE UNIVERSITY OF NEW YORK PRESS

Published by
STATE UNIVERSITY OF NEW YORK PRESS
ALBANY

© 2006 State University of New York

For information, address
State University of New York Press
194 Washington Avenue, Suite 305, Albany, NY 12210-2384

Production by Diane Ganeles
Marketing by Anne M. Valentine

Library of Congress Cataloging-in-Publication Data

Gu, Ming Dong, 1955–
    Chinese theories of fiction : a non-Western narrative system / Ming Dong Gu.
      p. cm. — (SUNY series in Chinese philosophy and culture)
    Includes bibliographical references and index.
    ISBN 0-7914-6815-1 (alk. paper) ISBN 0-7914-6816-X (pbk. : alk. paper)
    1. Chinese fiction—History and criticism. I. Title. II. Series.
    PL2415.G84 2006
    895.1'3009—dc22
                                           2005025463

10   9   8   7   6   5   4   3   2   1

To the memory of

my mother, Xu Hongzuo (1931–2000)

and

my father, Gu Shirong (1929–2000)

Contents

Preface

This book grows out of my long-term interest in Chinese and Western fiction and international fiction theory. It is a companion volume to my book *Chinese Theories of Reading and Writing* (2005). Like the other book, it represents my efforts to explore the conditions of Chinese literature, systematize Chinese literary theory, and bridge a series of gaps between ancient and modern Chinese literature, Chinese and Western literatures, and traditional and postmodern approaches to literary studies. Trained in both traditional and postmodern scholarship, I have always wanted to play the role of a mediator between different paradigms, approaches, and methodologies, but I have never underestimated the difficulties involved in mediation. Frank Kermode, an internationally renowned mediator between new and old ways of doing literature, humorously remarked twenty years ago that when there is a war on, "he who ventures into no-man's-land brandishing cigarettes and singing carols must expect to be shot at."[1] If one of the world's best critics admits his inadequacy as a mediator, I feel even more strongly my incompetence in initiating cross-cultural dialogues and negotiating ideal approaches to literary studies. What is fortunate for me is that now the dust of the "theoretical turn" has settled and academia is more receptive than ever before to new and innovative theories and approaches to literature.

As the manuscript goes to print, there are a few concerns that I wish to address briefly, having received feedback from some readers. First, as this book critiques and challenges some of the commonly accepted views on Chinese fiction, it may seem slightly polemic and even controversial at times. My critique, however, is conducted in the original sense of the word: to subject an idea to critical analysis that purports to reveal its strengths and limitations, and to consign it to a conceptual revision so as to endow it with more explanatory power. Thus, it should not be misunderstood as a rejection of the challenged views but should be taken as a reconsideration and reconception of them. At places where controversy may arise, I request the reader to judge the validity and value of an argument by considering whether it is a rational proposal based on reasoned analysis. Second, since this is a book on Chinese theories of fiction, it is necessarily conceptual and theoretical. At places, it may seem too abstract and metaphysical for readers who are interested in practical criticism only. I would like to explain why I think metaphysical abstraction is necessary. One central concern of this book is to internationalize Chinese fiction and fiction theory, and I think a most effective way to do that is to initiate meaningful dialogues between Chinese and Western traditions on the conceptual level. Comparison of individual works is surely a good way to start dialogues, but in my opinion it is like connecting two gigantic trees by the branches and twigs, not by the trunks and roots. I also believe metaphysical inquiries are the necessary basis for revealing the intrinsic nature of fiction in general and Chinese fiction in particular and for formulating new and innovative approaches to practical criticism. Third, as one of the objectives is to examine the general condition of Chinese fiction, this book cannot avoid traversing familiar grounds covered by previous scholarship. At such places, I request the reader not to focus on the familiar materials but to pay attention to how the familiar grounds are recrossed and what new insights the reexamination has yielded into the nature of Chinese fiction.

The publication of a book is not only a time to rejoice but also an occasion to acknowledge indebtedness. My study is built on the existent scholarship of fiction studies, both in Chinese and English. I have therefore owed an enormous intellectual debt to numerous scholars in the field of Chinese and world fiction, of whom I know only through their scholarship. Initially, I wanted to acknowledge my full indebtedness by preparing a long bibliography and full citations. Unfortunately, the need to save space forced me to cut citations to the minimum and to prepare a much shorter selected bibliography with works cited in this book only. To make up for this loss, I would like to avail myself of this opportunity to thank all scholars whose scholarship has influenced my study but is not cited in this book. My indebtedness to scholars whom I know personally goes to several quarters. First of all, I am indebted to my teachers and classmates at the University of Chicago, a bastion of literary and cultural studies, and a stronghold for Chinese fiction studies, where my knowledge of fiction was broadened, deepened, and systematized. Thanks are due to Professors Anthony C. Yu and W. J. T. Mitchell for their theoretical guidance on critical approaches to Chinese fiction in particular and world fiction in general, and to Professors David T. Roy, Edward Shaughnessy, Judith Zeitlin, and Xiaobing Tang, whose expertise in traditional and modern Chinese literature and culture considerably facilitated my study of Chinese fiction. Outside of Chicago, I owe my thanks to Professors William Nienhauser of the University of Wisconsin-Madison, Robert Hegel of Washington University at St. Lewis, Dore Levy of Brown University, Kang-i Sun Chang of Yale University, Chung-ying Chen of the University of Hawaii, David Rolston at the University of Michigan, Michael Puett at Harvard University, and Liangyan Ge of Notre Dame University, with whom I have frequently discussed ideas and issues concerning the study of Chinese literature over the past ten years. Working in the southern part of America where there is no East Asian library, I received generous assistance in locating research materials from Mr. Yiwen Li at the University of Chicago library, Professors Michael Puett at Harvard University, Chen Zhi at Hong Kong Baptist University, and Feng Li at Columbia University. I wish to take this opportunity to thank them for their indispensable assistance.

Several scholars have read different parts of my manuscript. Professor David Roy read early versions of chapters 1, 2, 3, 5, and 6; Professor Edward Shaughnessy read early versions of chapters 5 and 6; and Professors Anthony Yu and Liangyan Ge nearly read the whole manuscript. I am grateful to each of them for their criticism and suggestions for improvement. Some ideas in chapter 6 were first presented at a panel, "Redology beyond the Fin-de-siècle" that I organized for the Association for Asian Studies Annual Conference at Boston in 1999. I thank the panel members—Professors Robert Hegel of Washington University, Tina Lu of the University of Pennsylvania, Liangyan Ge of Notre Dame University, Dore Levy of Brown University, and Anthony Yu of the University of Chicago—for their comments. A slightly different version of chapter 5 was published in *Journal of Asian Studies* 63, no. 2 (2004): 333–56; some ideas in chapter 6 were presented in an article published in *Monumenta Serica: A Journal of Oriental Studies* 51 (2003): 253–82; and a short version of chapter 7 with ideas from the introduction and conclusion will appear as an article in *Narrative* 14 (2006). The Association for Asian Studies' and the journal editors' permission to use the respective published articles and ideas is hereby gratefully acknowledged.

In the long reviewing and revising process, I am very grateful to a reader who recognized the value of my manuscript and made a favorable recommendation. My final manuscript benefited a great deal from his or her discerning critiques and useful comments. I should also thank another reader, who, for reasons unknown to me, totally misread my manuscript but whose misrepresentation made me rethink some issues from the perspective of readers having a predilection for historical scholarship but little interest in or knowledge of conceptual inquiry into literature. I am most grateful to a third reader whose sagacity and expertise corrected the misrepresentation of the second reader and decided the acceptance of my manuscript. I also wish to thank Ms. Nancy Ellegate, the editor of the press, who showed as much interest and vision as she did with my first book and made the cooperation between author and editor an enjoyable and edifying experience. Finally, I want to thank my colleagues at Rhodes College—Professors Brian Shaffer, Valerie Nollan, Katheryn Wright, and Michael Leslie—for their encouragement and willingness to answer my scholarly queries; my wife, Ping Lu, who has always supported my intellectual pursuits and made no complaints while I worked on the book during weekends and holidays; and my son, Weining W. Gu, whose expertise in computing facilitated my word processing and manuscript production.

All translations not otherwise attributed are my own.

Ming Dong Gu
Wancheng Studio

ABSTRACT

Chinese Theories of Fiction:
A Non-Western Narrative System

Chinese tradition has a large amount of theoretical data on fiction. Fiction studies, however, are conducted on Western theories and tend to measure the achievements of Chinese fiction by the Western yardstick. Moreover, they are largely confined to historical scholarship or practical criticism and cherish little interest in conceptual inquiries into fiction. As a result, there has been so far no Chinese system of fiction theory that treats Chinese fiction on its own terms. This study attempts to fill that vacuum. Through an inquiry into the macrocosm of Chinese fiction, the art of some formative works, and theoretical data in fiction commentaries and intellectual thought, it examines the conceptual as well as historical conditions of *xiaoshuo* and explores its rise, origin, nature, function, definition, and relations to other literary genres, as well as theoretical issues like imitation, realism, historicity, fictionality, pure fiction, and fictional art. By describing how Chinese *xiaoshuo* evolved from its dependence on history and philosophy to the full-length novel in the local context of Chinese history and thought, and against the larger background of world fiction and general fiction theory, it argues that Chinese fiction does not follow the same route of development as its Western counterpart. Throughout its evolution, it came under the heavy influence of Chinese worldview and displays a fascinating mixture of diverse narrative modes, some of which did not appear in the West until modern times. Challenging the universality of realistic origin, this study argues a lyrical and psychological rise of fiction in China and uncovers a process of poeticization. It locates a creative drive in Chinese *xiaoshuo* toward pure fiction and an aesthetic turn that transforms storytelling into fictional art. It also identifies artistic features that have anticipated surrealism, magic realism, modernism, and postmodernism, and explains the reasons for their rise. It concludes that the Chinese system, while sharing some basic theoretical concerns with the

Western system, differs from its counterpart in conception, modes of representation, and ways of interpretation. As a whole, it constructs a Chinese theory of fiction that addresses the genesis, ontology, epistemology, conceptual vision, writing model, formal techniques, and hermeneutic practice of Chinese fiction in the international context of fiction studies.

Theory of Fiction:
A Chinese Perspective

INTERNATIONALIZATION OF CHINESE FICTION

Fiction is a slippery term that people have taken for granted for centuries across cultures. This is so not just for ordinary readers but also for fiction scholars. Terry Eagleton astutely observes that scholars may have been studying prose fiction for years, but "they never seem to have paused to ask themselves what prose fiction actually is. It would be like caring for an animal for years without having a clue whether it is a badger, a rabbit or a deformed mongoose."[1] But one thing is certain: fiction is a transcultural phenomenon. As a literary category, fiction evolved from storytelling in high antiquity. Since we know of no culture that has not a narrative tradition of stories, it is reasonable to hold as true such a claim as: "Nothing seems more natural and universal to human beings than telling stories."[2] Being universal, fiction as a form of narrative is transcultural and international. As Roland Barthes puts it, "Caring nothing for the division between good and bad literature, narrative is international, transhistorical, transcultural: it is simply there, like life itself."[3] When people in high antiquity began to discuss the nature and forms of fiction and make judgments about ways of telling stories, fiction criticism and theory came into being. If fiction as a verbal art is transcultural, do fictions from different cultures have similar origins, follow similar patterns of historical development, employ similar narrative modes and techniques, and display similar characteristic features? In fiction criticism and theory, do people from different cultural traditions share similar notions about fiction's genesis, nature, function, and ontological condition, and hold similar assumptions and attitudes in their reading and writing of fiction?

These are the major concerns of this book. My study, however, is not a general inquiry into these concerns through a conceptual study of data collected from different literary traditions. It is a comparative study of fiction theory using analytic and critical data from the Chinese tradition in the general context of international fiction studies. I have chosen this subject of inquiry and adopted this approach for a number of reasons. First, despite the fact that Chinese fiction is currently a hot subject for scholars of Chinese and comparative literature and there have been numerous studies of it, studies of fiction theory are almost nonexistent. There are, of course, some excellent studies of the art and narrative theory of Chinese fiction (*xiaoshuo*) in Chinese and English.[4] But their subject of inquiry is confined to methodologies of reading or "narrative" (*xushi*) defined in the broadest sense, which covers all discursive materials and does not focus on "fiction" as a literary and aesthetic category. Moreover, they are, with the exception of Andrew Plaks's seminal essays,[5] historically oriented and not conceptually concerned with the ontological and epistemological conditions of fiction. Second, except for haphazard remarks and random comparisons, there has been, so far, no book-length study in English that attempts to study Chinese fiction theory from the comparative perspective. Third, there is so far not a single book-length study in English that has as its objective the construction of a Chinese system of fiction theory in the larger context of the internationalization of fiction. A similar situation exists in China. There are numerous histories of Chinese fiction and even a few studies of fiction theory and fiction aesthetics, but there is not a single study that aims at formulating a Chinese system of fiction theory.[6]

Last but not least, I am concerned with two tendencies in the field of Chinese fiction studies. One emphasizes the unique nature of traditional Chinese fiction and considers fiction theory arising therefrom as something that must be evaluated using Chinese standards. The other, using Western fiction theory as the yardstick, implicitly views characteristic features of Chinese fiction as anomalies or even limitations. Ostensibly, the two tendencies differ, but in essence they share a commonality: both imply that Chinese fiction and its theory are difficult, if not impossible, to internationalize. I admit that Chinese fiction and fiction theory do possess some idiosyncratic features not found in Western fiction. For example, contrary to the Western view of fiction as arising from epic and romance, traditional Chinese fiction theory considered fiction as having evolved from street talk and popular gossip. In fictional practice, traditional Chinese fiction displays these interesting features: fiction commentaries may be printed alongside fictional works; a narrator may intrude into his fictional work as he pleases; author, narrator, commentator, and reader may all appear in the same fictional work; the narrator may declare a patently untrue account as relating true events that have happened in life or history; realistic tales may be structured in mythical or supernatural frameworks; in largely realistic stories and novels, gods and fairies, ghosts and demons, fox spirits and animal spirits, may become true-to-life characters who participate in the affairs of the human world; in generic forms, a prose narrative may be intermingled with storytelling, lyric poems, and dramatic songs; in narrative focus, an insistence on total vision and faithful recording of dialogues and events may tend to give rise to the rhetorical foregrounding of conflicting points of view; an extended fictional work may be organized on an episodic structure that sometimes shows no obvious connection between episodes; and the narrative language may range from the most literary and archaic classicism to the most vulgar vernacular of the illiterate.

By the standards of Western fiction theory predicated on mimesis and realism, most of these idiosyncrasies seem to be shortcomings or limitations. We may recall how one Western scholar, who measured the achievement of Chinese fiction by the yardstick of Western realist fiction, came to the hasty conclusion that Chinese fiction has an "undefinable inadequacy" and is "vaguely wanting."[7] What is interesting is that on the same narrative issue, a Chinese scholar and a Western scholar may come to entirely opposite opinions, with the expected outcome that while the Chinese scholar's opinion is positive, the Western scholar's opinion is negative. An interesting example concerns the organizational structure of the Chinese novel the *Shuihu zhuan* (the Water Margin). Zheng Zhenduo, an authority on Chinese literature in China who wrote a carefully researched textual study on the novel's evolution, comes to the conclusion that its structural organization is so close-knit that it deserves the word of praise "water-tight."[8] By contrast, Richard Irwin, a Western scholar who wrote perhaps the earliest thorough study of the novel in the West, said that it suffers "from . . . structural weakness," evinces "uneven narrative quality," and is "merely a collection of tales."[9] These judgments were prejudiced, and a few discerning scholars of Chinese literature voiced their disagreement. Regarding the Western reader's expected response to the differences of Chinese fiction, Cyril Birch sensitively points out, "Before we label these characteristics limitations we have the obligation to investigate the laws proper to the Chinese work itself, and these are laws that cannot be imposed from an alien tradition."[10] Nowadays, no scholar would make a judgment like Irwin's, but the view of the idiosyncrasies as limitations has not been adequately repudiated. Moreover, due to the lack of a systematic study of the laws of Chinese fiction, few scholars have realized that those idiosyncrasies are not symptoms of narrative weakness but signs of fictional artistry.

I argue that because Chinese fiction was produced in a tradition very different from that of the West, it has, in the process of development, formed a system of fictional practice and theory that cannot be adequately accounted for by the realistic tradition. I further contend that those idiosyncrasies are by no means shortcomings or limitations. They are characteristic features that grew out of the philosophical, social, cultural, and aesthetic conditions of a tradition and constitute contributions made by Chinese fiction to the general art of fiction. As I will demonstrate in this book, most of them are narrative ploys deliberately designed to advance the art of fiction, and some anticipate modern, modernist, and even postmodern techniques of fiction writing. But before we may come to a full realization of all these, the study of Chinese theories of fiction must internalize itself in theoretical and methodological orientations and be conducted from a comparative perspective employing a universal yardstick of human creativity. Only then will the study of Chinese fiction reveal fascinating insights into fiction as a transcultural phenomenon and converge with the international mainstream of fiction studies.

A CRITIQUE OF REALISM

Two phenomena have exerted a lasting impact, both positive and negative, on the study of Chinese prose fiction. One is the dominance of realism imported from the West. The realistic dominance has been so strong in Chinese fiction criticism that we may call it the "tyranny of realism." In discussing Chinese fictional works, realism and its variations—critical realism and naturalism—are undoubtedly the most frequently used concepts to describe Chinese fictional works, often to the complete neglect of a large number of Chinese prose fictional works, including short stories, novellas, or novels, that are composed with patently nonrealistic elements, supernatural motifs, fantastic details, and mythical narrative frames. Generally speaking, not many masterpieces of Chinese prose fiction were composed in strictly realistic modes, as defined by European realistic fiction. This is especially true in the field of the Chinese novel. Among the six commonly acknowledged masterpieces—the *Sanguo yanyi* (Romance of the Three Kingdoms), *Xiyouji* (Journey to the West), *Shuihu zhuan* (Water Margin), *Jin Ping Mei* (The Plum in the Golden Vase), *Rulin waishi* (The Scholars), and *Hongloumeng* (A Dream of Red Mansions), only the *Rulin waishi* can rightfully be viewed as an extended prose fiction written in a critically realistic mode and free from elements of supernaturalism, magic realism, and the fantastic.

The dominance of realism is symptomatic of the dominance of Western fictional theory in Chinese fiction criticism. The basic theoretical underpinning of realism is the archconcept of mimesis. Although I strongly believe that theory of mimesis exists in the Chinese tradition, and have gone to considerable length to construct a mimetic theory in Chinese literary thought, I do not think mimesis in China ever evolved into a major principle of fiction writing or was embraced as enthusiastically as in the West.[11] Even in the West today, some recent books on fiction theory have challenged the commonly accepted view that imitation of life is the ontology of fiction. Lubomir Dolezel and Dorrit Cohn, for example, both argue against the reduction of fiction to imitation by showing the inability of mimetic conception to explain situations involving fictional characters and their inner worlds. While both authors agree that fiction cannot be entirely free from imitation, they point out that since mimesis does not adequately account for the ontological and epistemological status of fiction, fiction cannot be defined by imitation alone.[12] I argue that dependence on imitation alone overlooks the different historical, philosophical, psychological, aesthetic, and other cultural circumstances under which

Chinese fiction rose and evolved into a mature form of literary art, and therefore it cannot adequately explain the ontological and epistemological conditions of Chinese fiction.

A CRITIQUE OF HISTORY

The second phenomenon is the dominance of history. History not only provides the source materials, plot structure, and narrative techniques for the creation of fictional works, but also exerts the most profound impact on fiction criticism and theory. Among various views of fiction, the historical view of *xiaoshuo* (fiction) is undoubtedly the predominant one. The scholarly consensus is that Chinese *xiaoshuo* as a literary category originated from historical writings, complemented historiography, and gradually departed from its maternal matrix to become a separate literary genre. Most recently, the history of Chinese fiction theory by Wang Rumei and Zhang Yu reaffirms this view: "Throughout ancient times *xiaoshuo* depended upon historiography for its maternal body. It was the son of historiography and oftentimes coexisted with historiography in a mother-son symbiosis. This was even more so at the beginning."[13] I argue that the biological metaphor of mother-son symbiosis completely overlooks the tension and struggle between *xiaoshuo* and historiography in historical development and critical discourses. In my view, a more appropriate analogy to describe the development of *xiaoshuo* would be a metaphor of political oppression and rebellion.

Xiaoshuo and historical writings grew out of entirely different creative impulses. While the former originated from the desire to seek psychological pleasure in narrating persons and events, real or imagined, the latter arose from the desire to record real persons and events for social and practical purposes. The different creative impulses endowed *xiaoshuo* and historiography with entirely different social positions: while the former was lowly regarded as something disruptive, immoral, and almost worthless, the latter was highly regarded as something lofty, moral, and extremely useful. A bird's-eye view of *xiaoshuo*'s relation to historiography tells us that whereas the former was always pushed to the margins, the latter always occupied the center of discourse; whereas the latter was always the master, the former was always its slave or, at best, its handmaiden. Historiography is to *xiaoshuo* as a government is to a rebelling force. From the outset, because of a different creative impulse, *xiaoshuo* always wanted to form a verbal genre of its own, but it was consistently repressed and oppressed by historiography, which sought to control it by containment or condemnation to oblivion. It rose many times in rebellion against historiography's oppression and, faced with its energy and power, history had to offer amnesty and enlistment to rebels (*zhaoan*). So it gave *xiaoshuo* an unimportant position in the power structure of discourse. Dissatisfied with its menial position, *xiaoshuo* constantly struggled against the official discourse until it eventually won its independence and became a literary category in itself. The history of *xiaoshuo*'s development is one of incessant struggle against history and a final winning of independence. This way of viewing *xiaoshuo* will not only give us a completely new perspective on *xiaoshuo*'s development, but also is capable of revealing the deep structure of *xiaoshuo*.

There is no denying the contributions made by history to the development of fiction. The impact of history, however, is a double-edged sword. In recent scholarship, scholars have begun to take note of the tension and conflict between history and *xiaoshuo*. In his study of Chinese fiction commentaries, David Rolston perceptively points out that traditional fiction commentators gradually felt the impact of history as a burden and made implicit attempts to liberate fiction from history.[14] Wang Rumei and Zhang Yu also pay some attention to the tension: "There are two kinds of views on *xiaoshuo* in ancient China: the historian's conception, which emphasizes the Dao, respects fidelity, and eschew fictionality; and the literary writer's conception, which loves the strange, employs fictionality, and values both fidelity and fictionality. While the two conceptions form a 'binary opposition,' they are also intrinsically related, interpenetrate, and influence each other."[15] Wang's and Zhang's view touches upon the conceptual differences of *xiaoshuo* from history, but their emphasis is still on how the two conceptions are related to and complement each other in historical development.

One of the consequences arising from the dominance of history is that fiction criticism was often conducted much in the way histories were examined, sometimes completely overlooking the differences between history as a narrative and fiction as a verbal art. Another consequence is that the dominant view of fictional development is one of fictional historiography. Scholars have generally followed the path charted by historiography, adopting a historical approach that describes how Chinese *xiaoshuo* evolved from its initially crude form of street talk through its mature form of storytelling to a narrative form close to modern fiction. Not many attempts have been made to adopt a conceptual approach to Chinese *xiaoshuo*. In the few attempts at conceptual inquiries, the dominant view describes in broad strokes how Chinese *xiaoshuo* underwent a transition from historicity to fictionality. No study has gone beyond a historical description of the transition. This description is certainly correct, but it only describes the surface development of Chinese *xiaoshuo*, leaving practically untouched how fictionality is achieved and how *xiaoshuo* evolved from a narrative discourse to a verbal art in the transition, and it is therefore inadequate in revealing the true nature and deep structure of *xiaoshuo*.

There are a number of reasons why I deem this history-to-fiction transition inadequate. The first reason is, of course, that this approach is descriptive in nature and pays little attention to such conceptual issues as the definitions of "historicity," "fiction," and "fictionality." Even in the description of the transition from historicity to fictionality, there are many areas that are left unexamined or explored incompletely. For example, the cardinal question "What is fiction or fictionality?" has practically been taken for granted.

The second reason is that this approach only takes note of changes in content: narratives are no longer preoccupied with retelling stories of real persons or real events in history and society, but are engaged in making fictional accounts that have no prototypes in history. This content approach seems to pay little attention to the fact that the transition from the early concept of "*xiaoshuo*" (petty talk) to *xiaoshuo* (fiction) is not only a shift in content but also a fundamental shift in form and aesthetic sensibilities. Essentially, what distinguishes the early form of *xiaoshuo*, scarcely distinguishable from history and philosophy, from its mature form of *xiaoshuo* as fiction is a perceptual, conceptual, and aesthetic shift in the way of telling stories. The third reason is that the content approach fails to take note of the deep structure of the shift. I argue that beneath the surface transition from historicity to fictionality, there is a gradual shift that is truly radical in nature. It is a shift from storytelling to the making of fiction as a form of verbal art. It is this shift that was largely responsible for Chinese *xiaohuo*'s development into an art form that was eventually capable of rivaling lyric poetry and classical prose and anticipating the coming of modern fiction.

A CRITIQUE OF THE POETRY-FICTION DIVIDE

My critique of the dominance of the realistic and historical should not be misconstrued to mean that realistic and historical approaches should be abandoned. I only mean that the dominance of these approaches tends to blind us to some characteristic features of Chinese fiction and that they therefore should be integrated with other approaches. Fiction as a verbal art is an aesthetic category. The historical approach should not be separated from an aesthetic approach. I suggest that the historical conception is the precondition for an aesthetic conception of *xiaoshuo* and for any conceptual inquiries into *xiaoshuo*'s development. While the transition from history to fiction characterizes the surface development of Chinese *xiaoshuo*, the shift from storytelling to fictional art underlies the deep structure of *xiaoshuo*'s long-term evolution. The two kinds of transition do not exclude one another. In fact, they complement each other and should give us a more adequate and profound understanding of the nature, function, and art of Chines *xiaoshuo*. To a certain extent, the existence of the two complementary shifts constitutes an obvious trend in the development of *xiaoshuo*. The question then arises: why has it not been given due attention in extant scholarship? The neglect is both curious and understandable. It is curious, because *xiaoshuo*'s development toward a form of art is so obvious. The neglect is understandable because the aesthetic turn is a subject of inquiry far more complicated and demanding than historical description. The artistic transition requires more conceptual and formal considerations than it does historical and content considerations. Whereas the changes in content are relatively easy to observe and describe, the changes in form and the shift to fictional art require more rigorous conceptual acumen and more heightened literary sensibility to conceptualize and characterize. In a word, the latter changes require us to undergo a shift in conceptual approaches. While we need to study *xiaoshuo*'s development from the perspective of what a fictional work narrates, we must examine its evolution from the perspective of how a particular fictional work presents its content.

Because of Confucian disparagement, in the mainstream literary establishment Chinese *xiaoshuo* was not deemed a form of verbal art worthy of respect until modern times. This prejudice relegated *xiaoshuo* to a position subservient to that of lyric poetry and classical prose. The unequal treatment of poetry and *xiaoshuo* gave rise to a dominant trend in literary scholarship throughout China's dynastic history: a separation of the two literary forms. This trend has persisted to the present day. I agree that poetry and fiction are different forms of literature and have distinctive features. I, however, suggest that the separation of *xiaoshuo* from poetry has overlooked the fact that both literary forms are inherently connected in their genesis, nature, function, and craftsmanship. Aesthetically, the deep structure of fictional art rests on poetry. Duly recognizing the radical distinction between fiction and poetry, John Stuart Mill makes a sagacious claim in his efforts to define poetry: "Many of the finest poems are in the form of novels, and in almost all good novels there is true poetry."[16] The German romantics had conceived of the novel as "super-poetry," and the French symbolists had experimented with composing prose narratives using the methods of poetry.[17] In the history of major literary traditions, first-rate fictional writers have often been concurrently poets either by temperament or profession. In the Chinese tradition, fiction writers like Yuan Zhen, Bai Xingjian, Shen Jiji, Feng Menglong, Li Yu, Ling Mengchu, Cao Xueqin, Ji Yun, Pu Songling, Wu Jingzi, Lu Xun, Guo Moruo, Yu Dafu, and others are both poets and fiction writers. In the Western tradition, one only need think of Goethe, Novalis, Friedrich Hölderlin, Hermann Hesse, André Gide, the Brontë sisters, Thomas Hardy, D. H. Lawrence, James Joyce, Virginia Woolf, or William Golding. I fully recognize the necessity for specialization in literary studies, but absolute specialization may turn a literary scholar into that ophthalmologist whom Qian Zhongshu satirizes in his hilarious story. The eye doctor wins a Nobel Prize for Medicine for specializing in the left eye and refuses to treat any patient's right eye.[18] Moreover, the separation of poetry from fiction overlooks an undercurrent in Chinese fiction's development. Historically and artistically, there has been an uneasy relationship between *xiaoshuo* and poetry, which exerted a considerable impact upon the aesthetic evolution of *xiaoshuo* into a verbal art. I will conduct an extensive inquiry into the poetic nature of Chinese fiction in chapter 4, and in the concluding chapter I will tell from a conceptual perspective the reason why a separation of fiction from poetry is not conducive to the study of fiction. For the time being, I suggest that poetry in its broad sense is the creative cement that united fiction, history, and philosophy into a symbiotic entity called *xiaoshuo* at the initial stage and exerted an impact in shaping fiction's long-term development.

Having critiqued the blind spots in the extant scholarship on fiction studies, I intend to adopt an integrated paradigm, which combines historical and content approaches with conceptual and formal approaches. Specifically, I will: (1) study Chinese fiction on its own terms and try to bring out its differences in conception and practice from history and historiography; (2) pay sufficient attention to central issues in *xiaoshuo*'s development, such as its definition, nature, function, and techniques; (3) place the study of *xiaoshuo* in the larger context of Chinese literature and culture and especially against the background of the dominance of the lyrical tradition; and (4) view *xiaoshuo* as a form of verbal art carefully crafted and explore how it was transformed from street gossip to fictional art by observing its techniques of making.

The movement from snippets of street gossip to fictional art consists of a series of interrelated and often overlapping processes of development. I describe these processes as a series of conceptual turns: (1) *xugou hua* (fictionalization); (2) *gushi hua* (storytelling); (3) *neihua* (internalization); (4) *chun xugou* (pure fiction); (5) *duoyuan hua* (multiplicity); and (6) *xingshi hua* (formal techniques). These processes could be subsumed under a fundamental turn to fiction as a verbal art, a general process of *yishu hua* (aestheticization), the core of which is *shihua* (poeticization). Thus, my study is essentially one of how the art of Chinese fiction is conceived and created in a fundamental evolution from historicity through fictionality to fictional art.

OBJECTIVES OF INQUIRY

Chinese tradition has a large amount of theoretical data on fiction. Studies of fiction, however, tend to be confined to historical scholarship or practical criticism and cherish little interest in conceptual inquiries into the conditions of fiction. As a result, there has been so far no systematic study of Chinese fiction theory that conceptualizes Chinese fiction and treats it on its own terms. The lack of an indigenous theory generalized out of Chinese fiction not only hinders fictional criticism but also obfuscates the understanding of fiction as a literary genre. This book attempts to fill that vacuum. Through an inquiry into the macrocosm of Chinese fiction, the art of some formative works like *The Plum in the Golden Vase* and *The Story of the Stone*, and theoretical data in fiction commentaries and intellectual thought, it examines the conceptual as well as historical conditions of *xiaoshuo* and explores its rise, origin, nature, function, definition, and relations to other literary genres, as well as theoretical issues like imitation, realism, historicity, fictionality, pure fiction, poetic fiction, and fictional art. It inquires how Chinese *xiaoshuo* evolved from street talk and parasitic writings of history and philosophy, through the popular forms of storytelling and the extended novel, to a full-fledge verbal art in the local context of the Chinese history and literary thought, and against the larger background of world fiction and general fiction theory, and argues that Chinese fiction does not follow the same route of development as its Western counterpart.

Throughout its evolution, Chinese fiction came under the heavy influence of the Chinese worldview and displays a fascinating mixture of diverse narrative modes, some of which did not appear in the West until modern times, with the result that some artistic features anticipated surrealism, magic realism, modernism, and postmodernism. Arguing for the inherently poetic nature of Chinese fiction, the book hopes to uncover what may be termed the poeticization of fiction in the Chinese tradition. In looking at Chinese theories of fiction, it addresses the genesis, ontology, epistemology, conceptual vision, writing model, formal techniques, and hermeneutic practice of Chinese fiction in the international context of fiction studies. For the purpose of comparative study, it will explore philosophical grounds for a new conception of fiction and makes some tentative suggestions for future work toward a transcultural theory of fiction.

A major objective of this study is partially revealed by the title. I have entitled my study "Chinese Theories of Fiction" rather than "Theories of Chinese Fiction." The distinction between the two indicates the emphasis of my study. While the former means Chinese ideas about fiction as a literary category irrespective of culture and tradition, the latter refers to views about Chinese fiction as the cultural product of a particular tradition. The chosen title indicates that in addition to being a study of Chinese fiction theory in particular, my book aims at an inquiry into fiction in general. In this connection, an alternative title would be "Theories of Fiction: A Chinese View." As a whole, my study hopes to achieve these objectives: (1) to reconceptualize theory of fiction from a transcultural perspective; (2) to pioneer a new approach to the study of Chinese fiction; (3) to discover new insights in traditional theoretical discourses as well as in fictional works; (4) to call for and contribute to a paradigm shift in fiction studies; and (5) to construct a non-Western system of fiction theory in the international context of fiction studies.

SCOPE OF INQUIRY

Prose fiction (*xiaoshuo*) in the Chinese tradition has a long history with numerous long and short fictional works and an abundance of critical and theoretical materials. It is not possible to deal with all of them; nor is it necessary for my purpose. The main focus of this study is on Chinese narrative works of pure fiction. The concept of pure fiction will be extensively discussed and formulated in this book, but tentatively I define it as a fictional work that does not rely on previous existent narratives such as histories, biographies, myths, legends, stories, and so on for its genesis and framework, but has its ontological status from and narrative strength in its own fictionality. Long as the Chinese history of fiction is, there are a few important stages in its evolution and development and some seminal fictional works that have exerted a formative influence upon later works and served as models for later writers to imitate and emulate. These representative works may be viewed as milestones of *xiaoshuo* on the long journey from its crude beginning through its stages of maturation to the advent of the novel. Some of them have had a monumental stature. A study of these works will offer a clear trajectory of *xiaoshuo*'s development and the most glorious moments in its history. My book, however, is not intended as a historical and critical study. It is an integrated study driven by a theoretical agenda. This means that while it conducts historical and critical analysis of chosen fictional works, its ultimate objective is to work out a poetics of fiction that is of conceptual and transcultural value.

The book consists of seven chapters, an introduction, and a conclusion. Chapters 1, 2, 3, and 4 offer a general view of Chinese fiction in terms of my proposed approaches and methodologies. They address the historical as well as conceptual conditions of *xiaoshuo*, and discuss its rise, origin, nature, function, definition, fictionality, and relations to other literary genres. This part attempts to offer a new view of how Chinese *xiaoshuo* evolved from its perceived dependence on history and philosophy to the popular form of full-length novel. Arguing against the commonly held view that sees the relationship between *xiaoshuo* and history as a mother-son symbiosis, it posits a new view that sees the relationship as a continuous struggle by *xiaoshuo* against the dominant official discourse, which ends with *xiaoshuo*'s complete independence as a literary category. Special attention will be paid to the conception of *xiaoshuo*, its denotations and connotations over the course of history, and other theoretical issues like imitation, realism, historicity, fictionality, pure fiction, and fictional art. Challenging the universality of mimetic origin of fiction, this part suggests a lyrical, psychological, and social rise of fiction in China. It also argues that there has been a creative drive in Chinese *xiaoshuo* toward pure fiction and poetic fiction, which brought about an aesthetic turn that transforms storytelling into full-fledged fictional art. Without this turn, Chinese fiction could never have become a full-fledged verbal art. This part also examines a fundamental change in writers' perception of language from a vehicle for conveying meaning to a creative force that structures narration and engenders meaning. The change in perception results in a change in the model of writing, and the new model brings about a linguistic turn to fiction as a verbal art. Chapter 4 is devoted to a study of the inherently poetic nature of Chinese fiction and discusses a process of poeticization of fiction. This part will form a historical as well as a conceptual basis for exploring the chosen fictional works, internationalizing Chinese fiction, and constructing a Chinese system of fiction theory, as well as bridging the gap between traditional Chinese fiction and modern Western fiction.

Chapter 5 focuses on the art of the *Jin Ping Mei* (*The Plum in the Golden Vase*), one of the four masterpieces of Ming fiction and the first full-length novel of pure fiction. Contrary to the widely accepted scholarly opinion, I argue that the novel does not have much in common with its predecessors in creative conception and fictional technique. As it was conceived as an extended pure fiction and displays a conscious awareness of the novelistic genre's unlimited possibilities for representation, the appearance of this novel truly marked the full maturity of Chinese fiction. It pioneered not only a tradition of pure fiction making but also a tradition of consciously open fiction making. By studying the novel in relation to Zhang Zhupo's (1670–98) and other scholars' commentarial work on it, I will explore how this novel contributes to the theory and practice of Chinese fiction. I will also examine the innovative tendency of this novel toward indeterminacy and multiplicity and the role of conscious making in the formation of open hermeneutic space. Finally, I will work out a poetics of pure fiction that weaves diverse narrative materials into a scheme of multiple dimensions. Chapter 6 studies the art of China's greatest traditional novel, the *Hongloumeng* (*The Story of the Stone*). I argue that the novel is as much a work of fictive representation as it is an unconventional treatise on fiction theory. In self-consciously addressing the interaction between fiction theory and practice, Cao Xueqin (1715–63) attempts to create a poetic fiction, a metafiction, a metanarrative, a total fiction, a grand narrative, and a kaleidoscopic fiction, and succeeds in accomplishing a summation of Chinese fiction theory through fictional practice. I also suggest that the author advances a system of narration that deliberately designs a complicated network of signification and representation capable of channeling our readings in different, opposite, and diverse directions. The novel exemplifies an open poetics of overdetermination based, among other things, on the author's profound insight into dreams, the poetic unconscious, and the novel as a literary form capable of multiple signification and representation.

Chapter 7 is the core of this study. All the preceding chapters serve to pave the way for its appearance. It will construct a Chinese system of fiction theory based on the conceptual insights that have been teased out of the theoretical data and chosen fictional works. It attempts to bring out a synthetic account of the ideas on the general conditions of Chinese fiction. I argue that the Chinese system of fiction theory, while sharing some of the basic theoretical concerns with the Western system of fiction theory, differs from its counterpart in some essential aspects. The last chapter attempts to synthesize the individual poetics of preceding chapters into a general poetics of fiction. The epilogue examines the philosophical foundation of Chinese fiction theory and, by examining its theoretical potentials in relation to Western fiction theory, attempts to formulate a new conception of fiction and uses it as a possible common basis for a transcultural theory of fiction. Through this book, I hope to demonstrate that although fiction in the Chinese tradition does not follow the same route of development as its Western counterpart and displays some seemingly unique features in its fictional products, the theory abstracted out of it has intrinsically nothing that resists internationalization.

ASSUMPTIONS AND METHODOLOGY

I have mentioned earlier that there has been no study that attempts to construct a Chinese system of fiction theory. This situation is perfectly understandable.

A great deal of traditional Chinese fiction criticism is to be found in *pingdian* commentaries. Written or printed on the margins of fictional works, *pingdian* commentaries are less concerned with conceptual criticism of the particular fictional work in question than with calling the reader's attention to its significant features of rhetoric and with passing evaluative judgments. The impressionistic brevity precludes any possibilities of a conceptual system. With few exceptions, even extended commentaries composed in the fashion of "how to read" the work were not intended as general inquiries of fiction. Because of their main concerns with a particular fictional work, few traditional fiction commentators were interested in conceptual and systematic inquires into the conditions of fiction as a literary genre. This situation spills over to modern studies of Chinese fiction.

My book is conceptually driven. It will lay emphasis on the interaction between theory and practice in the making of fiction art, and will thereby adopt a different approach to Chinese theories of fiction than that by previous scholars. In existent scholarship on Chinese fiction theory, as shown in the studies by Ye Lang, Wang Rumei, Zhang Yu, Meng Zhaolian, Ning Zongyi, Zhang Bibo, Lu Decai, Patrrick Hanan, Andrew Plaks, Sheldon Lu, David Rolston, and others, the general approach is a descriptive one that historicizes available data for fiction theory and critically analyzes the data to formulate critical assessments. This approach has both advantages and drawbacks. The main advantage is that it is capable of identifying, classifying, and synthesizing ideas and insights that have stood the test of time. Its drawbacks are twofold. On the one hand, it inherits the conceptual weaknesses and historical limitations emanating from the source materials. On the other, it is at least once removed from the fictional works, the original sources of critical and theoretical insights, and only in a secondary manner does it attempt to conceptualize ideas directly from fictional practice itself.

In their observation of the difficulties involved in the study of Chinese fiction theory, Wang Rumei and Zhang Yu have made a sagacious remark: "Fiction theory lags behind fictional practice. Theories contained within fictional works themselves are usually more abundant than those summarized by critics. Therefore, in the study of fiction theory of ancient *xiaoshuo*, attention should be paid to the theories and aesthetic ideas contained within fictional works themselves. To observe the aesthetic tradition and sum up the national features of ancient fiction, it is imperative to conduct integrated studies by relating fiction theory and fictional works."[19] Their suggested methodology shares a good deal with my approach to Chinese fiction theory. In my book, I will lay emphasis on the direct method that has been used by theorists from Confucius and Aristotle to Auerbach and Bakhtin—that is, the method of conceptualizing ideas of fiction by going directly to fictional development as well as to literary works themselves. In practical terms, I will conduct both macrostudies of Chinese fiction's development and microstudies of chosen fictional works, integrate conceptual insights derived from historical observation and critical analysis with those drawn from available theoretical data, and then synthesize all the conceptual insights into a Chinese system of fiction theory. The meager reference to historical development is intended not as a historical review but as a background to contextualize theoretical exploration.

Unlike previous scholarship on Chinese fiction theory, I do not rely solely on traditional theoretical data and only attach a secondary importance to traditional fiction commentary. This is not because I have a low opinion of traditional fiction criticism, but because I am aware of some of the limitations. Traditional criticism, as I have already noted, is generally spontaneous, impressionistic, and not very much concerned with the conceptual conditions of fiction as a literary genre. Some of the conceptual insights, because of their provenance in the reading of individual fictional works, are yet to be raised to the speculative and abstract level. Moreover, with few exceptions, traditional criticism shows little interest in exploring theory of fiction in a systematic manner. These limitations are understandable, because fiction criticism was, after all, intended primarily as reading guides for the public. It is unreasonable to expect it to conform to the conceptual rigor and systematicness of modern fiction studies.

Since this book attempts to formulate a Chinese system of fiction theory, I will not only treat a fictional work as a text produced by a certain writer at a certain historical time for a reading public, but also examine it as an art object that conforms to conceptual ideas, aesthetic values, and critical standards of all times. Methodologically, I will resort to an approach that treats a fictional work as a verbal construct predicated on the integration of ideology, psychology, and semiology. My study is neither a historical account nor a critical account. It aims at a poetics of fiction. "Poetics" has been used in several senses, ranging from the widest sense of "theory," which can be applied to almost any human activity, to the narrowest sense of "implicit principles" for a specific author. In this study, "poetics" is used to mean both "theory of fiction" and "fiction theory." In making a distinction between "theory of fiction" and "fiction theory," I am influenced by James J. Y. Liu's distinction between "theory of literature" and "literary theory": "the former being concerned with the basic nature and functions of literature, the latter with aspects of literature, such as form, genre, style, and technique."[20] To put it another way, I am concerned with both the conceptual conditions and the technicalities of fiction.

The major reason for my inclusive approach is that my main concern is with fiction as a verbal art. In *The Aesthetics of Chaosmos*, Umberto Eco suggests that Aristotle in his *Poetics* attempts to answer two basic questions in literary study: "What is art?" and "How does one make a work of art?"[21] If "poetics" is used to describe the program of a single author or a particular school of artists, it addresses the question, "How does one make a work of art according to a personal program and an idiosyncratic worldview?" When, however, the term refers to study of "the *differentia specifica* of verbal behavior" as defined by the linguistic, formal, and technical approaches to literature, "poetics" is "the study of the structural mechanism of a given text which possesses a self-focusing quality and a capacity for releasing effects of ambiguity and polysemy."[22] Whether it be in the broad sense or the narrow sense, poetics is concerned with the making of literary art. The technical aspect of making occupies a place at the center of reading and interpretation.

As my book is concerned with the art of fiction and the poetics of making, and, in addition to taking into account various aspects of fiction, it will lay a special emphasis on the use of language and techniques of fiction in the weaving of fictional elements into a verbal art. I do so for several reasons. First, fiction is a verbal construct, and the art of fiction is a language art. As early as the 1940s, Mark Schorer stated: "The difference between content, or experience, and achieved content, or art, is technique."[23] A fiction writer's technique is ultimately a craft of using language. As Roger Fowler, another theorist of fiction, puts it, "The structure of the novel and whatever it communicates are under the direct control of the novelist's manipulation of language, and concomitantly, of the reader's recreative sympathy, his desire and ability to realize and release the technique from verbal clues deposited by the author."[24] In the development of Chinese fiction, I have noticed a trend in which fiction writers increasingly resorted to manipulating language in their making of fictional art. In my study, I will describe in detail this significant trend and relate it to similar trend in the Western tradition. As a practicing critic, I believe in the saying that a theory that has no practical value is not a good theory. With a desire to identify insights for practical criticism, a considerable amount of my theorizing will be based on critical analysis of chosen fictional works.

Nowadays, Chinese fiction writers generally turn to Western masters for artistic inspiration and technical innovations. Such famed experimental writers as James Joyce, Henry James, Marcel Proust, Virginia Woolf, William Faulkner, Franz Kafka, and Ernest Hemingway have exerted their influence in one way or another on the practicing Chinese fiction writers, who have tried to emulate the Western masters' experiments with language, narrative techniques, or modes of representation. Some of them especially admire the magic realism of Latin American authors like Jorge Luis Borges, Gabriel García Márquez, and Alejo Carpentier. But ironically, even though this kind of experimentalism is not entirely new in the Chinese tradition, it has been almost completely overlooked. The earliest experiment can be traced to the *Jin Ping Mei*, a novel produced in the late sixteenth century. The author was engaged in exactly what has been attempted by Western modernist and postmodernist fiction writers. The experiment with language and technique in the *Hongloumeng* is even more pronounced. Lu Xun, who consciously absorbed both Chinese and Western traditions, is another fiction writer who experimented with language and techniques. Unfortunately, this aspect of fictional creation has not received due attention in the study of Chinese fiction. We should certainly introduce Western theories and methodologies of fiction, but we should not neglect the legacy bequeathed to us by traditional Chinese writers. My attempt to make connections between traditional Chinese writers and modernist experiments should not be misconstrued as implying that "China has it, and had it long ago," but should be understood as an effort to show the continuity between the past and present and the transcultural significance of Chinese fiction in the worldwide context of fiction studies.

CHAPTER ONE

Chinese Notions of Fiction

In the West, studies of fiction used to focus on the novel as a literary category, but since the 1960s, most theorists have agreed that there is no such thing as the novel. It is a literary category "that has no natural or positive existence" and that "arises and rearises in different regional cultures at different times"; and it is not a literary genre with a continuous history but a succession of works "bearing family resemblances to one another."[1] And most disconcerting to theorists who attempt to categorize it, it changes in relation to cultural and aesthetic changes. Curiously, the same can be said of Chinese *xiaoshuo*, which, as I will show, is a chameleon. In response to conceptual bewilderment, the study of fiction in the West has gone through a shift of conception from the novel to narrative. As one scholar puts it, the "death of the (realistic) novel, which attracted so much critical attention in America and France during the 1950s, coincided with the rebirth of narrative."[2] The replacement of the novel by narrative was necessitated by the conceptual and critical desires to be inclusive. As Andrew Plaks aptly puts it, "[I]t is adopted as a catch-all bracket for the chain of developments moving from epic through romance to novel."[3]

In the Chinese tradition, such a shift of emphasis is not necessary, for *xiaoshuo* has always been treated as narrative rather than fiction, even though the term *xushi* (narration) appeared later than *xiaoshuo*.[4] In 1977, Plaks edited a study of Chinese narrative. The book, entitled *Chinese Narrative: Critical and Theoretical Essays*, "attempted to provide a broad range of specialized studies covering the major works and genres of the Chinese narrative tradition."[5] Its use of the term "narrative" shows a sensitive awareness of the nature of narrative in the Chinese tradition as well as a timely response to the change of focus in the West. The word *xiaoshuo* is not as broad in scope as the general term "narrative," but it is also a "catchall basket" in the Chinese tradition, broad enough to necessitate a reconsideration of its denotations and connotations over history and a delimiting of its parameters. In the present study of Chinese *xiaoshuo*, I will go in the opposite direction from the Western trend and turn from a general approach to narrative to a narrow focus on prose fiction. I take this direction for two fundamental reasons. First, as scholars have noted, there has been a shift in *xiaoshuo* from being a general category of narrative to a specific literary form, which in the Chinese tradition shows a narrowing rather than a broadening of focus. Second, there is a visible transition in the development of Chinese *xiaoshuo* from historicity to fictionality. This transition also narrowed down the scope of *xiaoshuo* from a catchall category to a specific literary category, prose fiction.

In this part of my book, I will explore how the Chinese notion of *xiaoshuo* evolved from an amorphous category in the beginning to the modern notion of fiction culminating in the maturity of *zhanghui*-style *xiaoshuo* (the chaptered novel). In their influential study *The Nature of Narrative*, Robert Scholes and Robert Kellogg characterize studies of Western narrative in the middle of the twentieth century as "hopelessly novel-centered"[6] with assumptions about narrative and expectations from reading narrative works derived solely from the novel. In reaction against this dominant trend in narrative studies, they call for an almost opposite approach.[7] I understand their reaction against the hegemony of the realistic novel and the necessity to use narrative as a way to broaden views of literature, but I find their rejection of the novel as the final product of an ameliorative evolution somewhat problematic. My main objection is that their definition of the novel is a narrow one based on the realistic novels in the Western tradition. The realistic novel is certainly not the final product, but the novel as a literary genre has a sense of finality on two accounts. First, it is a literary form of totality and comprehensive capacity. Second, it never ceases to change and grow, and no one can predict when it will stop growing and what it will finally become. M. M. Bakhtin points out, "[T]he novel is a developing genre; they [symptoms of change] are sharper and more significant because the novel is in the vanguard of change. The novel may thus serve as a document for gauging the lofty and still distant destinies of literature's future unfolding."[8] The multifarious novelistic practice after the rise of the realistic tradition in the West and the diversified development of the novel in the Chinese tradition have confirmed the chameleonlike nature of the novel and its capability as a totalizing literary form. Because of its totalizing nature, the novel as a literary form is slippery and tends to resist conceptual categorization. D. H. Lawrence, who considerably enlarged the scope of the modern novel, once remarked: "Everything is true in its own time, place, circumstance, and untrue outside of its own place, time, circumstance. If you try to nail anything down, in the novel, either it kills the novel, or the novel gets up, and walks away with the nail."[9]

For these reasons, and in consideration of the evolutionary history of *xiaoshuo* in the Chinese tradition, I do not view the novel as "only one of a number of narrative possibilities" as Scholes and Kellogg do in the Western tradition. Instead, I consider the chaptered novel in the Chinese tradition as the final product of an evolutionary process and as the perfected narrative form that earlier forms of narrative—myths, legends, literary anecdotes, folk-tales, personal biographies, historical narratives, short stories, novellas, and so on—have helped to make.

A study of this evolution will involve two basic approaches: historical review and conceptual analysis. In existent scholarship, the former has taken precedence over the latter. I consider this a regrettable tendency. As early as the 1970s, Patrick Hanan, in his study of the classification of early Chinese *xiaoshuo* writings, sagaciously pointed out that although one should not ignore the importance of historical method, it should be subordinate to objective analysis.[10] I will try to bear in mind this advice. In a historical analysis of *xiaoshuo*'s evolution, I will describe a struggle between historical inertia and pure fiction in *xiaoshuo*'s movement away from historicity and toward fictionality, and examine its impact upon *xiaoshuo*'s journey from its modest beginning as a form of anecdotal snippets to its dominant position in the pantheon of modern Chinese literature. I am not content with a historical study of its development, however; I attempt to embark on a conceptual inquiry into the ontological and epistemological conditions of *xiaoshuo* as an aesthetic category in Chinese literature. In this chapter, I will conduct an inquiry into the Chinese concept *xiaoshuo* as well as into the rise and intrinsic nature of Chinese fiction.

CHINESE *XIAOSHUO* AND WESTERN "FICTION"

"Fiction" is a Western concept. It has two related meanings: (1) a literary category; (2) a mode of writing. As a literary category, it refers to a literary form in contradistinction to poetry and drama. As a mode of writing, it means composing prose works in the manner of fabrication. In this study, my concern is both with fiction as a literary category and with fictionality as the defining characteristic and core of the category, with an emphasis on the latter. To use the terminology from the Chinese tradition, the emphasis will be more on *xugou* ("fictitious construct," to construct in a fictitious manner) than on *xugou wenxue* (fictional literature). The closest term to the Western idea of fiction in China is, of course, *xiaoshuo* in its modern sense, which refers to the short story, the novella, and the novel in popular perception. The term, according to accepted opinion, acquired its present connotations quite late in the Chinese tradition, and there are some differences between Chinese *xiaoshuo* and Western "fiction," which must be clarified before we can come to a clear understanding of Chinese fiction. In his study of Chinese narrative, Victor Mair makes the following remark about the differences between Chinese *xiaoshuo* and Western fiction:

> [The] Chinese term for "fiction" is *hsiao-shuo* (literally, "small talk" or "minor talk"). This immediately points to a fundamental contrast with the English word, which is derived ultimately from the past participle of Latin *fingere* ("to

form" or "to fashion," "to invent"). Where the Chinese term etymologically implies a kind of gossip or anecdote, the English word indicates something made up or created by an author or writer. "*Hsiao-shuo*" imports something, not of particularly great moment, that is presumed actually to have happened; "fiction" suggests something an author dreamed up in his mind. By calling his work "fiction," an author expressly disclaims that it directly reflects real events and people; when a literary piece is declared to be "*hsiao-shuo*," we are given to understand that it is gossip or report. For this reason, many recorders of *hsiao-shuo* are at great pains to tell us exactly from whom, when, where, and in what circumstances they heard their stories.[11]

Mair's contrast succeeds in bringing out some of the major differences between Chinese notions of *xiaoshuo* and Western ideas of fiction, but the contrasting view growing out of the comparison presents some problems. First, the comparison is between an early notion of Chinese *xiaoshuo* and the modern Western idea of fiction. The problem does not simply lie in the contrast between an ancient idea and a modern notion. As I will show, in the accepted scholarly consensus the connotations of the early Chinese *xiaoshuo* that come close to the modern idea of fiction have been consistently overlooked, either purposefully or carelessly. Because of this neglect, the comparison is like one between oranges and apples, which both belong to the category of fruit and are round in shape, but taste different. It is therefore somewhat problematic to contrast them as though they were equivalent concepts. Second, the word *xiaoshuo* in the modern reader's mind does not evoke the negative associations that resulted from the Confucian prejudice against this genre in ancient times. True, *xiaoshuo* used to be a low literary genre in ancient Chinese society, but after the appearance of the *Hongloumeng* in the eighteenth century, and especially after Liang Qichao's call for a "revolution in *xiaoshuo* 小說革命" and other scholars' vigorous promotion of this genre in the early years of the twentieth century, *xiaoshuo* is no longer a despised literary genre. Third, as I will show, even in the earliest notion of *xiaoshuo* there were elements that are not much different from elements in the modern notion of fiction. I suggest that a fair comparison or contrast between Chinese *xiaoshuo* and Western fiction should not be confined to the etymological examination of their similarities and differences but should be conducted in a historical, conceptual, and aesthetic consideration of their origins, nature, function, and formal techniques.

In linguistic terms, *xiaoshuo* is a signifier. Moreover, it is a floating signifier whose signified has never been stable but has gone through a process of change and substitution, which engenders a gamut of meanings ranging from "petty talk" at its earliest inception to "fictional work" in its modern meaning. In ancient China, *xiaoshuo* is a catchall term for any writing that was not considered as serious, while it now refers to something similar to the Western conception of fiction. According to a popular dictionary of literary terms, fiction in English is a "vague and general term for an imaginative work, usually in prose"[12] and hence is also a floating signifier. Oddly enough, even though poetry and drama are both imaginatively contrived literary accounts, and therefore should be regarded as different forms of fiction, as Plato, Aristotle, and Northrop Frye[13] have viewed them, they are normally not included in the category of fiction. The situation is similar in the Chinese tradition. "Fiction," Y. W. Ma writes in his essay on Chinese fiction in the *Indiana Companion to Traditional Chinese Literature*, "may be defined as a composition written mainly in prose that creates an imaginative rather than factual reality. This permits the exclusion of drama and narrative poetry."[14] Since both *xiaoshuo* and "fiction" include the story, the novella, and the novel, *xiaoshuo* in its modern sense should be viewed as a rough equivalent of the Western term "fiction" with due attention to their nuances of difference. As a textual representation of interlocking events that have not happened in life but may happen by the law of probability, both Chinese *xiaoshuo* and Western "fiction" should be more appropriately called "narrative fiction in prose."

FROM "*XIAOSHUO*" TO *XIAOSHUO*

The title of this section is not a play on words. It is meant to succinctly capture a transformative process in the development of Chinese fiction. The "*xiaoshuo*" in quotation marks refers to an amorphous, nonliterary category, while *xiaoshuo* without quotation marks refers to the literary category of fiction. The distinction between "*xiaoshuo*" and *xiaoshuo* seems to support the scholarly consensus that the early notion of *xiaoshuo* and the modern notion of *xiaoshuo* have little in common, but this is not my intention. One of the aims of this chapter is to critically examine the accepted scholarly opinion and to find out to what extent it is true to the evolution of the term and to the intrinsic conditions of *xiaoshuo* as a literary form. In traditional China prior to modern times, *xiaoshuo* was a catchall term for writings that did not belong to official history, classics, or orthodox branches of learning. As Sheldon Lu notes: "It is no exaggeration to say that Chinese fiction is an anti-genre and anti-discourse in that it breaks down the hierarchies of the literary canon; it has always been an unsettling force to the literary establishment."[15] Indeed, *xiaoshuo* is such a slippery term that even if one thinks one has got a handle on it, one soon comes to the disconcerting realization that it has escaped one's grasp. Perhaps, rather than attempting to offer a hard-and-fast definition or an inclusive view of what *xiaoshuo* or the Chinese view of fiction is at this stage of my inquiry, a more meaningful approach may be to examine the denotation and connotation of the term *xiaoshuo* in its historical evolution. In my opinion, without first examining the concept *xiaoshuo*, we cannot adequately understand its intrinsic rise, true nature, internal structure, and even historical development.

With few exceptions, practically all studies of Chinese notion of fiction start with examining the etymology of the term in its historical development. While this approach may give us some valuable insight into the matter, the scholarly consensus based on this approach has left us in a state of bewilderment as to the relationship between the early and modern notions. An etymological inquiry into its origin seems to lead us to a conclusion that was allegorically imparted in the Chinese parable of the sword seeker: a man accidentally drops a sword into a river while sailing in a boat. Instead of jumping into the water to recover his sword immediately, he cuts a mark by the side of the boat where the sword has disapeared, and does not dive into the water at the mark to search for the sword until the boat arrives at its destination. His disappointment has been known to all educated Chinese through the ages. To put the scholarly consensus in semiotic terms, *xiaoshuo* is a signifier; its signified has never been stable. Indeed, its earliest signified and modern signified have little in common with each other. Practically all traditional and modern scholars have upheld this view. The earliest record of the expression *xiaoshuo* appears in the *Zhuangzi*: "If you parade your little theories (to fish for renown), you will be far away from the Great Dao."[16] In Xunzi's "Zhengming" (Rectification of Names) chapter, we find another expression, *xiaojia zhenshuo*[17] (the exotic theories of the minor schools), which has similar connotation to Zhuangzi's notion of *xiaoshuo*.

According to Zhuangzi's and Xunzi's usage, the term *xiaoshuo* refers to insignificant topics and ideas on metaphysical reasoning, moral advice, or political persuasion. As Hellmut Wilhelm rightly points out, "In both cases the word (說) is to be read *shui*, meaning 'political advice or persuasion' also in connection with the word (小), 'minor or petty'; and in both cases reference is made to the adornment or embellishment of such political advice."[18] It therefore has been generally accepted as having little bearing on the modern notion of *xiaoshuo* or fiction. I argue that even the earliest notion of *xiaoshuo* has something inherent that connects it to the modern sense of fiction. Ban Gu 班固 (32–92) was the first scholar in Chinese history to provide a description of *xiaoshuo*, but his notion of *xiaoshuo* has been misread by most scholars including Lu Xun. The misreading may be partially seen in an oft-quoted English translation of Ban Gu's definition in Lu Xun's pioneering study of Chinese fiction: "The *Hsiao-shuo* writers succeeded those of the Chou dynasty whose task it was to collect the gossip of the streets. Confucius said: 'Even by-ways are worth exploring. But if we go too far we may be bogged down.' Gentlemen do not undertake this themselves, but neither do they dismiss such talk altogether. They have the sayings of the common people collected and kept, as some of them may prove useful. This was at least the opinion of country rustics."[19] This understanding of early *xiaoshuo* writings as "the gossip of the streets," which has been reiterated time and again over history, is the source of the consensus that the early meaning of the word has little to do with modern fiction. Ban Gu's definition of *xiaoshuo*, as I will show later, has something that has been misunderstood or overlooked in existent scholarship. He listed fifteen categories of *xiaoshuo*, which cover diverse subjects such as historical events, miscellaneous discourses, witchcraft, medicine, and mathematical knowledge. One scholar's comment on Ban Gu's definition and classification represents a widely accepted opinion among Chinese and

Western scholars: "While it is true that presently the term *hsiao-shuo* is translated 'fiction,' in the Han dynasty its sense was very different. No serious modern scholar finds examples of early fiction (or early narrative precursors of fiction) among items in the first *hsiao-shuo* list, that of the Han-shu 'I-wen-chih'; much less would anyone argue that such examples were confined to that list."[20]

The history of *xiaoshuo* theory by Wang Rumei and Zhang Yu puts Ban Gu's definition of *xiaoshuo* into the historian's category. Their move is both correct and problematic. Correct because Ban Gu's classification is a historian's move; problematic because the content of the definition and the *xiaoshuo* writings that Ban Gu listed do not strictly belong to history. I would argue that Ban Gu's effort represents the first attempt by the orthodox discourse to control and contain the rebellious nature of *xiaoshuo*. Despite his low opinion of *xiaoshuo*, Ban Gu's classification reveals his sagacity and aesthetic sensitivity, which were seldom equaled by later historians. Though none of them is extant, the fifteen categories of *xiaoshuo* writings inform us by their titles alone that *xiaoshuo* is a form of writing different from historiography and close to the modern term "fiction."

Historians after Ban Gu, perhaps because of the deeper entrenchment of orthodox discourse, displayed more antipathy to *xiaoshuo* writings. Liu Zhiji 劉知幾 (661–721), the historian who composed China's first systematic theory of history writing, adopted Ban Gu's and enlarged Ban Gu's categories of classification, but he showed less aesthetic sensibility by classifying *xiaoshuo* writings into ten categories that have little to do with *xiaoshuo* as a form of literary writing: 偏記 (minor records), 小錄 (notes on insignificant matters), 逸事 (anecdotes), 瑣言 (scraps of remarks), 郡書 (biographies of local elites), 家史 (family histories), 別傳 (unofficial biographies), 雜記 (miscellaneous records), 地理 (geographical records), and 都邑簿 (records of cities and towns). In his classification, only a few categories include writings that may be viewed as fictional works today. Liu Zhiji emphasized the factuality and truthfulness of historical materials, and viewed *xiaoshuo* as a defective form of history or biography. Nevertheless, consistent with the Confucian literary policy of *zhaoan* 招安, he subsumed *xiaoshuo* under the larger category of historical records: "From this we know that *xiaoshuo* in the fashion of minor records forms a school of its own, but it can supplement official history."[21] They may have changed from philosophical writings to historical writings, but *xiaoshuo* writings, in his conception, were not any nearer to the genre of belles-lettres.

A comparative latecomer, Hu Yinglin (1551–1602) was perhaps one of the few scholars whose understanding of *xiaoshuo*'s intrinsic nature rivals that of Ban Gu. I agree with Wang Rumei and Zhang Yu's assessment: Hu noticed the aesthetic features and social function of *xiaoshuo*, recognized its differences from historiography, proposed to give it an independent status, and conducted fairly detailed classification of *xiaoshuo* writings.[22] But I disagree with their claim that Hu's study clarified and rendered accurate the concept of *xiaoshuo*.[23] Except for its larger scope and more detailed analysis, his understanding was not much different from that of Ban Gu. In discussing *xiaoshuo*'s relation to other schools of writing, Ban Gu wrote: "Among the ten schools of philosophical writings, only nine are worth examination."[24] Hu Yinglin restated Ban Gu's view: "As a category, the school of philosophical writings consists of ten branches. In the past, people only talk about nine. One of them they did not mention is *xiaoshuo*."[25] He more or less followed Ban Gu's classification and initiated a new method of dividing *xiaoshuo* into six branches.[26] Unlike Liu Zhiji, who subsumed *xiaoshuo* writings under the category of history, he reverted to Ban Gu's classification and put *xiaoshuo* back into the big category of philosophical writings. In view of the fact that by Hu's time the four big categories of writings—*jing* (classics), *shi* (historical writings), *zi* (philosophical writings), and *ji* (belletristic writings)—were well established, Hu's failure to classify *xiaoshuo* writings into the belletristic category is an eloquent proof that his understanding of *xiaoshuo*'s nature was not any closer to the modern notion of fiction. During the Qing dynasty, Ji Yun 紀昀 (1724–1805), the general editor of *Siku quanshu* 四庫全書, still viewed *xiaoshuo* writings as belonging to the category of philosophical writings and classified "the category of *xiaoshuo* writers" into three catchall categories: 雜事 (miscellaneous events), 異聞 (unusual hearsay), and 瑣語 (insignificant remarks).[27] Neither Hu Yinglin nor Ji Yun made a mention of vernacular fiction, which was circulating widely among readers at that time. It is not that they were unaware of the fictional writings of their times, but that they did not treat *xiaoshuo* as literary works. Their method of categorization that made no mention of *xiaoshuo* as a literary category seems to have corroborated the accepted view that the early notion of *xiaoshuo* has little to do with the modern notion of fiction. Lu Xun's pioneering study of *xiaoshuo* supports this view: "When it comes to the section on literature and art in the *Han Dynasty History*, *xiaoshuo* means 'the gossip of the streets,' which is closer to what is called fiction today. But it was still no more than a collection of small talk of the common people made by the king's officers so that they could study popular sentiment and customs. It is not the same as modern fiction."[28]

So the accepted scholarly opinion of *xiaoshuo* forces us to draw the conclusion that the early denotation of *xiaoshuo* and the modern denotation of *xiaoshuo* are a mismatch. It seems that the early notion of *xiaoshuo* indeed resembles the sword accidentally dropped into the river in that famous parable, and the modern notion of *xiaoshuo* is like the mark cut on the side of the boat. Just as the mark no longer correctly points to where the sword was dropped, the modern term is a signifier that has so radically deviated from its original signified that the two terms are different categories with only an identical name. In a word, the modern term seems to be a misnomer that has no relation to its erstwhile denotations and connotations.

I venture to contend, however, that the mismatch between the early and the modern notions of *xiaoshuo* has been exaggerated largely due to a two-thousand-year-long misinterpretation of Ban Gu's definition of *xiaoshuo* as only referring to "gossip of the streets." The modern term *xiaoshuo* for fiction (the short story, novella, and novel), commonly viewed as a concept born out of habitual use, is not entirely a misnomer. There is a continuity between the early and modern notions, but that continuity has been deeply buried under layers of history and discourse or overlooked because of prejudices and exegetical inertia.

To summarize the extant studies of the notion of *xiaoshuo*, there are three approaches: (1) an etymological approach, which analyzes the evolution of the term *xiaoshuo*; (2) a content approach that explores the similarity of *xiaoshuo* writing and fictional works in subject matter; and (3) a formal approach that analyzes *xiaoshuo* writings to show their similarity to modern notions of fiction. These approaches should be integrated with a conceptual approach that examines the ontological, epistemological, and aesthetical conditions of *xiaoshuo*. A single approach is incapable of recovering *xiaoshuo*'s continuity, still less its intrinsic features. I propose that we adopt an approach to the idea of *xiaoshuo* that combines studies of early critical discourses, analysis of *xiaoshuo* writings, and modern theories of fiction and narrative. Otherwise, we will be unable either to see the continuity between early and modern notions or to have an adequate understanding of *xiaoshuo*'s genesis, evolution, nature, and function. In the integrated approach, we need to conduct a conceptual inquiry by examining *xiaoshuo* writings as well as discourses on *xiaoshuo* in relation to contemporary theories of fiction, narrative, history, and fictionality.

THE CONTINUITY OF FICTIONALITY IN *XIAOSHUO*

My inquiry into the nature of *xiaoshuo* has uncovered a paradoxical situation. On the one hand, scholars in history generally agree that Chinese fiction evolved from the early *xiaoshuo* writings. But on the other hand, the extant theoretical materials concerning *xiaoshuo* seem to suggest that the early view of *xiaoshuo* as petty talk and the modern view of *xiaoshuo* as fictional works seem to refer to two entirely different categories. How can we reconcile this paradox? Zhang Xuecheng 章學誠 (1738–1801), a scholar of the Qing, found an easy way out and believed that the early meaning of *xiaoshuo* was lost and that the modern notion of *xiaoshuo* therefore was a misnomer. After reviewing the evolution of *xiaoshuo* through the ages from the inception of the term to its modern usage, he came to this conclusion: "[*Xiaoshuo*] originated from the petty officials of the court. This is recorded in the bibliographical treatise of the Han History. After three stages of transformation, it has completely lost its connection with the original sources in ancient times."[29] Zhang Xuecheng seems to suggest that the later meaning of *xiaoshuo* as fiction deviated entirely from its early connotations. I, however, suggest that if we grasp the intrinsic reason for the rise of *xiaoshuo* and the intrinsic value of fictional work, we will be able to see that the later concept of *xiaoshuo* not only evolved from its early namesake but also carried on its intrinsic connotations, despite changes in history, ideological orientations, and aesthetic tastes.

Traditional scholars have viewed the early notion of *xiaoshuo* and the later notion of *xiaoshuo* as two different categories simply because they did not view *xiaoshuo* as belonging to the realm of belles lettres. When we approach *xiaoshuo* as literary writings, we can find connotations similar to the modern sense of fiction. Zhuangzi's and Xunzi's remarks on *xiaoshuo* are too brief to merit much analysis, but extant records of the Han allow us to have a glimpse into its connotations when scholars of that time began to establish *xiaoshuo* as a school of scholarship. We need to restart from Ban Gu's definition in *Hanshu yiwen zhi* 漢書藝文志. Ban Gu adopted a Confucian approach to *xiaoshuo*, listing *xiaoshuo* writers in "Zhuzi lüe" ("Philosophers Section") and placing them last among the ten schools, which also include Confucianism, Daoism, Mohism, Legalism, Yin-yang theory, the Zongheng school, Logicians, the Miscellaneous school, and Agriculturists. Ban Gu's mention of fifteen schools of *xiaoshuo* with 1,380 individual pieces suggests that at that time there must have existed a large number of *xiaoshuo* writings. Unfortunately, practically all the listed schools of *xiaoshuo* have been lost, and only a few fragments have survived. Nowadays, inquiries into *xiaoshuo* rest on a few notes. But an investigation of these remaining notes will give us an inkling of what those *xiaoshuo* writings were.

Ban Gu's remarks on *xiaoshuo* constitute the earliest source for the nature of this category and have been regarded as authoritative. Unfortunately, due to the accepted opinion which does not view the early notion of *xiaoshuo* as having anything to do with the later notion, scholars have consistently overlooked its implications. A close reading of Ban Gu's remarks, guided by a desire to overcome exegetical inertia, will reveal that he treats *xiaoshuo* as imaginative creations of some kind. Let me quote again Ban Gu's statement on *xiaoshuo*. Wilhelm's English translation reads: "The trend of *Hsiao-shuo-chia* emerged from the (Board) of Petty Officials, *Pei-Kuan* (稗官). It was created by those who picked up the gossip of the streets and the sayings of the alleys and repeated what they had heard wherever they went 小說家者流，蓋出于稗官。街談巷語，道聽途說者之所造也。"[30] We should note a few intriguing but neglected points. First, the word *zao*, which means "invent" or "fabricate" in Chinese, has exactly the same root meaning as the Latin root of the Western term "fiction." Second, the scholarly consensus that equates *xiaoshuo* with gossip and rumors seems to be the outcome of a reading, based on a time-honored understanding, that did not take into account the whole context of the statement. In my opinion, Ban Gu's statement was incorrectly punctuated. *Jietan xiangyu* does not stand as an independent phrase meaning "gossip and rumors," but serves as a modifying phrase with the meaning of "street talk" parallel to *daoting tushuo*. The antithetical nature of the two phrases suggests that both are attributive phrases modifying the noun *zhe*. Thus, the statement should be punctuated as: 小說家者流，蓋出于稗官。街談巷語、道聽途說者之所造也。" According to this new reading, Ban Gu's statement should be translated as: "The school of *xiaoshuo* writings came from the petty officials of the court. They are fabrications by those who engaged themselves in idle talk in the streets and alleys and by those who heard gossip and rumors on the way." The main difference between the traditonal and new readings is that while the former views the rise of *xiaoshuo* as a trend started by the petty officials of the court, the latter attributes the origin of *xiaoshuo* to people in the streets who turned idle talk and gossip into fabricated accounts. My new reading entails a conclusion that people in the streets and gossipmongers were the original creators of *xiaoshuo* and the petty officials of the court were its secondary makers.

Thus, when *xiaoshuo* became records in the petty official's office, they had already gone through a process of selection, arrangement, and embellishment, and may have become quite sophisticated accounts. A close reading of Ban Gu's further statement tells us how early *xiaoshuo* writings were composed:

> Confucius said: "Even byways are worth exploring. But if one goes too far, he may be bogged down." Gentlemen do not compose *xiaoshuo* themselves, but neither do they dismiss *xiaoshuo* altogether. When moderately educated persons in the neighborhood encounter them, they have them stitched together so that they may not lapse into oblivion. If any of them may prove worth preserving, it is only because they represent the opinions of rustics and eccentrics.[31]

This passage and the preceding passage supply us with valuable information on the genesis and nature of early *xiaoshuo* writings. The sources of *xiaoshuo* are common people's words and opinions, but the common people themselves were not the creators of *xiaoshuo*; they only provided the raw materials for creating *xiaoshuo*. Because of the mundane nature of these raw materials, Confucian gentlemen would not deign to collect them, still less create *xiaoshuo* with them. People with moderate education were not collectors of raw materials, but creators of *xiaoshuo* in the true sense of the word. We should note the word *zhui* 綴. It means "stitch together" or "connect."[32] The petty intellectuals did not simply collect raw materials from life. Like a modern fiction writer, they "stitched together" (*zhui*) or wove their raw materials into *xiaoshuo* writings. The act of "stitching together" may range from plot arrangement to discourse embellishment. Not all petty literati could be the creators of *xiaoshuo*. Ban Gu tells us at another place in his treatise: "*Xiaoshuo* were composed by those with an untrammeled mind 放者為之." Thus, the genesis of *xiaoshuo* writings, in Ban Gu's characterization, is similar to that of later fictional works in the Ming and Qing periods: petty literati who, in close contact with the common people, defied the traditional belittlement of *xiaoshuo* as a literary genre and turned raw materials drawn from life into interesting stories.

What my reading has uncovered is a process of creation and re-creation: petty intellectuals collected the raw materials, from which they created *xiaoshuo* writings, and petty officials of the king's court re-created them in their editorial efforts. The end product of this process was not anecdotal snippets but fairly sophisticated *xiaoshuo* writings. Their sophistication can be gauged from the fact that Ban Gu listed fifteen schools of them in his treatise, even though only a few fragments have survived. Many of the *xiaoshuo* writings in Ban Gu's listed schools may have resembled the extant "Yan Danzi 燕丹子" and "Feiyan waizhuan 飛燕外傳" in content and form. Understandably, "Yan Danzi" and "Feiyan waizhuan" survived because both of them are literary accounts of true historical events. In this respect, history played a dual role. Under the protection of history, the *Mu Tianzi zhuan* 穆天子傳, perhaps the earliest specimen of Chinese historical fiction, came to be preserved.[33] All other *xiaoshuo* writings were consigned to oblivion, because Confucian disparagement and censorship would not allow them to exist. The surviving *xiaoshuo* writings from the Han consititute evidence that corroborates Ban Gu's view, and they have some of the features characteristic of the later *xiaoshuo* genres. It is reasonable to surmise that in the transition from the crude "discourse" heard in the street to sophisticated *xiaoshuo* writings produced in the petty officials' office, there was a complex process of fabrication, which suggests an artistry similar to the making of modern fiction, albeit on a smaller scale.

Huan Tan 桓譚 (c. 43 BC–AD 28) in his "Xinlun 新論" corroborated Ban Gu's view: "Those *xiaoshuo* writers, combining miscellaneous and short remarks with allegorical discussions taken from things at hand, created short writings. They are not lacking words worth examining for the sake of cultivating oneself and managing one's household."[34] Huan Tan's remark confirms that *xiaoshuo* writings were not all scraps of words passed on from mouth to mouth; some were compositions with allegorical meanings in figurative language. Liu Zhiji did not have a high opinion of *xiaoshuo*, nor did he view it as a category belonging to belles lettres. But in his treatise on history writing, his prejudiced comment reveals *xiaoshuo*'s genesis, nature, and mode of composition:

> When irresponsible people compose *xiaoshuo*, it becomes a perfunctory form of writing that records hearsay without annotations. As a result, the real and false are not distinguished, the right and wrong are confused. Guo Xian's *Dongming ji* and Wang Jia's *Shiyi ji* are such writings. These writings are completely composed of fictitious words intended to surprise the ignorant and vulgar folk. These show to what extent *xiaoshuo* can be harmful.[35]

Like Ban Gu, Liu Zhiji considered *xiaoshuo* as something composed by persons with an unconventional mind. He identified the mixture of the real and unreal in *xiaoshuo* writings, which is a characteristic feature of fiction. Most significantly, he came to the realization that some *xiaoshuo* writings are works composed in a fictitious manner with a fictitious subject matter. Inadvertently, he touched on the fictionality of *xiaoshuo*, the core of the modern notion of fiction. Although his identification of some essential elements of *xiaoshuo* writings was not consciously made, and certainly not intended to promote *xiaoshuo* as a literary genre, it inadvertently lends strong support to my argument that the early notion of *xiaoshuo* has similarities to the later notion. From a critical point of view, Liu Zhiji also correctly identified the *Dongming ji* and *Shiyi ji* as fictional works, the purpose of which is to appeal to popular taste. Although Liu Zhiji's comment was made on *xiaoshuo* writings after the Han, the continuity of the genre suggests that many of the early *xiaoshuo* writings may not have been very different from the tales of *zhiguai* 志怪 and *zhiren* 志人, genres in the Wei and Jin dynasties. These *xiaoshuo* writings of the later period were more likely fabricated tales than pseudophilosophy and pseudohistory writings that survived rigorous selection and censorship.

Lu Xun's speculative view, based on his annotations of Ban Gu, was this: "Generally speaking, some of these writings pretend to be written by ancients; some record ancient events. Those which claim to be written by ancients resemble philosophical writings but are shallow. Those which record past events come close to histories but seem absurd."[36] In his opinion, *xiaoshuo* at that time was a form of writing that is halfway between philosophy and history. This view has become the scholarly consensus up to the present day. When people talk about *xiaoshuo* before the Six Dynasties, few have looked upon them as literary works. But even in Lu Xun's speculation, *xiaoshuo* does have some characteristics that come close to the later notion of fiction. *Xiaoshuo's* recording of people is shallower than philosophical writings, and its recording of events does not adhere to facts. The first point shows *xiaoshuo* writing as a reflection of human life; the second point touches on fictionality. The combination of the two points comes close to the modern notion of fiction, which is a fictitious reflection of and on human life.

The lack of enough early *xiaoshuo* writings hinders our research into their nature, but this lack itself may give an idea as to why early *xiaoshuo* writings failed to survive the ages. The reason is not difficult to surmise. Apart from what I have labeled the "tyranny of history," it must have had much to do with the Confucian attitude. The putatively Confucian view of *xiaoshuo* reminds us of the origins of the Confucian classic, the *Shijing* or the *Book of Songs*. Many of the 365 poems in the *Book of Songs* were believed to have been collected by royal officials and were later believed to have been edited by Confucius. A note to Ban Gu's remark on *xiaoshuo* states: "Since the former kings wanted to learn of the customs and habits of the local neighborhoods and alleys, they set up the office of *xiaoshuo* to report them."[37] A comparative analysis of Confucius's supposed relation to both the *Shijing* and *xiaoshuo* will offer insight into the nature of early *xiaoshuo*, and allow us to speculate on what *xiaoshuo* writings looked like in the remotest past and its later uneasy relationship with poetry. Both *Shijing* poems and *xiaoshuo* writings were allegedly collected by royal officials from among the common people, but the two categories of writings received entirely different treatment by the reputed editor Confucius, who really represented the orthodox attitude toward the two different forms of writings. While the songs that were to make up the *Shijing* were favorably received and honored, the *xiaoshuo* writings from the alleys and streets received disparagement and were only given a minor role as something that could broaden people's knowledge. I bring up this point not only to show how the genre of *xiaoshuo* was mistreated but moreover to suggest two points for further discussions. First, *xiaoshuo* and poetry share a common ground because of their common provenance in the common people's natural and spontaneous literary creativity. This common ground may explain why Chinese *xiaoshuo* writing patently possesses features inherent in Chinese poetry. Second, the impact of the mistreatment is not entirely negative in *xiaoshuo*'s evolution into the modern notion of fiction. Both points I will discuss in detail in chapter 4. But for the time being, I think that the different treatment should be examined in two aspects: that of the content and that of its function. Let me deal with its function first. In the Confucian moral order, *xiaoshuo* functions as a supplement to the classics. Its generic function as a form of entertainment was almost completely overlooked until very late. Liu Xie's (c. 465–520) monumental study of Chinese literature up to his time, *Wenxin diaolong* 文心雕龍, discusses all the existent literary and nonliterary forms and genres, including historical and philosophical writings, but he left out *xiaoshuo* writings. Only in the chapter "Xieyin 諧隱" did he make mention of *xiaoshuo*:

> However, the place of the *hsieh* and *yin* in literature is comparable to that of the "Small Talk" [anecdotal writings which were considered as of no great importance] in the midst of the Nine Schools. For the petty officials collected these anecdotes to broaden their scope of observation. If one should allow himself to follow in their steps, would he be more advanced than [Ch'un-yü] K'un and [Tung-fang] So and the firm friends of Chan and Meng, the jesters?[38]

Liu Xie's brief remark echoes an idea mentioned in Ban Gu's discussion of *xiaoshuo*. Both of them traced the origins of *xiaoshuo* to the ancient office of the *bai-guan*, a minor scribe-official who was in charge of collecting the gossip of the streets and alleys for the royal court. Liu Xie was not free from the Confucian disparagement of *xiaoshuo*, but, it is to his credit that he implicitly noticed the main function of *xiaoshuo*, which is entertainment. As far as the function of entertainment goes, *xiaoshuo* must have dealt with the same subject matter that occupies the center of later *xiaoshuo* writings. Zhang Xuecheng (1738–1801) gave us a brief survey of the subject matter of *xiaoshuo*:

> *Xiaoshuo* came from the petty officials of the Zhou court. It deals with hearsay and insignificant topics of the winding alleys. Though the ancients did not abandon it, yet it is mostly idle fancy that has no credible basis. Generally speaking, it deals with miscellaneous subjects of ghosts and gods, and additionally tells of personal gratitude or grievances. The writings in the *Dongming ji* and *Shiyi ji* and the volumes of the *Soushen ji* and *Lingyi ji* became books that established themselves as a genre since the Six Dynasties. It was not until the Tang that *xiaoshuo* developed into individual stories, which formed a separate category of *Chuanqi*. . . . These stories usually tell of the love between men and women, of separation and reunion, sorrow and happiness: The story of Hong Fu tells of how the female protagonist deserts the Yang family to elope with Li Jing; the story of an embroidered coat narrates how Li Yaxian repays Zheng Yuanhe's love; Madame Han and Mr. Yu You become a couple thanks to red leaves; Miss Cui and Mr. Zhang fall in love through zither playing. While one tale tells of how Mingzhu dies of lovesickness and returns alive, another tale narrates how Huo Xiaoyu

retaliates against her perfidious lover after her death. Some of these tales are far-fetched accounts with seeming resemblances and some are blatantly groundless fancies. Though they are multifarious in feelings and situations, they share a general commonality. Initially, *xiaoshuo* writings were no more than extravagant reflections on ancient meanings, or the outcome of literati's consigning their emotions to wine, and they were not any different from the miscellaneous amorous poems of the Musical Bureau in the poetic genre. Since the Song and Yuan dynasties, *xiaoshuo* broadened into novels and was adapted into songs and plays. As a result, it allows the blind storytellers to sing it to the accompaniment of musical instruments and actors and actresses to perform it on stage. It appeals to people, irrespective of high or low tastes, male or female. All it does is to gratify the senses.[39]

While Zhang Xuecheng accused *xiaoshuo* writings of abandoning their ancient origin, his survey captures the continuity of *xiaoshuo* from its earliest appearance to its later development. He grasped the main characteristic of *xiaoshuo* both in content and form. In content, it deals with subject matters that are normally eschewed by more orthodox writings; in form, it pretends that the events it relates were real happenings. While his survey is valid in terms of the development of Chines *xiaoshuo*, his conclusion about the original conditions of *xiaoshuo* in antiquity is wrong. The subject matter of the early *xiaoshuo* and that of the later *xiaoshuo* did not change significantly over history. It is the mode of composition that changed over time.

Although Confucius never edited *xiaoshuo* as he was believed to have edited the *Shijng*, *xiaoshuo* in its early forms was "ghost-edited" by him. By this I mean that *xiaohuo* must have been collected, edited, and classified by his followers in accordance with the principles that he had established concerning the editing of the *Shijing*. The first editing principle is that the subject matter should be morally proper in terms of Confucius's saying: "Let there be no evil in your thoughts"; the second principle is that "Pleasure not carried to the point of debauch; grief not carried to the point of self-injury"; the third principle is that "the Master never talked of prodigies, feats of strength, disorders or spirits."[40] The subject matter that Zhang Xuecheng describes fails the criteria based on the Confucian principles of decorum and moral standards. From this, we can reasonably speculate on the main reason why all the fifteen schools of *xiaoshuo* collected before the Han are now lost. The main subject matter of early *xiaoshuo* writings must have been the same as that in the later *xiaoshuo* writings that has been criticized by Confucian scholars. What was allowed to exist by the Confucian standard in early *xiaoshuo* writings therefore came close to writings of history and philosophy that are morally acceptable and play a socially useful function in the Confucian world order of the Han, when Confucianism became the state orthodoxy. The rise of *zhiguai* and *zhiren* *xiaoshuo* in the Six Dynasties and of the *chuanqi xiaoshuo* in the Tang is at least partly explained by the slackening control of Confucianism.

THE INTRINSIC NATURE OF *XIAOSHUO*

The Confucian disparagement of *xiaoshuo* is probably responsible not only for the virtual nonexistence of early *xiaoshuo* writings before the Six Dynasties but also for an erroneous view in Chinese literary history expressed by Wen Yiduo:

> Stories and embryonic song-and-dance were not unheard of in China proper before then, but they had never developed into a division of literature. We have always seemed to be less than enthusiastic about telling stories and listening to stories. What we have shown interest in are didactic fables or factual history. We have never cultivated a taste for telling and listening to stories purely for the story's sake itself. At the least, we may say that it was the translation and preaching of Buddhist scriptures that are charged with a zest for stories which awakened in our native land a budding interest in story and which caused it then to combine with the comparatively advanced foreign forms to produce our own fiction and drama.[41]

Wen Yiduo's remark, emanating from an iconoclastic ideology that blinded him to the abundance of *xiaoshuo* writings before the Tang, is equivalent to saying that before the coming of Buddhist tales, Chinese writers were innately deficient in creative impulses for writing fiction. Likewise, the reading public lacked the innate desire to enjoy reading and listening to stories. Both kinds of abilities, innate to other nations, were cultivated through the introduction of Buddhism. As someone who grew up during the Cultural Revolution, I find this view as absurd as saying that in the historical period between 1966 and 1976, the virtual nonexistence of *xiaoshuo* writings in official publications in mainland China reveals the startling phenomenon that the Chinese nation suddenly lost her ability to create and enjoy fictional works. If anything, the lack of *xiaoshuo* writings during the Cultural Revolution should afford us an insight into why only a few *xiaoshuo* writings before the Six Dynasties have survived to this day. Governmental censorship and self-censorship were largely responsible for the disappearance of all but a few early *xiaoshuo* writings. The meager early *xiaoshuo* writings were able to survive only after they pledged their allegiance to historical writings.

Since Indian Buddhism has been identified by some scholars as the formative influence on the rise of Chinese fiction, we may as well examine the matter a little from the comparative perspective. In Western literary theory, fiction is believed to have had its origin in epic and drama. India also has an epic tradition, which may be taken to be the source of Indian fiction. When we look at the Indian tradition, however, we notice an interesting contrast with the Chinese tradition. While early China has an abundance of historical records but little fictional writings, early India has two world famous epics—the *Ramayana* and the *Mahabharata*—but has no early histories. This contrast does not imply that China had no epical and fictional impulse in its early development, nor does it suggest that India had no sense of history. I believe early civilizations have similar creative impulses. The contrast strongly suggests that different traditions channeled their creative energies in different directions, with the result that there were emphases on different literary forms. In early India, the creative impulse for writing histories was channeled into writing epics and dramas, the early forms of fiction. By contrast, in China, the creative impulse for writing fictional works was oriented toward writing histories. In his theoretical inquiry into Chinese narrative, Andrew Plaks makes a sagacious observation when he comments on the absence of epic tradition in early China: "But certainly the bearers of Chinese civilization have liked a good story as well as—or better than—the next man, and, what is more important, have produced what is perhaps the bulk of the world's corpus of narrative literature. The point here is simply to acknowledge the fact that historical writing, oriented towards the function of transmission, occupies the predominant position within the range of Chinese narrative possibilities, so that it is fiction that becomes the subset and historiography the central model of narration."[42]

In my opinion, in the early phase of Chinese civilization there was simply no place for a subset of fiction, due to governmental policies and self-censorship. As a result, fictional works led a parasitic existence by attaching themselves to historical records. If we closely examine some historical narratives, we will realize that some so-called historical narratives are fictional works in historical disguise. The *Mu Tianzi zhuan* (*An Account of the Travels of Emperor Mu*) (c. fourth century BC) is a typical example. For more than a thousand years after its discovery in AD 279, it was taken as a historical work; only in the Qing dynasty did Ji Yun, the general editor of the *Siku quanshu*, correctly classify it as belonging to the category of *xiaoshuo* writings. Ji Yun's correct classification was based on his perceptive understanding of the differences between historical records and literary fiction. With exceptional insight into its true nature, W. H. Nienhauser suggests that we should consider it a "historical fiction."[43] Following Ji Yun's and other scholars' cue, Deborah L. Porter conducts a study of the provenance, redaction, exegetical tradition, textual elements, and literary features in relation to historical records, and reconfirms Ji Yun's insights. She further argues that it is a literary representation of the Zhou dynasty's symbolic ways of dealing with traumatic crises and reestablishing dynastic identity, authority, and legitimacy.[44] Because of her reliance on a conceptual model of symbolism that presupposes a reconstruction of an absent referent in symbolization, she does not go any farther. In terms of available research, *the Travels of Emperor Mu* may be viewed as a Chinese epic. I may go even further and suggest that this extended historical narrative should be regarded as the first novel of magic realism as well as the first historical fiction in China. The narrative, composed and constructed on a principle of literary creation, was an imaginative representation of the creative spirit at work. In *Wenfu* (*Rhyme-Prose on Literature*), Lu Ji ably captures the creative spirit in these lines: "The writer envelops heaven and earth within shapes, and grasps myriad things with the tip of his brush"; "His spirit gallops to the eight limits of the earth; his mind roams ten thousand yards, up and down."[45] In a narrative form, *the Travels of Emperor Mu* presents an imaginative search comparable to Qu Yuan's spiritual search in poetic forms in many of his poems.

Having insisted on the continuity in the evolution of the term *xiaohsuo*, I must add that the early concept, in spite of considerable overlapping in meaning with the modern concept of fiction, differs from it significantly. The difference cannot be simply resolved by a distinction between a narrow sense of *xiaoshuo* and a broad sense of *xiaoshuo*. To pin down the difference, we must be able to answer this question: What distinguishes the traditional concept of *xiaoshuo* from the modern concept of fiction? I pose this question not just because I am interested in *xiaoshuo* as a conceptual category but also because answers to this question will give us a better understanding of the historical development of Chinese *xiaoshuo* and determine the choice of *xiaoshuo* or fictional works for this study. I think, the core of conceptual difference is fictionality. In discussing traditional Chinese theoretical discourses on *xiaoshuo*, Luo Fu 羅浮 voiced a most insightful opinion about the conceptual condition of *xiaoshuo*:

> What is *xiaoshuo* (small talk)? It distinguishes itself from what the *dayan* (big talk) talks about. First, it talks about the small (insignificant). It therefore will not talk about such important topics as heavenly classics and earthly meanings, the governance of the state and the education of the people, the Han Confucian scholars' exegeses of classics and their commentaries, or the Song Confucian scholars' efforts at cultivating the human heart through propriety and honesty. Second, it involves talk. But it will not talk about the ornate language and breadth of vision in Sima Qian's and Ban Gu's histories, the same artistry achieved by different means in Yang Xiong's and Sima Xiangru's writings, the different topics of sumptuous splendor, measured eloquence, and limpid restraint, and the different forms adopted to imitate the classics, to trace the origins of the Dao, and to analyze Sao poetry.[46]

Wu Gongzheng, in his *Xiaoshuo meixue* (*Aesthetics of Fiction*), rightly points out that Luo Fu drew a clear demarcation line between *xiaoshuo* writings and classics, histories, poetry, prose, and other forms of writing from the perspective of both content and form and established *xiaoshuo* as a distinct literary genre.[47] In Luo Fu's preface, he further narrowed down the idea of *xiaoshuo* in terms of subject matter and forms of expression:

> Its subject matter covers the minute details of the family, the relationship between father and son, daily necessities, food and drink, and social intercourse. Hence, it is called "small (trivial)." Its expressions are those of the idle talk on trivial matters among men and women of certain locations and places. Hence it is called "talk." Therefore, *xiaoshuo* writings with the utmost simplicity and the characteristics most easy to understand are the orthodox school of this genre.[48]

In Luo Fu's opinion, *xiaoshuo*'s subject matter is ordinary events of everyday life; its medium of expression is everyday language. He stressed simplicity and clarity as the defining characteristics of *xiaoshuo*. Wu Gongzheng again rightly points out that Luo Fu's idea of fiction had already formulated an inchoate idea of realism in fiction writing.[49] But Luo Fu's identification of *xiaoshuo*'s simplicity and clarity as the essence of *xiaoshuo* is only partially correct. It only grasps the formal aspect of *xiaoshuo*'s essence but misses the core element of *xiaoshuo*, which is the telling of fabricated stories. We have uncovered this core element in the early description of *xiaoshuo*, and it is clearly displayed in the evolution of this genre. It is found in *shuohua* 說話 ("speaking words," story-telling), the transitional genre connecting earlier and later *xiaoshuo*. *Shuohua* is an art form of storytelling that started in the Tang and existed until the Ming. Yuan Zhen 元稹, in his own annotation of a poetic line in his poem, "Time elapses during listening to stories," wrote: "[Bai Juyi?] once told the story of 'A Twig of Flower' at the Xinchang house; the telling lasted from midnight to the morning and the story was still not finished."[50] Clearly, *shuohua* means "telling stories" rather than just "talk." From *xiaoshuo* at the beginning through *shuohua* in the process of evolution to *xiaoshuo* again in the modern sense, we can see a discernable continuity.

THE PROBLEM OF
SELF-CONSCIOUS FICTIONALIZATION

The scholarly consensus in Chinese fiction studies holds that Tang fiction marks the full maturity of Chinese *xiaoshuo*. Nowadays, few scholars question this consensus, but why does Tang *xiaoshuo* represent the maturity of Chinese fiction? Lu Xun's view has been generally considered authoritative. In his opinion, *xiaoshuo* writings before the Tang resembled news reportage of modern times, and fiction writers did not intentionally create fiction as fiction:[51]

> *Xiaoshuo*, like poetry, witnessed a change in the Tang dynasty. Although it is still not far away from searching for the extraordinary and recording anec-dotes, yet its narration became subtle, and its diction ornate. Compared with the rough sketches of the Six Dynasties tales, its evolutionary traces were very obvious. What is most conspicuous is that by this time *xiaoshuo* writers began to consciously compose *xiaoshuo* writings.[52]

In Lu Xun's opinion, if the Wei and Jin marked the entry of Chinese literature into a period of self-conscious creation of literary works, the Tang represented the beginning of self-conscious creation in Chinese fictional development. In a most recent study, Lu Xun's opinion has been reaffirmed. *Zhongguo xiaoshuo yishuo shi* (History of Chinese Fictional Art) recognizes that the Wei, Jin, Northern and Southern Dynasties period is a period of self-conscious literary creation; the notion of fiction started to be born; and major elements necessary for fiction as a literary genre appeared. But because of various reasons, the *xiaoshuo* writings in this period, the *zhiguai* and *zhiren* tales, are still a far cry from genuine fictional works. In the title for the chapter discussing the *xiaoshuo* writings of this period, the new study simply restates Lu Xun's view: "Fei youyi zuo xiaoshuo de zhiguai zhiren" (*Zhiguai* and *Zhiren* Tales as Unconsciously Composed Fictional Works." By contrast, the study entitles the chapter discussing the Tang *xiaoshuo* writings as "Shi youyi wei xiaoshuo de Tang chuanqi" (Tang *Chuanqi* Tales as Fictional Works by Writers Who Began to Compose *Xiaoshuo* Consciously).[53]

My discussion in the introduction has already problematized this accepted view. The problem of conscious fictionality constitutes a theoretical issue not only for *xiaoshuo*'s historical development but also for its status as a literary genre. In this section, I will explore this issue from both historical and conceptual perspectives. What does the expression *youyi wei xiaoshuo* (consciously creating *xiaoshuo*) mean? In Lu Xun's words, it refers to a self-conscious intention to invent and fictionalize: "The writer deliberately indicates the fictitious nature of the narrated events 作者故意顯示著事跡的虛構."[54] Lu Xun's view was derived from Hu Yinglin's similar opinion:

> *Xiaoshuo* writings about changes and strange happenings flourished in the Six Dynasties, but most of them are transmitted records with errors and inaccuracies. They may not all be fictitious accounts with hypothetical words. By the time of the Tang, people intentionally hunted for the strange and made use of *xiaoshuo* to convey allegorical meanings.[55]

Both Hu and Lu Xun are of the opinion that the *xiaoshuo* writings before the Tang are radically different from those of the Tang because the authorial intention is different and only the Tang *chuanqi* tales involved conscious creation of fictional works. Recently, a few scholars have questioned this assessment. They cite authorial claims to authenticity at the end of a number of stories to argue that "it is not sufficiently convincing to treat 'self-conscious fictionalization' as the main characteristic feature of the Tang *xiaoshuo* and the reasons for its rise."[56] This questioning is provocative. Lu Xun's view of the Tang as the self-conscious age of *xiaoshuo* is valid, but his view that conscious fictionalization only started in the Tang is problematic because of conceptual as well as historical reasons.

Conscious fictionalization involves authorial intention. Theoretically, authorial intention is a very slippery category for literary studies. With the "death" of the author, it is difficult, if not impossible, to credit or discredit claims made by an author with regard to his intention in creating a literary work. Time and again literary theorists who uphold diverse views, ranging from those of New Criticism to postmodernism, have demonstrated that the pretextual and posttextual intentions are unreliable, misleading, or simply erroneous. In terms of contemporary literary theory, it is almost impossible to draw a line between self-conscious creation and mindless transmission. Historically, because of political, moral, and aesthetic reasons, a writer may try to hide his real intention in composing a fictional work. I will critically analyze the case of Gan Bao 干寶 (fl. 320), the Jin historian and literary man, to illustrate this point. Gan Bao collected *xiaoshuo* writings of his time into *Soushen ji* 搜神記. In the collected pieces, there is no sure way to ascertain that the writers of those tales, especially those that differ little from modern short stories, did not compose their tales with conscious fictionality in mind. Those writers did not leave behind any writings about their authorial intentions. But Gan Bao, who composed some tales in the collection, also wrote a preface to it that details his intentions in compiling it. Those intentions, whether we view them as pretextual or post-textual, not only testify to the unreliable nature of authorial intention but also reveal some hidden intentions that imply conscious fictionality.

He professes that his intention in collecting those *xiaoshuo* writings is to "illuminate the truthfulness of the divine Dao."[57] This has been cited as evidence that he was preoccupied with the truthfulness of factual records, not with the fictionality of literary imagination. But no scholar has so far read Gan Bao's words closely to understand his implications. All scholars have overlooked that what Gan Bao emphasizes is faithfulness to the divine Dao, not truthfulness of factual records. The divine Dao is the first metaphysical principle in Chinese thought. In his remark that the collected *xiaoshuo* writings adequately illuminate the truthfulness of the divine Dao, he only means that they may serve to exemplify the metaphysical principle that underlies myriad things, not that they attest to the faithfulness of what they record. Thus, Gan Bao's remark articulates a writing principle similar to Aristotle's mimetic principle of fiction based the law of probability. He defends his proposition with some strategies. One of them is that due to the lapse of time and the unreliability of human perception, even official histories supposed to record historical persons and events faithfully often cannot avoid being tainted with unverifiable events and outright errors. Furthermore, he declares that if official history tolerates the inclusion of untrue events, *xiaoshuo* as a category of writing meant to complement history is justified in writing about fictitious events. Most importantly, under the pretext of collecting *xiaoshuo* writings to complement historical records, he concludes his preface with a subtle allusion to the entertaining function of *xiaoshuo*: "I wish that in the future some busybody would collect the original forms of the *xiaoshuo* writings so that one can read them for entertainment without any worry about errors."[58] Here Gan Bao affirms the entertaining function of *xiaoshuo* and implicitly endorses conscious fictional creation under the pretext of collecting raw materials for historical writings. That he does not openly justify conscious fiction creation is understandable, because in the society of his time, scholars were still afraid of deviating from the Confucian admonition that *xiaoshuo* is something with which a gentleman should not get involved.

Gan Bao explicitly posed a distinction between the originally true account of an event and its imaginatively fictitious account, even though he considered the latter as arising from unreliable transmission. The distinction confirms that people of the Six Dynasties period did have a sense of what is true and what is fictitious, thereby seriously questioning Lu Xun's claim that: "People of the Six Dynasties period were not engaged in consciously creating fiction, because they treated the events of ghosts and those of men as the same; both kinds were regarded as real events."[59] Lu Xun's claim evidently underestimated the intelligence of the Six Dynasties period. In my opinion, scholars of the period treated *xiaoshuo* writings as though they were factual writings not because they could not distinguish between truth and fiction but because they were under the tyranny of history. Gan Bao's case is an eloquent illustration. An overview of Gan Bao's preface shows that his attitude toward *xiaoshuo* was ambivalent, paradoxical, and contradictory. His position was determined partly by his own dual role as historian and fiction writer and partly by what I have labeled the "tyranny of history." The tyranny of history stipulated that he, as a historian, was required to observe the sine qua non of factuality in history writing, but the creative impulse in him pulled him in the direction of fictitious creation. The conflicting impulses forced him to adopt a split attitude toward *xiaoshuo*: objectively he recognized its fictitious nature, but subjectively he denied that its fictionality was consciously willed by the author. His ambivalent position does not deny the notion of conscious creation but confirms the power and intensity of history's tyranny.

Kenneth Dewoskin's bibliographical and generic study of the *zhiguai* tales supports this view. Nowadays, it is commonly accepted that the *zhiguai* tales were leftovers from the materials that historiographers collected for compiling dynastic histories. Before the Tang, though they were classified in the category of defective historical records, they were still considered historical writings. Because of their literary nature, they fit uneasily in the category of history. Dewoskin observes that during the Six Dynasties, history and *zhiguai* tales began to diverge, and by the end of the period the separation between the two became so widely accepted that fictional pieces could be composed and read for literary purposes. But the Six Dynasties did not complete the process of separation, and there was still a compelling need for a rationale to compose fictional writings.[60] With the appearance of *Leishu* 類書, the dissociation of *xiaoshuo* writings from formal historiography was complete. It "freed writers inclined toward fiction from the restraints of historical methodology, freed them to borrow from the popular oral tradition and to elaborate plots and description in prose and verse. In short, writers were freed to indulge in the conscious fictionalizing that is the distinct feature of late Six Dynasties *chih-kuai* and the T'ang *ch'uan-ch'i*."[61] The process of generic divergence implies that it is not that *xiaoshuo* writers did not consciously create fictional works before the Tang but that there was no rationale that sanctioned consciously created fictional works, nor was there an appropriate category into which fictional works could fit.

It is difficult to imagine that, in a self-conscious age of literary creation, the *xiaoshuo* writers were engaged in mindless transmission of existent tales or unconscious transcription of other people's experience. Tao Yuanming's 陶

淵明 (365–427) literary activities concerning *xiaoshuo* writings alone should call the accepted claim into question. Tao compiled *Soushen houji* 搜神後記 (A Sequel to *Soushen ji*), a collection of *xiaoshuo* writings that narrate blatantly unreal and fantastic characters and events. The collection contains his famous utopian tale "The Peach Blossom Spring." The title has since become the Chinese equivalent to the Western term "utopia." Despite numerous attempts in history at locating the real setting for the tale, the utopian nature of this tale makes evident that it is fictitious. Utopia means "no place" in Greek. Whether it is Tao Yuanming's "Peach Blossom Spring" or Thomas More's *Utopia* or Plato's *Republic*, a utopian writing is created as a consequence of the writer's dissatisfaction with the conditions of the real world and his desire to imaginatively create a new world to his heart's content. Neither its fictitious nature nor consciously willed fictionality is to be doubted. The very fact that Tao Yuanming's tale is of a utopia suggests that the fictionality of the tale was consciously willed by the author. And that the author should have taken the trouble to compose a narrative poem to duplicate the tale further testifies to its conscious fictionalization.[62] If we take Tao's poem about the Peach Blossom Spring as a consciously written poem, by simple logic we must admit that his tale was consciously composed and its fictionality was consciously willed.

Critical analysis of *xiaoshuo* writings provides more solid evidence that before the Tang, there were plenty of signs of deliberate fictionalization. Here I would like to analyze one tale, "The Girl Who Sells Powder 賣粉兒," from the *Soushen ji*. The full text reads as follows:

> Once upon a time, there was a wealthy family with an only son. He was very pampered and given unusual freedom. One day, while strolling in the market, he saw a beautiful girl selling foreign powder and fell in love with her. As he had no proper ways to express his love for her, he pretended to buy powder from her shop. Everyday, he went to her shop to buy powder and then left the shop after he got it. At first, the girl had nothing to say about his coming and going. As time went by, the girl became suspicious and her suspicions deepened day by day.
>
> One day, when the boy came again, she asked him: "Sir, you buy this powder. How are you going to use it?"
>
> The boy answered, "I have fallen in love with you. I did not dare express it to you. But I wanted to see you every day. So, I made the excuse of buying powder from you."
>
> Deeply moved, the girl promised to make a tryst with him. It would have to wait till the next evening. As evening fell the next day, the boy went to bed joyously in his room, waiting for the girl to come. By night, the girl came as promised. The boy was overwhelmed with joy. Holding her arms, he said, "My long-cherished wish has been fulfilled today." He jumped with joy and unexpectedly died. The girl, terrified out of her wits, did not know what to do. So she fled from the room. The next day, she returned to the powder shop.

At breakfast time the following day, the boy's parents found it strange that he did not get up. They went to his bedroom to see him, only to find him dead in his bed. They laid his body in preparation for a funeral. Searching through their son's boxes, they found over a hundred bags of foreign powder. Some were packed in big bags, some in small bags. Altogether, the bags made a big pile. His mother speculated, "My son's death must have something to do with this powder." They then went to the market to buy all the available foreign powder. When they reached the girl's shop, they compared her powder with the powder found in their son's room. The two matched exactly. They therefore caught the girl and questioned her, "Why did you kill our son?"

Hearing their questioning, the girl burst into tears and told them the whole truth. The boy's parents did not believe her words and turned her in to the magistrate. The girl said, "I am no longer afraid to die, but I beg to see your son's body and mourn him to my heart's content." The county magistrate approved her request. The girl went straight to the boy's house. Holding his corpse with her hands, she wailed with deep sorrow. She moaned, "I did not expect bad luck to bring us to this pass. If your dead soul could show signs, what regrets do I have before I die?" All of a sudden, the boy came to life and retold the whole story. They became husband and wife and had many children thereafter.[63]

The fictitious nature of this story is clear as daylight. It is, however, a realistic tale with lifelike characters and a credible plot, except for the detail of the dead boy's return to life. Even this unrealistic detail is not out of place in a love story. Indeed, it may be viewed as a surrealistic or fantastic element, typical of many later stories in the Chinese tradition. In narrative technique, the story is quite sophisticated. It is narrated by an unobtrusive third-person narrator with cursory probing into the characters' mind. The boy's excuse, the girl's suspicion, the mother's speculation, the parental disbelief, and the use of temporal connectives—all are indicative of a unified creative vision, careful arrangement of details, and conscious intention to write an intriguing and credible tale. The ending is perhaps somewhat too abrupt. Otherwise, the tale would have been a perfect specimen of short realistic fiction with romantic elements. If it were placed into Giovanni Boccaccio's *The Decameron* (1351–53), a reader who has no previous knowledge of Boccaccio's story collection would mistake it for a tale produced in the romance tradition, the precursor of Western fiction.

As for its intentionality, there is little possibility that the author, whoever it was, intended to use it as a factual account for the transmission of extraordinary information. An educated guess would be that it was consciously intended to be an interesting love tale. In many other Six Dynasties tales, the characteristic features Lu Xun cited to describe the fiction of the Tang are all there. We may even say that many *zhiguai* and *zhiren* tales are already fictional works in the modern sense of the word, because they contain a kind of literariness that does not come from their imitation of the world but emanates from language's self-referentiality. Paul de Man's observation about the relationship between literature and language representation may lend support to this claim:

> Literature is fiction not because it somehow refuses to acknowledge "reality," but because it is not *a priori* certain that language functions according to principles which are those, or which are *like* (italics original) those, of the phenomenal world. It is therefore not *a priori* certain that literature is a reliable source of information about anything but its own language.[64]

Self-referentiality is a concept in postmodern literary theory. In some fantastic tales of the Six Dynasties, *xiaoshuo* writers seemed to have already become aware of it. "Yangxian shusheng" 陽羨書生 is a case in point. It tells of a character named Xu Yan. He meets a scholar on his way. Complaining of a hurt foot, the latter requests to be carried in Xu Yan's goose cage together with his two geese. Xu Yan takes it to be a joke, but the scholar goes into the cage. He does not dwindle in size, nor does the cage expand. The geese are not disturbed, and Xu Yan does not feel his load becomes heavier. When Xu Yan takes a rest, the scholar comes out of the cage and offers to entertain him. From his mouth he spits out a copper box, which holds all kinds of food and wine. After they drink and eat for some time, the scholar spits out a beautiful woman to keep them company. When the scholar becomes drunk and falls asleep, the woman spits out a young man from her mouth, who she says is her secret lover. When the scholar is about to awake, the woman spits out a tent, in which the scholar asks the woman to sleep with him. After both fall asleep, the second man reveals to Xu Yan that he himself has a secret love, and he spits out a young woman. She entertains the two men while they chat over wine. Hearing the scholar move in the tent, the second man swallows his woman in his mouth. The first woman comes out and swallows the second man in her mouth. When the scholar wakes up, he bids Xu Yan good-bye and swallows the first woman and all the utensils except a brass plate. He leaves the plate to Xu Yan as a souvenir.[65] I have omitted some details of the story. It is not just a tale about daydreams and secret desires. It is also an allegory about storytelling. The spitting out and swallowing of persons and things allegorically refers to the fabrication of fictional elements through language. Its fictionality is not only self-evident but also self-conscious.

In their study on the artistic history of Chinese fiction that I mentioned above, the authors, Meng and Ning, make a very meaningful distinction between myths and fables. According to them, "the fictionality of myths is unconsciously intended while that of fables is completed under self-conscious circumstances. It is the outcome of an intentional pursuit."[66] They correctly point out that the essential difference between myth and fable lies in a difference in compositional motive and textual effects. They further observe that "The fables in the philosophical writings of the pre-Qin eras were self-consciously employed for the sake of debates and persuasion. In emplotment, characterization, and other aspects, they are consciously created, very mature, and therefore are endowed with a great deal of fictionality."[67] Regrettably, when it comes to the question "When did the Chinese tradition start conscious fictional writing?" the authors retreat to the commonly accepted position first posited by Lu Xun.[68] They admit that there is conscious fictionality in the *zhiguai* tales of the Six Dynasties, but say it is very limited. Basing myself on the above conceptual inquiry and critical analysis, however, I think it reasonable to say that the scholarly consensus about the lack of conscious fiction making before the Tang is far too conservative and needs to be reconsidered and reevaluated.

CHAPTER TWO

The Nature of (Chinese) Fiction

I have examined a number of historical and ideological factors that have contributed to the complexity of Chinese fiction study, such as Confucian disparagement, the dominance of historiography, the conflation of early writing forms, and the problem of self-conscious fictionality. Because of these factors, the true nature of Chinese fiction has been shrouded in a mist of conceptual ambiguity. I think that we need to shift perspectives. Not only does *xiaoshuo* need to be liberated from the tyranny of historiography, but fiction theory needs to be emancipated from the dominance of related discourses. Rather than restricting the discussion of *xiaoshuo* as a literary genre to its relation to historical and philosophical writings, we ought to enlarge our horizons and examine the concept of fiction in its own right. There is in the history of Chinese literature a historical/narrative inertia that holds back the development of Chinese fiction, and Chinese *xiaoshuo* had to fight this inertia in order to gain full development into an art form. The motivating force that has transformed *xiaoshuo* into modern fiction is a drive toward pure fiction. Without this drive, Chinese fiction would still have remained a form of historical narrative or storytelling, and would not have been able to make the aesthetic turn to a full-fledged verbal art. The historical inertia has also adversely affected the study of Chinese fiction up to the present day. In practically all extant studies on Chinese fiction, the dominant paradigm is grounded on a historical perspective. In this chapter, I will not abandon the historical approach in its entirety, but will employ it to complement an analytic approach. Instead of trying to isolate fictional elements from a circumstantial perspective, I will first formulate a workable definition of fiction and use it as the yardstick to identify that which makes a narrative a fictional work and to locate landmark works that have contributed to the full maturity and artistic achievement of Chinese fiction.

A DEFINITION OF FICTION

The catchall category *xiaoshuo* seems to suggest that there is no conceptual equivalent to the modern concept of "fiction" in early Chinese history. Does this mean that fiction in the modern sense of the word did not arise until very late in China? This seems to be the widely accepted scholarly consensus. In chapter 1, I critiqued Wen Yiduo's view on the origins of Chinese fiction. His view was held by a number of renowned scholars of his time and enjoyed enthusiastic support by later scholars. In 1983, Victor Mair revisited the issue and wrote a provocative article, "The Narrative Revolution in Chinese Literature: Ontological Presuppositions." It became the central contention in a forum on Chinese fiction. In the article, Victor Mair employs comparative evidence on "Dunhuang transformation texts" (*bianwen* 敦煌變文) and Indian philosophical thinking to support a claim that has been made by a number of renowned Chinese scholars, including Wen Yiduo, Ch'en Yin-ko, Hu Shih, Ch'en Shou-yi, and others: the introduction of Buddhism into China exerted a tremendous influence on many intellectual aspects of Chinese culture; and in the field of literature, Chinese drama and fiction would not have arisen without the intellectual stimulus from Indian philosophy and thematic borrowings from Indian sources.[1] What is new and daring in Mair's study is his argument that "there is virtually nothing before the T'ang period that can properly be designated as 'fiction' (that which is feigned or imagined)"[2] and his contention that the introduction of fiction from India was the driving force for a virtual revolution in Chinese narrative.

Mair's view has been contested explicitly or implicitly by a number of scholars. It was directly challenged by Kenneth J. Dewoskin in his article "On Narrative Revolution," the thesis of which goes diametrically against that of Mair. Dewoskin argues that "invention—fiction writing—was an essential, perhaps *the* essential, mode of narrative in pre-Tang China, contrary to Mair's thesis that early narrative was *intended* (italics in the original) to be precisely and factually historical and became fictional only by rare (and regrettable) lapses in the discipline of factual recording."[3] Taking issue with Mair's narrow definition of "fiction" and his narrow focus on available evidence, Dewoskin concludes that "the revolution in narrative was not primarily a large-scale importation of fiction and drama (either the substance or the sensibilities), as Mair argues, but more plausibly a large-scale elevation and expansion of indigenous fictional and dramatic literature into written form by literati whose interest in them was newly stimulated. This explanation accounts for the manifest continuity in Chinese narrative—in terms of characters, themes, and sensibilities—that makes Chinese narrative recognizable as such from archaic to late imperial times."[4]

Employing R. G. Collingwood's two theoretical tenets in history writing—the "critical impulse," which refers to a historian's preference to select and reject his collected materials, and "constructive imagination," which refers to the process of imaginatively linking mere facts and making them intelligible and meaningful for the reader[5]—and Northrop Frye's emphasis on emplotment as the core of fictional narrative,[6] Dewoskin argues that in early Chinese histories, there is an abundance of fiction and fictionality. In his discussion of

Sima Qian's *Shiji* (Records of the Grand Historian), Dewoskin argues that with an intention to instruct posterity, Sima Qian, motivated by an extraordinary "constructive imagination" made bare documentary materials transmitted from the past into an enthralling collection of narrative plots: "There can be no question that a great deal of the Grand Historian's accounts of pre-Ch'in figures and events were 'made-up,' 'feigned,' or 'imagined.'"[7] Whereas Dewoskin argues from the perspective of thematic emplotment that there are fictional accounts in early Chinese history, William Nienhauser argues from the perspective of narrative technicalities that Chinese fiction originates from early history writings and miscellaneous writings. In his article "The Origins of Chinese Fiction," he analyzes fictional techniques of some early historical writings and suggests that "works demonstrating fictional techniques occur . . . much earlier" in Chinese history.[8]

I agree with Dewoskin, Nienhauser, and other scholars that fiction arose very early in the Chinese tradition. I, however, must point out that Mair's thesis is very sophisticated, and is not only based on the views expressed by renowned modern scholars but also supported by authoritative ancient scholars. The view of fictional elements in the pre-Tang *xiaoshuo* as an accident is derived from Liu Zhiji's 劉知幾 (661–721) theoretical discourse on historical narratives. In the *Shitong* (*Generalities on History*), Liu Zhiji viewed *pianji xiaoshuo* 偏記小說, the closest category to fictional works, as a result of a lamentable lapse by *wangzhe* 妄者 (irresponsible persons), *bizhe* 蔽者 (ignorant persons), *miuzhe* 謬者 (persons with erroneous views), and *yuzhe* 愚者 (foolish persons).[9] To contest Mair's thesis with a concept of fictionality that valorizes imaginative reconstruction of existent materials and the ample use of fictional techniques as patent signs of fiction is not addressing the core issues. The fictional elements that the opposing scholars have identified are certainly signs of fictionality, but they may indeed be incidental elements of fiction, not intended to serve any authorial plan to create a fictional work. The counter-argument is therefore not entirely persuasive. We therefore need to contest Mair's view directly by providing hard evidence supported by conceptual rigor. This requires us not only to search for the origins of fiction in early writings but also to conceptualize the notion of fiction.

All too often, historical and theoretical studies of Chinese fiction search for the roots of fiction in the *zhiguai* and *zhiren* tales of the Six Dynasties. But most modern scholars of Chinese fiction agree that the earliest elements of fiction can be found in narratives that predated the Six Dynasties. Dewoskin rightly points out, "[T]he earliest moments of Chinese fiction . . . were in fact the earliest moments in Chinese narrative writing itself, the classical histories and certain sections of the classical philosophical works."[10] The question then boils down to how to separate fictional elements from nonfictional elements. Previously, scholars have adopted a historical approach, trying to designate a genre or a period as marking the point when fiction and history diverged from each other.[11] This approach has its advantages, but it also has a problem. Due to the lack of clear definitions of fiction and history in traditional China and the blurring of the line between what really happened and what is imagined in *xioashuo*'s development, it is almost impossible to designate a genre or period as marking the birth of fiction. If, however, we had a hard-and-fast definition of fiction, the task would be much easier. In my foregoing analysis, I have problematized various notions of fiction in history. Now I am going to try to formulate a workable definition of fiction.

An adequate definition of fiction must take into account two related aspects: (1) fiction as a literary genre, and (2) fiction as a metaphysical category. Generically, fiction is a literary genre that combines the function of language for communication and that of history and philosophy for the consideration of human life and the world, but as it affirms neither function explicitly, it tells no specific historical truth or philosophical truth. It is a form of discourse that aims at a social function without a definite social purpose other than entertainment. Otherwise, it becomes a form of propaganda, not a verbal art. Of course, all fictional works are implicitly or explicitly writings of propaganda, because their authors consciously or unconsciously propagate some ideological or moral positions, but for a fictional work to be a verbal art, it must transcend its intended ideology. Metaphysically, a definition of fiction needs to answer the question: What is fiction in its ontological and epistemological dimensions? As an initial idea for further conceptual fine-tuning, let us define fiction tentatively as *a narrative of events that have no prior temporal existence in the real world but are true to life*. The reason this definition is tentative is that it is still inadequate in a number of conceptual aspects. For example, it cannot explain why narrative materials with circumstantial elements of fiction should not be regarded as literary fiction. To remedy the inadequacy of the initial definition, we need to introduce "intentionality" into the definition of fiction and propose to measure fictional works by their own intended fictionality. The coupling of "fictionality" and "intentionality" will facilitate a fine-tuning of my idea. By "intended fictionality" I mean *the ontological condition of a narrative work that is consciously intended not as a faithful record of reality but as an imaginative account of fabrication, whose coming into being is not intended for the transmission of knowledge but for aesthetic pleasure.* In simple words, the fictionality is not accidental or circumstantial; it is consciously willed. A narrative with this kind of fictionality may be said to have attained the status of pure fiction.

To summarize, I propose that *fiction as a literary genre is a kind of prose narrative about actions and events that may not necessarily have prior temporal existence but are nevertheless true to the law of probability in life, and it is intentionally created not primarily for the transmission of information but for the sake of entertainment and aesthetic appreciation.* With the formulated definition as the yardstick, it should be easier to subject narrative materials to a conceptual examination and separate fictional elements from nonfictional elements.

FICTIONALITY:
THE CONCEPTUAL CORE OF *XIAOSHUO*

Early forms of *xiaoshuo* were viewed as a category of writing halfway between history and philosophy. This notion suggests that *xiaoshuo*'s survival depended on the two categories of writing, especially on history. But as I have argued earlier, *xiaoshuo*'s indebtedness to history is a paradoxical one. Thanks to history, *xiaoshuo* writings were granted a right to existence. This right to existence, however, was also a pledging of allegiance and a forfeiting of certain natural rights. While giving *xiaoshuo* a place to exist, history took *xiaoshuo* captive, assigning to it a servile status. History became the master, and *xiaoshuo* its servant or slave. Chinese *xiaoshuo* was compelled to fight its master, history, in order to gain full development. Previously, scholars of Chinese fiction have noticed this paradoxical situation. David Rolston has observed that fiction critics adopted two strategies in dealing with history: "The simplest was to claim that individual works of fiction are just like historical works in general or some historical work in particular. . . . A less explicit and more dangerous approach was to argue that fiction is different from history and not to be slighted for that fact. In general, fiction critics made use of the prestige of history until they felt fiction had become mature enough to discard that crutch and walk on its own."[12] Correspondingly, Sheldon Lu argues in his study that Chinese fiction theory and criticism have experienced a transition from an emphasis on historicity to that of fictionality.[13]

To adequately define *xiaoshuo*'s sense of fiction in the Chinese tradition, we have to examine the relationship between history and fiction and discuss fictionality, the core of fiction, in conceptual terms. We may start from Aristotle's position. Aristotle did not theorize on the relationship between history and fiction, but he drew a distinction between history and poetry, with poetry meant as a general term for fiction in its broad sense. He stated in his *Poetics*:

> [I]t is not the function of the poet to relate what has happened, but what may happen—what is possible according to the law of probability or necessity. The poet and the historian differ not by writing in verse or in prose. The work of Herodotus might be put into verse, and it would still be a species of history, with meter no less than without it. The true difference is that one relates what has happened, the other what may happen.[14]

Aristotle's idea of probability clarifies the difference between history and fiction. His distinction helps us clarify a number of crucial issues in the study of fiction in general and Chinese fiction in particular. His view of fiction as a conceptual category rather than a generic or formal category suggests that fiction may exist in different forms of writing: poetry, drama, or prose. It is therefore proper to say that formal elements should not be the single most important criteria in identifying works of fiction. What then is the decisive factor? Aristotle's idea of probability plus a formalistic commonsense may provide an answer. In discussions of literary forms, fiction generally refers to the story, the novella, and the novel. What is common to the three genres of fiction is not just that they are all written in prose; one intrinsic quality common to all three genres is that they narrate events in a hypothetical way that may not be true to facts but is true to life. Thus, fiction in the normal sense of the word is a form of fictive narrative in prose. Hence, the decisive factor for fiction is fictionality.

This is not very difficult to see, but a more difficult question then arises as to what fictionality is. In consideration of its ontological status, fiction is always related to the opposition between truth and falsity. In a scientific approach to truth and falsity, fiction refers to "a false connection between words and things, or reference to something that doesn't exist."[15] In literary studies, fiction is generally perceived to be a representation of what does not exist but may exist through the use of language. This view emanates from the philosophical tradition committed to a mimetic view of the relation between concepts and the world, a tradition that has tried to maintain an epistemological distinction between truth and falsity, reality and imagination. Fiction as a literary form in the modern sense of the word, however, does not mean "untrue," "unreal," or "something that has never existed or happened." The word "fiction" comes from the Latin *fingere* and has the basic meaning of "to form," "to fashion," and "to invent." It has similar connotation to the Chinese word *zao* or *zuo* (to create, make). Fictionality is a paradoxical notion. On the one hand, it means "untrue or unreal accounts"; on the other, it claims to be true by the principle of probability. What unifies the opposite impulses in the concept is the idea that fiction may not be true to verifiable facts, but is true to life.

In traditional Chinese fiction criticism, there was no exact equivalent to "fictionality" until the appearance of the modern concept of *xugouxing* (the qualities or properties pertaining to fiction). However, there were many near equivalents, such as the popular expressions *wuzhong shengyou* 無中生有 (to create something out of nothing), *pingkong niezao* 憑空捏造 (to invent something out of the blue), and *pingkong zaohuang* 憑空造謊 (to create lies out of thin air), and more imaginative expressions like *kongzhong louge* 空中樓閣 (a tower in the air), *jinghua shuiyue* 鏡花水月 (flowers in a mirror and the moon in water), *haishi shenlou* 海市蜃樓 (sea mirage), and *haiwai sanshan* 海外三山 (fairies' mountains beyond the sea).

In the Chinese tradition, history follows the creative principle of *shu'er buzuo* (transmission of past events and not creation of events) or *yishu weizuo* (to use transmission as creation). Historical fiction in the Chinese tradition deviates considerably from this principle, but does not abandon this principle altogether. In terms of Aristotle's distinction between history and fiction, we may say that Chinese historical novels, which constitute a major current of traditional Chinese fiction, can be regarded as both fiction and nonfiction.

They may be viewed as nonfiction, because those historical novels narrate what has happened in Chinese history. Indeed, often a historical novel is an artistic extension of official history with a faithful adherence to chronology, persons, events, and settings—so much so that readers often confuse historical fiction with histories. In *A Brief History of Chinese Fiction* (1924), Lu Xun cited an interesting example. He says the *Sanguo yanyi* (*The Romance of the Three Kingdoms*) is made up of 70 percent history and 30 percent fiction. As a result, many reader mistake the novel for a factual account of history. As Lu Xun pointed out, even a learned poet-scholar like Wang Shizhen 王士禎 (1634–1711) made the mistake of treating a fictitious place in the novel as a real place and sincerely composed an elegiac poem to mourn the death of Pang Tong, a character who is described to have died at that place.[16] Precisely because of the fictitious parts, historical novels are fictional works. In their detailed characterization of historical personages, events, settings, and even plot arrangements, they do not doggedly adhere to historical accounts in official history and instead narrate what may have happened by the law of probability. For instance, in the *Sanguo yanyi*, after Zhao Yun, one of his generals, has gone through a life-and-death fight and brought Liu Bei's baby son to safety, Liu Bei throws his rescued baby to the ground, saying that because of this baby, he has almost lost a great general. This episode did not actually happen, but the author of the novel imaginatively thought that it might have happened in view of Liu Bei's characteristic way of winning devotion from his subordinates. It is these kinds of fictional accounts that entitled Chinese historical novels to a place in the domain of fiction. However, since the historical novel generally follows the development of history, they cannot be regarded as "pure fiction," a term which I will further clarify, but for the time being can be taken to mean representation in language of events that has never happened.

Even in official histories, fiction is not entirely absent. Zhang Xuecheng, for example, is of the opinion that history writers may invent, fabricate, and fictionalize within reasonable limits sanctioned by the law of probability. The fabrication and invention on the part of the historian are allowed particularly in dealing with the delineation of characters' inner thoughts and putting words in their mouths:

> In regard to the method of recording speeches, there is no invariable rule for addition and reduction. It all depends on what the author wants. But the [author] must infer what was in the speaker's mind on that day. In that case, the addition of a thousand words is not too many. But when [the author] comes up with what was not in the speaker's mind on that day, the addition of one word is fabrication as well, even though the words make up a good composition.[17]

Zhang Xuecheng's method of fiction writing contains precious insights that have been employed by recent Western scholars who challenge the definition of fiction in terms of imitations of life alone.[18]

Robert Scholes reconceptualizes Aristotle's distinction between history and poetry in terms of C. S. Peirce's triadic model of the sign and develops a refined distinction between historical narrative and fictional narrative. It offers a clearer understanding of fictionality or pure fiction. Scholes makes a semiotic attempt to clarify some aspects of "story" by examining the process of encoding and decoding stories in terms of the Peircean triad of semiosis: sign, object, and intepretant. He correlates the Peircean triad with the essential elements in a story's creation and interpretation: "The object of a story is the sequence of events to which it refers; the sign of a story is the text in which it is told (print, film, etc.); and the interpretant is the diegesis or constructed sequence of events generated by a reading of the text."[19] He calls the three aspects of a story the "events," the "text," and the "interpretation."

Scholes views historical narrative and fictional narrative as having both similar and different features. As far as similarity goes, "Both history and fiction assume the normal flow of events, and the interpretation of both kinds of texts involves the construction of a diegesis in which this flow is re-created by the interpreter with every event in order and all relationship as clear as possible."[20] As for differences, "History is a narrative discourse with different rules than those that govern fiction. The producer of historical text affirms that the events entextualized did indeed occur prior to the entextualization. Thus it is quite proper to bring extratextual information to bear on those events when interpreting and evaluating a historical narrative."[21]

Fictional narrative differs from historical narrative in one essential aspect, which I may consider as the essence of fictionality: "[I]n fiction the events may be said to be created by and with the text. They have no prior temporal existence, even though they are presented as if they did. As Sidney rightly pointed out four centuries ago, the writer of fiction does not affirm the prior existence of his events, he only pretends to through a convention understood by all who share his culture."[22] By this standard, even historical fiction is, strictly speaking, *not* pure fiction, because its major events have prior temporal existence that can be verified by history. In no small degree, historical fiction depends upon real historical events in the way a parasite depends upon its host; or to put in a benign way, a fetus owes its survival to its mother via the umbilical cord. Just as a fetus is not a viable, separate life before the severing of the umbilical cord, Chinese *xiaoshuo* did not gain its full-fledged fictionality before it ceased to rely on histories in the broad sense of the word. It is my contention that only a *xiaoshuo* writing with full-blown fictionality can be said to have attained the ontological status of pure fiction. From a philosophical point of view, pure fiction reverses the conception of the relationship between the world of appearance and the world of ideas in Plato's theory of artistic imitation. Plato conceives of the world of appearances as the result of modeling after the world of ideas. The latter is related to the former, but it is a separate and transcendental entity. Pure fiction imitates events in life but transcends the imitated events. In the final analysis, it is this transcendental quality that lies at the heart of pure fiction.

A DEFINITION OF PURE FICTION

I have provided a general definition of fiction and briefly discussed "pure fiction" in early sections. Now I would like to further elaborate on the idea of pure fiction and offer a more refined definition. I will then use this definition as a guide for further inquiries into the nature of Chinese fiction and conceptualizing fictional art. *By "pure fiction" I mean a fictional work that does not rely on previous narratives or stories for its genesis and has its narrative strength in its own fictionality.* The definition has two complementary aspects. First, a pure fiction narrates a unified and coherent story that does not depend on extant narratives, whether in official history, local history, personal biography, circulated myths and legends, or extant stories. Second, pure fiction does not exclude the incorporation of existent sources, but the incorporated sources are only raw materials to be woven into the macrostructure of the whole fictional work and should not play the role of structuring the main narrative plot. By this definition, histories fall far short of being pure fiction. Even historical fiction does not measure up to the criteria of this definition.

The reader may wonder why I use pure fiction as a standard and subject historical fiction and adaptations of previous works to its arbitration. Let me briefly explain why. First, my proposal has much to do with the question of imagination and originality. Pure fiction is closer to originality than other forms of fiction based on previous writings. Historical fiction generally follows the developmental pattern of recorded histories. A history is written by an author or authors, known or unknown, and historical fiction based on it is an imitation. It is not an imitation of life or nature, as the Aristotelian theory of imitation proposes. It is a second-order imitation, because it imitates previous works. Adaptations and extensions of previous works are second-order imitations, too. Like historical fiction, they are relatively farther away from creative originality than pure fiction, simply because second-order imitation has less originality than first-order imitation. Edward Young, who expressed a sound view of the relationship between imitation and originality, pointed out: "Imitations are of two kinds; one of nature, one of authors: the first we call originals, and confine the term imitation to the second."[23] Young did not object to imitation of other authors altogether. But he added a twist to the imitation of ancient masters. For him, the proper object of imitation is not the work of an ancient master, but his "spirit" and "taste": "Let us build our compositions with the spirit, and in the taste, of the ancients; but not with their materials."[24] Even with this allowance, we must admit that successful imitation of the spirit or taste of an ancient master, say the Grand Historian, Sima Qian, yields less originality than successful works that imitate life and nature or build on imaginative simulation.

Second, as I have mentioned in the introduction, in the development of Chinese prose fiction *xiaoshuo* emulated and competed with lyric poetry and cherished the ambition of becoming an esteemed form of art like poetry. In artistic form, *xiaoshuo* can never hope to rival poetry, but it can rival poetry through a special content. This special content is pure fictionality. Narrative prose in its pure fictionality is closer to lyric poetry than to history or historical fiction in genesis and ontology. It does not follow the generative principle of a history book, which imitates real events and has therefore a generative principle of second-order imitation. Pure fiction shares with lyric poetry the expressive principle of genesis, and its ontological status comes from a special use of language. Its art lies in the infinite possibilities with which a writer may make use of language. In the next few chapters, I will discuss in detail the essence of fictional art. For the time being, I only wish to say that pure fiction, because of its independence from finite reality, is conducive to multiple associations and interpretations, and accounts for a great deal of fictional art.

INTRINSIC REASONS FOR THE RISE OF FICTION

About the specific origins of *xiaoshuo*, the accepted view has identified three sources: (1) it arose from mythology; (2) it originated from collections of gossip and street talk by feudal lords' petty officials; and (3) it evolved from historiography. While this scholarly consensus provides an adequate historical (extrinsic) view of *xiaoshuo*'s genesis, it fails to account for the conceptual (intrinsic) rise of *xiaoshuo* as a literary genre; nor is it able to distinguish *xiaoshuo* from other forms of writing and describe the internal tensions between *xiaoshuo* and historiography. By tracing the evolution of the term *xiaoshuo* in Chinese history, I have partially dealt already with the extrinsic reasons for the rise of fiction in China. In both Chinese and Western studies of fiction, a great deal of attention has been paid to other external reasons for the rise of fiction: the appearance of cities, the spread of book printing, the rise of a reading public, the demand for entertainment, the commercialization of literature, and so on.[25] In his comparative study of the full-length *xiaoshuo* and the Western novel, Plaks considers Ian Watt's *The Rise of the Novel* theoretically flawed, but he accepts Watt's sociological thesis on the origins of the novel: "[T]hese extraliterary factors, rather than the purely literary qualities mentioned earlier, may indeed be credited with the emergence of the novel form."[26] Plaks extends it to the Chinese tradition: "[T]he putative relation between the Western novel and its social and economic background is nearly duplicated in the Chinese context."[27] After accepting the theoretical notion of the novel by Georg Lukács and Abel Rémusat that the novel form "grows out of the increasing cultural complexity of the modern era" and appears "as a response to the sheer weight of history and culture at a certain stage in the development of civilization," he expresses a dissatisfaction with the theory's inability to explain the rise of the Japanese novel, the *Tale of Genji*, which, while conforming to a number of the defining characteristics of the novel form, came into being in a social and intellectual milieu that had few social, economic, and intellectual prerequisites for the rise of the modern novel. His dissatisfaction touches upon the limitations of an external approach to the rise of the novel.

The Chinese case exposes the limitations from an opposite direction. Studies of Chinese fiction have confirmed that by approximately the same historical period as the *Tale of Genji*, the social and cultural conditions for the rise of the novel already existed in the capital of the Northern Song (960–1127) and were fully developed by the Southern Song period (1127–1279).[28] In a study of the relationship between urbanization and the maturity of popular fiction, Jaroslav Průšek compares the Chinese case with its European counterpart and draws the conclusion that "the Chinese soil [for popular fiction] is richer and more finely prepared. . . . In all these [social and cultural] respects, China was far ahead of contemporary Europe and bears some resemblance rather to Europe in the era of early capitalism."[29] During the Song dynasty, however, storytelling flourished, but nothing like the *Tale of Genji* (eleventh century), *Don Quixote* (1605), or *Robinson Crusoe* (1719) appeared, not to mention the English realistic novels of the eighteenth century. The delayed appearance of similar novels in the Chinese tradition suggests that the rise of fiction cannot be adequately accounted for by an external approach alone. The seemingly odd case of the *Tale of Genji* requires us to adopt an intrinsic approach as well. According to Japanese literary history, the novel was the result of a single genius, Lady Murasaki Shikibu, who, as a lady-in-waiting in the Japanese court, had a lot of time on her hands and wrote it to entertain herself as well as others.[30] Thus, the genesis of the novel could be attributed to the author's intention to seek pleasure through writing.

To fully account for the rise of fiction or the novel, we must deal with the intrinsic reasons, which, among other things, include the author's creative impulse and pretextual intention, and the reader's desire for reading fiction. Fiction, like other forms of literature, has two basic functions: didacticism and entertainment. While didacticism is more concerned with the extrinsic function of fiction, entertainment is more concerned with the intrinsic function. In the earliest discourse on *xiaoshuo*, scholars only emphasized its didactic function, which is the extrinsic reason for the use of fiction. The official attitude toward *xiaoshuo*, set by Confucius, is an ethical and utilitarian one. It stresses the didactic function of *xiaoshuo*, and fails to see its function of entertainment. Because of the emphasis on social function, the early view of *xiaoshuo* failed to note why people created *xiaoshuo* and enjoyed hearing or reading them. As a result, it failed to grasp the intrinsic reason for the rise of *xiaoshuo* and its intrinsic value.

In the Chinese tradition, the idea that literature is to give pleasure appeared very early. In his *Rhyme-Prose on Literature*, Lu Ji 陸機 (261–303) stated: "One can find joy in this endeavor [literature], / which has been revered by wise men and worthy men."[31] Lu Ji spoke of the pleasure produced by literature in general and made no distinction between different forms of literature. The creative impulse for poetry and that for fiction are basically the same, for they both represent the desire for pleasure. But I argue that there is a difference in the ways of seeking pleasure. In the Chinese tradition, literary creation is perceived to be the positive result of suffering. Sima Qian conceptualized this in a famous theory of literary creativity: *fafen zhushu* 發憤著書 "to give vent to one's grievances by composing books." According to him, King Wen extended the *Zhouyi* because he was imprisoned; Confucius wrote the *Spring and Autumn Annals* because he was down on his luck; Qu Yuan composed *Li-sao* when he was exiled; Zuo Qiu wrote *Guoyu* [the *Discourse of States*] after he became blind; Sun Bing composed a discourse on the art of war because he was maimed; Lü Buwei compiled *Lü's Spring and Autumn Annals* after he was banished from the court; Han Fei composed the discourses "Shuonan" and "Gufen" after he was imprisoned in Qin; and the three hundred poems in the *Book of Songs* were generally compositions by sages and saints who had grievances.[32] All the persons mentioned by Sima Qian suffered physical or mental inflictions, but the suffering became the motivation and inspiration for creation. After observing the intimate relationship between suffering and creativity, Sima Qian drew his conclusion: "These people all had some pent-up emotions, which could not be channeled to their proper destinations. As a result, they narrated their past experiences as a way to contemplate events to come 此人皆意有所鬱結，不得通其道也，故述往事，思來者。"[33] Sima Qian voiced an expressionist theory of poetry, which has been simplified into a famous Chinese saying: "A poet is born out of profound indignation 憤怒出詩人." It is a different way of stating the time-honored theory about the genesis of poetry expounded in the Great Preface to the *Book of Songs*: that it is a natural and spontaneous growth.

The very fact that Sima Qian pioneered a writing pattern of historiography and was held in esteem as the forefather of historical fiction should allow us to formulate an expressionist theory of the rise of Chinese fiction. I will further discuss this issue in chapter 7. Sima Qian's conclusion touches on a facet of creative impulse, which has been neglected by scholars: all the writings he mentioned retell past events and think of the future. We may recall the Aristotelian distinction between history and poetry: the former narrates what has happened while the latter narrates what may happen. Sima Qian's theory complements Aristotle's idea. Poetry may also describe past events. This is why some scholars maintain that Chinese poetry is often the result of a direct response to an empirical situation. But while poetry may be in response to an event that has happened, it may also have in mind events that have not happened and may likely happen in the future. In fiction, the narrated events are unreal, but fiction narrates those never-happened events as though they had happened in the past.

Ostensibly, Sima Qian provides a psychological as well as a sociological explanation for the rise of literature. The writer of serious literature has some pent-up painful emotions in his heart that cannot be released through proper social channels. He therefore resorts to a substitute form to channel his repressed emotions. But aesthetically, he identified a tendency in Chinese historical writings and prose fiction that, as I will discuss in detail in chapter 4, is poetic in nature. Scholars in China have set great store by Sima Qian's theory of literary creativity, generally viewing it as appropriate for describing the rise of literature and art in general, especially poetry. Though his theory never mentions *xiaoshuo*, it has a direct relevance to prose fiction in two ways. First, he himself is a historian whose task is to narrate past events. Second, his theory makes a special mention of the narration of past events with an eye to the future. Thus, his theorizing is concerned with both poetry and narrative. Since Sima Qian's theory exerted a formative impact on the theory and practice of literature, the dual concern endows Chinese narrative with the dual quality of being both lyrical and narrative in nature. When prose fiction evolved from the writings of history, this dual quality gave Chinese prose fiction a series of characteristic features that distinguish it from its Western counterpart: features of being lyrical, nonmimetic, unrealistic, and, in a word, poetic. This dual quality of Chinese fiction is clear in all forms of Chinese historical fiction, from the earliest to the latest productions.

We must note that among the writings Sima Qian mentioned, all are canonical texts, be they prose or poetry or non-literary writings. None of them comes close to *xiaoshuo* in the remotest sense. All of them are serious in intent. They form a striking contrast with *xiaoshuo* as street talk. This may be why Sima Qian's theory about the rise of literature is believed not to cover the rise of *xiaoshuo* or fiction. Hence, scholars have turned to other channels for supplementary theorizing. In his study of Chinese fiction, Lu Xun may be said to have supplied a complementary theory to account for the rise of both poetry and fiction. In his conception, poetry arose from labor and religion, while fiction resulted from relaxation:

> When people were engaged in manual labor, they would use songs and chants to amuse themselves so that they could forget about the toil. But when it came to the time of rest, they had to seek some way to while away leisure time. One way is to engage in telling stories to one another. And this kind of storytelling is nothing but the origin of fiction.[34]

Lu Xun's theory complements Sima Qian's theory about the rise of literature and art and directly touches upon the rise of fiction. In a way, Lu Xun's theory may be rephrased as: "Poetry grows out of suffering; fiction, out of pleasure." This rephrasing may not only grasp the intrinsic reason for the rise of literature, but also make clear a distinction between the intrinsic values of poetry and fiction. In traditional Chinese literary thought, some scholars affirmed the pleasure-seeking nature of fiction, but they also emphasized the expressive nature of fiction. In the Ming dynasty, a scholar with the pseudonym Tiandu Waichen 天都外臣 (fl. 1584) wrote in a preface to the *Shuihu zhuan* 水滸傳序 on the social reason for the rise of fiction:

> The rise of *xiaoshuo* began with the reign of Emperor Ren of the Song. At that time people in the empire enjoyed a well-to-do life, and border invasions did

not occur yet. With a laissez-faire rule, the emperor had leisure time at hand. He ordered the bureau of entertainment and office of music to appropriate folk stories from society, set them to songs, and perform them by a motley group of actors and actresses. After its initiation, this kind of performance became very popular and spread inside and outside the court. Although it did not conform to traditional propriety, it nevertheless constituted an enjoyable endeavor in a time of peace and reflected the vestiges of ancient times when folks naturally burst into songs after having a full stomach, stamping their feel on the ground as accompaniment.[35]

His view was quite lopsided in some ways, but it correctly identified the relationship between the rise of fiction and the human demand for entertainment irrespective of historical time. Another scholar of the same period with the pseudonym of Youyang Yeshi 酉陽野史 expressed a similar view: "*Xiaoshuo* is the popular sayings of society. It is therefore not official history or proper records. Its function was no more than providing entertainment to while away long days and nights. Some people dispelled their boredom and sorrows with it and gave vent to a moment of pent-up feelings."[36] This view makes a clear distinction between official history and fiction and affirms fiction as a kind of literature the purpose of which is to entertain people. The same preface also makes a distinction between author's pleasure and reader's pleasure: "The composition of this novel was intended no more than to give vent to the author's grievances for a moment and to entertain people for thousands of years to come." Here we may see the strong influence of the dual concern in Sima Qian's conception. Li Zongwei, a modern scholar who studies Tang *chuanqi*, the mature form of Chinese fiction, points out that one of the creative intentions for *chuanqi* writers is to give free rein to flights of imagination and to seek pleasure in fiction writing.[37] From the creative point of view, the author may want to give vent to a pent-up feeling; from the perspective of reading, fiction can entertain readers for generations to come.

In literary psychology, poetry and fiction are both ways of seeking pleasure, but they differ in the nature of the pleasure sought. A poet writing poetry is, in a way, like someone who suffers pain or discomfort because of a sickness. The curing of the sickness gives pleasure because it gets rid of suffering. Thus, poetry arising from the desire to reduce emotional tensions tends to produce something that contributes not to the generation of pleasure but to the reduction of suffering. The rise of poetry thus follows a principle that might be characterized as "negative pleasure." Writers of fiction may also be motivated by the desire to seek negative pleasure, but as a rule, the prevalent motive is to entertain others as well as the writer. Thus, the writer (and reader) of fiction is like a healthy person who takes narcotic drugs with the aim not to reduce pain, as many drug addicts usually do, but to experience pleasurable sensations that will not arise naturally. Thus, fiction arising from the conscious desire to seek wish fulfillment is not aimed at reducing suffering but at seeking pleasurable mental experiences. It follows a pleasure principle. It therefore can be called "positive pleasure."

Why can fiction give pleasure to the writer and reader? Fiction, as I have argued, is a form of writing about events that have never happened but may happen by the law of probability. Fiction, in other words, is the result of an act to invent situations and occurrences that have not existed, thereby giving the author and reader an imagined control of situations that are actually beyond their control. As such it is a form of fantasy, a kind of daydream, a castle in the air. Why do people fantasize in life? Obviously they want to use fiction to satisfy certain physical, emotional, and spiritual needs, the fulfillment of which gives pleasure. Writers of fiction create fantasies; readers of fiction consume fantasies. Both writing and reading give pleasure. Freud's psychological study confirms this insight: "The motive force of phantasies are unsatisfied wishes, and every single phantasy is the fulfillment of a wish, a correction of unsatisfying reality."[38] In a study of the origins of fiction, Marthe Robert suggests that a tension between the ideal and the real lies at the heart of modern fiction. She argues that to trace the origin of fiction, one needs to think about the creative impulse in the fiction writer. Pressurized by the creative urge and faced with undesirable reality, the writer must turn to fiction for relief. Frustrated in the fulfillment of wishes, the writer wants to rebel against reality, to destroy the real world and to re-create another world in accordance with his or her wishes.[39] Evidently, her idea of the rise of fiction is based on the psychoanalytic model of daydreaming. Somewhat narrow as it is in scope and perspective, this model nevertheless offers a valid insight into the rise of Tang *xiaoshuo*. Yu Ji 虞集 (1272–1348) of the Yuan wrote on why the Tang literati created fictional works:

> Among the literati of the Tang, not many had original insights into the classics, arts, the Way, and scholarship. They only set their mind on composing embellished writings. When they had time on their hands and had nothing to occupy their minds, they would imagine mysterious creatures and extraordinary encounters and indulge in an entranced use of their talents. They then gave their idle fancies far-fetched meanings and used them as substitutes for poetry and prose in their social intercourse. At places where they met, each of them produced a writing to amuse one another. What they wrote did not have to be true events. It was therefore called *chuanqi*, "transmitting the strange."[40]

The Tang literati were not as morally rigid as their predecessors and posterity. They enjoyed life in imaginative ways. For them, writing is not just for annotating classics; it could provide pleasure. Writing could amuse oneself; it could also amuse others. What is most important in Yu Ji's observation is the remark: "to amuse each other." This remark touches on the essential difference between the pleasure of poetry and that of fiction. Poetry tends to amuse the poet himself. Fiction tends to amuse others. This difference may not only explain the commercial nature of fiction, but also account for the decline of poetry in modern times. There is a witty remark that there are more poetry writers than poetry readers nowadays. It is an apt comment on the self-amusing function of poetry. But in the initial stages, fiction was meant to entertain the writer himself more than his readers. Self-amusement, primarily aimed at the fulfillment of unrealizable wishes, constitutes another facet of the creative urge. In traditional society, the literati's aim in life can be summarized as success in the civil service examination, appointment for a high official post, and marriage to a beautiful woman—ideally, to a beautiful daughter of a high-ranking official, or most ideal of all, to a daughter of the emperor. But in real life, the road to success in the civil service examination is exceedingly narrow; the road to success in officialdom is even narrower. Those who achieved success are only the minority; the majority of the literati had to confront the harsh reality of failure. They, therefore, often resorted to daydreams to make unrealizable ambitions come true. In many ways, *xiaoshuo* became the most effective vehicle for their unrealized daydreams. In many *xiaoshuo* writings, ranging from the Tang *chuanqi* (Bai Xingjian's 白行簡 "Li Wa zhuan 李娃傳," for example) to the *xiaoshuo* of the Qing (Pu Songling's 蒲松齡 tale, "Pianpian 翩翩"),[41] we frequently come across stories that have the same *datuanyuan* (grand denouement): the protagonist comes out first in the civil service examination, marries a beautiful daughter of the prime minister or emperor, produces several sons who are equally successful, and lives happily to a ripe old age.

The daydreaming nature of the Tang *xiaoshuo* may be seen in the fact that many of the Tang *chuanqi* are titled with the word *meng* (dream). One of them, Shen Yanzhi's 沈亞之 (ca. 781–ca. 832) "Qinmeng ji 秦夢記," is a daydream almost literally transcribed in *chuanqi* form. In the story, the protagonist has the same name as the author. With his extraordinary talent, he helps the Duke of Qin conquer a large piece of land. The duke appoints him to a high post, makes him wealthy, and gives him a princess as his wife. Thus, the life goals of the literati in the traditional society are all fulfilled to the letter. In other dream tales, even though the authorial intention might be ironical or satirical, the same life objectives constitute the subject matter. In "Nanke taishou zhuan 南柯太守傳," "Zhenzhong ji 枕中記," and "Yingtao qingyi 櫻桃青衣," the male protagonists all experience the same success in their dream adventure. The ironical endings of the stories reveal a self-conscious introspection of daydreams and suggest that the authors were able to poke fun at the daydreams of the literati at that time.

People from different walks of life and in different situations may have different kinds of fantasies. Freud classifies all the fantasies into two categories: ambitious fantasies that "serve to elevate the subject's personality" and erotic fantasies that satisfy a person's erotic desires unlikely to be fulfilled in real life. Freud's theory and Robert's theorizing on the origin of fiction corroborate both the nature of *xiaoshuo* and the historical development of Chinese fiction. Myths and legends dated before the Han and records of extraordinary persons and things created during the Six Dynasties and the Tang obviously belong to the first category of fantasies. Stories and tales about secret trysts, illicit affairs, love and romance, and happy marital life obviously belong to the second category of fantasies.

The Tang *xiaoshuo* marked the first explosion of interest in sex and sexuality. Among them some tales deal with the subject matter of courtesans and going to brothels. Typical examples include "Li Wa zhuan" (The Story of Miss Li) and "Huo Xiaoyu zhuan" (The Story of Huo Xiaoyu). Some other stories are erotic daydreams that narrate chance meetings with beautiful women who are either fairies or courtesans. A typical example is Zhang Wencheng's 張文成 "You xianku 遊仙窟" (A Chance Visit to the Fairies' Cave). In this tale, the male protagonist accidentally visits a cave inhabited by beautiful fairies in the mountains. He flirts with the fairies in the cave and goes to bed with the most beautiful and talented among them. At the end of the story, he leaves those fairies with reluctance and regret. In this story, the fairies are bold and forward in their amorous behavior. The place they inhabit has the ethos of a fairyland, but reminds one of a house of prostitution. The beauties inside are lifelike women who are the objects of desire for both the male writer and reader. The daydreaming nature of the tale is revealed by a number of signs. First, it uses a first-person narrator who is also the male protagonist. Second, the narrative features a disjointed temporal sequence. Third, there is a strong note of wish fulfillment: whatever the male protagonist wishes comes true. The opening of the story has these words: "I felt as though my body was in flight and my soul in a dream 身體若飛，精靈似夢."[42] "You xianku" is a long tale, as long as a modern novella. As a tale of erotic daydreaming, it is well conceived and well written. Its disappearance in China and its rediscovery in Japan speak a good deal about the difficulty in preserving *xiaoshuo* in a predominantly Confucian society.

The creative impulse to seek erotic pleasure gave rise to tales that border on pornography. Liu Zongyuan's 柳宗元 (773–819) "Hejian zhuan 河間傳" (The Biography of Hejian) is an example. It is a story of a virtuous woman who turns into a sex maniac under pernicious influences. In the story, there are graphical descriptions of sex acts and an orgy. The appearance of such a story by one of the famed masters of the ancient style prose shocked his contemporaries as well as posterity. People adopted an allegorical approach to the story, reading it as a moral lesson on the difficulty of preserving virtue and choosing friends. As one scholar puts it, "The story of the change from exemplary virtuous woman to monstrous sex maniac becomes an allegory of human relationships in a patriarchal society."[43] Even though the author himself claimed that he wrote this story as an allegory, I must point out that the use of explicitly pornographic description cannot but force the reader to perceive the creative motive as paradoxical: on the one hand, the author seems to have wanted his tale to be an cautionary one, but on the other, he seems to have nursed the secret wish to satisfy a physical desire.

Myths and legends represent the early development of fiction and are not the mature form of fiction, because they, as Freud points out, are "distorted vestiges of the wishful phantasies of whole nations, the secular dreams of youthful humanity."[44] In other words, myths and legends were created not by single authors, but collectively invented by the nation. That is why we have no way of knowing the authors of myths and legends. Accordingly, myths and legends, tales of the extraordinary persons and events cannot be the mature form of *xiaoshuo* or fiction. The mature form of *xiaoshuo* or fiction generally builds on fantasies of the second kind with the complement of the first kind of fantasies. It is interesting to note that in the Tang tales, there are many stories that are written as both love romances in content and dream adventures in form. Typical examples are Shen Yazhi's 沈亞之 (ca. 781–ca. 832) "Yimeng lu 異夢錄" (Record of a Strange Dream) and "Qinmeng ji 秦夢記" (Record of a Dream in the Qin), Bai Xingjian's 白行簡 (776–826) "Sam meng ji 三夢記" (Record of Three Dreams), Shen Jiji's 沈既濟 (740–800) "Zhenzhong ji 枕中記" (The World in a Pillow), Li Gongzuo's 李公佐 (770–848) "Nanko taishou zhuan" (Biography of the Magistrate of Nanke), Li Men's (fl. 835) "Zhang Sheng 張生" (Scholar Zhang), and Wang Tu's (fl. 614?) "Gujing zhi 古鏡記" (Records of an Ancient Mirror). Some of the dream tales have become stock subject matter for later writers of fiction and drama, and Shen Jiji's "Story in a Pillow" and Li Gonzuo's "Biography of Nanke" have been told and retold numerous times. Among the most famous adaptations, we find the *Huangliang meng* 黃粱夢 (A Dream of Yellow Millet) by Ma Zhiyuan of the Yuan (ca. 1250–1323); two Ming plays, *Handan ji* 邯鄲記 (A Record of Handan) and *Nanke mengji* 南柯夢記 (A Dream of South Branch) by Tang Xianzu (1550–1616), and the short story "Xu Huangliang 續黃粱" (A Sequel to Yellow Millet) in Pu Songling's (1640–1715) *xiaoshuo* collection, the *Liaozhai zhiyi* 聊齋志異. The mere fact that the dream stories become stock motifs points to the archetypal nature of the daydreams themselves. The adaptations and readaptations not only mark technical advances in daydreaming, but also show how sophisticated later authors had become in imparting aesthetic pleasure, which, as Freud points out, is a fore-pleasure that "make[s it] possible for the releases of still greater pleasure arising from deeper psychic sources." Moreover, the aesthetic advance makes it possible for the reader to enjoy his own daydreams without self-reproach or shame.[45]

There are many reasons for the maturity of *xiaoshuo* as a form of fiction in the Tang. But the intrinsic reason lies in the *xiaoshuo*'s capacity to fulfill wishes that cannot be realized in reality—to furnish writers and readers with physical, emotional, and spiritual pleasure. While poetry can play the same role, *xiaoshuo* or fiction is especially effective in providing erotic pleasure. Hu Yinglin, in his attempt to explain why people from all walks of life enjoy *xiaoshuo*, rightly put his finger on the entertaining function of *xiaoshuo*:

As for the gentlemen of great taste, they know the absurdity [of the *hsiao-shuo*] in their heart, but rush to tell it with their mouth. In the daylight they repudiate its erroneousness, but in the dark they quote and use it. It is like licentious sound and beauty in women; people hate it but cannot stop loving it. The more the people love it, the more the people tell it. And the more the people tell it, the more the authors write it. Why should it be strange?[46]

On the surface, Hu Yinglin expressed an ambivalent attitude toward *xiaoshuo*, comparing it to sex and women. As Sheldon Lu rightly points out, "Men's love and hatred for fiction are comparable to their love and hatred for sex and beauty."[47] But from another perspective, Hu was touching on the intrinsic reason for the rise of *xiaoshuo* or fiction: it gives pleasure to the writer as well as the reader. Moreover, he intuitively grasped the reason behind the love-and-hate attitude toward *xiaoshuo*. The pleasure that *xiaoshuo* gives to people is often questionable socially, morally, and aesthetically. Socially, the pleasure is a subversive force that challenges the dominant position of canons. Morally, it is not sanctioned by the reigning morality as it originates from people's repressed instinctual desires. Aesthetically, the pleasure is expressed in a form akin to the idle fancies in dreams and to gossip in the streets and alleys, and is far removed from the lofty and venerable aesthetic forms of poetry and prose. But Hu had to admit the raison d'être of *xiaoshuo*: that it arises from the deep recess of the unconscious. "People cannot stop loving it." This enables us to see why people derive pleasure from reading fiction. Norman Holland, a renowned psychoanalytic critic, came to the same realization several hundred years later with the aid of Freud's psychoanalytic theory: "Literature transforms our primitive wishes and fears into significance and coherence, and this transformation gives pleasure."[48] Chinese *xiaoshuo* as a literary form is, in the final analysis, an aesthetic transformation of the writer's unconscious fantasies and appeals to the reader's unconscious desires.

HISTORICAL AND NARRATIVE INERTIA

Fiction is a most amorphous and open literary form. But when we observe the macrodevelopment of Chinese fiction from its early stages to modern times, we will notice an obvious phenomenon. Negatively speaking, it is a kind of creative fixation on early narrative materials and models. To put it in less-negative terms, it is "historical inertia." It is a history-oriented inertia, but it goes far beyond a dependence on histories. On a broader dimension, there is a reluctance to explore new subjects for fiction creation, a penchant for adapting and rewriting existent stories, and a tendency to use time-honored fictional techniques. A more exact term would be "narrative inertia." Chinese *xiaoshuo* has been aided by historical narrative throughout its development. Historicism played an inestimable role in the maturity of Chinese fiction. It, however, is a double-edged sword. On the one hand, it provided Chinese fiction with all it needed for its evolution from anecdotal snippets at the beginning to fiction in the modern sense of the word. In this sense, the indebtedness of Chinese *xiaoshuo* to historical narrative cannot be overestimated. On the other, historicism was also a hindrance for *xiaoshuo* to gain full maturity, because it hindered Chinese fiction from developing into a literary form that stands on its own strengths and merits. *Xiaoshuo* must fight its benefactor in order to achieve its full maturity. A struggle took place between the historical inertia and the creative impulse for pure fiction. The historical inertia is deeply embedded in all aspects of Chinese fiction from literary creativity to fiction studies.

First, it is to be found in the output of fictional works. The appearance of the novel marked the full maturity of Chinese *xiaoshuo*. As I have stated in the beginning of this book, the *zhanghui xiaoshuo* (chaptered novel) in the Chinese tradition was the perfected narrative form that earlier forms of narrative—myths, legends, literary anecdotes, folktales, personal biographies, historical narratives, short stories, etc.—have striven to become. After the first appearance of chaptered novel, the historical novel became the dominant literary genre, and the major novel output is in one way or another an artistic extension of histories, biographies, and existent stories. At the end of the Yuan and the beginning of the Ming, the *zhanghui*-style novel came to maturity. The first batch of novels produced then were almost all history based: the *Sanguozhi yanyi* 三國志演義, *Shuihu zhuan* 水滸傳, *Sansui pingyao zhuan* 三遂平妖傳, *Can Tang Wudai yanyi zhuan* 殘唐五代演義傳, *Sui Tang liangchao zhizhuan* 隋唐兩朝志傳, and so on. In the mid-Ming, *zhanghui xiaoshuo* witnessed a period of great prosperity. In this period, novels were counted by hundreds, and most of them deal with the subject matter of histories. As one recent study points out, "The *zhanghui* style novels at the beginning developed from historical narratives of the Song and Yuan (講史平話). They generally base themselves on subject matters of existent historical narratives, and create new forms of narrative by following the old narrative and promoting their development. This situation existed and largely developed into the mid and late Ming periods."[49] As for the literary achievement of this period, Robert Hegel's study suggests that the greatest success is to be found in novels with historical themes.[50]

The appearance of the *Jin Ping Mei* changed the direction of *xiaoshuo* somewhat, but it did not significantly alter the history-oriented trend in Ming and early Qing fiction. Even with the rise of the *Hongloumeng, Rulin waishi*, and other novels of pure fiction, the historical inertia was not generally overcome. Historical narrative reigned throughout the premodern periods. It is common for fictional writers to rework existent themes. Modern authors are as eager as their traditional predecessors to write on historical themes. Even an original writer like Lu Xun could not keep from wanting to. He originally planned to write a historical novel based on the stories of Yang Guifei, the favorite imperial concubine of Emperor Xuanzong of the Tang. In the latter part of his creative career, he did not compose a single story that may be counted as a pure fictional work. Instead, he produced a collection of historical tales, *Old Stories Retold* 故事新編. It consists of nine stories; each of them is a reworked account of a myth, a legend, a parable, or a historical tale.[51] The Cultural Revolution (1966–76), which was supposed to sweep away all old ideas, customs, and habits, failed to eradicate the predilection for historical fiction. Fiction writing practically came to a total halt in this period. There were only two novels, and they appeared toward the end of the Cultural Revolution; one of them was Yao Xueying's historical novel, *Li Zicheng* 李自成. Recently, historical narrative has seen an upsurge. A good number of historical novels have appeared one after another. Among them, *Zeng Guofan* 曾國藩, *Yongzheng huangdi* 雍正皇帝, *Kangxi dadi* 康熙大帝, *Qianlong huangdi* 乾隆皇帝, and *Hanwu dadi* 漢武大帝 are only some of the well-known titles. The major difference in the modern trend is that instead of narrating a historical period, modern writers of historical novels focus on the histories of historical persons. My brief examination of the historical predilection in fiction creation in Chinese history proves beyond doubt that there has existed a dependence on history in Chinese fiction.

Second, the historical inertia is reflected in discourses on the theory of Chinese fiction. It gave rise to an erroneous attitude towards creativity and imagination that was not overcome until modern times. The view was that literary representation of real events is difficult and therefore demonstrates high literary quality; by contrast, literary creation based on pure imagination is easy and therefore reveals little artistic quality. Mao Zonggan 毛宗崗 (fl. 1660) is a most vocal proponent of this view:

> The *Romance of the Three Kingdoms* is superior to the *Water Margin*. The realism of the former is to be preferred to the fantasy of the latter, yet the author created his narrative ex nihilo and started or ended episodes at will. The *Water Margin*'s literary craftsmanship was not as difficult as that of the *Romance of the Three Kingdoms*, which narrates predetermined material that brooks no changes, and therefore reveals the intricacy of the author's artistic mind.[52]

In his opinion, writers of historical novels are limited by historical facts and can only exercise their imaginations within a definable space, and they therefore are faced with a more difficult task than those who write novels of pure fiction. Thus, Mao Zonggang privileged truthful narrative over fictionality. Cai Yuanfang 蔡元放 (fl. 1730–67) agreed with Mao in his "How to Read the *Dong Zhou lieguo zhi* 東周列國志讀法":

> It is easier to write fictitious *xiaoshuo*. Since novels like the *Fengshen yanyi*, *Shuihu zhuan*, and *Xiyou ji* are fictitious accounts with no factual basis, the writers could supplement, prune, and make connections of events at will to get a coherent composition. The *Lieguo zhi* is based on facts. The writer must narrate events episode by episode and could not make use of the artistry of tailoring. As a result, the wording turns out to be not as good as that of the fictitious account.[53]

These opinions obviously reflected the impact of the dominance of history in Chinese narrative theories. They in fact challenge the very foundation of fiction—that is, fictionality, which in the Chinese tradition is the very expression that Mao Zonggang argued against: *wuzhong shengyou* 無中生有 (to produce a fictional account out of nothing). Both in theory and practice, these opinions are erroneous. In theory, they overlook the difference between history and fiction and underestimates the importance of imaginative fabrication for fictional creation. In the practice of fiction writing, they neglect the difficulties involved in pure fiction making. Historical fiction relies on history for its general structure and organizational principle. In this respect, pure fiction has nothing to rely on. For plot arrangement, characterization, and settings, pure fiction also has nothing to fall back on. True, pure fiction allows an author a free hand in exercising his imagination, but a fictional work totally dependent on free imagination without proper organization and artistic rendering would result in unconvincing account that violates verisimilitude and therefore cannot rise to the level of high-quality art.

The impact of historical inertia has also been felt in critical practice. Because of the penchant for the historical, a major current in fiction criticism is dominated by what might be called "fictional historiography": a kind of fiction scholarship devoted to the study of the history of a given work, including its origin, dating, transmission, emendations, and editions. In many cases, fictional historiography developed into examinations of authors' and characters' biographies, sometimes to the total neglect of the fictitious nature of fictional works. Interestingly, this kind of fictional historiography was started by erudite historians. Chen Yinke 陳寅恪, a renowned modern Chinese historian, may be said to have started this scholarship. One of his studies, which employs historical data for the analysis of literary works, was once hailed as a "milestone in scholarship." However, his exploration of the prototypes of literary characters sometimes lapses into conclusions that totally ignore the fictitious nature of fictional characters. For example, after elaborate research, he came to the conclusion that the female protagonist in "The Story of Ying Ying" was not a girl from a noble family but a female entertainer.[54] Recently, another scholar further promoted Chen Yinke's idea and, after much evidential study, he argued that Ying Ying was a foreign entertainer.[55] Needless to say, one of the dominant approaches in the *Hongloumeng* scholarship—that of the autobiographical school—was also initiated by historians like Hu Shi.

Third, the historical inertia spills over to other subject matter and other literary forms. As a result, historical inertia should be broadly defined to cover the penchant for using already existent narrative materials. Biographies of historical persons were certainly a subject matter. After all, Chinese histories consist of interlocking individuals' biographies. Other subject matter came from old stories and stock narratives. "Ying Ying zhuan" became such a stock story. Since its appearance in the Tang, it has been adapted into several much longer versions not restricted to fictional form. The same story appears in Dong

Jieyuan's 董解元 *Xixiangji zhugongdiao* 西廂記諸宮調 in the Jin, Wang Shifu's 王實甫 *Xixiangji* 西廂記 in the Yuan, Li Rihua's 李日華 and Lu Tianchi's 陸天池 *Nan Xixiangji* 南西廂記, Zhou Gonglu's 周公魯 *Fan Xixiangji* 翻西廂記 in the Ming, and Cha Jizuo's 查繼佐 *Xu Xixiang zaju* 續西廂雜劇 in the Qing. I do not mean that none of these works shows admirable originality and artistry; but each of them falls short of being pure fiction. Strictly speaking, this inertia is no longer historical in nature. In a way, it becomes a creative inertia.

There are many reasons for the historical inertia: reverence for histori-cal truth, overemphasis on the value of second-order imitation, the historical sense of the reading public, the psychological pleasure of repetition, and so on. But it seems to me it has something to do with a lack of clear distinc-tion between historical narrative and pure fiction and with an incorrect atti-tude toward originality in literary creation. Jin Shengtan 金聖歎 (1610–61), a perceptive commentator on Chinese fiction, was perhaps the first theorist who noticed the distinction between historical narrative and pure fiction. He agreed with the idea that writing history is more difficult than writing fiction, but he did not consider the former as superior in artistry:

> In the *Records of the Grand Scribe*, words are used to convey events, while in the *Shuihu zhuan* events are produced from the words. When you use words to convey events, you first have events that have taken place in such-and-such a way, and then you must figure out a piece of narrative for them. Even though the Grand Scribe was a great talent, it was still a hard job. To use words to produce events, on the other hand, is quite different. All you have to do is follow where your pen leads. To cut down what is tall and make tall what is short are both up to me.[56]

In his opinion, in writing history language is only a vehicle that serves to con-vey historical facts. In writing fiction, the writer follows his creative impulse, and language is not just the means of representation; it is also a way to create themes. The latter idea is remarkable in that it is close to the modern idea of fiction, which views language not just as a means of representation but also as a means to discover themes. Thus, Jin Shengtan made an apt distinction between history and fiction in terms of their ways of creation. At the heart of the distinction is fictionality. In Jin's remarks, *sheng* (to give birth to) is to fictionalize and create what is nonexistent. The crux of the matter concerns fic-tionality and creativity. By comparing the *Sanguo yanyi* with the *Shuihu zhuan*, Jin Shengtan came to a different conclusion as to whether historical fiction is superior to pure fiction in fictional artistry:

> In the *Romance of the Three Kingdoms*, historical persons and events speak too much. As a result, the author's pen drags along and has few twists and turns. The author acted as an attendant to an official, who passes on messages. He can only use his voice to transmit what he has been told. Indeed, how dare he add or subtract a word by himself.[57]

The comparison of the *Sanguo yanyi*'s author to a hired runner who passes orders of the magistrate is a fit way of describing the weakness of the said historical novel in particular and historical fiction in general. In his opinion, the *Shuihu zhuan* is superior to the *Sanguo yanyi* because it does not adhere rigidly to historical facts like the *Sanguo yanyi*, which has less room for the writer to exercise his imagination. Xie Zhaozhi, an earlier contemporary of Jin Shengtan, expressed a bold opinion that historical writings were too close to histories and deficient in literary qualities:

> The *Sanguo yanyi, Qiantang ji, Xuanhe yishi, Yang Liulang* and other historical romances are vulgar and have no taste. Why? Because their subject matter is too close to reality and borders on staleness. They may entertain children in back alleys, but are not worthy topics for the literary gentlemen.[58]

In modern times, scholars tend to agree with Jin Shengtan and Xie Zhaozhi. Hu Shi, for one, is critical of the *Sanguo*'s rigid adherence to historical facts: "*Sanguo yanyi* adheres to historical events too rigidly. As a result, it displays too little imagination and too thin a creativity."[59] Zheng Zhenduo 鄭振鐸 expresses a similar opinion: "Because historical narratives or historical novels were written solely on history, they cannot ride on the author's flight of imagination. . . . How can one write well if he is restricted on the left and right? This is why historical fiction rarely produces first-rate works."[60]

Modern scholars have overlooked the drawback of historical narrative: that it is a second-order imitation and lacks fictionality. Liu Tingji 劉廷璣, a scholar of the Qing, correctly identified the ontological status of *yanyi*-style novels: "The historical novel is based on events of prior existence, which it amplifies, reconstructs, elaborates, and extends. It cannot be compared with narratives that create something out of nothing."[61] Consciously or otherwise, Liu recognized the lack of fictionality in historical romances. In the final analysis, deficiency in fictionality is a sign of the lack of creative impulse to pursue originality. In the Chinese tradition, histories served as a walking stick for fiction, but as the walking stick was used for so long that a kind of inertia set in and the walking stick became an artificial leg for many historical fiction writers. The walking stick was a necessary aid to the lame, but it was an impediment to the strong. The movement of *xiaoshuo* from historical narrative to pure fiction required a strong writer who did not rely on the aid of historical narrative. This strong writer was the author of the *Jin Ping Mei*. The appearance of this novel marked a fundamental break from the historical inertia. Even in this novel of pure fiction, however, there are still traces of historical inertia. They can be seen in the use of an episode in the *Shuihu zhuan* to start the novel. Its ample use of existent materials, however, does not diminish its nature as pure fiction, for the sources were used as raw materials, ingeniously woven into a fictional fabric with a totally new design. The novel pioneered a new way of writing, which is the modern way of fiction writing.

FROM STORYTELLING TO FICTIONAL ART

Chinese *xiaoshuo* went through two fundamental shifts: a transition from street talk and gossip to mature form of storytelling and a shift from storytelling to fictional art. The second shift was more important for the evolution of *xiaoshuo* into an aesthetic category. The two shifts did not exactly come one after the other; rather, they overlapped each other, and characteristic features of earlier stages persisted long after *xiaoshuo* became a mature form of fictional art. But when *xiaoshuo* succeeded in making the transition from storytelling to fictional art, the aesthetic turn in Chinese fiction was complete.

The reader may ask: How can you distinguish between storytelling and fictional art? Clive Bell's famous aesthetic hypothesis may offer us some assistance. Bell suggests that there must be some quality common to all works of art, without which a work of art cannot exist. By pinning down that quality to something that provokes our aesthetic emotions, he propounds his famous hypothesis: "'Significant Form' is the one quality common to all works of visual art" and "significant form is the essential quality in a work of art."[62] Li Zhehou, a renowned Chinese aesthetician, points out that Bell's theory of significant form, despite its fascinating insights, has the drawback of tautology: the significant form of an object decides whether it can arouse aesthetic emotion, and aesthetic emotion comes from its significant form. He supplements Bell's significant form with his own theory of aesthetic sedimentation: "From representation (imitation) to expression (abstraction), from realism to symbolism—this is a process of sedimentary shift from content to form. It is also the original process of how beauty came to be 'significant form.'"[63] Li theorizes that the reason why significant form is a form that carries meaning is that in the process of evolution, the original meaning of an object gradually becomes an abstract form. Bell's significant form is derived from the study of visual arts. When it combines with Li Zhehou's aesthetic sedimentation, it has some significance for any form of art, including verbal art like fiction. In my opinion, the production of significant form through aesthetic sedimentation is essentially an aesthetic transformation of meaning into form via the route from imitation to expression or realism to symbolism. Significant form is, in the final analysis, a content in form or a form with content. This revised idea of significant form may provide an adequate understanding of the difference between fictional art and nonfictional art.

Bell's discussion of why some descriptive pictures are not works of art is particularly useful in understanding the difference between mere storytelling and fictional art. Bell admits that many descriptive pictures possess, among other qualities, the essential quality in a work of art—that is, formal significance—and they are therefore works of art. But many descriptive pictures do not possess formal significance. They may interest viewers, and even move them in many ways, but they are not works of art, because "they do not move us aesthetically. . . . They leave untouched our aesthetic emotions because it is not their forms but the ideas or information suggested or conveyed by their forms that affect us."[64] Storytelling differs from fictional art in its nature, function, and techniques. As far as their basic nature is concerned, storytelling and fictional art are essentially similar; both are a kind of narrative in prose form. But in function and formal techniques the two differ from each other radically. We must admit that many stories narrated in the storytelling fashion are works of verbal art, but many more of them are not, because, like most descriptive pictures, their function is to impart ideas and information, not to elicit aesthetic appreciation. From its earliest appearance in primitive societies, storytelling had had two main functions: to entertain and to educate. But fictional art, apart from having the two practical functions, has an aesthetic function that often transcends the practical functions. Fictional art has all the techniques that pertain to storytelling and has a lot more to offer. The most fundamental difference between storytelling and fictional art is that the latter provides the reader with opportunities for aesthetic appreciation of its significant form in addition to opportunities for hearing an enthralling story. In other words, apart from imparting interesting ideas and information, a fictional work of art possesses a significant form aesthetically conceived and skillfully crafted. In visual art, significant form exists in combinations of lines and colors that move spectators. In a verbal art like fiction, significant form is to be found in a skillful use of language that imparts information as well as aesthetic values beyond the narrated information. As far as modes of presentation are concerned, fictional art starts with realistic imitation, but ends up with symbolic expression.

Our exploration, then, narrows down to the question: What is the aesthetic value of Chinese fictional art? Here again, a look at the judgment of aesthetic value in other forms of art may offer some insight. Aestheticians generally agree that art can only have an "open" definition,[65] and aesthetic value is an open category, too. Nevertheless, many aestheticians concur that art is essentially a surplus form with nonfunctional values. Take a chair, for example. The function of a chair is to allow people to sit comfortably. To meet the functional requirement, a chair needs to have a flat surface supported by four legs and to have a back that supports the body. People may add more things to it: they may supplement it with arms and wrap it with soft pads. But these added elements still serve a functional purpose and do not turn a chair into an object of art. If, however, one carves the legs, arms, and back of the chair into beautiful shapes, the chair undergoes a fundamental change. The carvings are not necessary to the function of the chair. They only supply surplus ornaments to the chair, but as a result of the functionally unnecessary ornaments, the chair becomes an object of art. In terms of Immanuel Kant's conception of the beautiful, the chair becomes an object of art not because of "objective purposiveness, i.e. the reference of the object to a definite purpose," but because of "formal purposiveness, i.e. a purposiveness without a purpose."[66] The unnecessary ornaments evoke in the viewer of the chair a disinterested appreciation of its form, which imparts a surplus value that transcends practical function. From this reasoning, we may conclude that art is an object with surplus value whose realization is accomplished by surplus form. A work of verbal art must also have surplus signifying value; in addition to imparting surface information, a work of verbal art must convey more meaning than meets the eye, and do so through its carefully crafted language form.

Fiction is a verbal art. The function of a verbal discourse is to communicate information. A story is also a verbal discourse. It imparts information either to entertain or to educate. The capability to make people happy or to teach people ideas about society is the function of a story. By its function alone, a story cannot be regarded as an object of verbal art, because its function does not transcend the communication of information. For a story to be a work of fictional art, it must have surplus value. In an artistically crafted chair, the surplus value is created by the surplus ornaments. In term of my proposed conception of surplus value as the core of fictional art, a story must have something beyond an interesting story for it to be viewed as a verbal art.

It may be reasonably said that except for some short stories, practically all Chinese fictional works narrated in the storytelling fashion had the overriding aim of telling an intriguing story. The small number of stories that may be counted as fictional works with artistic traits transcend the dominant aim of storytelling. For ordinary stories, once the tale is told, it is over. There is little worth further reflection. Those stories that have attained certain amount of fictional art are endowed with surplus signifying values. Here I may cite just a few examples: "The Story of Ying Ying," "The World in a Pillow," "Du Shiniang Sinks the Jewel Box in Anger," and "The Oil Peddler Courts the Courtesan." These stories have significance beyond an interesting tale. Apart from telling a love story, "The Story of Ying Ying" offers a profound insights into the complexities of the human psyche. The jewel box in "Du Shiniang Sinks the Jewel Box in Anger" is more than a detail in the story. By its shape and ownership, it symbolizes the gendered status of the female protagonist. With its hidden content, it symbolizes her concealed worth unrecognized by the male protagonist. When it gets recovered by a character who once helps Du Shiniang, it conveys the idea of poetic justice. The oil peddler story is on the surface a story of visiting a brothel, but besides the oil peddler's moving account, which turns a conventionally debased motive into a moral action that wins readers' sympathy, the author wove a subtext. It is a quasi-religious dimension. The oil peddler's persistence in saving enough money for a night with the courtesan, his reverent attitude toward her on that night, and his immense satisfaction at serving her while she is drunk and totally ignores him are permeated with an air of religiosity as though he were on a pilgrimage and had the rare chance of seeing a god. Indeed, the story informs us, to the male protagonist the courtesan is "a goddess from heaven," and he felt as though he were having a "dream rendezvous with a goddess."[67] Interestingly, the latter two stories were popular stories told by professional storytellers but were later rewritten by scholars. The rewriting added surplus signifying values and evidently accounted for much of their fictional art.

In my theorizing on the rise of Chinese fiction, I have identified daydreaming as a major source of early Chinese stories. Daydreaming, however, is obviously not an art, because it is naive, egoistic, and simplistic, far removed from any verbal art imaginatively crafted. In fact, daydreaming may not even be counted as an interesting story, for, as Freud points out, daydreaming without formal embellishment will not give pleasure; on the contrary, it will only repel the reader. "The essential *ars poetica*," Freud suggests, "lies in the technique of overcoming the feeling of repulsion in us."[68] How does the writer accomplish this? Freud provides an aesthetic answer: "The writer softens the character of his egoistic daydreams by altering and disguising it, and he bribes us by the purely formal—that is, aesthetic—yield of pleasure which he offers us in the presentation of his phantasies." He calls this technique "incentive bonus" or "fore-pleasure."[69]

In early Chinese fiction, some stories that bear clear traces of daydreaming have already attained a considerable measure of verbal art, precisely because their authors already knew how to soften the egoistic nature of the daydreaming, how to give their tales "incentive bonus," and how to supply aesthetic pleasure as well as egoistic pleasure. "The World in a Pillow" is a case in point. Ostensibly, the story follows a conventional daydreaming formula: how the protagonist leaves the world of reality to enter a world of fantasy, where he enjoys great success in his official career and the happiness of family life, only to wake up to find all is only a dream. What makes the story verbal art is the formal frame that sandwiches the story proper: its polemic beginning and ironic ending. The story begins with a discussion of what happiness is and ends with the conclusion that "The happiness of human life is but a dream." By emphasizing the fact that the millet the innkeeper has been cooking before the protagonist falls asleep is not yet ready, the author deliberately pokes fun at daydreaming. In so doing, the author self-consciously maintains a distance necessary for the reader to engage in disinterested contemplation. Without this distance the story is only a daydream far off from the aesthetic conditions of a verbal art.

CHAPTER THREE

The Aesthetic Turn in Chinese Fiction

In his study of the four masterpieces of Ming fiction, Andrew Plaks argues convincingly that contrary to the popular belief that the four great novels are the products of popular imagination, they were really the "self-conscious artistic constructs" crystallized out of transmitted source materials, antecedent narratives, and alternate recensions by the refined imagination of the literati.[1] Proclaiming the four masterpieces to be "literati novels," he suggests that these novels "defined and shaped the generic outlines of the serious novel form in Ming and Ch'ing China." More daringly, he dissents from the accepted view, which attributes the rise of the novel to urbanization, mercantilism, and the rise of middle-class culture, and instead relates its rise to aesthetic conditions such as "patterns of composition, critical theories, and prevailing intellectual trends more characteristic of the literati milieu."[2] He draws a most enlightening conclusion: "[T]he mature literati novel stands as a new synthesis of the whole range of literary developments of the Ming period, drawing upon the aesthetic qualities and techniques of late Ming prose style and poetics, compositional principles of the *pa-ku* essay, the informal spirit and rhetorical devices of *hsiao-p'in wen*, and the structural patterns and intellectual attitudes of the literati drama, as well as certain storytelling devices that eventually go into the formation of the colloquial short-story genre."[3]

Plaks's study contains a vision of Chinese fiction that implicitly advocates a paradigm shift in the study of Ming and Qing prose fiction. I wish to broaden his vision to cover traditional Chinese fiction as a whole. I venture to argue that in contradistinction to European fiction, which arose from a mercantile demand for entertainment and catered to the popular taste, Chinese fiction as a mature form of verbal art, despite its genesis in the popular demand for entertainment, came into being as a result of both the visible and invisible influence of the literati culture and a self-conscious emulation of and competition with the dominant literary genres, which were lyric poetry and classical prose. Indeed, it may well be said that from the outset, Chinese *xiaoshuo* went through a long and extended aesthetic turn.

THE INITIAL TURN TO FICTIONALITY
IN EARLY *XIAOSHUO*

The aesthetic turn started from high antiquity when fiction was still indistinguishable from other forms of writing. Important as it is, the movement at this stage is not so much a turn to verbal art as a turn to fictionality. Because of the almost complete loss of early *xiaoshuo* materials, it is hard to speculate on how the turn came about. As Hellmut Wilhelm aptly puts it in his study of Zhou fiction, "to establish the existence of, and describe, a literary genre from material which is entirely nonexistent" belongs to "the category of forbidden games."[4] We are therefore compelled to be content with describing and isolating elements of fiction. On the basis of the meager information left about Zhou fiction, Wilhelm speculates that earliest *xiaoshuo* writings were derived from political persuasions, especially from the legendary episodes in the *Zuozhuan*, *Guoyu*, and *Zhanguo che*, and *xiaoshuo* as a literary category might have existed before Ban Gu's times.[5] His speculation, though somewhat narrow in focus, is justified by the preserved historical materials. In the development of Chinese fiction, early historical narratives made perhaps the greatest contribution to the maturity of Chinese fiction, but in my opinion, none of them can be viewed as fiction per se. Historical narratives, like the *Zuozhuan*, *Guoyu*, *Zhanguo che*, and *Shiji* profess to record historical events as they truly were, and, incidentally, they represent the highest achievement of early Chinese narrative literature. Early histories contain more fictional elements than later official histories, because they were often written by a single author and with more imagination. Later official histories are the collaborative projects of many authors who wanted to use history as providing lessons for the future. What was discarded by later historical writings is precisely the elements of fiction to be found in early histories. But from a purely literary point of view, early histories are not yet fictional works in the modern sense of the word; they are not even on a par with historical novels of later times like the *Sanguo yanyi*. Consider the case of Winston Churchill's monumental history of World War II. The book was awarded the Nobel Prize for Literature, but the selection has often been cited as an example of poor judgment. In the same way, early histories can only be counted as protofiction with elements of fictionality.

Nowadays, scholars generally agree that in the historical period before the rise of fiction in the modern sense in the Tang, four categories of writing may be viewed as fiction on their own elements of fictionality: (1) some historical writings; (2) myths and legends; (3) parables and allegories in philosophical writings; and (4) records of extraordinary things and people in the Six Dynasties.[6] Many historical episodes in the first category can be read as interesting stories of fiction if we do not know that they were meant as historical records. Even some historical writings that have been regarded as histories should be properly treated as fiction, or at least historical fiction on account of their unrealistic details and fantastic episodes. The *Mu Tianzi zhuan* (*An Account of the Travels of Emperor Mu*) (c. fourth century BC) is an example. Many myths and legends in the second category were consistently classified into the broad category of *xiaoshuo*, and their fantastic way of presentation was later absorbed into stories of the extraordinary and in a way anticipated what nowadays is called magic realism. But we must note that their fictionality was not consciously intended. The third category consists of episodes taken from the philosophical writings of thinkers, and many of them have always been read as interesting stories. These stories and parables were created for the sake of argument, and their fictionality was consciously intended. Nevertheless, they are only episodes in a philosophical work and not independently composed stories. The fourth category consists of tales of extraordinary things and people collected in *Lieyi zhuan* 列異傳, *Shenyi jing* 神異經, *Shizhou ji* 十洲記, *Hanwu dongming ji* 漢武洞冥記, *Bowu ji* 博物記 , *Soushen ji* 搜神記, *Youming lu* 幽明錄, and thirty-odd other collections. Some of the stories in these collections of *zhiguai* and *zhiren* tales are narratives of considerable length and with carefully conceived plots. Some extant tales in the *zhiguai* and *zhiren* collections differ little from later fictional works in their representation of events, characterization, plot arrangement, and fictional techniques. By the formulated definition of fiction, these tales can be counted as fictional works.

There are many tales in the extant *zhiguai* and *zhiren* collections that resemble modern short stories. Tales like "Zhao Feiyan waizhuan 趙飛燕外傳," "Dongfang Shuo liezhuan 東方朔列傳," "Han Wu neizhuan 漢武內傳," "Shennü zhuan 神女傳 ," "Du Lanxiang biezhuan 杜蘭香別傳," "Dong Yong 董永," "Dinggu ci 丁姑祠," "Pang Ah 龐阿," and "Liu Chen and Ruan Zhao 劉晨阮肇" display comparable narrative sophistication and conscious desire for creating fiction. "The Unofficial Biography of Zhao Feiyan" is exceptional. It centers on a love triangle among two sisters and an emperor. It gives a detailed narration of events in the inner court of the palace, and depicts two vivid characters with entirely different personalities. Its structural arrangement, description of settings, emphasis on characterization, exploration of the characters' inner world, conversations between characters, and apt use of language all testify to its status as a full-fledged fictional work. It anticipated the rise of the Tang *chuanqi* tales. Hu Yinglin's comment is an apt observation: "The story of Zhao Feiyan is the first of *chuanqi* genre tales 飛燕，傳奇之首也 ."[7] They should give us enough reason to revise Lu Xun's view that tales of the Six Dynasties are too brief and sketchy 六朝之粗陳梗概 and lack the conscious creative intention of the Tang *chuanqi*. In my opinion, such tales differ from the Tang *chuanqi* tales only in length and degrees of sophistication, not in intention of conscious creation and fictional techniques. As there is a visible continuity from the Six Dynasties *zhiguai* and *zhiren* tales to the Tang *chuanqi* tales, there was no narrative revolution in the Tang; there was only the culmination of an evolutionary process. The Tang *chuanqi* tales only greatly enriched and improved the narrative tradition in the Six dynasties.

In the early forms of fictional writings, then, we can find most of the elements of modern fiction, but I must qualify this claim by adding that no single form of early writing contains all the elements of modern fiction. A category may contain one element, but lack others. The main reason that the four kinds of narratives may be considered early forms of fiction is that, whether long or short in length, they all tell stories, real or imagined. Technically and formally, they conform to the requirements described by Scholes in his conception of "story": "A story is a narrative with a certain very specific syntactic shape (beginning-middle-end or situation-transformation-situation) and with a subject matter which allows for or encourages the projection of human values upon this material. Virtually all stories are about human beings or humanoid creatures. Those that are not invariably humanize their material through metaphor and metonymy."[8]

Another reason why I say they may be viewed as fiction is that they all contain elements of modern fiction. The common element that entitles them to be regarded as fiction is fictionality. If fictionality is defined as that which has no prior temporal existence but is true to life, all the four forms of early Chinese narrative qualify as fiction. Even supposedly factual historical records such as the *Zuozhuan* and *Shiji* contain episodes that surely could not have happened in real life, past or present. However, nonfactuality alone is not what makes a writing a fictional work. There are other essential elements. Fictional works are a result of representation or imitation of life. Nonfictional *xiaoshuo* is just a heap of topics; by contrast, a work of fiction is a linguistically organized (or manipulated) entity. Since representation or mimesis is done through language in fictional works, the ontological condition of fiction must be subjected to linguistic inquiry.

Literary theorists that take a linguistic approach view fiction as a hollow use of language. In terms of J. L. Austin's speech-act theory of language, theorists of fiction suggest that "fiction is not exactly false, non-existent, or imaginary; it is just oddly empty."[9] Barbara Herrnstein Smith, a theorist who makes use of speech-act theory of language in her theorizing on fiction, suggests that fictional works, especially those in the form of novels, "are usually imitation of nonfictive writing acts, such as the production of histories and biographies."[10] She argues that "the essential fictiveness of novels . . . is not to be discovered in the unreality of the characters, objects, and events alluded to, but in the unreality of the alludings themselves."[11] According to her argument, fiction should be defined as pretended speech-act. In terms of her theory, the early forms of Chinese narrative are pretended speech-acts by those writers, be they mythmakers, philosophical thinkers, or scribes, who attempted to speak to the public and posterity.

Having proclaimed the four kinds of early narrative as early fictional writings, I must hasten to add that except for a sizable number of *zhiguai* and *zhiren* tales, they are, strictly speaking, only forms of protofiction, because they fall, in one way or another, short of the modern conception of fiction. The first shortcoming common to most of the early fictional narrative is their short length. Aristotle said, "Tragedy is an imitation of an action that is serious, complete, and of a certain magnitude."[12] Although Aristotle was talking specifically about tragedy, the point is valid for literature generally. His mimetic theory emphasizes the narration of an action that is complete and has a certain length. It reveals a limitation of early *xiaoshuo* writings as narratives of extended events. Narrative, as the word indicates, is a kind of verbal account that contains narratability, or that which can be narrated. Narrative is a temporal category. As Scholes points out: "Only one kind of thing can be narrated: a time-thing, or to use our normal word for it, an 'event.' And strictly speaking, we require more than one event before we recognize that we are in the presence of a narrative."[13] Thus, a narrative is an account that narrates a series of events in a time sequence. Many *zhiguai* tales (records of the strange) and miscellaneous anecdotes before the Tang cannot be strictly considered narrative, simply because they often narrate a single event.

Although myths, legends, and most *zhiguai* tales are abundant in fictionality, they have another deficiency in terms of the modern concept of fiction. Except for some tales, these early pieces of fiction display no obvious desire on the part of the author to create a fictional work. Reworking Lu Xun's idea of conscious fictionalization, Y.W. Ma draws a line between fictional works and some early *xiaoshuo* writings: "It [fiction] not only creates an imaginative reality, but brings about a reality which is the result of a conscious act on the part of the author. This helps to draw lines between fiction on the one hand and parables, folklore, and various components of mythology on the other."[14] While myths, legends, and *zhiguai* and *zhiren* tales are short, historical narrative is certainly long. But it falls short of fictional work in the strict sense of the word in another way: its fictionality is not strong enough. The problem of fictionality even in later historical novels is still an issue that troubles critics and theorists of fiction.

Examination of the development of Chinese *xiaoshuo* up to the Tang reveals that practically all major elements of fiction can be found in *xiaoshuo* writings produced before the Tang. This suggests that Chinese fiction followed an evolutionary path. There is visible continuity from the earliest notion to the appearance of Tang *chuanqi* tales, but no narrative revolution. Great changes took place gradually. Narrative revolution in the sense of abrupt, large-scale changes in modes of writing occurred perhaps only once in the whole history of *xiaoshuo*. It was the revolution in *xiaoshuo* initiated by Liang Qichao and other scholars at the turn of the twentieth century and completed by the writing practice of Lu Xun and other modern fiction writers. The narrative impetus that drives the evolutionary process of Chinese *xiaoshuo* is the motivational force of pure fictionality. This evolutionary view of Chinese *xiaoshuo* with a drive towards pure fiction will be a red thread that runs through my study of Chinese fiction.

THE TURN TO REALISM AND INWARDNESS

I have problematized Lu Xun's view of self-conscious fictionality as the hallmark of Tang *xiaoshuo*. But his view that Chinese fiction went through a radical change in the Tang is certainly a correct observation. What, then, are the salient features that distinguish the Tang *chuanqi* from its predecessors? In my opinion, it is first a drastic turn to realism and then a turn to simulation and inwardness. Early signs of the first turn can be found in the tales of the Six Dynasties. In a very recent study of Chinese *xiaoshuo*, a Chinese scholar makes this sagacious observation: "The human beings in the *zhiguai* tales, like their counterparts in the *zhiren* tales, are all imitations of human beings in reality. To put it another way, the narrator who is a person in real life and the characters in the stories share a common nature and are located on the same level of existence. In earlier writings, the narrator only represented an area known to the 'outside' world and the collective, but in the tales of the Six Dynasties, the narrator turned his attention to himself and to the human groups in real life closely related to him."[15]

Like early Western fiction, the realistic turn finds its expression in an unusual preoccupation with truth in fiction. In the early stages of Western fiction, there is a similar situation. We may recall how the narrator in Cervantes's masterpiece, *Don Quixote*, frequently assures the reader that what is written is either what he has observed with his eyes or what is recorded in authentic history books.[16] The Chinese turn to realism manifests a much more concentrated interest in the subject. The unusual preoccupation takes the form of a paradox. In Tang *chuanqi* tales, there is almost a formulaic pattern: at the end of a tale, the author claims that the story's content is true because he either had witnessed the events himself or someone he knew has witnessed it, even though the events obviously are unreal. This formulaic pattern appears to be necessary for the achievement of a "willing suspension of disbelief" on the part of the reader. It is meant to have the reader interact with the narrator, and may be viewed as a precursor for what Patrick Hanan finds in later Chinese vernacular fiction: the "simulated context," which is "the context of situation in which a piece of fiction claims to be transmitted."[17] Hanan's notion supports my psychological explanation for the formulaic pattern: "[T]he simulacrum is that of the oral storyteller addressing his audience, a pretense in which the author and reader happily acquiesce in order that the fiction can be communicated."[18] In his study of fictional theory, Michael Riffaterre identifies as a clear sign of fictionality the "constant coincidence between textual features declaring the fictionality of a story and a reassertion of the truth of that story."[19] The Chinese formulaic pattern comes from a similar fictional consciousness: it describes a blatantly unreal story but declares it to be true. The conflicting and paradoxical authorial intrusion is indicative of conscious fictionality.

There are a number of other explanations for this narrative ploy. One is that the traditional view privileges transmission over creation. It started with Confucius, who modestly claimed that he did not create but only engaged in transmitting what was passed on to him (*shu er bu zuo*). Another has to do with *xiaoshuo*'s relation to history. Starting from the Han, the historical narrative model pioneered by Sima Qian had been praised by Liu Xiang, Yang

Xiong, and Ban Gu for its faithful, straightforward recording of historical events (*shilu*). Zhang Xuecheng remarked: "[Sima Qian's] writing is direct, and the events are verifiable. He did not indulge in empty praise, nor did he conceal evils. This is why it [the *Shiji*] has been called truthful recording (*shilu*)."[20] The early notion of *xiaoshuo* was that it was a branch of scholarship closely related to history. Liu Zhiji, the first Chinese scholar who conducted a systematic study of history, simply viewed *xiaoshuo* as an unofficial and defective form of history, unreliable in its content and defective in its form. Since *xiaoshuo* was viewed as a defective form of history, writers attempted to rival history for the sense of *vraisemblance*. In their attempt to sidestep the charge of untruthful fabrication, they self-consciously emphasized the *zhen* (real) in their stories with the aim to achieve a sense of *shi* (the solid, the factual, the actual) in the writing of history. This might have influenced the practice of ending a story with a statement about its authenticity, but in many stories the narrated events are, as I said, anything but believable. Take Shen Jiji's "Rensi zhuan" (Miss Ren), for example. The story opens with the categorical statement: "Miss Ren was a fox-spirit," and then tells of her love triangle with two men and her eventual demise. Evidently, this kind of tale requires "willing suspension of disbelief." In spite of the author's intrusion into the tale toward the end to assure the reader of the truthfulness of his account, no sensible reader except children and the most gullible will believe in the authenticity of the story. On the contrary, as Eagleton rightly observes, "If an author breaks off to assure us that what she is now asserting is acutally true—that it really, literally happened—we would take this as a fictional statement."[21]

Finally, there is an aesthetic explanation for why the ending claim to truth was so prevalent. I have demonstrated that the rise of Tang *xiaoshuo* was largely the result of daydreaming or idle fancy by the Tang literati. Traditional Chinese literature valued the historical sense of truth and reality and frowned on daydreams. The Tang literati who created *xiaoshuo* must have acutely felt the need to justify their idle fancy and to defend against the accusation of indulging in daydreaming. From a comparative perspective, in the West, fiction writers in the seventeenth and eighteenth centuries were accused of the same act of indulging in idle fancy and, feeling guilty as charged, they began to produce more realistic and believable tales, which culminated in the realistic novel. The result is not a substitution of truth for fiction but only a better-disguised fiction. Tang *xiaoshuo* writers took great pains at the end of their stories to say how real their tales are, not so much to rival historical writings in factual representation, but to achieve a reality effect comparable to that in historiography. In his study of history, Barthes says that the writing of history does not aim at presenting the "real" but creating a "reality effect."[22] This idea is especially useful for an understanding of the Tang *xiaoshuo* writers' claim to the real. In trying to approximate real events, Tang *xiaoshuo* does not exactly attempt to rival history in the degree of the real and factual, but attempts to create an artistic effect that could be called verisimilitude or the "real effect."

The desire to achieve the "real effect" is the hallmark of realism, but this is not something new in Chinese literature. Historical writings have long achieved great success in literary realism, or verisimilitude. But that kind of realism is based on historical truth, not on the genuine verisimilitude that is a characteristic feature of fiction. In claiming that something obviously unreal is real, Tang fiction meant not only to inject historical realism into literature, but also to finalize an aesthetic turn, the signs of which had appeared earlier. As I've said, the *zhiguai* or *zhiren* tales of the Six Dynasties had already contained essential qualities that endow them to be called fictional works in realism. By proclaiming real a series of potentially unreal events, Tang *xiaoshuo* writers were declaring a principle that is similar to the Aristotelian law of probability: a fictional work is not necessarily about something that has happened; it can be about something that might happen with a stretch of the imagination. The unabashed presence of the author seems to suggest that fiction has the same claim to existence as history or other forms of literature. This, I claim, is one of the hallmarks of *xioashuo*'s coming close to the modern sense of fiction.

The claim to truth in a tale the content of which is obviously untrue foretells that Chinese fiction would develop in a direction fundamentally different from Western fiction grounded on mimesis and realism. It was endowed with a subversive power to confound the boundaries of truth and fiction by problematizing the duality between model and copy in realistic imitation. By declaring a truthful representation of reality, *xiaoshuo* writers were conscious of the mimetic function of *xiaoshuo*; but since what they represent is patently untrue, they were aware, quite self-unconsciously, that a *xiaoshuo* writing is a simulacrum in which the copy (what is represented in *xiaoshuo*) does not have to imitate the model (events in nature or life) in a strictly realistic fashion. This insight that I have teased out of the convention may enable us to see the deep dimension of why in the early stages of Chinese *xiaoshuo* there was already an abundance of fantastic plots and phantasmagoric fictional techniques that may well be described as belonging to magic realism.

"[T]he simulacrum is not simply a false copy," says Deleuze; "it places in question the very notations of copy and model."[23] In numerous Tang *chuanqi* tales, the writers were effectively questioning the relationship between model and copy. I have suggested in the previous chapter that the ironical ending of "Nanke taishou zhuan 南柯太守傳" may be a self-conscious look at daydreams or an act of poking fun at the daydreams of the literati at that time. From another point of view, it may be seen as an act of simulation that problematizes the relationship between model and copy. The protagonist's successful career is a credible imitation of that of a successful civil service candidate. But the ending places the narrated events in a simulated framework. The successful story is only a simulation of what might have been going on in the kingdom of ants located at the foot of a big locus tree. This kind of duplication can no longer be explained by the Aristotelian logic of imitation. It can only be accounted for by the theory of simulation, which is "the generation by models of a real without origin or reality: a hyperreal."[24] The ending is perhaps meant as an artistic maneuver to deter every real process and to short-circuit all the realistically represented events. This kind of ending is just the opposite of the claim to truth at the end of other tales, but both endings serve the same aesthetic objective of fictional creation, which was articulated by Cao Xueqin in the *Hongloumeng*. The couplet inscribed on the stone arch in the Land of Illusion, "Truth becomes fiction when the fiction's true; / Real becomes not-real when the unreal's real,"[25] is not just a hint at the content of that specific novel; it is a view of fictional representation in general. In the *chuanji* tale's claim to truth, it is implied that fiction is a mode of writing that, unlike history, is meant to erase the demarcation between truth and fiction, the real and unreal. The claim to truth at the ending of some *chuanqi* tales, then, is an act of subversion taken to emancipate *xiaoshuo* from the hold of history. By declaring the truthfulness of a *xiaoshuo* writing, the author was not entirely under the influence of faithful representation; he was also proclaiming in a mocking manner that *xiaoshuo* as a form of narrative is fundamentally different from history. This implication of unreality complements *xioashuo*'s turn to realism.

The second hallmark of realism is the internalization of the narration of persons, events, and experience. Early *xiaoshuo* writings, because of their short length, were incapable of extended exploration of characters' inner world. The extended length of Tang *xiaoshuo* made inner probing possible. Many of the *chuanqi* tales certainly depict unrealistic persons, creatures, and events, but mainstream Tang tales, and the most brilliant of them that can be regarded as fiction in the modern sense, deal with themes related to the family, the relationship between man and woman, and the human experience in real life. In her study of the origins of fiction, Robert suggests that "family romance" can be regarded as the fountainhead of fictional inspiration. Whether it is popular or highbrow, old or new, classical or modern, fiction comes from the personal folklore made up of the set of infantile complexes created by family life.[26] "Family romance" and "family complexes" are phrases coined by Freud in his study of infantile sexuality, especially the oedipal wishes. As Freud showed in his essay "Family Romance"[27] and his *Introductory Lectures on Psychoanalysis*, the infantile mentality during the oedipal stage is pervaded with sexual curiosity, incestuous desires, rebelliousness, and parricidal attempts.[28] The infantile complex emanating from family romance is the universal psychic phenomenon of humankind. All kinds of artistic forms can reproduce these complexes, but fiction is the most convenient form for representing them, because while poetry and drama are restricted in the use of language or space, fiction is not subject to any formal restrictions if the writer frees himself or herself from mental and aesthetic inhibitions.

The Tang was a time of emancipation from the repressive morality of Confucianism. The emancipation accelerated the transformation of Chinese *xiaoshuo* from the *zhiguai* and *zhiren* tales of the Six Dynasties to the Tang *chuanqi*, which comes close to fitting the modern notion of fiction. The emancipation enabled another hallmark of internalization to appear. It is the internalization of narration in the characters' inner worlds. It is a scholarly cliché that traditional Chinese fiction, with a few exceptions, is exclusively concerned with external narration and has little interest in exploring the characters' inner worlds. In contesting this cliché, Andrew Plaks sagaciously points out: "In most cases where the narrative texts fail to clearly set forth the internal deliberation leading up to specific actions, it is less a case of disinterest in human motivation than an implicit understanding between narrator and audience that the causes of human behavior usually need not be spelled out, or are better off left unstated."[29]

In view of the historical development of *xiaoshuo*, I may offer another reason for the seeming disinterest in psychological exploration of the characters' inner worlds. I suggest that the dominance of historical truthfulness impeded the rise of interest in fictional characters' minds. Dorrit Cohn observes in her study of fiction theory that speech-acts encountered in fiction are not always imitations of natural speech-acts, and there is at least one kind of speech that has no natural correspondent: the narration of life "as experienced in the privacy of a character's consciousness."[30] She argues that in everyday life no one can know, much less report, the intimate thoughts of a fellow human being in various situations. Therefore, the reenacting of someone else's inner thoughts in the first person is a linguistic act that occurs only in fiction. This point may afford us an insight into why early traditional Chinese fiction writers did not show as much interest as their Western counterparts in the description and narration of the characters' inner worlds. History is to record observable words, actions, and events of historical persons. In Chinese history, scribes seldom recorded the inner consciousness of historical persons, because historical records are supposed not to be speculative. As fictional works wanted to rival the authenticity of history, they followed the practice of historical writings and refrained from entering the minds of their characters.

But with the rise of pure fiction, as the dependence on history was weakened, Chinese fiction became more and more preoccupied with the exploration of characters' inner worlds. This trend started with Tang *chuanqi* tales, deepened in the *Jin Ping Mei*, and culminated in the *Hongloumeng*. Some Tang stories show a remarkable psychological penetration into characters' behavior. "The Story of Ying Ying" is a case in point. This story has so many innovative features that it deserves an important place in the development of Chinese fiction. One of its innovations is the detailed description of the female protagonist's psychology as revealed by her hesitation over the male protagonist's seduction. After Mr. Zhang professes his love through his poems, she lures him into meeting her at night, and then rebukes him for taking advantage of having helped her family. After Mr. Zhang completely despairs of ever winning her love, she suddenly capitulates and goes to offer herself to him on another night. She is thus depicted as having two selves: one self adheres to the Confucian morality of proper behavior for a young woman, and the other self seeks individual fulfillment and rebels against the moral restraints. The split selves reveal the author's in-depth insight into the female psyche in a Confucian society.

The author's psychological acumen is also revealed in the characters' understanding of each other. Before Mr. Zhang leaves for the scheduled civil service examination, Ying Ying guesses correctly that he would be leaving her for good. Her guess is based on in-depth analysis of the situation. She says to Mr. Zhang: "To seduce someone and then abandon her is perfectly natural [for a man], and it would be presumptuous of me to resent it. It would be an act of charity on your part if, having first seduced me, you were to go through with it and fulfill your oath of lifelong devotion."[31] She understands clearly that without the proper arrangements for marriage, their love is doomed from the very beginning. This story also pioneers the practice of mixing narrative with poems and letters. In the European history of fiction development, Samuel Richardson's (1689–1761) epistolary novels *Pamela, or Virtue Rewarded, Clarissa Harlowe*, and *Sir Charles Grandison* pioneered the novelistic tradition of exploring the psychological aspects of characters. According to English literary history, Richardson wrote his first epistolary novel while he was an apprentice in a printing shop working on a manual of letter writing. The compiling of the manual not only gave him the impetus to write the first psychological novel in Europe but also contributed significantly to the inwardness of the narrated events.[32] It is not by mere accident that the first Chinese story that achieves psychological inwardness also features the inclusion of letter writing.

In a way, "The Story of Ying Ying" may be viewed as the first epistolary fictional work in the Chinese tradition. In her letter to Zhang, Ying Ying expresses her profound love for him and tells him of her miserable existence because of his absence. Yet she is clearly aware of her fate: "How could I have foreseen that our encounter could not possibly lead to something definite, that having disgraced myself by coming to you, there was no further chance of serving you openly as a wife?"[33] She understands that her love has been doomed by the double standard for men and women in her society. There are more details worth psychological analysis. The lovers's changing emotions, such as longing, hope, despair, and grief, are depicted with rare psychological insight that deserves to be regarded as "modern" in the psychology of human emotions. The story has been accused of an inconsistency in plot development, especially with regard to the male protagonist. I, however, suggest that neither Mr. Zhang nor Ying Ying is a "flat character" whose personality development is constructed on a single idea or quality, as in most of the *zhiguai* and *zhiren* tales of the Six Dynasties. Both of them are "round characters" in E. M. Forster's words, who are capable of surprising the reader in a convincing way.[34] Ying Ying's apparently abrupt change of behavior from assumed moral rigidity through total abandon to willing acceptance of her fate makes her a character with modern sensibilities. "The Story of Ying Ying" has value not only in providing the themes for later writers of drama and fiction, but also in pioneering new ways of characterization, psychological exploration, and plot development. With the advent of this story, Chinese fiction completely came of age, and *xiaoshuo* became an established literary genre in the modern sense of the word, even though it would still take a long time for the literary establishment to recognize it.

THE TURN TO MULTIPLICITY IN THE FULL-LENGTH NOVEL

As *xiaoshuo* developed from the predominantly short episodes of *zhiguai* and *zhiren* tales in the Wei, Jin, and Six Dynasties period to the short stories of the Tang, to the *huaben* (storyteller's prompt-books) of the Song and Yuan, to the extended discourses of the novels of the Ming, it took another turn in its evolutionary process. It is the turn to multiplicity in representation conducive to multiple interpretations. With this turn, *xiaoshuo* acquired an open conception; it was no longer content with presenting a single creative vision but aimed at facilitating multiple interpretations. Indeed, it gained so much complexity in narrative scope, creative visions, authorial intentions, plot arrangement, and mimetic technicalities that it became a literary form of multiplicity, and in many ways an open literary form in Umberto Eco's conception of the term. In his study of James Joyce's fictional masterpieces, Eco, who views *Ulysses* and *Finnegans Wake* as exemplifying the notion of open work par excellence, formulates a poetics of openness and considers openness as a hallmark of modern fiction.[35] Openness in theory means that a literary text is not an enclosure of words with finite and limited messages, but a hermeneutic space constructed with verbal signs capable of generating unlimited interpretations. In common usage, it means that a literary text has no "correct" interpretation, or has multiple interpretations.

Fiction is an open literary form for a number of reasons. A fictional work is theoretically open because events in it have no prior temporal existence, and there is no extratextual correlation to limit its interpretation. Barbara H. Smith perceives this open tendency of fiction as emanating from its unlimited relations: "Among any array of narratives—tales or tellings—in the universe, there is an unlimited number of potentially perceptible *relations*. These relations may be of many different kinds and orders, including formal and thematic, synchronic and diachronic, and causal and non-causal."[36] In the Chinese tradition, the openness of *xiaoshuo* has three aspects of meaning: (1) it is a totalizing genre; (2) it is an open form; and (3) it is open to diverse interpretations.

First, *xiaoshuo* is an amorphous literary genre that is difficult to classify in Chinese history. There have been many attempts in Chinese history to categorize *xiaoshuo*, but none is satisfactory, because it simply resists any attempts to be pigeonholed. Hu Yinglin (1551–1602) was one of the scholars to attempt a viable classification of *xiaoshuo*, but he had to admit to the fluidity of the genre and the difficulty involved in classification:

> *Hsiao-shuo* belongs to the branch of philosophical writings. But in discoursing
> on principles and truth, some come close to the Classics and others resemble
> commentary. In recording and narrating events, some interpenetrate with
> historiography, and others resemble the record and the biography. Anecdotal
> poems by Meng Ch'i and the lyrics by Lu Huan are sampled in poetic criti-
> cism [*shih-hua*] and literary discussions and appended to the division of *belles
> lettres*. But an investigation of their style and format would show that they
> really belong to the branch of *hsiao-shuo*. As for the miscellaneous writings
> in the division of philosophy, they are much entangled with the *hsiao-shuo*.
> [Cheng Ch'iao, 1103–62, a Southern Sung historian] said that there were
> nine kinds of ancient and modern writings that could not be distinguished
> from each other, but he did not know that the easiest one to get mixed up
> was the *hsiao-shuo*.[37]

Xiaoshuo as a literary genre is really a pivot point upon which different forms
of writing converge. In the West, the modern novel is a synthesized form of all
conventional literary genres: epic, tragedy, comedy, lyric poetry, prose, epistolary
writing, and other literary genres. In the Chinese tradition, *xiaoshuo*, in addition to the conventional genres listed in the Western tradition, incorporates
history, biography, philosophy, and belletristic prose. What makes fiction in
the modern sense distinguishable from other literary genres is that while other
literary forms are limited to one or more established modes of writing, fiction
incorporates all modes and transcends the limitations of all literary modes. As
a result, its impact upon the reader in the process of reading is all-pervasive,
multidimensional, and all-penetrating. As D. H. Lawrence argues, "The novel
is the one bright book of life. Books are not life. They are only tremulations
on the ether. But the novel as a tremulation can make the whole man alive
tremble. Which is more than poetry, philosophy, science, or any other book-
tremulations can do."[38] Fiction as a late literary form in all literary traditions is
largely due not only to the complexity of the mastery of all literary forms, but
also to its rebellious nature that always transcends the human effort to define
and confine it. In this sense, fiction is an open literary genre.

Second, *xiaoshuo* as an extended narrative is a totalizing form of representation that can deal with any subject matter and often weaves a heterogeneous
group of themes into a single volume. D. H. Lawrence once says: "The novel is
a great discovery: far greater than Galileo's telescope or somebody else's wire-
less. The novel is the highest form of human expression so far."[39] The main
reason why he has such a high regard for the novel is that he views it as a
bright book of life. Whatever life has, fiction can represent. What life does
not have, fiction can create also. Chinese *xiaoshuo* manifested this characteristic trait very early. In traditional *xiaoshuo*, there were no limitations by time
and space, and the boundaries between animate and inanimate things, life and
death, humans and animals, and cold and heat were often transcended or simply collapse. Not only that, but in those stories it is always the case that the

strange and extraordinary things or events have been witnessed or experienced by persons in real life. This blurring of the real and unreal not only influenced great novels like the *Hongloumeng* but also anticipated the modern technique of magic realism.

Third, fiction is a text open to interpretations. In Peirce's semiotic theory, interpretation involves semiosis, a process of producing incessant interpretants. By "semiosis," he means "an action, or influence, which is, or involves, a cooperation of three subjects, such as a sign, its object, and its interpretant."[40] The triadic relationship is likely to make interpretation open. In reading fiction, interpretation is even more open because of the fictitious nature of fiction. We can recall Scholes's reconceptualization of Aristotle's distinction between history and poetry in terms of Peirce's triadic model of the sign in an attempt to define fictionality. Fiction tells a story that may be long and short. In the process of reading a story, the Peircean triad of semiosis—sign, object, and intepretant—can be correlated with the essential elements in a story's creation and interpretation: "The object of a story is the sequence of events to which it refers; the sign of a story is the text in which it is told (print, film, etc.); and the interpretant is the diegesis or constructed sequence of events generated by a reading of the text."[41] The object is "events" in a story, the sign is the material "text," and the interpretant is what is produced out of the diegetic process of correlation, called "interpretation." The three elements are all open in a story. The object of a story is a fictional account that has no correlation with real facts in reality. The text is woven out of the materiality of signs, which are slippery because of the loose correlation between signifier and signified. The interpretant is invariably different for every interpreter. In reading history or other factual accounts we can still have something to lay hands on, but in reading fiction, there is nothing to grasp. It is in this sense that we may call fiction an open form of literature.

THE DRIVE TOWARD PURE FICTION

In spite of the fact that historical fiction occupies a center place in the development of Chinese fiction, there is a visible movement of Chinese *xiaoshuo* from historical narrative to pure fiction. This drive toward pure fiction is the most crucial turn in Chinese fiction. In this movement, there have been many recognizable milestones. In this section, I will briefly examine some of the milestones and assess their contributions to Chinese fiction in terms of pure fiction. Tang *xiaoshuo* as a whole constitutes the first milestone in the development of Chinese *xiaoshuo* toward the modern notion of fiction. All the ingredients of modern fiction, such as realistic representation of life, characterization, psychological exploration of characters, plot arrangement, and so on, are present in Tang fiction. It even features unrealistic ways of representation, which anticipate modern modes of representation such as surrealism, magic realism, and the fantastic. All that later *xiaoshuo* writers had to do was combine those fictional elements and weave them into extended narrative discourses. Later fictional works, whether they were the *huaben* of the Song and Yuan or the *nihuaben* of the Ming and Qing or *zhanghui xiaoshuo*, are improvements on Tang *xiaoshuo* in methods of writing; but they were not entirely innovations. The greatest innovation of later fiction lies in the complex structural organization of extended narration and multiplicity of narrative perspectives. In this respect, the *Sanguo yanyi*, the *Xiyou ji*, and the *Shuihu zhuan* made great contributions to the culmination of Chinese *xiaoshuo* in the *Jin Ping Mei*, the *Rulin waishi*, and the *Hongloumeng*. Mao Zonggang correctly identified the contributions made by historical novels, especially the *Sanguo yanyi*, to the organization and artistic control of long and extended narrative as compared with those in histories:

> [I]n the case of *The Romance of the Three Kingdoms* . . . the basic annals, hereditary houses, and biographies are combined to form a single composite work. When things are treated separately, the text of each section is short and it is easy to exercise artistic control, whereas when things are combined, the text becomes long and artistic success is more difficult to achieve.[42]

Although the *Sanguo yanyi*, *Xiyou ji*, and *Shuihu zhuan* each contributed to the artistic development of Chinese *xiaoshuo* in their own ways, they are all short of pure fiction in one way or another. And their distance from pure fiction has much to do with their dependence on history or historical inertia. All of them were aided by historiography or official biography, but each was restricted by their source materials. In varying degrees, each of them was created as a writing in the form of *yanyi* (historical extension); some are still a bit distant from romance, one of the precursors of modern fiction. In his critique of the translation of *yanyi* as "romance," Anthony C. Yu provides a comparison between the two that helps explain why historical fiction is not pure fiction: "Because the word *yan* can mean both to popularize and to expound in a detailed and exhaustive manner, *yanyi* is hardly a 'baseless story with exaggerated and fanciful details' or 'an account of heroic exploits in an imaginary setting,' which constitutes a part of our contemporary dictionary definition of romance. The Chinese term is better thought of as a story that purports to provide an alternative perspective or propound a systematic development of hidden meanings, and that takes on the semblance of an extended allegory."[43]

What he has said is certainly true of the *Sanguo yanyi*. There is no doubt about its dependence on official history. Mao Zonggang in his comment on this novel, praised its achievement as a narrative based on historical facts and not on fiction, and said it can be compared with classics and history. Of course, it is not entirely based on history. As Zhang Xuecheng said, "[I]t is a narrative account of which 70 percent is fact and 30 percent fiction. Because of this, readers have often been confused with it."[44] For generations, numerous Chinese readers have read it as history. Many more have acquired their knowledge of the Three Kingdoms period from reading this novel. For this simple reason, it cannot be considered "pure fiction." Hu Shi expresses an idea that goes much further than mine. He considers the novel as short of being a literary work and as having little literary value because the author adheres too doggedly to historical facts and displays little imaginative creation: "The author of the *Sanguo* is most poor in selecting his materials. His skill lies in collecting bamboo ends and sawdust, scraps of iron and brass, without omitting anything. Because of his poor ability at tailoring his materials, the novel cannot be regarded as a literary work."[45] His judgment seems too harsh, for it neglects the novel's achievement in other aspects.

In contrast with his low of opinion of the *Sanguo yanyi*, Hu Shi highly praises the *Shuihu zhuan* as a fictional work with superb imaginative creativity: "The *Shuihu zhuan* is pure imagination, and it therefore can achieve extraordinary brilliance."[46] This comment is not entirely accurate. The *Shuihu zhuan*'s dependence on history and biography and early legends differs from that of the *Sanguo* only in degree, not in kind. The *Shuihu* was based on several related sources. First, it drew its source materials from official history. The historical record of Song Jiang's rebellion is found in a number of individual biographies of the Song History. A comparison between the novel and historical records shows that the basic story line of the novel deviates little from official history. Second, the artistic rendering of the historical figures had already existed in previous scholars' writings. According to recent research, even the nicknames of the main characters in the novel had already appeared in previous writings.[47] In *Da Song Xuanhe yishi* 大宋宣和遺事, many of the heroic episodes of the novel were artistically portrayed and the basic plot of the novel was already outlined, sometimes briefly and sometimes in detail.[48] By the time of Yuan, dramatic productions further enriched the stories of the *Shuihu zhuan*. Although the novel evidenced more imaginative fabrication than the *Sanguo yanyi*, by the time the authors (Luo Guanzhong and Shi Nai'an) wrote the final version of the novel, most ingredients as well as plot arrangements were already there. That is why some scholars view the novel as the product of collective creation. For these reasons, the *Shuihu zhuan*, like the *Sanguo yanyi*, cannot be viewed as pure fiction. Its episodic structure is also a factor that distances it from the carefully woven modern novel.

If both the *Sangguo* and *Shuihu* are more or less artistic extensions of history or extant stories and therefore cannot be regarded as pure fiction, the *Xiyou ji* seems to be largely a fictional account. Zhang Xuecheng, for example, remarked, "Novels like the *Journey to the West* and the *Jin Ping Mei* are solely based on fiction."[49] However, if we examine the evolutionary history of it, we have to say that it still depends on an unofficial history. The original source of the *Xiyou ji* was the pilgrimage undertaken by Xuanzhuang, a Buddhist monk in the Tang, to India. His disciple Bianji 辨機 wrote a famous record based on his pilgrimage, *Ta Tang xiyue ji* 大唐西域記. His two other disciples, Huili 慧立 and Yanzong 彥宗, wrote another record of his pilgrimage, *Da Tang Ci'ensi Sanzang fashi zhuan* 大唐慈恩寺三藏法師傳. Both books are records of basically real persons and real events. These two books provided the basic narrative structure for another book, *Da Tang Sanzang qujing shihua* 大唐三藏取經詩話. This book is no longer a factual account of the pilgrimage but a fictionalized account. It already has a fairly well portrayed Monkey King and narrates a series of episodes with extraordinary encounters and visits to strange and hazardous places. The characterization and plot episodes laid the structural foundation for the later novel. The *Journey to the West* is permeated with flights of fancy and shows a fascinating imagination. It is largely a fictional account, but in two aspects it is short of being a modern novel. First, structurally it is dependent on biographical records. Second, its subject matter is far removed from those of modern fiction, which has its focus on human life in this world. Jin Shengtan was aware of this limitation: "The *Xiyou ji* is too fantastic. The author just made it up paragraph by paragraph. It is like setting off fireworks on New Year's Eve—they explode one group after another with no connecting link [*kuan-ch'uan* 貫串] between. When we read it, we can stop at any place."[50] The *Xiyou ji, Sanguo yanyi*, and *Shuihu zhuan* are certainly important milestones in the evolution of Chinese *xiaoshuo* into the modern novel, but they have been found to fall short of modern fictional works in one way or another.

By the standards of pure fiction and modern fiction, there are three great achievements that are indispensable for the full and complete transition from traditional *xiaoshuo* to modern fiction. They are the *Jin Ping Mei, Hongloumeng*, and Lu Xun's fictional works. The *Jin Ping Mei* is the first extended prose narrative whose structural framework, subject matter, and narrative techniques are totally invented by a single author. It therefore should be regarded as the first novel of pure fiction in Chinese history. It pioneered the fictional mode of weaving a diverse cast of characters and a heterogeneous series of events into a well-conceived and carefully written novel. Before the appearance of this masterpiece, all novels were fictional works with an external focus. If the *Shuihu zhuan* marked the beginning of an inward concern with family life and individual's inner world in the development of full-length Chinese novel, the *Jin Ping Mei* continues that beginning, radicalizes it, and brings it to an unprecedented height. While the *Jin Ping Mei* marked the beginning of conscious aesthetic consideration of the total conceptualization of fiction, fictional form, fictional techniques, and psychological exploration of characters' inner world, the *Hongloumeng* brings all those aesthetic concerns to an apotheosis. Its self-conscious preoccupation with form, discourse, and language departs radically from the traditional construction of a diegesis in terms of representation and interpretation. It anticipated postmodern concern with metafiction, and by problematizing the entire process of narration, it forces the reader to get out of the closed habit of reading and anticipates open fiction. Lu Xun's fictional writings appeared at the historical juncture when traditional Chinese *xiaoshuo* and Western modern fiction confronted each other. By assimilating narrative techniques from both traditions, his fictional works not only bridged the gap between traditional and modern aesthetics but also played a decisive role in the complete transition of Chinese fiction from *xiaoshuo* to the modern concept "fiction."

A CHANGE IN MODEL FOR FICTION WRITING

Due to the overlapping of early and later forms of fictional writings, it is rather difficult to identify a time when the transition from storytelling to fictional art was completed. Conceptually, however, we may locate a certain signpost that signifies the completion of the aesthetic turn. This signpost is the appearance of pure fiction, not in the form of short stories but in the form of extended narrative, which is the novel. I have identified the *Jin Ping Mei* as the first novel of pure fiction in Chinese history. It is therefore the signpost that signals the completion of the aesthetic turn. The reader may wonder why I attach so much importance to the concept of pure fiction, so let us examine this issue from a conceptual perspective.

The reason pure fiction, especially in the form of the novel, is significant for the completion of the aesthetic turn is that it is indicative of a fundamental change in conceptual models of fiction writing. This change in conceptual models is a complex issue, but to describe it in as simple a way as possible, it marks a shift from a model of fiction writing based on the concept of symbol to a new model based on the concept of sign. In her study of the novel, Julia Kristeva argues that the emergence of the novel as a linguistic form in Europe was due not so much to the disintegration of the epic system, which started toward the end of the Greek antiquity, but to a fundamental change in people's way of thinking, a change in the perception of the sign itself, which started at the beginning of Renaissance. She calls this change "a passage from the symbol to the sign" and argues that "the novel is a narrative structure revealing the ideologeme of the sign."[51]

By coincidence, the change from historical novel to the novel of pure fiction in the Chinese tradition may be explained conceptually by the shift from the perception of the symbol to that of the sign. Let us first look at the difference between symbol and sign in semiotics. In semiotic theory, the word "symbol" is sometimes used interchangeably with "sign." For example, in Peirce's system of signs, the three terms are respectively icon, index, and symbol. Among them, the symbol really means "sign" in Saussure's system, for it "refers to the object that it denotes by virtue of a law, usually an association of general ideas."[52] In other words, the relationship between a Peircean "symbol" and its referent is arbitrary. In Saussure's system, "One characteristic of the symbol is that it is never arbitrary; it is not empty, for there is the rudiment of a natural bond between signifier and signified."[53] Thus, the fundamental difference between "symbol" and "sign" is that while the relationship between symbol and its referent is one of natural correspondence, however slight it may be, the relationship between the sign and its referent is arbitrarily willed.

This distinction will be of great importance for distinguishing historical fiction and pure fiction.

Historical fiction and pure fiction are composed on different models. Simply stated, the difference is that while the former is composed on the model of the symbol, the latter on the model of the sign. The *Sanguo yanyi* and the *Jin Ping Mei* are two good examples to illustrate the difference. The former is composed on the model of the symbol because, despite its literary nature, the novel is a text that refers back to a series of events that actually existed in history. The writer may use his imagination to supply colorful episodes sanctioned by the historical events, but he can only move within the narrative space marked by the historical events. In terms of the linguistic model constructed by Saussure, which is an opposition between the signifier and signified, the hermeneutic space of historical fiction is limited, because the signifier may be colorful and diverse, but the signified is fixed and unchangeable. In nonconceptual language, the text of the *Sanguo yanyi* is the signifier while the historical period is the signified. There is a natural correspondence between the text and the history in the same way the signifier and the signified in a symbol are naturally related.

Of course, the relationship between the signifier and the signified in a symbol is not entirely one of natural correspondence. A symbol is a symbol by virtue of the absence of a posited counterpart, which may often be transcendental universals. There is a transcendental aspect of the symbol in historical fiction, because "the symbol does not 'resemble' the objects it symbolizes. . . . The symbol assumes that the symbolized (the universals) is irreducible to the symbolizer (markings)."[54] In the *Sanguo yanyi*, the narrative is not intended simply as a record of the historical events. Apart from narrating the events during that historical period, the author was aiming at representing some transcendental universal ideas, such as "kingly way," "legitimacy," "benevolence," "loyalty," "heroism," "courage," "wisdom," "virtue," and so on, and their opposites like "hegemony," "illegitimacy," "despotism," "treason," "cowardice," "fear," "folly," "wickedness," and so on. In his commentary on the novel, Mao Zonggang systematically discussed these universal ideas.[55] These transcendentals may be presented in dazzling ways, but they are restricted in connotation by the function of the symbol. From a comparative perspective, we may observe a similar phenomenon in European literature. In her study of European literature and art that developed till around the thirteenth century, Kristeva observes that: the model of the symbol "is a cosmogonic semiotic practice where the elements (symbols) refer back to one or more unknowable and unrepresentable universal transcendence(s). . . . Mythical thought operates within the sphere of the symbol (as in the epic, folk tales, *chansons de geste*, etc.), through symbolic units that are *units of restriction* in relation to the symbolized universals ("heroism,' 'courage,' 'nobility,' 'virtue,' 'fear,' 'treason,' etc.). The symbol's function, in its vertical dimension (universals-markings), is thus one of restriction."[56]

The restricted hermeneutic scope of the symbol may be seen in studies of other historical writings. In her study of the *Mu Tianzi zhuan*, Deborah Porter employs a symbolic approach to the text and comes to the conclusion that the text is not a historical representation but a symbolic representation, and is therefore a literary text. Nevertheless, she also points out that the literary text is built on a symbolic text encrypted within the surface text, which, though absent to the casual reader, can be reconstructed through a symbolic reading.[57] Her symbolic approach builds on two premises: "(1) the *Mu T'ien-tzu chuan* is a symbol for the obstacle to being that led to its own generation, namely, a crisis of legitimacy experienced by the Chou court after King Chao's startling death; and that (2) this symbolic level of reference is communicated through allusions to cosmogonic myths which themselves tacitly transmit information pertaining to their own generation."[58]

I commend Porter's "(Re-)reading Chinese fiction from the perspective of symbol formation that does not assume the conscious intent of the author as its hermeneutic maxim or heuristic baseline," but her effort to extend the symbolic approach to Chinese fiction as a whole reveals a deep-seated longing for historical referents or her unawareness of the inherent limitations of the symbolic approach. The symbolic model is an effective tool for the study of historical writings, but as it is predicated on the decoding of "encrypted narrative," locating of "collective trauma," and construction of "the absent symbolic text,"[59] it displays obvious limitations for the study of fiction, especially pure fiction. The symbolic model is not appropriate for pure fiction precisely because the relationship between the signifier and signified is not entirely empty; it still betrays the rudiments of a natural link. In the historical development of Chinese fiction, the symbolic model of historical fiction was gradually called into question, challenged, and eventually replaced by the model of the semiotic sign. There arose the idea of pure fiction, which is composed with words as pure signs, referring not to an existent reality, but to a reality that exists by the law of probability.

Thus, at the conceptual roots, the difference between historical fiction and pure fiction is one between the symbol and the sign. To fully understand this difference, I will take some space to elaborate the conceptual difference between the traditional conception of the symbol and the semiotic conception of the sign. The semiotic sign stands in contrast to the symbol, though it assumes some characteristic features of the latter. The sign retains the fundamental characteristic of the symbol, such as "irreducibility of terms, that is, in the case of the sign, of the referent to the signifier, of the signified to the signifier, and based on this, irreducibility of all the 'units' of the signifying structure itself."[60] Nevertheless, as Kristeva suggests, while the symbol primarily signifies vertically, the sign has both vertical and horizontal functions. In its vertical function, the sign "refers back to entities of lesser dimensions that are more concretized than the symbol. These are reified universals, which have become objects in the strongest sense of the word. . . .

The semiotic practice of the sign thus assimilates the metaphysical strategy of the symbol and projects it on to the 'immediate perceptible.'" In the sign's horizontal function, "the units of the sign's semiotic practice are articulated as a *metonymic chain of deflections* [*écarts*] that signifies a *progressive creation of metaphors*. Opposing terms, which are always exclusive, are caught up in a system of multiple and always possible deflections . . . giving the illusion of an *open* structure that is impossible to terminate, and which has an *arbitrary* ending."[61] Ultimately, the difference between the symbol and the sign is a semiotic distinction: "[I]n the case of the symbol the signified object is represented by the signifying unit through a restrictive function-relation; while the sign, . . . pretends not to assume this relation which in its case is weaker and therefore might be regarded as arbitrary."[62]

The basic reason pure fiction is a better form of art than historical fiction is that pure fiction is based on the model of the semiotic sign, which has these basic characteristics: (1) "It does not refer to a single unique reality, but evokes a collection of associated images and ideas"; (2) "It is part of a specific structure of meaning [*combinatoir*] and in that sense it is *correlative*: its meaning is the result of an interaction with other signs"; and (3) "It harbours a principle of *transformation*: within its field, new structures are forever generated and transformed."[63]

Kristeva argues that in the West, starting from the late Middle Ages, there began a fundamental change in the perception of the sign that shifts from the conception of the sign as a symbol of transcendental closure to a linguistic practice that is an open-ended structure.[64] I have observed a similar change around the same historical period in the Chinese tradition. The earliest indication of change can be found in Tang *chuanqi* tales, but the dominant model of fiction then was still that of the symbol. The symbolic model was not challenged until the rise of the novel. The first large-scale challenge came from the composition of the *Shuihu zhuan*. The novel is based on historical personages and events, but does not follow the creative principle of historiography. The appearance of this novel marked the weakening of the symbolic model and ushered in a gradual transition. Once the relationship between the signifying unit (the fictional text) and the referent (historical personages and events) had been weakened, the fictional text became more and more independent until it finally forgot its "origins." The *Jin Ping Mei* marks this forgetting of "origins." The novel opens with an episode taken from the *Shuihu zhuan*. That episode itself had no historical origin. In the linguistic model of the sign, the signifier and signified have no natural relationship. On the chain of signification, the signifier incessantly slides from one thing to another. Its meaning is in relation to another signifier, which in turn entails still another signifier ad infinitum. The fictional model based on the model of the sign gives rise to fictional works that have no origins and are only an open system of transformation and generation. This kind of discourse sanctions limitless reading and interpretation. The replacement of the symbolic model by the sign model ushered in the coming of pure fiction and signified the completion of the aesthetic turn from historicity to fictional art in the Chinese tradition.

THE LINGUISTIC TURN TO FICTION AS VERBAL ART

The change in the conceptual model entails a linguistic turn to fiction as a verbal art. In Western fiction, the linguistic turn to fictional art may be said to have started with Laurence Sterne's *Tristram Shandy* (1759–69). It was then followed by a period of inactivity due to the dominance of realistic art, and completed with the appearance of modernist fictional works by James Joyce, D. H. Lawrence, Virginia Woolf, Ernest Hemingway, William Faulkner, and others. In the Chinese tradition, the linguistic turn started much earlier, albeit sporadically at first. The signpost for the completion is the appearance of the *Jin Ping Mei*. Before it, there were a number of fictional works showing signs of the linguistic turn. Its apotheosis is the appearance of the *Hongloumen*. In the following chapters, I will explore the linguistic art of these two novels in detail, but in this section, I would like to discuss the nature and rationale of the linguistic turn.

The linguistic turn, as its name indicates, is concerned with the role of language in the composition of fiction. Before the turn, language was generally viewed as a vehicle for representing settings, events, and characters, constructing plots, and characterization. With the linguistic turn, the view of fiction's language as a mimetic vehicle only was changed. Metaphysically, fiction was no longer viewed as a vehicle for transmitting the Dao, or expressing one's pent-up emotions, or representing social realities. In addition to all its conventional roles, the language of fiction became the means for fiction to become an art form in its own right. Thanks to the changed perception of language, fiction came into its own ontological and epistemological being, independent of all other existential purposes, and become totally separated from writing forms like history and philosophy. In a word, with the linguistic turn fiction no longer needed to model itself on historical or philosophical writings. Of course, the linguistic turn did not mean the abandonment of the early functions of language. It only enriched and expanded the early functions. As a result, it opened up new representational and hermeneutic space for the fictional form.

To facilitate a discussion of the linguistic turn, the art of Chinese calligraphy offers an apt analogy. Although Chinese calligraphy uses language as the material basis, it does not primarily rely on language's signifying and representational capacities. Its artistic being and appeal do not reside in the representational or hermeneutic field, but in the field of visual perception and aesthetic appreciation. In a similar way, fiction as a verbal art relies on language as its medium for representation, but does not solely rely on language's representational function for conveying ideological, metaphysical, and moral meanings. To put it another way, it does not view representation of reality as its exclusive objective. Of course, fictional art is still concerned with representing reality (real or imagined), expressing emotions (pent-up or untrammeled), and depicting human conditions in straightforward or symbolic ways. But in addition to all these concerns, fictional art is self-consciously concerned with its ontological and epistemological being beyond all those conventional concerns. It aims at using the fictional form to convey subtle meanings and inspires disinterested appreciation of its raison d'être. The linguistic turn to verbal art is based on a similar rationale to that of the calligraphic art. When a calligrapher creates a piece of calligraphy, he or she may write a poem or some poetic lines or some meaningful words on the page. The content of the writing definitely conveys meanings. But the calligrapher is not primarily concerned with the meaning of the words on the page but with the shape, contour, texture, and structural arrangement of the brushstroke. The ordering of the material aspect of the words is meant not to underscore the meaning of words on the page but to transmit a subtle aura, an ethereal pneuma, and a subjective feeling. Such things constitute the essence of the calligraphic art.

In linguistic theory, the linguistic turn to verbal art is predicated on language as a second-order semiotic system. It draws strength from the sign structure of connotation, metalanguage, or what Barthes calls "myth." In connotative semiotics, there are two systems: the first system is the plane of denotation and the second system is the plane of connotation. A connotative system is "a system whose plane of expression is itself constituted by a signifying system."[65] And "a metalanguage is a system whose plane of content is itself constituted by a signifying system; or else, it is a semiotics which treats of a semiotics."[66] In *Mythologies*, Barthes calls metalanguage "myth" in the sense that the signification hides a second-order system and implies concealed meanings related to culture, history and ideology: "[M]yth is a peculiar system, in that it is constructed from a semiological chain which existed before it: it is a second-order semiological system. That which is a sign (namely the associative total of a concept and an image) in the first system, becomes a mere signifier in the second."[67] In fictional works with a self-conscious linguistic turn, there are two, three, or even more levels of signification and representation. The surface level of the fictional text may represent an interesting story, but its second-order signifying system may conceal or convey several levels of meaning.

In the reminder of this section, I will analyze Pu Songling's 蒲松齡 (1640–1715) tale, "Shuchi" 書癡 (Bookworm) to explain second-order signification and the linguistic turn. The tale is a fictional extension of a popular poem that urges young men to study hard in order to gain sucess in life. Attributed to Emperor Zhenzong of the Song (r. 998–1022), it reads:

Books naturally contain houses of gold.	書中自有黃金屋，
There, a thousand bushels of grain are found.	書中自有千鍾粟，
There, horses and carriages are plenty.	書中車馬多如簇，
There, girls as beautiful as jade abound.	書中有女顏如玉。[68]

Superficially, the tale seems to be a fictional rendering of Emperor Zhenzong's poem. In the tale, the desirable outcomes expected from reading books are all achieved literally by the protagonist in the same way as they are enumerated. One day, while chasing a page of a book blown by a wind, he stumbles into a hole in which a jar of grain is hidden. Although the grain is already rotten, the incident makes him believe that "There, a thousand bushels of grain are found." Another day, he discovers a gold model carriage hidden in the stack of books at home. He becomes skeptical about the saying "Books naturally contain houses of gold" after he finds out that it is only a gilded carriage, but someone persuades him to donate it to a Buddhist temple where it may be used as a shrine. Pleased with his devout act, a high-ranking official rewards him with gold and horses. This makes him believe the poetic line: "There, horses and carriages are plenty." The literal way the poetic lines are fulfilled alerts the reader that the tale is not just an extension of the poem but perhaps also a kind of parody. The major plot of the tale centers round the idea expressed in the third poetic line: "There, girls as beautiful as jade abound."

If Pu Songling stopped at simply writing a story based on the theme of that poem, his tale would be a conventional story. It is interesting, and may even be read as a parody. But it certainly could not be counted as a specimen of verbal art. What turns a potentially conventional story and comic parody into a verbal art form is his awareness of the various possibilities of language and his self-conscious utilization of some of them. In other words, the art of the tale does not lie in the literal fulfillment of social successes, but in a literalization of language for creating multiple levels of meaning. The naming of the protagonists, for example, shows that the tale could not be an imitation of social reality in life. The male protagonist has the surname "Lang," which is the Chinese word for a male, a lover, or a bridegroom. The female protagonist has the surname "Yan" and the given name "Ruyu." The full name means exactly "a girl beautiful as jade." The naming of the characters is only a clever use of language; what constitutes an artful use of language is the literalization of the poetic line. As a whole, the plot of the tale grows out of this literalization. A literal reading of the poetic line enables Pu Songling to create a romantic tale of love, devotion, separation, and retribution, written in the style of magic realism.

Pu Songling's use of language typifies an artistic feature in Chinese fictional art, which, while sharing some affinity with the contemporary Western conception of literary language, differs from its counterpart in a significant way. Jacques Lacan, Roland Barthes, Jacques Derrida, Paul de Man, and others hold that all writing is concerned with its own activity as language, and because language is slippery, unreliable, and contains within itself the potential of signifying the opposite of what it is supposed to mean, literary narrative often tells the story of its own inability to tell a story.[69] The Chinese literary narrative shares some of this view, but it accentuates language's ability to generate stories. The creative desire to maximize language's ability to tell stories emanates from a different model of composition.

The compositional model that Pu Songling employed is that of calligraphy. Like a calligrapher who creates a piece of calligraphic art out of an existent poem, Pu was not interested in turning the content of that poem into a fictional tale, but he is concerned with transforming it into a piece of narrative art. Its artistry is manifold. He treated words as materials like a piece of clay in the hands of a sculptor. He manipulated the language medium to fashion a plot for expressing ideas beyond the conventional level of signification and representation. Through linguistic manipulation, he created several dimensions of representation. The first is a realistic dimension in which a conventional tale is narrated to cater to the popular taste. The plot in this social dimension is realistic and credible. The second is a magical dimension in which the female protagonist appears and disappears like magic. The third is an ironic dimension. The tale is both a credible story and a parody. The authorial intention is ironic and hard to determine. A reader of conventional taste may read the tale as encouraging people to study hard. But this is not what was meant. The satirical characterization of the book-crazy male protagonist shows the conventional re-presentation of the poem's theme to be ironic. What is most ironic in the tale is the detail: the beautiful girl whom the male protagonist wins through his assiduous reading turns out to admonish him against avid reading and goes so far as to stop him from reading by disappearing a couple of times.

The fourth is an intellectual dimension. The story is a tale of enlightenment. It tells how the male protagonist grows from innocence to experience. This dimension is made ironic by the fact that it is the beautiful girl in the book who guides him through the process of learning basic life skills. The last is a metaphysical dimension. By narrating a tale of edification, the author gives the tale a philosophical twist and turns a fantastic story into food for thought. He seems to imply that book learning has its positive and negative aspects, and that too much diligence without a proper direction is not only useless but may bring harm to the hardworking person, literally turning him or her into a "bookworm." The girl's admonition—"The reason you cannot make rapid advances in your life is precisely because you are consumed with nothing but reading"—may be taken as a coolheaded assessment of the negative aspects of book-learning.

In his own preface to the *Liaozhai zhiyi* 聊齋志異, Pu Songling professed that his fictional works were a continuation of the classical tale tradition pioneered by the *zhiguai* tales of the Six Dynasties.[70] Judith Zeitlin's in-depth study has confirmed this view from both the cultural and literary perspectives. Her excellent study reveals that Pu Songling made many advances in fictional techniques in comparison with his predecessors.[71] It is unnecessary to restate her insights here. I will only add that in the "Bookworm" alone, Pu Songling employed some techniques of writing that may be considered modernist and postmodern: irony, parody, intertexuality, fantastic details, second-order signification, magic realism, and so on. It is not for nothing that Franz Kafka showed admiration for some of Pu's stories that he read in translation. He considered those tales to be "exquisite."[72] The high artistic achievement of Pu Songling's tales comes to us as no surprise, for before his coming to the scene of writing, the aesthetic turn to fiction as a verbal art was already completed. Fictional writers had long ago started to compose fictional works with as much attention to the use of language as poets who compose lyric poetry.

CHAPTER FOUR

The Poetic Nature of Chinese Fiction

In traditional Chinese literature, there is no doubt that lyrical poetry occupies an exalted position and that fiction is only its handmaiden. In the study of Chinese literature, scholars have generally separated the study of fiction from that of poetry. While this separation is justified in view of the traditional separation of poetry and prose from fiction and drama and the necessary specialization in literary scholarship in classical and modern times, it neglects the inherent relationship between poetry and fiction in *xiaoshuo*'s evolution toward a form of verbal art. Certainly, it has blinded us to the internal driving force that moved Chinese *xiaoshuo* from its earliest form of snippets of street talk to the modern form of fiction. In existent scholarship on Chinese *xiaoshuo*, scholars have explored in detail the history-to-fiction pattern of development of *xiaoshuo*. While fully recognizing the significance of this process, I venture to argue that the most significant and far-reaching process in *xiaoshuo*'s development is what I wish to call a process of "aestheticization."

The process of aestheticization involves many branches of Chinese art: poetry, poetics, drama, classical prose, calligraphy, painting, and so on. Andrew Plaks provides a fascinating account of how classical prose, especially *bagu wen* (the eight-legged essay), drama criticism, and painting theories exerted a formative impact on the rise of the Chinese novel.[1] I would like to emphasize the impact of lyric poetry on the aesthetic turn of *xiaoshuo* into a verbal art. Scholarly studies of *xiaoshuo* have generally concurred that historical writings exerted a salutary influence on the development of Chinese fiction, whereas the dominance of lyric poetry stunted its growth. While duly recognizing the correctness of this consensus, I believe this commonly accepted view should not be pushed too far for two reasons. First, as I have argued, the initial dependence on history was not entirely a positive factor in *xiaoshuo*'s development, because it gradually evolved into a historical inertia that impeded the full development of Chinese fictional art. Second, although the dominance of the lyric has generally been blamed for the belated rise and underdevelopment of Chinese *xiaoshuo*, it has exerted an unexpected positive impact that has been completely overlooked. It forced *xiaoshuo* to compete with its oppressor, sharpened its aesthetic sensibility, and eventually helped it develop into a verbal art. Thus, while *xiaoshuo*'s friendly and cooperative relation to history is not entirely positive, its uneasy and often tense relation to lyrical poetry is not all negative.

I argue that a significant part of *xiaoshuo*'s aestheticization is a movement driven by (un)conscious impulses to emulate and rival lyric poetry. In the development from storytelling to fictional art, the poetic impulse in *xiaoshuo* played a decisive role in effecting the fundamental shift. Without the lyrical impulse to imitate or emulate lyrical poetry, which is the predominant form of literature in Chinese history, Chinese *xiaoshuo* would not have been able to develop into a verbal art. In a way, that which made the shift possible is what I wish to call a process of poeticization, a movement to aestheticize Chinese *xiaoshuo* in terms of lyric poetry. It not only changed the course of development for Chinese *xiaoshuo* but also altered its essence. The poeticization is the key development that allowed *xiaoshuo* to extricate itself from its dependence on history and the conventions of storytelling and to evolve into a mature form of verbal art. Poeticization gave rise to poetic fiction, which is the core of pure fiction. The apex of poeticization is the appearance of the poetic novel, a representative of which is the *Hongloumeng*.

Investigation of the impact of lyricism upon the historical development and aesthetic form of Chinese fiction is a fertile ground. It seems, however, that only a few scholars have done some research in this area. In a short study of the impact of the lyric tradition upon the creative vision of Chinese fiction, Yu-Kung Kao explores how a "lyric vision" underlies the conception of the *Hongloumeng* and the *Rulin waishi*.[2] In another study of the *Hongloumeng*, Wong Kam-ming briefly mentions that the novel's structure "has as much affinity with lyrical poetry as with conventional novels."[3] Had more scholars done work in this direction, they might have opened up an interesting field. In this chapter, I will comprehensively explore how lyricism affected the totality of Chinese fiction in its genesis, conception, structure, and representation, and how it contributed to the completion of the aesthetic turn.

THE LYRIC UNCONSCIOUS OF CHINESE FICTION

In his psychoanalytic system, Freud speaks of three interrelated terms that refer to both mental processes and topographical mapping: the conscious, preconscious, and unconscious. The conscious is easy to understand because, as Freud puts it, it is "the same as the consciousness of philosophers or of everyday opinion."[4] Everything else in the mind is unconscious. The unconscious refers to dynamically repressed mental processes. It is further split into the unconscious and the preconscious. The latter is that "which is latent" but is "capable of becoming consciousness." In the dynamics of the mind, the divisions are not absolute or unchangeable. A state of consciousness is very transitory, but everything unconscious can be made to become conscious. Consciousness is attached to the ego, a coherent organization of mental process that controls an individual's actions.[5] To borrow the Freudian mental system as an analogy, I may describe the internal development of Chinese fiction in terms of three related terms: the fictional conscious, lyric unconscious or preconscious, and historical unconscious. The aesthetic drive toward a separate, independent literary form is the fictional conscious. The desire to compete and emulate with lyric poetry and classical prose is the lyric preconscious. The shaping force that constantly exerts an influence on the aesthetic conditions of fiction is the historical unconscious. Fiction writers realize that history and fiction are two different aesthetic categories, but an unconscious sense of history always sways their creative activities willy-nilly. The desire to compete with lyric poetry is largely unconscious, but it is also a fairly clear objective. That is why it may also be called lyrical preconscious. An aesthetically viable fictional consciousness is unable to appear before the fictional preconscious is made conscious and before the repression of the historical unconscious is overcome. A Chinese aesthetics of fiction is born out of the interaction among the three creative forces.

To continue the analogy with Freud's system, both lyricism and historicism may be viewed as playing the role of the superego in the creative mind of Chinese fiction. But there is a difference. Psychoanalysis conceives of the superego as a structure in the unconscious built up by early childhood experiences. It consists of an inhibiting agency and an ego-ideal.[6] In Chinese literary history, historicism is the inhibiting agency with its dos and don'ts, while lyricism is the ego-ideal with a standard of perfection. In other words, historicism lays down some dogmatic rules for fiction to obey. By contrast, lyricism sets itself up as the ideal model with which fiction seeks to identify.

Predictably, there is a heavy presence of poetry in fictional works. The practice of mixing prose narrative with lyric poetry is so prevalent that even storytelling meant to cater to the illiterate could not forgo it. In his study of early Chinese short stories, Patrick Hanan identifies a group that he calls "virtuoso pieces." He describes this group as follows:

> In each of them the hero is a poet, in most cases an actual poet and not a fictional one. A large part of the function of many of these stories is to provide a context for the poems that the hero composes at will. The plot, such as it is, is that context and little more. The high points in the story do not really concern the plot, but rather the poet-hero's own existence, his reactions, especially his response in verse to the situation in which he is placed by the plot.[7]

In other stories in which the protagonist is neither a poet nor a man, versification is a prominent feature as well. Take the well-known stories "Li Cuilian 李翠蓮" and "Chengfo ji 成佛記," for example. Hanan points out: "The most important part of the Li Ts'ui-lien story consists of her rhymed and patterned diatribes, while one important part of the other story consists of the girl's verse riddles."[8]

This practice is not simply an attempt by fiction writers to show off their knowledge of poetry or poetic talent. It is symptomatic of the lyric unconscious at work in the deep structure. In fictional development, the attempt to fuse poetry and prose did not always work out well, especially in the hands of storytellers who did not possess poetic talent. Consequently, the practice brought about a reaction. In his study of the Chinese fiction commentaries, David Rolston provides a detailed account of the reaction. Traditional commentators became increasingly harsh in criticizing the quotation of poetry by the narrator and the inclusion of poems composed or recited by the characters. Displeasure at these practices led quite a few commentators to excise a large number of poems in the existent fictional works or to rewrite them according to their own ideas of how lyric poetry should be combined with narration.[9] Despite the harsh measures, the practice of mixing poetry with prose narrative remained an eye-catching feature of Chinese fiction up to modern times. After criticizing previous fictional practice of showing off the author's talent in composing poems in the narrative, Cao Xueqin himself composed many poems in his masterpiece. Why did the practice persist? Traditional commentators are of the opinion that it comes from the author's desire to preserve his or her own poetry. For example, the Zhiyan zhai commentary claims that one of Cao Xueqin's intentions in writing his novel was to preserve and transmit his own poetry.[10] I think there is an entirely different explanation. The persistence of lyric poetry in narrative is indicative of a special feature of the deep structure of Chinese fiction: the existence of the "lyric unconscious" in Chinese fiction.

The "lyric unconscious" is a term that I have invented to reveal the deep structure of Chinese fiction. This term helps me to formulate a model in my approach to the uneasy relationship between prose fiction (*xiaoshuo*) and lyric poetry (*shi*). It has several layers of meaning. In psychoanalytic psychology there are a number of expressions which depict the unconscious as "uncharted terrain," "unknown regions," and "processes that are of a different order from conscious processes." Similarly, the lyric in Chinese prose fiction has remained a "dark continent," a metaphor Freud employed to describe the unknown mechanism of the mind, especially the structure of female sexuality. In the topographical model of the mind, the relationship between consciousness and the unconscious is presented as an algorithm with consciousness above the bar of repression and the unconscious below it. Let us examine the two following diagrams:

consciousness		fiction	
--------------	(repression barrier)	--------------	(historical repression)
unconscious		lyricism	

The diagram on the right reflects my conception of the relationship between fiction and lyric poetry with history as the repressive force. With this diagram, I wish not only to show the separation between the two literary genres but also to suggest that while fiction constitutes the surface structure, lyric poetry forms the deep structure that constantly exerts an invisible impact on the structure of fiction. Just as the unconscious may overcome repression and finds ways of release in consciousness, so lyric poetry may surmount the barriers of historical repression and generic differences and find expression in fictional discourse.

I have constructed this model not only to map the dynamic interactions among history, poetry, and fiction but also to reveal the the intrinsically poetic qualities in Chinese fiction. Conceptually, it may be better understood in terms of Roman Jakobson's psycholinguistic theory. Lyricism and narration result from two different creative impulses. While lyricism grows out of a spontaneous overflow of powerful feelings, narration is born out of discursive desires to represent a series of events, episodes, and actions. In his study of the relationship among psychology, language, and literature, Jakobson realizes that the two Saussurean principles of linguistics—the paradigmatic (associative) and syntagmatic functions—not only govern the operations of language but also underlie the deep structure of literature. Through his studies of aphasia, he discovers two fundamental modes of thinking: metaphorical and metonymical thinking. These two modes of thinking play different roles in literature: the metaphoric mode tends to be foregrounded in poetry, while the metonymic mode tends to be foregrounded in prose. In his linguistic analysis of romantic and symbolist poetry and the realistic novel, Jakobson observes that poetry is predominantly metaphorical, since the poet has the urge for "compulsory parallelism," while realistic fiction is predominantly metonymic, since the novelist, obsessed with synecdochic details, "metonymically digresses from the plot to the atmosphere and from the character to the setting in space and time."[11]

Jakobson sees symbolist poetry and the realistic novel as separate catergories, but they are fused together in Chinese fiction, especially in the mixture of prose narrative and lyric poetry. In his conceptual exploration of Chinese narrative, Andrew Plaks points out, "If it is a truism of all literary theory that the possibility of realizing any form of 'pure' lyric or narrative within a single work remains a hypothetical one, so that it is always the mixing of the primary modes that is at issue in practical criticism, the interrelation of the two strains in the traditional Chinese genres goes perhaps farther in this direction."[12] In fictional criticism, Yu-kung Kao perceptively notices the lyrical vision of Chinese narrative and its impact upon the thematic composition of the *Hongloumeng* and *Rulin waishi*.[13] In the present book, I will try to demonstrate from the conceptual and critical perspectives that lyricism constitutes the deep structure of Chinese fiction and is the motivating force that drives *xiaoshuo* toward fictional art.

Over the course of historical development, lyric poetry became the unconscious for fiction in the way literature served as the unconscious for psychoanalysis.[14] The process of becoming was marked by a transition from manifest display of poetry in surface narration to latent use of poetic structures and qualities in structural form, emplotment, setting description, characterization, and narration. This transition is very important, because only after lyricism was repressed and entered into the deep structure of the fictional consciousness did it become the lyric unconscious of fiction and came to exert a lasting aesthetic impact. Scholars have recognized that lyric poetry and prose fiction are two very different but related literary genres. In his discourse on *xiaoshuo*, Ban Gu implicitly suggested that *xiaoshuo* writings came from the same provenance as *shi* (lyric poetry) in the *Book of Songs*. That is, both had their origins in the common people's spontaneous expressions and were collected by court officials appointed by the kings to gauge people's opinions. In chapter 2, I have identified the reason why *xiaoshuo* was declared a "foundling" immediately after its "royal birth," while lyric poetry was chosen as the "prince royal" of belles lettres: the Confucian exaltation of *shi* (lyric poetry) and disparagement of *xiaoshuo* (fiction). But this is not the whole reason. In the West, fiction had a similar fate. As late as the nineteenth century, fictional works "remained for critics the stepchild among literary forms, popular with the mass reading public but not considered serious in the way of the lyric or the long poem."[15] The similar fate suggests that *xiaoshuo* (fiction), despite the same origin as that of poetry, always had something unrespectable about it and was therefore not regarded as a serious form of writing on a par with poetry.

Throughout the dynastic ages, lyric poetry was the dominant genre in the Chinese literary tradition. In terms of power discourse, lyric poetry may be viewed as the master discourse of traditional belles lettres. By contrast, prose fiction was in a subservient position. It was therefore the servant discourse. Because of the lyrical dominance, Chinese *xiaoshuo* was underdeveloped in its early stages. To gain space for development, the servant discourse had to fight its master as well as pay homage to it. By imitating and competing with the master, the servant discourse established itself as a master in a different discourse. In literary terms, the narrative impulse in Chinese literature had to wrestle with the lyric impulse. In the struggle, the desire for narrative pleasure overcame the lyrical impulses sporadically and in some measure succeeded in neutralizing the lyric dominance and even taking the lyric captive. The captured or domesticated lyric impulse in fiction became a repressed creative consciousness pushed to the background of fiction. It fit into its new position uneasily at first, but gradually, in its repressed state of existence, it was transformed into the lyrical unconscious of Chinese fiction and turned into a pillar of the deep structure of Chinese pure fiction. Lyricism is the core of poetry, and poetry in its broad sense is the core of literature. Lyricism occupies different positions in poetry and fiction. While lyricism is the conscious or even self-conscious core of poetry, it is the unconscious or subconscious structure of fiction. In the Chinese tradition, since fiction had the same origins as lyric poetry in common people's spontaneous expressions, and it has always kept a considerable measure of lyricism in its content and form. This is the broad background against which Chinese fiction underwent the aesthetic turn in its development.

POETICIZATION OF PROSE FICTION

In a previous chapter, I have argued that Chinese pure fiction is not the result of mere imitation but is often the result of spontaneous expression of pent-up emotions. The blending of imitation and expression brought about poetic fiction. Poetic fiction is a kind of prose fiction with some features characteristic of lyric poetry. In the development of Chinese fiction, the process of poeticization is not easily recognizable. Because of the dominance of historical romance and retold stories, poeticization provided the impetus toward pure fiction. Indeed, without this process of poeticization, the tyranny of history could not have been overcome and Chinese pure fiction would not have matured in the sixteenth century. Chinese poetic fiction started quite early. It may be traced to some *zhigui* and *zhiren* tales of the Six Dynasties and some short stories of the Tang. But sustained effort at creating poetic fiction may be said to have started with the advent of the *Jin Ping Mei*. My suggestion that the *Jin Ping Mei* is a poetic novel may come as a surprise or even a shock to the reader. There is certainly not much poetry in the content or subject matter of the novel, as it deals with mundane, decadent details of everyday life and erotic, downright pornographic themes. The poetry lies in its formal structure, as I will later show. Poetic fiction reached its peak in the *Hongloumeng*, was further enriched in Lu Xun's fiction, and continues to the present day.

My concept of poetic fiction has much in common with Ralph Freedman's idea of the "lyrical novel."[16] While the Western lyrical novel came into being as a result of dissatisfaction with the realism of the classical novels of the eighteenth century and the conventions of nineteenth-century naturalism, Chinese poetic fiction grew out of a discontent with the dominance of historical romance and the conventions of both love stories and tales of adventure and strange experiences. In the opening section of Cao Xueqin's *Hongloumeng*, the narrator expresses through the mouth of the stone a strong reaction against the conventions of historical and other romances:

> Your so-called "historical romances," consisting, as they do, of scandalous anecdotes about statesmen and emperors of bygone days and scabrous attacks on the reputations of long-dead gentlewomen, contain more wickedness and immorality than I care to mention. Still worse is the "erotic novel," by whose filthy obscenities our young folk are all too easily corrupted. And the "boudoir romances," those dreary stereotypes with their volume after volume all pitched on the same note and their different characters undistinguishable except by name. . . .[17]

This passage expressing a dissatisfaction with the subject matter of romances is followed by a blast against conventional ways of writing:

> The trouble with this last kind of romance is that it only gets written in the first place because the author requires a framework in which to show off his

love poems. He goes about constructing this framework quite mechanically, beginning with the names of his pair of young lovers and invariably adding a third character, a servant or the like, to make mischief between them, like the *chou* [clown] in a comedy.[18]

The author also bridles at the features accompanying the conventional styles of writing: the stilted, bombastic language, and the inanities and absurdities. If the author of the *Hongloumeng* voiced his displeasure with the dominance of different kinds of romances, the author of the *Jin Ping Mei* showed his antipathy by his writing practice. The genesis of the novel is still open to investigation. I am inclined to this idea: it might have started from an attempt to satirize popular romances of the day. The fact that it takes an episode from the *Shuihu zhuan*, a heroic romance, and reverses the outcome of many borrowed episodes as well as the destinies of the borrowed characters in that novel seems to lend support to the hypothesis. Of course, it ends up as a new novel that recasts imaginatively old materials and pioneers a new form of fiction.

Chinese poetic fiction shares some basic features of Western poetic fiction in Freedman's conception of "lyrical novel," but it differs from its Western counterpart in some significant aspects. First and foremost, while European fiction came into existence as a separate genre from drama and especially from poetry, Chinese fiction was always related to poetry in one way or another even at the outset. In the early stages of fiction development, protofictional works were written mostly by literati who were poets. This is especially true with fictional works produced in the Tang dynasty, when Chinese fiction came to full maturity. Famous fiction writers like Yuan Zhen, Bai Xingjian, Liu Zongyuan, Shen Jiji, Niu Zhenru, Li Gongzuo, and others were at the same time first-rate poets. Because of their poetic training and poetic temperament, they consciously or unconsciously created fictional works in the same way they wrote poetry, quite unlike early European fiction writers, who were as a rule not poets. (It is interesting, however, to observe that lyrical novels flourished in Germany and were composed by great poets like Goethe.) The poetic tint in early Chinese fiction had a profound impact on the content and form of early Chinese fiction. Because of writers' poetic temperament, early Chinese fiction was colored by an expressive intent, which resulted in the appearance of the strange, fantastic, and supernatural in the content of Chinese fiction. As for form, early Chinese fiction tended to be very short in structure. This was obviously a characteristic trait of lyric poetry. Poetry comes into being as a result of the spontaneous overflow of emotions. The poetic impulse is not as sustainable as narrative impulse. Once it runs its full course, it will stop. Characteristically, its course is short in contradistinction to that of narrative impulse. The *zhigui* (records of extraordinary things) and *zhiren* (records of extraordinary persons) tales that played a role in the early stages of *xiaoshuo*'s development are generally so brief that they read like snippets of lyrical descriptions of an observed person, scene, situation, or event. Indeed, many of them present verbal pictures of a moment's impression. As I will show, the short, episodic, pictorial, and impressionistic features are precisely those often found in lyric poetry.

Second, the lyrical novel, as its name shows, deals with extended narratives. In the Chinese tradition, poetic fiction may refer to fictional works of any length. It may be a short story, a novella, or a novel. Third, Chinese poetic fiction does not share the limitations of the lyrical novel in Europe. In his discussion of the lyrical novel, Freedman identifies these limitations: "an underemphasis on character and an overemphasis on image, dream-like encounter, or allegory. The excitement created by the plot is largely absent and the excitement instilled by the expectations of the lyrical process does not usually make up for it."[19] The lyrical novels he has in mind include Laurence Sterne's *Tristram Shandy*, James Joyce's *Ulysses* and *Finnegans Wake*, Virginia Woolf's *Waves*, Djuna Barnes's *Nightwood*, Marcel Proust's *Remembrance of Things Past*, Hermann Hesse's novels, André Gide's novels, Franz Kafka's novels, and some of D. H. Lawrence's novels. These novels, because of their poetic vision, conception, and techniques, are endowed with aesthetic qualities that are not found to a great degree in realistic, naturalistic, and critically realistic novels. As Freedman points out, lyrical novels have certain advantages over novels of manners. He says, "[N]o detailed examinations of conscience, no discussions of motives, sensibilities, or realistic portraits of manners can make up for the intensely inward projection of experience in which the lyrical novel excels. Few other forms allow the author, or his *persona*, to penetrate so directly into the very act of knowledge and to represent it in immediately accessible portraiture."[20]

In my functional analysis of the genesis of poetry and fiction, I conceive of their differences in these words: poetry arises from the (un)conscious desires to reduce emotional and psychological tensions, while fiction comes into being as a result of the (un)conscious desires to produce and seek pleasure. Critics agree to the aesthetic achievements of lyrical novels, but to the general reading public, lyrical novels have much less appeal than novels written in a predominantly realistic manner. Except for literary critics, how many among the reading public have finished reading Joyce's *Ulysses* and *Finnegans Wake?* Chinese poetic fiction has a different characteristic feature. The *Hongloumeng*, as I will show, has many of the same poetic qualities as the Western lyrical novel, but it has never lost its grip on the primary function of fiction: entertainment. For over two hundred years, it has been avidly read by generations and generations of readers, old and young, well educated and moderately literate. And many of them read it more than once. Evidently, the Chinese poetic novel attaches great importance to intellectual and aesthetic appeal as well as the function of popular entertainment.

THE RISE OF POETIC FICTION

In the previous section, we have noted the common origins of lyric poetry and prose fiction. But despite their common provenance, lyric poetry and prose fiction seemed to have followed separate routes of development. Since "poetic fiction" is a concept that I have invented to describe the deep structure of Chinese fiction, there is no theoretical data that address the rise of this hybrid genre, still less data to characterize its nature. The closest conceptual source material about it may be drawn from Lu Ji's *Wenfu* (*Rhyme-Prose on Literature*). In his discussion of different forms of writing, Lu Ji made this famous remark: "Lyric poetry (*shi*) arises from affective emotions and is sensuously intricate. / Rhyme-prose (*fu*) gives formal shape to objects and is clear and bright."[21] Of the two poetic lines, the first affirms affective feelings as the original source of lyric poetry and expresses a view of poetry that differs from the Aristotelian conception of poetry as the imitation of an action but comes close to Wordsworth's idea of poetry as arising from an overflow of powerful feelings. The second line discusses a special literary genre in the Chinese tradition: the *fu* or rhyme-prose. As a literary genre, it may be translated as "poetic exposition" or "poetic narrative." As a mode of expression, it means "direct composition in plain words." As the literal English translation shows, "rhyme-prose" is a hybrid genre, halfway between poetry and prose, even though it has generally been viewed as a form of lyric poetry. Lyric poetry (*shi*) in early Chinese tradition was seldom used as a means to compose extended description or narration. Rhyme-prose, however, was employed widely to compose compositions that extend to hundreds of lines. Lu Ji's *Discourse on Literature*, the first sustained discussion of literature in the Chinese tradition, was written in the *fu* form. Liu Xie's *Wenxin diaolong* (*Literary Mind and the Carving of Dragons*), the first comprehensive treatise on literature in China, was also composed in the *fu* form. Even though we may not consider rhyme-prose as the precursor of Chinese poetic fiction, I am disposed to think that its structural principle and expository mode of writing must have had considerable influence on the appearance of Chinese poetic fiction.

As I have said, Chinese poetic fiction arose from a conscious or unconscious desire to emulate and compete with lyric poetry. This desire gave rise to a unique feature to traditional Chinese fiction. In its surface structure, traditional Chinese fiction displays some structural features that are totally alien to fictional works in other literary traditions, especially the European tradition. When Chinese fiction developed into storytelling, the storytellers were not writers with poetic talent. But because of their desire to emulate creative poets, even popular stories meant to cater to the popular tastes were colored by a superficial tint of poetry. This poetic tint has been preserved in *huaben xiaoshuo* (prompt-books for storytellers) as well as in literati novels. A popular tale usually opens with a poem and ends with another poem, with poetic lines or whole poems scattered throughout. As a rule, the poems were quoted from historical poets by storytellers, obviously with the aim to flaunt their literary knowledge. Thus, even the moderately educated storytellers nursed aspirations to ascend to the exalted status of poets. For all that, these superficial poetic elements do not add much to the poetic qualities of popular fiction, but they represent a conscious and unconscious desire of Chinese fiction to emulate and compete with the time-honored literary forms of lyric poetry and classical prose.

Because of the poetic impulses, mature Chinese fictional works such as short stories, novellas, and novels developed a unique structural design that may be called "poetic sandwiches." By this term I mean that the narrative is sandwiched into a poetic framework that displays an opening poem at the beginning, a poem at the ending, and one or more poems in the middle of the narrative. In extended fictional works, the title of each chapter is a poetic couplet. In fictional works with more artistic qualities, the poems were no longer taken from existent poetic collections but were composed by fiction writers themselves and formed an integral part of the narrative. These originally composed poems carried on the role of the quoted poems in popular stories and went beyond that: they sometimes served as descriptions of persons and scenes, sometimes as authorial comments, sometimes as summing up of what had gone before, and sometimes as moral judgment. They look extrinsic to the narrative and may at most be viewed as a conscious desire on the part of the fiction writer to emulate poets; but from a different perspective, they reveal the strong impact of the poetic tradition on fiction writing and are indicative of the presence of the poetic impulse in the making of fiction. This idiosyncratic feature represents one distinct difference from Western poetic fiction: while Chinese fiction started from its outset with strong emphasis on lyricism, the European fiction, because of the Platonic-Aristotelian restriction of poetics to imitation and narration,[22] underplayed the lyric impulses in the beginning.

It is, of course, the literati with poetic talent who substantially changed the course of development for Chinese fiction in the direction of poeticization. The *Sangu yanyi, Xiyouji,* and *Shuihu zhuan* were all based on popular versions, but the writers who wrote the final versions were all literary men with poetic talent. In those novels, the poems that lead each chapter and end the chapters are no longer poems taken readily from existent sources, but are original poems composed by the authors to express certain feelings and responses inspired by the narrated events. Most of them are poetry of considerable lyricism and add literary qualities to the fictional works. Although these poems are already woven into the formal structure of those fictional works, they are still quite extrinsic to the internal structure of those fictional works. It is the *Jin Ping Mei* that started the poetic conception of fictional works in the Chinese tradition and it is the *Hongloumeng* that brought the process of poeticization to completion and culmination.

The (un)conscious desires to write fiction in the manner of writing poetry constitutes the major force that overcame the tyranny of historicity and paved the way for the rise of pure fiction. Moreover, in the Chinese tradition, poeticization had a sociological impact on the perceived legitimacy of fiction as a literary form. Before the appearance of the *Hongloumeng,* fiction was consistently deemed a low form of literary writing catering to the popular, and often vulgar, tastes of the lower classes, and was considered unworthy of the writing efforts of the elite. Confucius's admonition that gentlemen should not engage in fiction writing became an almost inviolable literary tenet. In spite of some scholars' vehement protest against this prejudice, the lowly status of fiction remained unchanged for most of Chinese literary history. With the advent of the *Hongloumeng*, however, Chinese fiction finally rid itself of the odium of lowliness and became a respectable literary art on a par with venerable lyric poetry and classical prose. After Cao Xueqin's novel started circulating in society, there was a popular saying: "If one opens a talk without mentioning the *Hongloumeng*, / He has read the *Classics of Poetry* and *Documents* in vain." Scholars have generally taken this saying to mean that Cao Xueqin's novel achieves an artistic excellence equal to that of time-honored literary classics. I would add that this saying also represents an acknowledgment of the poetic qualities of the novel and confirms from a sociological perspective that the *Hongloumeng* marks the completion of poeticization of fiction in Chinese history and is a poetic novel par excellence.

I have discussed the process of poeticization and the circumstantial evidence of poetic fiction. Without clearly explaining the rationale and intrinsic properties of poetic fiction, my suggested idea of poeticization would not be totally convincing. In the following section, I will explain why I call the chosen fictional works "poetic fiction." Poetry and fiction are distinctly different literary categories, but the distinction is not so great as to rule out the intermingling of the two categories. Greek epics are narrative poetry. Yet in Georg Lukács' opinion, they are a kind of fiction and only happened to be written in verse form. In the same vein, Bakhtin calls the Greek epic the "Greek novel."[23] Conversely, some fictional works are prose in form, but they are essentially poetry and only happened to be written in prose. In the Chinese tradition, due to the fact that lyric poetry was the dominant literary form and all fiction writers were trained in the art of poetry and were in one way or another poets, some of the fictional works were composed with the conscious and unconscious intention to use fiction to rival lyric poetry. In the Tang, there was the so-called practice of *wengquan* (warming up compositions before civil service examinations): candidates who wished to be patronized by high-ranking officials in the court wrote imaginative fictional works and presented them to potential patrons, who were often examiners or powerful officials who controlled the selection process. This practice may perhaps be considered the beginning of the poeticization of fiction in China.

The works of Chinese fiction are characterized by a heavy presence of poetic features. Some of them may indeed be said to be poetic works that happened to be written in prose form. To truly understand the compound word "poetic fiction," we need to clarify in what way a fictional work is endowed with poetry or poetic qualities. And to tackle this issue, we need first of all to briefly examine the question: "What is poetry?" There are numerous definitions of poetry. I have picked one that has cross-cultural implications and is directly related to the issues at hand. In his treatise "What Is Poetry?" John Stuart Mill makes light of scholarly attempts to distinguish between poetry and prose, because he believes that both kinds of writing may act on human feelings. He agrees that "the faculty of the poet and the faculty of the novelist are as distinct as any other faculties," but he also maintains that "many of the finest poems are in the form of novels, and in almost all good novels there is true poetry."[24] In his opinion, "poetry, which is the delineation of the deeper and more secret workings of the human heart, is interesting only to those to whom it recalls what they have felt, or whose imagination it stirs up to conceive what they could feel, or what they might have been able to feel, had their outward circumstances been different."[25] Mill's conception of poetry is not significantly different from that of Wordsworth: "[P]oetry is the spontaneous overflow of powerful feelings; it takes its origin from emotion recollected in tranquility: the emotion is contemplated till, by a species of reaction, the tranquility gradually disappears, and an emotion, kindred to that which was before the subject of contemplation, is gradually produced, and does itself actually exist in the mind."[26] Nor is it significantly different from the time-honored Chinese conception of poetry as expressed by the Great Preface to the *Book of Songs*:

> Poetry is where the intent of the heart [mind] goes. Lying in the heart [or mind], it is "intent"; when uttered in words, it is "poetry." When an emotion stirs inside, one expresses it in words; finding this inadequate, one sighs over it; not content with this, one sings it in poetry; still not satisfied, one unconsciously dances with one's hands and feet.[27]

The three definitions have one fundamental idea in common: poetry is a spontaneous expression of powerful feelings, and those feelings are, more often than not, recollections of events in the past that wait for a channel of expression. Scholars are still debating the authorship of the *Jin Ping Mei*, but according to a self-styled close friend of the author, the novel came into being as a result of the author's attempt to facilitate the channeling of common people's pent-up depressed feelings and performed the same function as poetry and the Dao.[28] The author of the *Hongloumeng* states in the opening section that: despite his failure in society and poverty-stricken life, he could not forget his past life spent with some extraordinary girls, and his irrepressible creative impulse expressed itself in the form of the novel.[29] Lu Xun's masterpiece, *The True Story of Ah Q*, has a similar genesis. The author confesses that for several years, he had been obsessed with the story of Ah Q. After considerable hesitation, the author was about to give up the project, but "in the end, as though possessed by some fiend, I always came back to the idea of writing the story of Ah Q."[30] Cao Xueqin's obsession with writing his life story and Lu Xun's "fiend" are different ways of expressing Plato's idea of the "divine madness" and D. H. Lawrence's artistic "demon," the original source of poetic inspirations.

The reader may object to my citing the genesis of the two masterpieces as evidence for poetic features. He or she may say that almost all fictional works have such a genesis. In what way can one justify the cited geneses as evidence of poetic features? My first answer to this question comes from Mill's treatise: "in almost all good novels there is true poetry." My second answer is that poetry and fiction have different kinds of genesis. As I have argued, both poetry and fiction emanate from the conscious and unconscious desires to seek pleasure, but while poetry achieves pleasure through a reduction of emotional tension, fiction derives its pleasure by gratifying conscious and unconscious fantasies. The reason that I consider the geneses of Cao Xueqin's and Lu Xun's fiction as having a poetic nature is that both fictional work were composed with the explicit purport of ridding the author of an emotional burden. It is reasonable to say that poetry essentially arises from an expressive impulse, while fiction mainly grows from a mimetic impulse. Poetic fiction, of course, is still a form of imitation, but its genesis is mainly the outcome of poetic expression. The author has pent-up emotions, and that cluster of emotions finds a chance occasion to express itself, often after being triggered by an incident or event. Witness the genesis of Proust's masterpiece, *Remembrance of Things Past*. In her well-known essay on fiction making, "Mr. Bennett and Mrs. Brown," Virginia Woolf tells us of how an incidental encounter with an old woman and a middle-aged man on a train evoked in her heart a strong creative urge to "manufacture a three-volume novel about the old lady's son, and his adventures crossing the Atlantic, and her daughter, and how she kept a milliner's shop in Westminster, the past life of Smith himself, and his house at Sheffield."[31] The main reason why Woolf was able to compose an extended narrative out of a chance encounter is that the incident was only a trigger, and the old lady was one of "unlimited capacity and infinite variety; capable of appearing in any place; wearing any dress; saying anything and doing heaven knows what." Ultimately, "she is, of course, the spirit we live by, life itself."[32] I will try to show in the following section that what Woolf discussed with regard to the genesis of a new form of fiction that differs from the realistic novel is exactly what gave rise to the writing of the *Jin Ping Mei* and the *Hongloumeng*.

INTRINSIC POETIC QUALITIES IN FICTION

Since all fictional works contain elements of poetry, an exploration of the nature of poetic fiction from the perspective of genesis and creative impulse cannot lead us very far. In my opinion, poetic fiction distinguishes itself from other forms of fiction by its poetic concerns with formal presentation. The name "prose fiction" itself suggests that it is a prosaic form of writing not constrained by rigid rules of ordering the verbal discourse. But that does not mean that prose cannot contain poetry. Coleridge made the apt remark: "[P]oetry of the highest kind may exist without meter, and even without the contradistinguishing objects of a poem."[33] However, poetry does have some distinguishing features that separate it from fiction, and poetic fiction consciously or unconsciously emulates those features. The first poetic feature of poetic fiction is the tendency to express emotions in an intensified and concentrated way. This is especially prominent in some classical tales written in *wenyan* (literary language) and in some of Lu Xun's short stories. The major reason I compare these fictional works to poems is that they are written with such a spontaneous flow of intense emotions that they fit into the Chinese definition of poetry: poetry expresses what the mind is intent on. The outpouring of emotions in poetic fiction is so spontaneous that the author can scarcely hide his presence behind the pages.

The intensification of emotions in fiction writing endows Chinese fiction with some idiosyncratic features that are often viewed in a negative light. One characteristic feature of Chinese *xiaoshuo* is the heavy presence of the author. Be it a classical tale or a vernacular story, one almost always encounters some authorial comments on the narrative. Since Henry James propounded the concept of point of view in fiction writing by insisting that the narrative voice be purged of any authorial commentary that may interfere with the narrative flow, authorial intrusion has always been viewed as a drawback in fiction writing. I beg to differ. In my opinion, the heavy authorial intrusion in *xiaoshuo* is a reflection of the poetic impulse that seeks to express rather than represent. The fiction writer cannot help but intrude into the narrative, because, like a poet, he simply cannot suppress his pent-up emotions. Note that D. H. Lawrence was also criticized for his authorial intrusion. In his critical comment on *Lady Chatterley's Lover*, Joyce satirically remarked that because the author talks too much through his characters, the novel should really be renamed "Lady Chatterbox's Lover."[34] By no mere accident, Lawrence is a poet of free verse and his novels are marked by a strong desire for expression and have a distinct poetic quality.

Poetic fiction differs from realistic fiction in that it has a different approach to the relationship between self and the world. As Freedman notes, "The 'I' of the lyric becomes the protagonist, who refashions the world through his perceptions and renders it as a form of the imagination. . . . The lyrical process expands because the lyrical 'I' is also an experiencing protagonist. The poet's stance is turned into an epistemological act."[35] The *Hongloumeng* and Yuan Zhen's "The Story of Ying Ying" adopted a lyrical approach to the narration of the story. In Yuan Zhen's story, though the narrative has a third-person protagonist and a first-person narrator, the story is autobiographical in nature.[36] The autobiographical genesis allows us to view the protagonist, the narrator, and the author as one and the same person—that is to say, Yuan Zhen himself. The autobiographical genesis places the story in the same order as lyric poetry in the Chinese tradition, which is often an immediate response to an event or situation, and that may explain why the story attained an inwardness rarely achieved by fictional works of traditional *xiaoshuo* of the author's time. In the *Hongloumeng*, the author confessed that its genesis depended upon the intimate relationship between self and society, lyrical "I" and epistemological act, the author and his personae. The novel opens with the author's claim that it is a personal account of his experiences with a group of girls:

> Having made an utter failure of my life, I found myself one day in the midst of my poverty and wretchedness, thinking about the female companions of my youth. As I went over them one by one, examining and comparing them in my mind's eye, it suddenly came over me that those slips of girls—which is all they were then—were in every way, both morally and intellectually, superior to the 'grave and mustachioed signior' I am now supposed to have become. . . . I resolved that, however unsightly my own shortcomings might be, I must not, for the sake of keeping them hid, allow those wonderful girls to pass into oblivion without a memorial.[37]

Thus, the genesis of the novel is the result of an epistemological act and subsequent enlightenment. And the process of composition is a further epistemological act that seeks to discover the meaning of life. Nevertheless, the protagonist is first an incarnated stone, and then a playboy in an aristocratic family. The stone becomes the bearer of the narrative, the narrator, and the protagonist. And finally, the narrator becomes the editor of the novel. As a result of the metamorphosis of the roles, the author, narrator, protagonist, and editor become interchangeable. The interchangeable roles are indicative of a writing process alien to realistic fiction, but compatible with poetic fiction.

Poetry differs from prose in the repetition of patterns, rhythm, and regulated meters. Fiction cannot rival poetry in this respect, but poetic fiction emulates poetry by organizing the narrative in terms of recurrent motifs, repetitive patterns, and regulated structures. Historical fiction follows the set pattern of historical events, which is a natural pattern. Poetic fiction organizes its narrative materials on a consciously designed structural pattern intended to convey certain surplus meanings. This is especially prominent in the *Jin Ping Mei* and *Hongloumeng*. The former has a schematic design centering on the alternation between heat and cold which symbolizes the fluctuation of fortune and misfortunes, happiness and sorrow, and the physical exhaustion of the antihero parallels the political and economic depletion of the state. In the latter, the poetic pattern is set on the appearance and disappearance of the stone, which symbolizes the collective unconscious, the male protagonist, and the novel itself. In both novels, the structural pattern resembles that of a classical Chinese poem composed in regulated meter with the set pattern of opening, connection, furthering, and ending. If we care to look into the deep structure of other masterpieces, we will realize that some repetitive patterns are also the result of a poetic impulse.

Chinese fiction has often been charged with the structural limitation of being episodic in nature. It is said to lack a tightly knit structural pattern that binds disparate narrated events into a unified, coherent framework. In his response to this charge, Andrew Plaks acknowledges that "The well-founded indeterminacy of the conception of the event in the Chinese context does

present, and cannibalism imagined and real. All the cannibalistic images serve to convey the theme of the story: the four-thousand-year history of China is a history of cannibalism.[43] Lu Xun is a recognized fiction writer, but he is also a poet who composed ancient-style poems. Many of his essays are really poems in prose form. His fondness for using images to convey profound ideas is recognizable in almost all his fictional writing: the image of the wreath and crow in "Medicine," the cake of soap in "Soap," and the pigtail worn by various characters in the *True Story of Ah Q* and some other works. Many of Lu Xun's short stories do not read like stories; they appeal to the reader like poems. A random list would include "Kong Yiji," "My Old Home," "Village Opera," "The Comedy of Ducks," "In the Tavern," "Rabbit and Cat," "White Light," and, above all, "Regret for the Past."[44]

Not only his essays but almost all Lu Xun's stories are also poems in prose form. Scholars of Lu Xun have often regretted that he did not write a novel and have speculated on the possible reasons. One widely accepted explanation is that when Lu Xun went to the historical sites associated with Emperor Xuanzong and his imperial concubine Yang, he was repelled by the dilapidated bleakness of the legendary places. His long-cherished desire to write a novel on Concubine Yang vanished without a trace. But there is another plausible reason. By temperament and education, Lu Xun was a poet—not a narrative poet, but a lyrical poet. Lyricism bursts forth in a moment and cannot sustain long and extended narrative. Su Shi's view of literary creation strongly supports this speculation. In his commentary on his own literary works, Su Shi talks about how poetic inspiration comes and goes. When poetic inspiration grips him, he says,

> my writing resembles a spring with millions of buckets of water and seeps out from underground without choosing places for outlet. On level ground, it flows in torrential streams and covers a thousand *li* in a day without any difficulty. When it encounters mountains, stones, and twists and turns, it changes into shapes in correspondence with the landscape. How this is done I myself cannot tell. What may be known is that it will move when it should move and it will stop when it must stop. That's all there is to it![45]

Su Shi's idea may explain why Lu Xun's stories are always short and read more like a poem in prose, and why he did not write a novel. Despite the short length, his fictional works are all objects of verbal art, because they transcend the telling of an interesting story and convey surplus implications beyond the surface meanings.

I am now returning to an idiosyncratic feature in Chinese fiction that I mentioned but did not discuss: the episodic structure. In the novel, this feature is especially marked: many novels are episodic in structure with the different episodes connected by a loose structural frame. Historically, the episodic structure may have been due to the influence of official histories. Sima Qian pioneered the paradigm of history writing, which groups together biographies of individual historical personages around a very thin organizing structure. The episodic narration in novels like the *Water Margin*, *Journey to the West*, and the *Scholars* is symptomatic of the influence of the historical paradigm. The episodic structure of the Chinese novel may also, however, have been the consequence of the poetic impulse at work. The lyric impulse in poetic composition works by installments and is therefore episodic in nature. It is short, transient, and incapable of sustaining long and extended narratives. When the spontaneous overflow of powerful feelings surges, the flow of narrative will endure for a certain length. But the narrative focus cannot last long, because the aesthetic pleasure arising from the release of powerful feelings is a negative pleasure or a reduction of unpleasure. By contrast, the pleasure coming from narrative impulse can go on and on, because it is a positive pleasure that can be consciously prolonged. When pent-up emotions are released, the poetic impulse ebbs, and the narration will stop or change directions. In the composition of novels, it means changes in topics, which give rise to new episodes.

The poetic structure may therefore offer insight into another special feature in Chinese fiction: the insertion of episodes that seem to have no direct relation to the narrative line. This idiosyncrasy was once considered a limitation of Chinese fiction, but it is again a poetic feature attributable to the poetic unconscious or even the conscious poetic impulse at work. We may recall the results of Jakobson's research on language and literature. His conclusion was that poetry is largely grounded in metaphor, while prose in metonymy.[46] If poetic fiction in China were often structured on the principle of metaphor rather than on metonymy, the insertion of seemingly unrelated episodes into a coherently presented narrative would not be a narrative oddity that impedes the flow of narration but an aesthetic feature that strengthens the quality of the fictional work. Take one of the six greatest traditional Chinese novels, the *Scholars*, as an example. It opens with a chapter of the poet-recluse Wang Mian, who is set apart from the rest of the novel by a century and has no ostensible relation whatever to the novel's narrative thread or other characters. To a critic trained in Western narratology, this way of opening an extended narrative with a seemingly unrelated episode must look exceedingly odd. But if we look at the opening in light of the foregoing argument, we cannot but admire the author's poetic vision. In his pioneering study of the lyric vision in the *Scholars*, Yu-kung Kao perceptively locates the inherent role of connection palyed by lyricism in the episode: "[D]espite the fact that Wang Mien's name is not mentioned after this point, he remains the model for readers against which to measure all the other figures striving for fame or competing in the examination system. . . . Finally in the epilogue, again with several decades intervening, we get at least a refracted vision of Wang Mien again in the cameo presentation of four latter-day artists living in solitude and enjoying their own artistic pursuits."[47]

Yu-kung Kao also notes that the conventional Chinese fictional practice of "employing a 'frame-tale' or a prologue-epilogue structure to symbolize within a single episode the meaning of a full-length novel" should be understood as "a metaphor for the novel as a whole."[48] Indeed, in terms of the principle of metaphorical composition, we may always find lyric relations of all seemingly unrelated episodes to the general narrative thrust of a fictional work. The reader just needs to broaden his or her vision so as to see not just the narrative thread but also the implied poetic qualities. From a conceptual as well as critical perspective, it appears that "episodic structure" is a misnomer for what should be properly called "poetic structure."

A DEFINITION OF POETIC FICTION

In addition to telling an interesting story, poetic fiction aims at endless signification of meanings in the presented story. From this point of view, poeticization of fiction in the development of Chinese *xiaoshuo* brought about a quantum change to Chinese *xiaoshuo*. It effectively transforms *xiaoshuo* from a kind of storytelling to a narrative art comparable to the highly respected form of poetry. In this section, I will provide a definition of "poetic fiction." By the name alone, "poetic fiction" is a compound word. It is neither pure poetry nor pure fiction, but is a combination of the basic features of both poetry and fiction. The combinatory nature of this concept may be seen in both directions. Despite its poetic features, it is still a form of fiction with the ontological and epistemological features of fiction. Ontologically, it is predicated on the conception that fiction imitates life and must be true to life. Epistemologically, it mainly employs associational thinking and represents life primarily through the narration of episodes, events, characters' actions, and psychological explorations. But it also possesses distinctive features of poetry. It employs imagistic thinking and lays an equal emphasis on expression of emotions. It pays so much attention to the use of imagery that it has a kind of pictorial or spatial quality. In creative uses, a writer of poetic fiction professes to write a fiction, but he actually writes as though he were writing a poem. To summarize all the discussed characteristics, I may define poetic fiction thus: it is a kind of fictitious narrative that possesses the characteristic features of poetry and aspires to be poetry in fictional form. In contradistinction with narrative poetry, we may call poetic fiction "poetic narrative."

LYRICAL REALISM AND MYTHICAL REALISM

A unique feature of fiction in the Chinese tradition is an unrealistic tendency that may rightfully be characterized as "magic realism" in modern fictional terms. Of course, the Chinese version of magic realism is quite different in genesis from its modern counterpart, which arose as a self-conscious reaction against the dominance of realism in literature and art. Up to the appearance of the magic realism pioneered by Latin American fiction writers, Western fictional tradition seldom endorses the mixture of supernatural elements with realistic narrative. By contrast, in the Chinese tradition, the use of the supernatural had its rightful place in fiction almost from the very beginning. This phenomenon does not mean that Chinese fiction writers who employed supernatural elements believed in the existence of the supernatural. Rather, it is an indication of poetic qualities in fictional works and attests to the poetic imagination at work. The literary mind responsible for the creation of realistic fiction follows the mimetic principle of being true to reality. By contrast, the poetic mind does not have to follow the realistic principle and frequently transcends the limitations of the realistic mind. In Lu Ji's *Rhyme-Prose on Literature*, he describes how the poetic imagination works in these poetic lines: "The creative spirit flies to the eight extremities of the earth, / the mind roams to a height of ten thousand yards."[49] In many traditional Chinese poems, the line between the human world and supernatural world, the living and the dead, heaven and hell, and past and present was completely eradicated. In Quan Yuan's poem *Lisao* (Encountering Sorrow), Song Yu's rhyme-prose "The Goddess," and Cao Zhi's rhyme-prose "the Goddess of the Luo River" the human persona is able to communicate with goddesses, and sometimes engages in love affairs with them. In fictional creation, the mixture of the supernatural and the realistic was used in a dazzling array of representations. Gods and goddesses, ghosts and demons, fox spirits, snake spirits, fish spirits, and other animal spirits—all may become major characters that play a role in the affairs of the human world. Ideologically, this phenomenon may have to do with pantheism in Chinese religion and the idea of the equality of all things under heaven in philosophy. In storytelling, it is certainly employed to create an intriguing tale. But in terms of the poetic mind at work, I suggest that the use of the supernatural shares an aesthetic function like that of magic realism.

Magic realism started with the visual arts and did not become an established concept in fiction criticism until the 1980s. It has been narrowly used to describe the works of Latin American novelists such as Jorge Luis Borges (1899–1988), Gabriel García Márquez, (1928–), Alejo Carpenter (1904–), and others, and broadly applied to fictional works by E. T. A. Hoffmann, Franz Kafka, and even Salman Rushdie. The most eye-catching characteristic features of magical realism fiction include "the mingling and juxtaposition of the realistic and the fantastic or bizarre, skilful time shifts, convoluted and even labyrinthine narratives and plots, miscellaneous use of dreams, myths and fairy stories, expressionistic and even surrealistic description, arcane erudition, the element of surprise or abrupt shock, the horrific and the inexplicable."[50] Interestingly, all these features are abundant in traditional Chinese fiction. The disruption of linear time sequence, the expressionistic and surrealistic tendencies in fictional narrative, and the blending of the realistic, the strange, and the fantastic are all indicative of a creative impulse that is lyrical in nature. In creative vision, it represents the author's surrealistic response to the relationship between self and society, ideals and reality, life and art.

In fictional technique, it presents a hyperreality that simulates social conditions or mental states that realistic techniques are incapable of capturing. Many traditional Chinese fictional works feature themes of the supernatural, encounters with the strange and inexplicable, dream adventures, relationships with gods and goddesses, ghosts and animal spirits, and other unrealistic experiences. The creators of these fictional works succeeded in producing what Freedman calls "romantic irony," a creative vision "achieved by author intrusions and frame-story devices," which suggests that they attempted "to break the aesthetic illusion and to produce the portrait of a hero simultaneously in life and art."[51]

"Romantic irony" may provide a partial explanation of why there has been an abundance of stories and tales with authorial intrusions and frame-story devices. It is a lyrical state of mind, which generates an awareness transcended by the "true presence of the spirit." Through it, the demarcation between the real world and the imagined world is abolished. As Freedman aptly puts it, "[T]he world of objects is transformed and dissolved into a world of 'magic'— a freedom gained in fairy tale and myth—which mirrors a passive hero's finite awareness in a spiritual state."[52] The frequently used dream-adventure frame in traditional Chinese fiction, as in "The World in a Pillow," and the mythical frame used in the *Shuihu zhuan* and *Hongloumeng* are the results of a poetic mind with romantic irony at work. In the light of this poetic (un)consciousness, the metamorphosis of the stone in the *Hongloumeng* should not be too difficult to explain in analytical and reflexive terms.

From the perspective of depth psychology, the Chinese fondness for magic realism in fictional works serves a creative purpose often known only to the poetic unconscious or subconscious. Take the characterization of ghosts and animal spirits as beautiful females for example. These nonhuman characters are endowed with human qualities such as loving tenderness, selfless devotion, and moral integrity, and have physical beauty. A modern reader may wonder: why would the traditional fiction writers be engrossed with portraying lovely female characters as nonhuman beings? The answer seem to be that these nonhuman characters reflect and refract the male unconscious and subconscious perceptions of and visions about the female. A beautiful female in fiction is an ambivalent figure who objectifies the male unconscious and subconscious. The frequent portrayal of beautiful females as supernatural creatures brings to light the contradictory attitude of the male toward the female: she is both an object of desire and an object of fear. She is a desirable object of love, because she is both beautiful and virtuous, but at the same time, she is non-human and therefore arouses the male fear. The prevalent use of the supernatural in Chinese fiction embodies an inquisitive spirit that attempts to search for the unknown, to discover the unconscious, and to reveal the deep layers of meanings in social reality. It compensates for the relative lack of psychological exploration of characters' minds elsewhere in Chinese literature. When it is used to construct the structural form of a fictional work, as is done in the *Hongloumeng*, it anticipates and is truly worthy of the name of magic realism in modern fiction.

As the highest achievement of Chinese fiction, the *Hongloumeng* is a poetic fiction par excellence. As a whole, it exemplifies Wordsworth's definition of poetry: it is the artist's conscious reconstruction of unconsciously assembled impressions recollected in tranquility. In terms of psychological realism, it is reminiscent of Proust's "involuntary memory," which unites the time-bound physical world and the timeless mental world. Metaphysicaly, the creative mind of the *Hongloumeng* touches upon Bergsonian ideas concerning the concept of the moment. Indeed, we may say that the whole novel is constructed on a concept of the moment: it begins with the stone's birth and ends with the stone's full story symbolically inscribed on its back. In its human form, the stone experiences life as a poem as well as a narrative. In this respect the novel's conception of the stone parallels Coleridge's conception of the interaction between primary and secondary imagination. In the primary imagination, the narrator tells a coherent story, credible, realistic, and even naturalistic. In the secondary imagination, which, as Coleridge states, "dissolves, diffuses, dissipates, in order to recreate,"[53] the narrator tells a hyperreal tale of self and society in a fantastic, surrealistic, and magically realistic mode. Because of its intermixture of the expressive, lyrical, romantic, and realistic qualities, there is ample reason to term this mode of representation "romantic realism" or "lyrical realism."

Whether we call it romantic realism, lyrical realism, magic realism, or romantic irony, the fact remains that it is hard to explain the prevalent use of the supernatural in Chinese fiction. To fully account for the supernatural phenomenon in Chinese fiction, perhaps we should call it "mythical realism." All Chinese fictional works with the presence of the supernatural and the fantastic can be read both as mythical tales and realistic fictional works. First, mythical realism is the result of the integration of myths and realistic tales. It incorporates the traditional meaning of the word, "myth," which "tends to signify a fiction, but a fiction which conveys a psychological truth,"[54] but it also embodies the modern meaning of "myth" in semiological representation. In Roland Barthes's conception, a modern myth is a second-order semiological system in which a sign (i.e., the associative total of a concept and an image) in the first system becomes a mere signifier in the second system. In one of his illustrative examples, a picture showing a Negro soldier saluting a French flag is a first-order semiological system, which ostensibly signifies what it is. But it is only a signifier in a second-order system with a signified, which conveys a patriotic message: "France is a great Empire, [and] all her sons, without colour discrimination, faithfully serve under the flag."[55] As I have already pointed out, the strong presence of the supernatural in Chinese fiction does not mean that traditional writers believed in the supernatural. Rather, it serves the "myth" function in Barthes's conception. For example, the common theme of love between a human protagonist and a supernatural being, apart from telling an enthralling tale, conveys miscellaneous messages about the conditions of love in the societies of the time.

AESTHETIC SUGGESTIVENESS:
HALLMARK OF FICTIONAL ART

In the history of Chines *xiaoshuo*, there are many cases in which the definitive version of a fictional work came from the rewriting of an existent story by a literatus. Take the *Shuihu zhuan*, for example. There were several popular versions circulating among the reading public in seventeenth-century China, but scholarly research demonstrates that it was by the pen of the literati that the final version came to be written, the version that displaced all other, less-literary versions. In a recent study of the novel, Liangyan Ge provides a fascinating account of how the novel gradually evolved into an artwork through the interaction between written culture and popular orality, and a rewriting of storytellers' accounts by literary persons.[56] The rewriting process is a process of aestheticization in general and poeticization for some masterpieces. One way of aestheticization is to embellish the popular version by literally adding surplus signifying discourses. This can be most clearly seen from the genesis of the *Xiyou ji*, *Shuihu zhuan*, and *Sanguo yanyi*. The literati who rewrote those stories not only polished their languages but also transformed their formal presentation at large. They added a great deal to the existent stories. What they added is both literally and figuratively surplus discourse elements that carry surplus signifying values. This process of aestheticization finds the most concentrated expression in the rewriting of the three great Ming novels and the short stories collected by Feng Menglong. But before the appearance of the *Jing Ping Mei*, rewriting did not deviate completely from the transmitted materials, and the surplus signifying value is largely imparted by the newly added discourse elements. Thus, the surplus value is largely content based. It is literally "surplus" value that comes into being as a result of telling an interesting story.

There is another kind of rewriting undertaken on the principle of pure fiction making. The fiction writer no longer followed the theme, structure, story line, and narrative details of existent stories, but used them for a radical conception of a new narrative project. In this kind of endeavor, attention is paid as much to the content as to the form. Such a fictional work is conceived of on the principle of fictional art and aspires to the condition of poetry with aesthetic suggestiveness as its hallmark. In such a work of fictional art, the surplus signifying value is generally not to be found in its content but in its structure and form. Or, to be more exact, it resides in the form of content. The *Jin Ping Mei* exemplifies this representational trend. In a detailed study of this novel, I have shown how the novel's form carries additional themes and its stylistic features convey surplus meanings.[57] The multifarious ways in which images are presented, scenes described, events narrated, motifs repeated, or story line plotted represent the surplus ornaments of a verbal discourse that can be described in terms of Kant's "formal purposiviness" and "purposiveness without a purpose." They are the formal aspects of the novel that convey surplus signifying value. *Essentially, I argue that the core of fictional art is a formal network that produces additional meanings beyond the stated meaning.* Here, we may see an intimate relation between Chinese *xiaoshuo* and traditional poetry. In traditional Chinese poetics, the surplus value in a verbal discourse may be called "aesthetic suggestiveness." It has been expressed in these sayings and notions: *yi zai yanwai* (what is intended should go beyond words), *yanwai zhi yi* (a text should convey meanings beyond the expressed words), *xianwai zhi yin* (sound off the string), *xiangwai zhi xiang* (images beyond the image), *weiwai zhi zhi* (flavors beyond the flavor), *hanxu* (subtle reserve), and Zhong Rong's famous saying, "The text may come to an end but the implications abound."[58]

In the Chinese tradition, Zhong Rong's famous saying represents the highest aesthetic state a poem can attain. It is also a state that the Chinese poetic fiction and Western lyrical novel aspire to. Joyce's *Ulysses* narrates the simple story of a day in the lives of three characters. The chronological pattern of the day's events supplies the only narrative plot in the novel. For those who enjoy realistic stories, there is nothing of interest in *Ulysses*. But through a superb use of language, Joyce weaves so wide a range of subjects into the narrative that the novel is believed to represent practically everything under the sun. The multiplicity of the novel's themes lies in the endless signification of the novel's language, which the Chinese would call "endless meanings." In terms of contemporary theory, multiplicity of meanings is called literary openness. In fictional studies it may be termed open conception and open representation. In the final analysis, the essence of fictional art lies in whether a fictional work is endowed with aesthetic suggestiveness or literary openness. Fictional openness does not come out of the blue. Aesthetically, it was influenced by open ideas in Chinese poetics. In traditional Chinese poetics, there may be said to have been a tradition of open conception of poetry. Admittedly, poetry is different from fiction, but the open position advocated for poetry is only a few steps from an open conception of fiction. Indeed, the chosen fictional works in this book all show indebtedness to the open conception in poetics, especially the idea of aesthetic suggestiveness. And as my study of chosen fictional works will show, they all display a varying degree of fictional openness. It may even be claimed that fictional openness most adequately represents the essence of fictional art.

Chinese fiction, as represented by the three great novels, the *Sanguo yanyi*, *Xiyou ji*, and *Shuihu zhuan*, had sought to deal with the narration of interesting histories, legends, and folklore, and other story-oriented events. The author of the *Jin Ping Mei* saw the *Shuihu zhuan* as the most successful work of storytelling-oriented fiction, but at the same time, he seems to have realized that it represented the climax of the historical method and storytelling technique. He also seems to have been aware that storytelling could not develop any further as an art form without taking a new direction and without the introduction of new narrative techniques. The *Jing Ping Mei* pioneered such a new direction in narration. It does not abandon the traditional regard for telling intriguing stories; it just pays more attention to producing a narrative that constructs a network of formal purposiveness. It ushered in a poetic manner of narration that converts traditional storytelling into a carefully crafted network of verbal representation and weaves together a variety of poetic elements such as imagery, symbolism, allegory, recurrent motifs, patterned emotions, and the projection of self onto narrated scenes, events, and actions. Even the quotidian routines like eating, sleeping, visiting, and sexual intercourse[59] are often remolded into a symbolic vision. As a result of the artistic inspiration, the daily acts of the characters are endowed with feelings that are normally the subject of poetry. The *Hongloumeng* further develops the symbolically suggestive trend. In it, vivid scenes become "moments of vision" that stand out in the flow of narrative; landscapes become features and emotions that transmit surplus meanings; objects enmesh their contours with the fate of characters; and formal representation implicates the author, narrator, and characters in a network of signifying relations imparting endless meanings. In my detailed study of this novel, I will show that it stands as the peak of traditional Chinese fictional art precisely because it is capable of yielding endless surplus meanings in addition to narrating an intriguing story.

CHAPTER FIVE

The Art of the *Jin Ping Mei:* Poetics of Pure Fiction

Scholars of traditional Chinese fiction generally agree that the *Jin Ping Mei* 金瓶梅 is a most important milestone in the transition of Chinese narrative from historicity to fictionality. One of the so-called Four Wonder Books of Ming fiction, it has been viewed as fitting into the same category of fiction to which the *Sanguo yanyi* 三國演義, *Shuihu zhuan* 水滸傳, and *Xiyouji* 西遊記 belong, and as the continuation and culmination of the novelistic tradition perfected by the other three novels. I venture to suggest, however, that except for being written in the same historical period and having some similar thematic concerns and the same *zhanghui* style of fiction writing, the *Jin Ping Mei* does not have much in common with the other three novels in the domains of subject matter, creative impulse, artistic vision, and techniques of self-conscious fictionalization. This chapter will address these differences and examine the original contributions the novel has made to the transition of Chinese fiction to pure fiction and verbal art.

If I argue that the *Jin Ping Mei* does not have a great deal in common with the other three novels, scholars may agree with me about the comparison with the *Romance of the Three Kingdoms* and the *Journey to the West*. As for its comparison with the *Water Margin*, scholars may not be easily persuaded, for the accepted critical opinion is that the *Jin Ping Mei* is heavily indebted to the *Water Margin* and that its difference from the latter is one of degree rather than of kind. While duly recognizing the *Jin Ping Mei*'s indebtedness to its predecessors, I venture to argue that the greatness of the novel precisely lies in its radical break with the novelistic tradition established by the other great masterpieces of Ming fiction in the areas of subject matter, creative impulse, artistic vision, and techniques of writing. It was conceived as a new form of novel and pioneered for the Chinese tradition a conception of fiction that does not rely on artistic extension of history, legends, or extant story lines.

The reader may ask: if you claim that the *Jin Ping Mei* does not have much in common with the other three novels, how can you explain the fact that the novel itself is an elaboration of an episode from the *Shuihu zhuan*? Well, it is true that the *Jin Ping Mei* is indebted to the *Shuihu zhuan*, just as the latter is indebted to the previous legends and stories about outlaws. One may even accept the widely circulated claim that without the *Shuihu zhuan*, the *Jin Ping Mei* could not have come into existence. Nevertheless, there is a fundamental difference. While all the major characters and their actions in the *Shuihu zhuan* had already existed in official history (*Songshi* 宋史), historical stories (*Da Song Xuanhe yishi* 大宋宣和遺事), and Yuan plays,[1] the *Jin Ping Mei* employs a few characters from the *Shuihu zhuan* merely as a point of departure. Quantitatively, the subject matter of the *Jin Ping Mei* differs from that of the *Shuihu zhuan* not just in degree but in kind. Moreover, the novel was conceived as a new form of extended narrative with a novelistic conception that conforms to the modern notion of the novel and even anticipates some postmodern fictional techniques of fiction writing. In this chapter, I am going to explore these issues: Was the novel written with a conception of fiction different from that of its predecessors? If so, what new conception underlies the novel's construction? How did the new conception affect the way of fiction writing? Does the new conception help us construct a Chinese system of fiction theory?

A SELF-CONSCIOUS TURN TO PURE FICTION

In his seminal study of Chinese fiction, Lu Xun considers consciously writing fiction as a hallmark of the maturity of Chinese fiction. His view applies to the novel in the Chinese tradition as well as other traditions. In a history of the English novel, Walter Allen emphasizes conscious making as an important prerequisite for the development of the English novel as an art: "The notion of the novel as a literary form having something to do with art in the sense of being consciously made and shaped to an aesthetic end is quite new. Though there have been few more consummate artists in the novel than Fielding and Jane Austen, for the greater part of its course in England the novel has been naive, the product of men of genius modest enough to believe they were fulfilling their duty as long as they were pleasing an unexacting public."[2] The same may be said of the situation concerning novel writing before and during the sixteenth-century China. The writers of novels other than the *Jin Ping Mei* were largely carrying out their political, moral, and social duties as fiction writers. They were not engaged in consciously writing the novel to create a verbal art.

The author of the *Jin Ping Mei* initiated a self-conscious turn to pure fiction and fictional art. Instead of bringing to its perfection the novelistic tradition stemming from a seemingly slavish commitment to the Confucian notion expressed by the phrase, "to transmit but not to create," the *Jin Ping Mei* marked a major departure from that tradition. This radical break is to be found not only in subject matter but also in the creative conception and poetics of novel making. Though some scholars have noticed the radical departure from the earlier tradition, the emphasis has always been placed on the shift from the artistic extension of historical records (*lishi yanyi*) to the fiction of social manners (*renqing xiaoshuo*), and little attention has been paid to the novel as exemplifying a self-conscious turn to pure fiction with multiple visions. Because of insufficient attention to this new turn, the *Jin Ping Mei* has remained a most misunderstood and most controversial novel in the Chinese tradition. It has been surrounded by a cluster of mysteries concerning its authorship (single or multiple), authorial intention, composition, themes, settings, language, artistic achievement, and critical assessment. The controversy concerning the novel has been going on for several hundred years and is very likely to continue for a long time to come. I venture to suggest that if we do not recognize the novel as being constructed on a novelistic conception totally different from that of its predecessors, we can never hope to find any satisfactory solution to the controversy.

Though the scholarly consensus is that the *Jin Ping Me* continues the novelistic tradition pioneered by the three great Ming novels, few would deny that it evinces some differences from its predecessors. One obvious difference is that it employed a unitary plot to replace what Patrick Hanan describes as a "system of linked plots" widely used in long and extended fictional works like the *Shuihu zhuan* that were commonly thought of as "novels."[3] Another difference, which looks like continuity to the casual reader, is that while previous novels are largely artistic extensions of official records, unofficial histories, legends, and folklore, the *Jin Ping Mei* viewed existent narratives as raw materials and borrowed them selectively to suit the need for constructing a purely fictional account. A more important difference, which often escapes our attention, is that while the major themes of previous novels are fairly easy to summarize, the *Jin Ping Mei* resists attempts to pin it down to a single theme. It is not that previous novels only have single-faceted themes. The previous novels sometimes had more than one theme, but those themes were generally compatible with each other, while the multiple themes of the *Jin Ping Mei* differ from one another to such an extent that they actually contradict and mutually exclude one another. What are these themes? Even that is debated. Several hundred years have already passed and there has been no consensus on the perceived general vision of the novel. Before modern times, scholars said it was a political allegory, a moral tract, an individual's attempt to seek revenge on a family foe, a book on filial piety 苦孝說, a book meant to wreak pent-up emotions, a book that incriminates wealth and sex, a work of pornography, and so forth. On top of these premodern views, modern scholars have added a few more new views: a novel of exposé, a novel of social manners, a novel with an antitraditional tendency, a novel on the rise of the bourgeoisie, a novel about the awakening of individualistic consciousness, a book of hedonism, and so on.[4] And these are only some of the major views of the novel. One can say that these perceived themes are but the different results of different interpretations by different readers, but the fact remains that nothing of the sort occurred with the reading of the other three novels.

As for the authorship, its artistic achievement, and its impact upon the development of the Chinese novel, opinions differ even more drastically. Whereas more and more scholars have accepted the opinion that the novel was created by a single author with considerable planning and great care for artistry, some scholars insist that it is the result of a collective authorship, because it exhibits glaring inconsistencies and uses language borrowed from sources spanning several dynasties from the Song through the Yuan to the Ming. While from the very beginning some scholars had attributed the novel to the hand of a great literatus, many others were of the opinion that the novel was composed by a person of inferior education. So far, the number of possible authors suggested by scholars over the world has already exceeded thirty.[5] As for the achievement of the novel, critical evaluations are so polarized that acclaim and detraction often totally contradict one another. Those who think highly of it extol it to the sky; those who think lowly of it trample it to the ground.[6] In a word, no other literary work has aroused such polarized views as the *Jin Ping Mei*.

It is no wonder that a novice of the *Jin Ping Mei* can feel overwhelmed by the conflicting and mutually exclusive views of the extant scholarship. What is even more disconcerting is that few of the expressed opinions are easily dismissible; most of them are based on solid research or sensitive readings. Evidently, the difference in opinion is not just a question of difference in aesthetic tastes, nor even of difference in methods of reading. Its root cause must have to do with the inner structure of the novel itself. The novel apparently embodies an entirely new conception of fiction making that is based on a remarkably pluralistic creative vision. It is on these grounds that I claim that the novel marked a self-conscious turn not only to pure fiction but also to open fiction.

So the *Jin Ping Mei* was conceived as a new form of novel that was not animated by a single ideological vision or constructed according to a single narrative form, and an exploration of this new conception and creative vision may put us in a position to come to terms with the conflicting and contradictory readings of the novel and locate conceptual insights that contribute to the Chinese theory of fiction. I would like to examine the novel's conception of fiction in relation to traditional commentarial work and focus on how the new conception was carried out in the actual making of the novel. In the process of my inquiry into its making, I will attempt to construct a poetics of writing and reading in terms of contemporary theories of narrative and explore its significance for the making of pure fiction in the Chinese tradition.

A NOVELISTIC CONCEPTION OF WEAVING

"With the possible exception of the *Tale of Genji* (1010) and *Don Quixote* (1615)," notes David Roy, "there is no earlier work of prose fiction of equal sophistication in world literature."[7] I agree with some Chinese scholars on their assessment of the novel: "Whether one examines the novel by placing it on the abscissas of the Chinese novels of manners or explores it by placing it on the ordinates of novels of similar subject matter in the worldwide context, it will not lose its status as a brilliant masterpiece."[8] I also agree with those scholars that because of narrow, outmoded, and poorly constructed methodologies of reading and interpretation, we have failed to do full justice to the art of this unconventional masterpiece, which came into being ahead of its time in aesthetic consciousness and writing techniques.

Readers familiar with Chinese erotic narrative literature may regard the *Jin Ping Mei* as the culmination of this narrative tradition, but even a casual comparison with representative erotic fictional works will reveal their differences. The *Jin Ping Mei* shares with other erotic narratives the narration of erotic themes, but it differs from them in situating erotic themes in the large context of human desires in general and weaving different kinds of desires into a network of interpretive spaces coordinated by a self-consciously constructed poetics of writing. An overemphasis on its erotic themes obscures the fact that the novel is a specimen of verbal art carefully crafted by an extraordinary mind with an innovative artistic vision. I suggest that the novel is a brocade of human desires, and its principle of composition is a poetics of weaving. It is not just a network of characters, scenes, events, incidents; in its totality of subject matter and artistic form, it is a woven fabric of human desires couched in linguistic signifiers, mapped with a self-adjusting design that intends to make the novel appealing to different tastes and amenable to different interpretations.

In commenting on the *Shuihu zhuan*, the predecessor of the *Jin Ping Mei*, Jin Shengtan made a famous remark, which has often been quoted as a differentiation between history and fiction. He views history like the *Shiji* as a discourse in which "words are used to carry events [*yiwen yunshi*]," while fiction like the *Shuihu zhuan* is a discourse in which "events are produced from the words [*yinwen shengshi*]."[9] The *Shuihu zhuan* is certainly not a historical novel, nor is it a novel of pure fiction. It is a hybrid, a novel of transition. Because of its heavy indebtedness to historical records and previously existent sources, much of its narrative still follows the principle of "using words to carry events" and is the result of a second-order imitation. The *Shuihu zhuan* is therefore not entirely a work of pure fiction. The *Jin Ping Mei*, despite its borrowed opening from the *Shuihu zhuan*, is a work of pure fiction, because it follows the principle of "generating events out of words." As I will show, the narrative of the *Jin Ping Mei* was almost literally produced out of the words in the borrowed episode from the *Shuihu zhuan*.

The fundamental difference of the novel from its predecessors lies in a new conception of fiction executed through innovative techniques of writing. This conception is based on a poetics of fiction making that is not sustained on the time-honored mode of historical narration, but on a mode of fiction making very close to the modern conception of creative writing as an act of weaving. Structurally, the novel is constructed on a principle of fiction making that may be called "spider's weaving." The act of weaving consists of two inter-related aspects: the weaving of raw materials gleaned from different sources and the weaving of signifiers in the novel's language. As early as the late Ming, the anonymous commentator who left comments on the Chongzhen edition of the novel praised it as a complex network of narration (*xu de cuzong bianhua* 敘得錯綜變化) with wonderful needlework (*hao zhenxian* 好針線).[10] But it was Zhang Zhupo 張竹坡 (1670–98), one of the most brilliant fiction commentators in traditional China, who, after a systematic study of this novel, first identified its characteristic features of weaving and adopted a systematic approach to its weaving conception. In no uncertain terms, he declared it to be a piece of intri-cately woven fabric: "a volume of a thousand stitches and ten thousand threads 一部千針萬線 ."[11]

In the making of any extended narrative, one cannot dispense with these prerequisites: a creative vision, raw narrative details, and plot arrangement. Scholars of fiction often compare the writing of a novel to the construction of an architectural edifice: creative vision is the style for the building that one wants to construct. Plot arrangement is the blueprint for a certain style of building. Narrative details such as characters, setting, scenes, and episodes are the building materials, its bricks, stones, timber, and mortar.[12] But the analogy is valid only up to a point, because the architectural model has a mechanical aspect and cannot fully capture the flow of creative thought that gives shape to a narrative discourse. The creative imagination is a stream of consciousness. It does not obey a rigid preplanned model and often changes course due to free association. The architectural model of a novel's construction is very effective for viewing a completed novel, but is incapable of completely explaining the process of a novel's making. Perhaps for this reason, Chinese narrative theory has another model, which is given a more prominent place. The favorite model is that of weaving. Zhang Zhupo adopts both models of analogy for the structure of the *Jin Ping Mei*, but he prefers the model of weaving and views the novel as the outcome of an elaborate process of weaving. Even in using an architectural model, his emphasis is on the seamless interconnections of ele-ments, as can be seen from this statement: "Therefore, to compose a writing is like building a house. The writer must join all the tenons and mortises of beams and columns so closely that not a single seam is visible. In reading a writer's writings, however, one must act as though one were dismantling a house, mak-ing every single tenon of a beam or column appear before one's eyes."[13]

In the preface to the Chinese version of *The Four Masterworks of the Ming Novel*, Andrew Plaks points out a phenomenon in the studies of Ming-Qing fiction in China: traditional commentarial work has been primarily used for research into authorship, editions, and dating of the works concerned. Only in a secondary way has it been put to use in critically studying those works.[14] In his preface to the English edition, he expresses the opinion that in spite of their shortcomings, traditional commentaries can still compare favorably with modern scholars' studies in critical achievement.[15] His opinion is especially sound concerning Zhang Zhupo. Zhang Zhupo's commentarial work on the *Jin Ping Mei* is perhaps the most comprehensive and systematic study of the novel before modern times. Its degree of systematicness is rare even among modern commentaries. It has *zonglun* (general treatises) that set out its guiding theory; *huiping* (chapter comments), which are elucidations of the general theory through detailed analysis; *jiapi* (interlinear comments); and *meipi* (comments in the upper margins). In the exploration of the novel's artistry, few studies have surpassed it in insights. As a treatise on narrative theories, Zhang's commentary is remarkably modern and discerning. Compared with the systematic and theoretical rigor of Zhang's commentary, modern studies of narrative theories concerning the novel look somewhat pale.

Since David Roy first called our attention in the mid-1970s to the significance of Zhang Zhupo's commentary for the understanding of the novel and Chinese narrative,[16] a great deal of critical work has been done in relating Zhang's commentary to the *Jin Ping Mei* in particular and to Chinese narrative in general. But not much conceptual work has been done in relating Zhang's commentary beyond the novel itself to the theoretical conception of fiction making and narratology in spite of Roy's discerning suggestion that Zhang's "How to Read the *Jin Ping Mei*" is "the closest thing . . . in the Chinese language to a poetics of the novel."[17] In this regard, Ye Lang's study of Zhang Zhupo's narrative aesthetics is perhaps the most outstanding.[18] Ye Lang is indebted to Zhang Zhupo in many ways, from brilliant critical insights concealed amid a welter of details to a poetics of the novel, the embryonic form of which had already taken shape in Zhang's complete commentarial work. Zhang's commentary on the *Jin Ping Mei* is a rich lode of gold that has not yet been fully mined, especially with regard to the theoretical making of the novel. Through a study of Zhang's commentarial work in relation to modern narrative theories as well as the details of the novel, I will attempt to construct a poetics of making that not only sheds light on the composition of the *Jin Ping Mei* but also provides food for thought for the making of fiction in general.

CREATIVE IMPULSE AND MOTIVATION FOR FICTION MAKING

For an inquiry into the making of any fiction, we cannot ignore the creative impulse or motivation lying behind the making. The motivation to write a novel is commonly known as authorial intention. With regard to the *Jin Ping Mei*, there are a number of supposed authorial intentions: (1) the writing of the novel was motivated by a desire to wreak vengeance in a family feud; (2) a scholar who had a lot of time on his hands observed his master's decadent life and wrote this novel to express his disapproval; (3) the novel was written by someone with the intention to satirize the decadence of the time.[19] They might have been among the original motives, but modern theories on authorial intention have convincingly argued that the pretextual intention is unreliable and misleading, and cannot help us come to a better idea of how the novel was made. While it is harmless to take note of the transmitted pretextual intentions, we must focus on the in-text intention of the author. By "in-text intention of the author," I mean a mental complex that comprises the author's motivation for writing, the conscious act of shaping the properties of the text for certain intended purposes, and the unconscious creative impulses and fantasies buried in the materiality of the text. In other words, I conceive of the in-text intention as a creative totality that incorporates what the author had in mind at the moment of the creative act, embodied in the work, supported by transmitted pre-textual intentions, and verifiable by textual evidence.

In Xinxin Zi's 欣欣子 preface to the *Jin Ping Mei* 金瓶梅詞話序, there is a statement that looks like a statement of a pretextual intention, but it partially reveals the in-text intention of the author. In the preface, Xinxin Zi claims to be a friend of the author and to know his intention. He has either been suspected of being the real author or been dismissed as a mouthpiece for the novel's publisher. Whoever he might have been, his statement nevertheless throws some light on the in-text intention of the author:

> A person has seven dispositions, of which chronic depression is the worst. People of high intelligence were born with the ability to disperse it in the way fog is dispersed and ice broken. It is therefore unnecessary to talk about them. People with somewhat less intelligence also know how to disperse it by themselves through logical reasoning, thereby freeing themselves from its nuisance. People with low intelligence neither know how to expel it from their bosom unaided, nor have poetry, books, the Dao, and things of beauty for diversion. As a result, few of them can avoid falling sick because of it. With this in mind, my friend, the Scoffing Scholar, composed this novel with all the knowledge he has accumulated in his life. It consists of a hundred chapters. It was written in fresh and marvelous language and has enjoyed great popularity. . . . It is hoped that it may enable readers to enjoy a good laugh and to forget their worries.[20]

Xinxin Zi may be said to be an understanding friend of the author (though many scholars have doubts about his true identity), for he seems to have really grasped the intention of the author, which is the making of fiction to cater to ordinary folk's need for entertainment. In his exploration of the relationship between the reading public and the rise of the English novel, Ian Watt, the noted scholar on the rise of fiction in England, points out an accepted opinion: "The novel was widely regarded as a typical example of the debased kind of writing by which the booksellers pandered to the reading public."[21] All fiction serves two basic functions: didacticism and entertainment. A comparison of the *Jin Ping Mei* with the other great novels shows that there is a shift in emphasis on the two basic functions in the development of novels through the Ming. In the other three great novels, didacticism is seldom as explicitly emphasized as it is in the *Jin Ping Mei*, but it seeps through the pages. By contrast, in the *Jin Ping Mei*, although didacticism is constantly harped on throughout the novel, it seems to be rendered hollow because of the implicit motive for entertainment. Indeed, taking the novel as a whole, the reader often gets the impression that the didacticism is nothing but lip service paid by the author to avoid the odium of promoting moral depravity. The shift in emphasis in the *Jin Ping Mei* not only decided the different nature of this novel, but also had considerable impact on the way it was written.

The shift in emphasis may be said to have been one of the major causes for the rise of fictionality in the Chinese tradition. For the purpose of entertainment, nothing excels the discharge of emotional pressures. To provide emotional release through literature, nothing excels writings that do away with sexual inhibition. To loosen the grip of moral inhibition, nothing excels a direct confrontation with human sexuality. Literary theories and practices in China and the West have suggested that in the confrontation with human sexuality lies the creative impulse for pure fiction. In her work on the origin of the novel, the French scholar Marthe Robert argues that to trace the origin of fiction, one needs to think about the creative impulse in the fiction writer. Pressured by the creative urge, the writer must turn to fiction for relief.[22] Her argument fits exactly the creative mentality as described by Xinxin Zi, who claimed to have known intimately the creative impulse of the author of the *Jin Ping Mei.*

Robert also suggests that the "family romance" can be regarded as the fountainhead of fictional inspiration, and fiction itself is only the extension of the writer's unconscious wishes. Whether it is popular or highbrow, old or new, classical or modern, fiction comes from personal folklore, which is the set of infantile complexes and fantasies created by family life, the so-called family romance.[23] As an archetype for fiction, "the Romance will not reach a more lively stage until sexuality appears on the scene with notions of *otherness*."[24] Sexuality plays an important role not only in creating fiction but also in reading fiction. As the noted literary theorist Norman Holland points out, the so-called "primal scene fantasies," which grow out of an intense curiosity about sex and sexuality, are responsible for a child's later interest in watching drama and other performances.[25] Harold Bloom, another literary theorist, further links the primal scene with fantastic fiction.[26] On the basis of these theoretical explorations, I have argued in an essay that conscious and unconscious curiosity about sex and sexuality underlies not only the desire to read fiction but also the impulse for creating fiction.[27] The explosive interest in sex and sexuality in seventeenth-century Ming fiction and the appearance of the *Jin Ping Mei* seems to support this argument. Earlier erotic narratives may also lend support to this suggestion,

Since I have mentioned that the confrontation with human sexuality provided inspiration for the rise of pure fiction, a reader familiar with traditional Chinese fiction may ask: Why do the erotic narratives before the *Jin Ping Mei* not qualify as "pure fiction"? For example, in Xinxin Zi's preface he mentioned several earlier erotic narratives, one of which, *Ruyijun zhuan* 如意君傳 (*The Story of Mr. Delightful*), is extant. My answer is very simple: *The Story of Mr. Delightful* was based on an unofficially transmitted account of Wu Zetian's (r. 684–704) erotic life and has little description of family life that amounts to a "family romance." Nevertheless, those earlier erotic narratives should be considered as the beginning of the change toward a new form of fiction making, for they displayed an inchoate shift of Chinese fiction from historicity to fictionality, from didacticism to entertainment, and from the external approach to grave matters of social life to the internal approach to quotidian issues of family life and personal desires.

From a more narrowly focused perspective, Tony Tanner highlights a commonly observed phenomenon in the Western tradition: that nineteenth-century European novels that have been canonized as "great" and felt to be profound in exploring the spirit of their age center on adultery.[28] As far as novelistic form is concerned, he suggests: "The novel, in its origin, might almost be said to be a transgressive mode, inasmuch as it seemed to break, or mix, or adulterate the existing genre-expectations of the time."[29] His observations are quite pertinent to the *Jin Ping Mei*. Before the appearance of the *Jin Ping Mei*, there were quite a few long narratives, but none of them is as preoccupied with adultery, sexuality, family life, and diverse literary genres as the *Jin Ping Mei*. I, therefore, suggest that *it is not by mere accident that the author of the* Jin Ping Mei *should have chosen from the* Shuihu zhuan *an episode dealing with family life and adultery as the basis for the plot development and full representation of a long novel.*

The author of the *Jin Ping Mei* was equipped with the right prerequisites and poised at the right time to embark on the route to a new form of novel making that completely turned its back on history. He had the creative impulse for entertainment, was free from psychological inhibition, and was aware of the limitless formal capacity of the novel. But compared with his predecessors, while he was free in many ways, he was also at a disadvantage in the actual making of the novel. For his predecessors who wrote historical novels, almost everything was ready at hand: subject matter, plot, characters, and even structuring principles. But for the author of the *Jin Ping Mei*, everything had to be found by himself. What was ready at his service was only his creative impulse for writing something both didactic and entertaining, plus his knowledge of some existent fictional writings. All he could do was to follow his creative impulse and the outcome was the emergence of a novel of pure fictionality, which is open to different interpretations. Among the multiple interpretations, each is capable of capturing a facet or facets of the novel, but none of them is capable of capturing the totality of the novel. This is because the author was engaged in writing a work that is also an open fiction.

In his characterization of Freud's theory of dream formation, Terry Eagleton employs an interesting analogy: "[T]he unconscious has the admirable resourcefulness of a lazy, ill-supplied chef, who slings together the most diverse ingredients into a cobbled-together stew, substituting one spice for another which he is out of, making do with whatever has arrived in the market that morning as a dream will draw opportunistically on the 'day's residues,' mixing in events which took place during the day or sensations felt during sleep with images drawn deep from our childhood."[30] The author of the *Jin Ping Mei* may give the reader the impression of also being such a chef. Scholars have shown that the work incorporates a diverse variety of source materials gleaned from widely different historical periods, literary genres, and written records.[31] Whoever the author may have been, however, he was by no means lazy; nor was he engaged in an unconscious making of fiction in the way the unconscious works in the creation of dreams. Unlike the unconscious in dreams, he consciously makes use of free association, the basic mode of creation in the formation of dream contents, to combine materials gleaned from different sources into a dazzling embroidery of words.

There is a Chinese saying: "One cannot make a piece of embroidery out of gunnysack." Just as an embroiderer needs a piece of quality cloth to serve as the basis for a piece of embroidery, the author of the *Jin Ping Mei* was in need of a subject matter for his verbal embroidery. He found in the *Shuihu zhuan* the primary source for his verbal embroidery. In choosing a long episode from an existent novel as the basis for his own fiction making, the author of the *Jin Ping Mei* departed radically from the previous mode of novel writing and created a new model of writing, which may be called the "weaving of signifiers into extended narrative discourse." The weaving of signifiers may be a most appropriate model for the composition of the novel. It is capable of explaining the rationale of the novel's construction.

To probe the poetics of weaving, I wish, first of all, to deal with the source materials that went into the making of the novel. Like a master rug weaver, the author borrowed ready-made materials from previous writing on a massive scale. As he wove along, he invented his own yarn. By weaving the ready-made fibers and his own yarn into desired patterns, he succeeded in creating a superb tapestry with many interlocking figures and patterns. Some scholars have viewed the author's borrowing in quite a negative light and criticized the incorporation of songs, lyrics, quotations from existent poetry, drama, and fiction as signs of the author's inability to maintain a consistent tone.[32] In their most positive opinion, they maintain that the author had turned what is trash into a work of miraculous art. It seems to them that the borrowing was done as a random act to make up for the lack of ideas and materials.[33] Nothing could be further from the actual process of making. The borrowing was done deliberately to serve the purpose of weaving a verbal fabric. If the borrowed material did not suit the purpose well, the author would make alterations. The borrowed episode from the *Shuihu zhuan* was tailored in this manner. A collation with the original material reveals that the reworked material in the *Jin Ping Mei* is not only much longer but also much more complicated in details.

The alterations of, and additions to, the old materials were made to suit the authorial purpose of making a verbal fabric.

The author's use of the episode from the *Shuihu zhuan* is an astute choice that reveals his vision for pure fiction, for the ingredients of family romance and human sexuality in it were most concentrated. A brief survey of the other three great novels tells us that no other episode in the previous novels could match the chosen episode in vivid description of familial conflicts, man-woman relationships, seduction, and adultery. By intuition and calculated observation, the author of the *Jin Ping Mei* sensed in the borrowed material the potential for developing an enthralling narrative plot. We know that the borrowed episode largely centers on a story of seduction. In the story, Old Woman Wang plays a significant role. In fact, she could be compared to the director of a drama, having drawn up a detailed script of how the seduction is to be conducted. Everything in the real seduction scene goes ahead as smoothly as she has plotted. If Old Woman Wang's plotting of the seduction is a story leading to another story, the author of the *Jin Ping Mei* adds another episode of seduction to increase the dose of family romance and sexuality. Zhang Dahu, the wealthy old man who attempted to seduce Jinlian, is only a pale figure briefly mentioned in the *Shuihu zhuan*. But in the *Jin Ping Mei*, he becomes a fully portrayed character. He seduces Jinlian, angers his wife, marries Jinlian off to Wu Da, and continues to have illicit relations with her. Finally, he dies of sexual indulgence. His story may be said to anticipate the seduction of Jinlian by Ximen and the latter's eventual demise at her hand. For the same purpose of fuller portrayal, the author makes some changes to the character of Wu Da. He is portrayed with more negative features: shorter in stature, uglier in appearance, and more hapless in life. The more negative portrayal contrasts with the beauty and accomplishment of Jinlian, thus enhancing their incompatibility and paving the way for her attempted seduction of Wu Song and her own seduction by Ximen.

The rewriting of the seduction episode from the *Shuihu zhuan* provides the author with a good start for the making of pure fiction, but on this start alone it is impossible to weave a novel of one hundred chapters. The author has to bring his own invention to the weaving of the narrative discourse. In the course of weaving, he has two major kinds of raw materials for his narrative threads: sex and wealth, the root causes of human desire. Zhang Zhupo makes this apt comment:

> The reader should pay attention to where the author displays superb writing skills and where he makes methodical arrangements. Where are these places? Look at how he develops a great topic with two persons. One of them wants to sell sex; the other wants to steal wealth. This is where methodical arrangements are made and where the author's writing brush is as big as a beam.[34]

Sex and wealth are the two dominant elements in the novel. They form the two pivotal points around which the major characters revolve. Indeed, an overview of the novel tells us that each of the characters lives and dies by one or the other of the two elements. For subject matter, the two elements serve as the material for the warp and woof in the author's weaving efforts. The interaction and interlocking of the warp and woof on the basis of the *Shuihu zhuan* episode gave substance to the result of the weaving and formed the canvas of the verbal embroidery.

THE INVENTION OF CHARACTERS AND PLOT

In order for the novel to tell an enthralling story, it must be populated by characters. In previous novels, the characters were provided by official history, personal biographies, anecdotes, legends, and so on. The author of the *Jin Ping Mei*, as I have mentioned, does not have these readily available resources. So he had to invent his own cast of characters. His principle of invention was a self-generating principle based on free association and conscious selection in terms of naming. In the borrowed episode, some major characters are already provided: Ximen Qing, Pan Jinlian, Wu Da, Wu Song, Old Woman Wang, and others. From these existent characters the author conjures up a whole cast of more than one hundred characters for his extended narrative.

Zhang Zhupo wrote an interesting discourse, "Yuyi shuo" (A Discourse on Implied Meanings). It is an important commentary. It is, in fact, the guiding theory for his miscellaneous commentaries. But so far scholars have not taken it seriously. While some scholars have acknowledged a minor relevance of this allegorical theory to the novel, the general opinion either deems it "a low form of art"[35] or dismisses it as an absurd way of interpretation that reads too much into the novel.[36] No one seems to have realized that Zhang Zhupo's discourse at least touches upon the writing principles underlying the novel and has the potential to be developed into a mode of writing or a method of reading. The theory of reading may be called "paronomastic reading," the rationale of which I will elaborate in the analysis of the novel. But as I understand it, Zhang Zhupo himself does not recognize it as a way of reading. On the contrary, he considers it a way of novel writing, a theory of composition that underlies the making of the novel. As a theory of writing, it may not always fit the *Jin Ping Mei*. Zhang Zhupo's "allegorical theory" constitutes a mode of writing that one may term "intertextual dissemination," a notion that conceives of reading as a process of unlimited semiosis, and of the text as tissue, "hyphology" or a spider's weaving.[37] It is also a notion of the necessary intertexuality of all discourse as each text is an interweaving or "textile of signifiers" whose signifieds are by definition intertextually determined by other discourses.[38] To help illuminate the relation of "intertextual dissemination" to Zhang Zhupo's theory, I wish to point out that Zhang's advocated mode of writing also conceives of a text as a tissue, or a spider's web, that builds on the materiality of discourse: its sound, shape, sense, and constituent principles, and induces a form of reading that treats a text as an interweaving or "textile of signifiers" whose signifieds are intertextually determined by other signifiers. Zhang Zhupo's discourse opens with these lines:

> Fiction is allegory. It invents a character and makes up an event. Although what it narrates is an account of wind and shadows, it must conjure up rocks as though they were lying on a mountain and stir up waves as though they were borrowed from the sea. The *Jin Ping Mei* is a novel with no fewer than a hundred named characters. If one wishes to explore their origins and implications, over half of them belong to allegory. The author derived many of them from objects and entrusted them with representing situations so that he was able to compose this novel of a hundred chapters full of twists and turns.[39]

Here, by emphasizing that events and characters are linguistically generated, Zhang is not simply reiterating the traditional Chinese writing principle of "creating events out of writing 因文生事"; he has located a variant principle of "creating events out of names 因名生事." What he has discovered is a modern principle of fiction writing that unequivocally stresses the fictionality of *xiaoshuo* and the causality of fictionality. He views the *Jin Ping Mei* as an allegory that evolves out of the interconnection between the naming of characters and the development of plot. Then he gives a full account of how the naming of characters is related to the making of the novel.

Zhang's theory of allegorical naming is in fact an extension on a massive scale of the accepted view with regard to the naming of the novel. At the time the manuscript of the novel started to circulate, scholars agreed that *Jin Ping Mei* is a composite title consisting of the Chinese characters from each of the three major female protagonists. Yuan Zhongdao (1570–1624) wrote in 1614: "The so-called 'Jin' refers to Jinlian; 'Ping' refers to Li Ping'er; 'Mei' refers to the maid, Chunmei."[40] What is innovative in Zhang's theory is that he views the major plot of the whole novel as growing out of an intricate network of names. In his opinion, all the characters were derived from the already available characters in the borrowed *Shuihu zhuan* episode. Li Ping'er comes into being as a result of Ximen Qing's name: "Li Ping'er's name means that Ximen Qing, because of his indulgence in gratifying his carnal desires and doing evil deeds, has withered his body and exhausted his life blood as completely as a vase is emptied of its content. For this special meaning, Li Ping'er was so named." A vase is for storing flowers. So Li Ping'er's husband gets his surname "Hua 花." Since he is a character invented to keep the narrative going, he gets the name Zixu 子虛 (fictitiousness). Ping'er's nurse Ruyi 如意 who becomes her surrogate, comes into the plot and gets her name because of the same rationale: "Ruyi is the surrogate Ping'er after the latter's death. Her maiden name is Xiong (bear) and she has the married surname Zhang. What is valuable in a bear is its gallbladder. This Ruyi is meant to be a bladderlike inner container of a vase." Chunmei 春梅, the other female protagonist, also came into the plot because of Ping'er: "With a plum flower in a vase, the spring scene is nearly over. While the emptying of the vase content symbolizes an invisible withering of [Ximen's] bone marrow, the plum flower in the vase suggests another not-too-distant decaying and decline." If the name of Ximen Qing gives rise to a series of characters, Pan Jinlian's name also gives rise to a fair share. Chen Jingji 陳敬濟, the other male protagonist (who is essentially Ximen Qing's reincarnation), comes out of Jinlian's name: "*Lian* (lotus) and *Ji* (water chestnut) belong to the same category. *Chen* means 'old' and decaying. *Jing* is a homophone for the stem of a plant. That both the lotus and water chestnut have decaying stems is suggestive of a bad end for Jinlian. Therefore, [in the novel,] Jinlian is ruined by Jingji." Some other characters enter the plot as a result of the associations with Jinlian's name. Lotus grows in a pond, its flower above water and its root buried in mud. This image gives rise to a series of characters. The names of Chen Jingji's father, Chen Hong 陳洪 (puns with 陳紅 displaying the red), and Xia Longxi 夏龍溪 (dragon stream in the summer) both hint at Jinlian's situation during her ascendecy. A few other characters are related to Jinlian but hint at her in decline: Shui (water) Xiucai 水秀才, Wen (warm) Xiucai 溫秀才, Ni (mud) Xiucai 倪秀才, and Wang Chao'er (lost to the tide) 王(亡)潮兒. Still more characters are associated with Jinlian: Song Huilian 宋蕙蓮, Wang Liu'er 王六兒, and Wang Jing 王經. Song Huilian is a rival with Jinlian, since they are two kinds of lotus. Wang Liu'er puns with Huang Lu'er 黃蘆兒 (yellow reed). Wang Jing puns with Huang Lujing 黃蘆莖 (yellow reed stem). "Both *lu* reed and *di* reed serve as a foil to the lotus. For this reason, it may be said that these two characters were created to complement Jinlian."[41]

In his commentary, Zhang Zhupo elaborates on the naming of practically all the major characters who play a role in the development of the novel. It is unnecessary to give an exhaustive account of his elaborate scheme. What needs some further elaboration is that in Zhang Zhupo's opinion, the naming association not only supplies new characters for the plot development but also provides inspiration for details of the plot. For example, Ximen's proper wife is called Yueniang (Moon Lady), as she was born during the mid-autumn festival. She is the head of the house and presides over all the other ladies, because the moon shines on all the flowers. The *gui* (sweet osmanthus) flower 桂花 is in full bloom in mid autumn; so the Moon Lady has an adopted daughter called Gui'er 桂兒. The moon follows a cycle of waxing and waning; so the Moon Lady has times of happiness and times of sorrow. Since the Moon Lady was born in mid autumn, she has a maidservant called Zhongqiu 中秋 (Mid Autumn). She has another maid called Xiaoyu (Little Jade). "Xiaoyu is the legendary rabbit in the moon. Both she and Zhongqiu are at Yueniang's service."[42] According to legend, when the moon is full, the rabbit in the moon has fully grown; a corresponding event is that Xiaoyu (Little Jade) the maidservant gets married. Her marriage is a forced one, because she has been seduced by Ximen's male servant Dai'an. The seduction is an act of "stealing jade 竊玉." The Moon Lady is forced to arrange the marriage at her own expense and pay for it both literally and figuratively. All this follows the rationale that after the moon becomes full, it starts to wane.

Another male servant, Ping'an, bearing a grudge against the Moon Lady for not giving him the same favor, steals some jewelry from the Ximen family's pawnshop. Among the stolen goods there is a gilded crescent. Ping'an goes to hide himself at a place called Nanwazi (Southern Tile). Zhang Zhupo believes that this incident is an imaginative reenactment of the waning of the moon: "No sooner had Xiaoyu gotten married at the time of the full moon at mid-Autumn than Ping'an stole a golden crescent. Scarcely had he hidden at the Southern Tile for a whole night when the moon like a golden crescent shone upon the Southern tile." Ping'an's crime is judged by the newly promoted patrol inspector Wu Dian'en 吳典恩, who used to be Ximen's butler and came to get an official appointment through his connection with Ximen. The patrol inspector's name means "this person does not repay a single jot for the favor he has received." The implications of his name lead to a chain of plot development. He forces Ping'an to testify falsely that the Moon Lady arranged for Dai'an to marry Xiaoyu because the Moon Lady herself had had an illicit affair with the male servant. But for Chunmei's intervention, the Moon Lady would have met with serious trouble. "An inquiry into whether the moon has waxed or waned should be directed to the plum. Therefore, no sooner had the Moon Lady asked Chunmei for help than Wu Dian'en got humiliated." Why would Chunmei be willing to intercede for the Moon Lady, who did not treat her favorably when she was still a maid in the Ximen household? "The moon is the master of plum flowers. So, the Moon Lady maintains a relationship with Chunmei."[43]

Towards the end of the novel, the Moon Lady has a dream in which she and her entourage including Xiaoyu, are all killed by Ximen's erstwhile friend Yun Lishou 雲裏守. Zhang Zhupo believes that this dream is a representation of the idea that the moon is shrouded by clouds and the moon rabbit disappears altogether. "The moon must be hidden by clouds. Therefore, the dream of Yun Lishou is invented."[44] Zhang Zhupo's scheme is so elaborate that, as we have seen, he takes the trouble to link the qualities associated with a character's name to his/her personality, behavior, and outcome in the novel. For example, he goes so far as to relate the sexual habits of Ping'er and Ruyi to their symbolism: "Li Ping'er loves having sex from behind; Ruyi prefers to suck Ximen's male organ—their sexual preferences are associated with the characteristic features of a vase and its inner container."[45]

Zhang Zhupo is so dedicated to his idea of how the novel was consciously made that his entire commentary on the *Jin Ping Mei* is guided by this theory. We as readers, of course, cannot buy his scheme lock, stock, and barrel. But one may ask: To what extent does Zhang Zhupo's scheme of naming conform to the actual situation in the novel? And more importantly, how does his scheme help us better understand the novel? And what benefit can we reap from Zhang Zhupo's scheme in our attempt to construct a poetics of making or reading?

Well, Zhang Zhupo's scheme certainly captures a significant aspect of the novel's poetics of making. A careful reader of the novel would not dispute the following stated in Zhang's discourse:

There are even cases in which a single event gives rise to a number of characters. In this sort of situation, several named characters share a similar allegorical meaning. For instance, Che Dan (talking nonsense), Guan Shikuan (meddling in others' business), You Shou (idling about), Hao Xian (loafing around)—these four characters share one allegorical meaning. For another example, Li Zhi (plum stem) and Huang Si (yellow the fourth) refer to the withering yellowness of the plum flower and plum fruit, which hints at a late spring scene. These two characters share one allegorical meaning. For still another example, before the episode in which Ximen had a sexual battle in the bathtub, three characters were mentioned: Nie Lianghu (holding between the fingers two lakes), Shang Xiaotang (going into the tiny pond), Wang Beiyan (going to the northern bank)—the three characters share one allegorical meaning. For one more example, An Zhen (indulging in pillow comfort) and Song Qiaonian (ruining one's old age) allude to the damage done to the body by indulgence in sex. The two characters' names share one allegorical meaning. There are also situations in which a character begets a series of characters' names: Ying Bojue (inveterate sponger), style name Guanghou (empty throat); Xie Xida (thanks for giving me favors), style name Zichun (paying lip service); Zhu Shinian (taking abode for ten years); Sun Tianhua (heavenly talk), style name Boxiu (feeling no embarrassment); Chang Shijie (habitual borrower); Bu Zhidao (know-nothing); Wu Dian'en (utterly devoid of gratitude); Yun Lishou (a hand inside clouds), style name Feiqu (fly away); Bai Laiguang (merely come to scrounge), style name Guangdang (loiterer); Ben Dichuan (gossipmonger); Fu Zixin (betraying one's own heart); Gan Chushen (not related by blood); Han Daoguo (doing mischief). All these characters get their names because of Ximen's improper behavior.[46]

Some scholars may say that this use of allegorical names is only a word game and may be considered at most a low form of artistry. I venture to argue that wordplay on names is used on such a massive scale that it constitutes a creative principle for pure fiction making. In chapter 30 of the novel, a wordplay on a name permits us to have a glimpse of how this principle works. Ximen sends his servants with lavish birthday gifts to see the corrupt prime minister Cai Jing 蔡京 (1046–1126) in the capital. Because of the lavish birthday gifts, Cai Jing wants to give Ximen something in return. He asks whether Ximen has any official appointment. When he receives a negative reply, he decides to give Ximen a government appointment. According to the narrative, Ximen is to fill a position vacated by an official called He Jin 賀金. The name of this official is made up of two characters that mean "congratulatory money." A reader does not need much pondering to see the connection between the official's name and the bribes submitted by Ximen. In sending the prime minister lavish birthday gifts, Ximen has spent a good deal of money. There is a big hole in his amassed wealth. That hole has to be filled by a government appointment that can earn for Ximen wealth several times the birthday gifts. Of course, the naming of the character could have taken place afterward. The plotline of this episode might have been conceived first, and the character later named as an implied critical comment. Whichever is the case, this episode paves the way for the narrative account of Ximen's corrupt career as an official.

In his study of the novel, Plaks follows one of Zhang Zhupo's ideas and gives a detailed analysis of how the name of Pan Jinlian gives rise to Song Huilian (who used to have the same given name, Jinlian), how the same name determines their rivalry, how the word *jinlian* 金蓮 relates to bound feet and women's shoes, and how a series of episodes center around the loss and recovery of Pan Jinlian's shoes.[47] Plaks's critical analysis confirms the correctness of Zhang Zhupo's insight: several characters, incidents, episodes appear in the novel because of the author's imaginative use of the word *jinlian*.[48] Moreover, it demonstrates beyond doubt that the creative use of naming is not just a word game; it is a significant creative principle for pure fiction making.

Having discussed Zhang Zhupo's theory of allegory at considerable length, let me summarize its significance for the making of the novel. As I have demonstrated, the way of naming certainly has a structuring and generative function in the making of the novel. It functions in two directions. In one direction, the author may have an idea in mind and want to incorporate the idea into the text proper. He might search for a proper name or coin a name that bears same relation to the word in sound, shape, or sense. Ying Bojue 應伯爵, Che Dan 車(扯)淡, Guan Shikuan 管世(事)寬, You Shou 遊守(手), Hao Xian 郝(好) 賢(閑), and Li Waichuan 李外傳 are created by this method. The author might also make use of already available names, allow them to beget new names somehow related to the old names through associations in sound, shape or sense, and develop narrative details in accordance with the associations that these new names evoke. Yueniang 月娘, Song Huilian 宋蕙蓮, Wang Liu'er 王六兒, Li Guijie 李桂姐, Yun Lishou 雲裏守, Wu Dian'en, 吳典恩, and others are created by this method. While the first kind of naming supplies new characters to populate the landscape of the narrative and hints at allegorical meaning, the second kind provides the narrative impetus and details to keep the story going.

A DISSEMINATIVE PARADIGM OF READING/WRITING

The creation of narrative details and their interconnections through the impetus of association shares some affinity with the ways Marcel Proust conceived of his masterpiece, *A la recherche du temps perdu* (*Remembrance of Things Past*). In that masterpiece, the narrative impetus is free association, which gives rise to involuntary memory in the mind of the narrator. According to *Le temps retrouvé*, the genesis of this novel was a series of trivial incidents that happened to the narrator: his stumbling over an uneven cobblestone, hearing the clink of a spoon against a cup, and wiping his mouth with a napkin, and so on. These chance incidents trigger involuntary memories of a past that lay hidden from his consciousness. They not only provide source materials for a work of art but also help him discover the latent pattern in his life, which gives structure and form to the artistic efforts of rendering that we experience in fiction.[49] Of course, the associational narrative impetus in the *Jin Ping Mei* as described by Zhang Zhupo is considerably different from that of Proust's novel. One difference is that while Proust's novel employs association through events, the *Jin Ping Mei* makes use of association through characters' names as well as events. In other words, the Chinese fiction writer was following the principle of "creating events out of *wen* 文 and *ming* 名." Another difference is that while Proust's novel is autobiographical in nature, it is unlikely that the *Jin Ping Mei* has any autobiographical elements.

Zhang Zhupo's allegorical reading evidently grasps a key to the narrative impulse of the *Jin Ping Mei*, which is the conscious use of free association in the making of fiction. As a method of reading, his theory is perfectly tenable. But as an insight into the novel's making, it may have some problems. In many cases, he has stretched his allegorical theory too far, thereby producing some unconvincing explanations. For example, his idea of how Li Ping'er's name evolves out of Ximen Qing's name is rather far-fetched. His claim that "not a single name in this novel does not carry a profound intention"[50] may be an overstatement, for it is simply impossible to decide in some cases whether an explanation of a certain name is the implication intended by the author or is an implication conjured up by the reader. There may be several explanations for the same name or event. For example, Zhang Zhupo's rationale about the naming of Chen Jingji and his role in the plot development is impossible to verify. Zhang's explanation is an interesting one, but readers could come up with other explanations. One could argue, for example, that *chen* is a near homophone for *cheng* 承; *jingji* 敬濟 in the Cihua 詞話 edition is written as 經濟. It is a homophone of 經紀 (managing or manager). According to some scholars, Chen Jingji in the latter part of the novel is really a reincarnated Ximen. Wen Long 文龍 (fl. 1870–86), who wrote an extended commentary on the novel, regarded Chen Jingji as "truly Ximen Qing Jr.," "Ximen Qing's split self."[51] This is a very sound view, for Chen Jingji is not only as wicked, licentious, and immoral as Ximen, but he also literally carries on Ximen's immoral life, engaging in illicit affairs with Pan Jinlian, Chunmei, and other women characters. Moreover, he is Ximen's son-in-law. On one occasion in the novel, Ximen proclaims that since he has no son, he treats Jingji as his son, at least a "half son." In the light of these narrative details, it is not far-fetched to say that Chen Jingji's surname means *cheng* 承 (continue or inherit). He inherits Ximen's robe and bowl and carries on his immoral life. The name Jingji 經濟 or 經紀 reinforces this implication. Ximen is a businessman who manages a large family business. Before his death, Chen Jingji is practically his general manager. In comparison with my view, Zhang Zhupo's explanation of *chen* as "worn-out" and *jing* as "stem" seems quite unnatural.

Although we can never be certain that Zhang Zhupo's theory of allegory always fits the author's conception and making of the novel, one thing we can be quite sure of is that his ideas may be viewed as constituting a theory of pluralistic reading. Zhang's theory of reading can be linked with a method of writing that Derrida calls "dissemination." The essence of this kind of reading is the attention paid to the indeterminacy warranted by the materiality of the sign—its sound, shape, and sense. It does not simply emphasize the representational quality of the sign; it pays close attention to the sign itself and views its materiality as carrying other than surface implications. This theory of reading is predicated on the fluid signifying process in the context of the text. In attempting to grasp the implications of a key word or name, one first ponders its sound when pronounced, its shape when written, and its sense, and all the possible associations that the materiality of the word or name may evoke, then situates the possible associations within the context of the text, and finally selects implications that fit most properly into the context. The implications thus produced are very different from the surface meanings or the meanings represented by the word or name alone.

Since the context of the text is not monolithic but consists of numerous details, scenes, and episodes, it is multifaceted. Each facet of the context would put the associations of a word or name in a new situation, thereby making it possible to yield fresh and different interpretations. This theory of reading is thereby capable of opening up the text to different readings, and by thus opening up the text, it endows the text with an open hermeneutic space that may or may not be there at the time of making the text.

Here let me give a few examples to show how this theory of reading opens up intended and unintended hermeneutic space. In chapter 9 of the novel, Wu Song accidentally beats to death a *yamen* runner who has leaked information to Ximen Qing. The runner's name is Li Waichuan 李外傳. The implication of the runner's name is deliberately intended by the author as can be seen from the fact that he makes a special mention of the detail in the novel: this character has a nickname Li Waichuan 裏外傳 (He passes information in and out). But this may not be the only implication of the novel. Wen Long expressed a different but more intriguing idea in his comment on chapter 9: "This chapter breaks away from the *Shuihu zhuan* and leads into the *Jin Ping Mei* proper. The character *chuan* '傳' should be read in its falling tone. This reading truly fits the proper theme of the novel. Therefore, this character is used to let Ximen go free. The *Shuihu zhuan* is an inner story; this novel is an outer story."[52] In other words, the character Li Waichuan serves as an indication of the author's intention to leave behind the source text and to embark on a literary creation of his own making.

Employing the paronomastic method, one can see the character in a different light and read the character's name as having some other implications. First, one can read the name as punning on "li wai zhuan 理外傳," *qingli zhi wai zhi zhuan* 情理之外之傳, meaning that the episode centering on Wu

Song is a story that goes against the normal order of things that a reader familiar with the *Shuihu zhuan* might expect. Unlike the Wu Song in the source book, this Wu Song fails to kill Ximen and gets himself exiled. Second, one can read the name as punning on "li wai zhuan 理歪傳," *buzheng zhi li zhi zhuan* 不正之理之傳, meaning that this episode warns the reader that by allowing Ximen to survive Wu Song's revenge, the author was going to write a novel that is a story of the improper order of human affairs. It is not about heroes who fight or die for justice and propriety but about antiheroes whose immoral life makes a mockery of *tianli* (heavenly principle). The combination of the two ideas may serve as a caution to the reader: Do not read the *Jin Ping Mei* in the same way you read the *Shuihu zhuan*, or you may simply miss the message of the whole novel. Considering that the author continues to draw source materials from the *Shuihu zhuan*, there is good reason to believe that this implication might well be a possible cue to the reader. After all, since the novel came into the world, readers have continued to compare the borrowed episodes with the sourcebook. And many of them claim that the rewritten episodes are inferior. Obviously, they have completely missed the point that the author hoped to put across. In his comment on the role of the character Yun Lishou in chapter 100 of the novel, Zhang Zhupo offers a similar warning: "A hundred foreign pearls are woven into the dreams of Commander Yun. This shows the author in the clouds hinting at the implications of the dream for the 100-chapter novel. But readers of this 100-chapter novel may be still in the clouds and in a dream, and may not necessarily be able to understand the author's painstaking efforts."[53]

What is it that the author took pains to labor at? A possible answer may be: he was engaged in writing a new novel, a pure fiction. There are many signs indicating this intention. I have mentioned that scholars have ferreted out quite a few discrepancies in the novel, which form a glaring contrast with the painstaking care that characterizes most of the novel. Some discrepancies may have been slips of the pen when the novel was circulating in its manuscript form. But some other discrepancies may have resulted from the authorial attempt to break from historical fiction and to make pure fiction. In the preceding chapters, I have conceptually explored the negative effect of historical tyranny and narrative inertia. In the *Jing Ping Mei*, deviations from historical facts might have been consciously intended to overcome narrative inertia. In the making of the novel, the author incorporated many historical personages into the text. A close examination of these historical persons reveals that details concerning these persons are more often than not discrepant with historical facts. There are numerous examples in the text. Here I will cite only a few examples that cannot be explained away by carelessness. The ending of the novel states that after the cataclysm of war and destruction, the Song was divided into two dynasties with two emperors: the Jin 金 state established the puppet emperor Zhang Bangchang 張邦昌 (1081–1127) in the north, and the Song 宋 loyalists proclaimed Prince Kang 康土 as the new emperor Gao Zong 高宗 (r. 1127–62) in the south. When we have a look at the history of the Song, it is obvious that the ending statement deviates drastically from real history. Zhang Bangchang was the puppet emperor for only approximately thirty days. Shortly afterward, he pleaded with Emperor Gao Zong and asked for the bestowal of death. A few months later, for a certain crime, the emperor did order him to commit suicide.[54] A revisionist use of historical details is a common occurrence in novels before the *Jin Ping Mei*, because of a given author's dissatisfaction with historical facts. In the *Jin Ping Mei*, however, the author's artistic manipulation seems to have gone beyond the purpose of revising history. Some textual evidence suggests that the author might have intended his revision to hint that he was writing a pure fiction, not an artistic version of history.

A revealing detail is found in chapter 17. Yuwen Xuzhong 宇文虛中, a minister of the Song court, writes a memorial to the emperor calling for the indictment of venal officials. Yuwen is positively portrayed as an upright minister with high moral standards who would not be afraid to risk his life in order to fight against corruption and appeasement. But in real history, Yuwen Xuzhong 宇文虛中 (1079–1146) was almost the opposite. Instead of calling for resistance to aggression, he several times went to the enemy camp as a negotiator. On his last negotiating mission, he was detained by the Jin state and afterward surrendered. He participated in the Jin state's strategic planning to invade the southern part of China. For some time, he was respected by the Jin people as the "state teacher 國師." Although he was eventually executed by the rulers of the Jin for treason, he was by no means a loyal minister of the Song.[55] The reason for the positive characterization may have to be sought in the making of the novel. Yuwen Xuzhong's name puns with 余文虛中, which may be rendered as "My text is fictitious inside." Thus, he might have been a character to hint at the author's intention to create pure fiction. His action in the novel is fictitious; so is the implication of his name. It is perhaps largely for this reason that Zhang Zhupo makes this remark: "If one reads the *Jin Ping Mei* as an account of facts, he will be deceived by it. One must read it as a work of literature so as not to be deceived by it."[56]

THE POETICS OF FABRICATION

In the making of pure fiction, I have dealt with two aspects: the characters who populate the narrative landscape and the narrative details that keep the story going. What remains to be dealt with is the constructive principle that is often compared to the blueprint of a building. I have argued against using the architectural analogy to describe the construction of a text. Instead, I have opted for a model of embroidery. It is a fitting and proper model because a text, by its etymological definition, is a kind of braided entity, a tissue, a woven fabric. This is precisely what Zhang Zhupo understands the *Jin Ping Mei* to be. In his complete commentarial works, he again and again talks about the weaving of the novel. Here are just a few examples. In "How to Read the *Jin Ping Mei*," he refers to the novel as "a volume of a thousand stitches and ten thousand threads 一部千針萬 線."[57] In "Zhupo's Random Remarks," he tells us that the intricately woven texture of the novel is what had attracted him: "I love the novel, because though it consists of a voluminous total of 100 chapters, its thousand stitches and ten thousand threads emanate from a single source, and despite the thousand twists and ten thousand turns, not a single thread is exposed to the eye. . . . If I do not reveal the golden needle of such a wonderful text, wouldn't people be likely to overlook the author's painstaking efforts over a long time!"[58] In the same discourse, he points out the nature of the novel as a woven fabric:[59] "The details of this novel are as fine as the hairs of an ox, which are numbered by the thousands and tens of thousands, yet all belong to a single body and are sustained by the same circulatory system. Although the needle-work is concealed, even widely separated elements are interconnected."[60] In his comment on chapter 1, he compares the conceptual structure to a braided pigtail: "A book with 100 chapters ties its thousands of threads into a whole in the first chapter in the same way one ties the hairs on one's head into a braid with a single string."[61] In his comment on chapter 32, he refers to the totality of weaving: "I therefore know that only by taking the 100 chapters as completely conceptualized at one time can one realize that the novel was sewn into a seamless whole by stitches and threads."[62] In another short discourse, "The Cold and Hot Golden Needles 冷熱金針," he views the novel as a fabric woven with two golden needles pulling the two threads of "cold" and "heat."

If we compare Zhang Zhupo's metaphor for the novel as a woven texture with the French concept of a text, we will be surprised at its modernity. In contemporary literary theory, some theorists no longer view a piece of literature as a wrought work but regard it as a woven text. In their theorizing on the nature of the text, they use the act of weaving as a favorite analogy. Barthes, for one, makes the remark that:

> The text, while it is being produced, is like a piece of Valenciennes lace created before us under the lacemaker's fingers: each sequence undertaken hangs like the temporarily inactive bobbin waiting while its neighbor works; then, when its turn comes, the hand takes up the thread again, brings it back to the frame; and as the pattern is filled out, the progress of each thread is marked with a pin which holds it and is gradually moved backward: thus the terms of the sequence: they are positions held and then left behind in the course of a gradual invasion of meaning. This process is valid for the entire text. The grouping of codes, as they enter into the work, into the movement of the reading, constitute a braid (*text, fabric, braid*: the same thing); each thread, each code, is a voice; these braided—or braiding—voices form the writing: when it is alone, the voice does not labor, transforms nothing; it *expresses*; but as soon as the hand intervenes to gather and intertwine the inert threads, there is labor, there is transformation.[63]

We may compare Barthes's analogy with Zhang Zhupo's miscellaneous remarks on weaving, and especially with another extended statement: "These hundred chapters were not written in a day, but they were conceived on particular days at particular times. If you try to imagine how the author conceived of this wealth of individually structured episodes you will come to realize how much planning, interweaving [*ch'uan-ch'a* 穿插], and tailoring [*ts'ai-chien* 裁剪] was required."[64] The comparison cannot but compel us to marvel at the closeness of Zhang Zhupo's idea of the novel to the modern conception of the text. Although Zhang Zhupo does not talk about his idea of the novel from the perspective of highly abstract theories, his commentarial work touches on most of the important aspects of a text. Of course, Zhang Zhupo did not have had access to modern literary theories. His ideas grew out of his sensitive understanding of the *Jin Ping Mei* and his own creative conception of how fiction should be made. Before writing comprehensive commentaries on the novel, he even attempted to rewrite the novel so as to demonstrate his idea of novel making:

> More recently, oppressed by poverty and grief, and goaded by "heat and cold," when time weighed heavily on my hands, I came to regret that I had not myself composed a book about the way of the world in order to relieve my depression. Several times I was on the point of setting pen to paper but was deterred by the amount of planning that the overall structure required. And so I laid aside my pen and said to myself, "Why don't I carefully work out the means by which this predecessor of mine constructed his book on 'heat and cold'?" In the first place, my elucidation of the work of my predecessor can count as an equivalent for my own planning of a book in the present.[65]

In his conception of the novel's making as a weaving of myriad threads, Zhang Zhupo picks out two major threads as the warp and woof for the whole woven fabric. They are the ideas of "cold" and "heat," which he considers as the key to an adequate understanding of the novel's theme and structure:

> The *Jin Ping Mei* opens its discourse with two words, "cold" and "heat." Who does not know they constitute a golden key to the whole novel? Nevertheless, where is the pivotal point of the novel? I say: it lies in the naming of two characters, Wen Xiucai and Han Huoji. Why do I say so? *Han* puns on "cold," another word for "chilly"; *wen* puns on "warmth," the residual quality of "heat." Han Huoji appears after Ximen receives his official appointment, symbolizing cold amid heat (prosperity), whereas Wen Xiucai does not enter until after the episode of polishing the mirror, being a herald of "cold." This arrangement implies that fortune and misfortune are immanent in each other and may transform into their opposites; it is the way of heaven that winter and summer steal each other's essence.[66]

In spite of the fact that Zhang Zhupo's reading was based on the Chongzhen 崇禎 version that differs significantly from the Cihua 詞話 version, especially in chapter 1, his view of the whole novel as being constructed on the binary opposition of cold and heat and their explicit and implicit meanings is pertinent to all versions. In his understanding, cold and heat are endowed with literal and symbolic meanings. Literally, they represent changes in temperature, weather, and the four seasons. Symbolically, they represent changes in the major protagonist's swings of mood, the vicissitudes of fortune, the highs and lows of sexual desire, and so on. With Zhang Zhupo's insight as a basis, Andrew Plaks has conducted a fascinating study of the correlation of heat and cold with the development of the novel's plot and the vicissitudes of the characters.[67] Plaks' study emphasizes the impact of certain aspects of traditional Chinese philosophy on the aesthetic features of the novel's construction. Here I want to emphasize the linguistic, conceptual, and artistic implications of Zhang Zhupo's understanding. The wordplay on *han* and *wen* not only generates new characters for the plot but also supplies details for the ongoing plot. In this sense, the binary opposition of cold and heat is a complementary principle to the principle of free association that I have discussed as the narrative impulse.

I have mentioned above that the *Jin Ping Mei* differs significantly from Proust's novel. Since his novel is autobiographical in nature, Proust could draw raw materials from his own life experience. The author of the *Jin Ping Mei* could also draw upon his own experience of life, but the disparate nature of his other source materials would compel him to find a constructing principle other than the autobiographical. Since he was engaged in writing a fiction, he had to invent his materials as he wrote. To coordinate materials drawn from observations and materials that came out of thin air, the author was in need of a writing principle that could take care of the vertical and syntagmatic progression of the narrative thrust. The binary opposition between heat and cold and their interpenetration may be viewed as another structuring principle.

Because of his own predilection, Zhang Zhupo devotes a lot of space to the discussion of cold and heat and their significance for the whole novel. As he puts it, the whole novel is a "book on heat and cold."[68] On the basis of Zhang Zhupo's idea, we could abstract a general principle of the novel's making. Indeed, if we read the novel closely, the binary opposition does not limit itself to cold and heat. It extends to a series of oppositions: real/false, fortune/misfortune, death/birth, leisurely/occupied, happy/sad, positive/negative, superior/inferior, master/servant, mistress/maid, and so on. Binary opposition also figures prominently in the division of chapters, the wording of espisodes within a chapter, the arrangement of chapter structure, and the whole novel's structure. Plaks has paid much attention to the antithetical structure of the novel's formal arrangement. He also rightly relates it to the ancient-style essays and traditional critical theories concerning poetry and essay writing. I would add that in the creation of fiction, the writer uses binary opposition and antitheses as a way to give form and structure to the disparate elements of the narrative. The source of inspiration might not have been solely the theories of classical essays; it may have been a conscious or unconscious use of the author's education in poetry writing. A scholar who has been trained in writing old style poetry will frequently relapse into writing poems in that style even though he consciously renounces it in favor of a more modern style. Witness the cases of Lu Xun, Hu Shi, Chen Duxiu (1879–1942), and even Mao Zedong (1893–1976). The author of the *Jin Ping Mei* consciously or unconsciously organized his materials in accordance with the poetic writing techniques of antithesis, parallelism, and alternation between opposite and complementary images, colors, sensations, qualities, characters, situations, and so on. This is the fundamental reason why I have claimed in a previous chapter that the *Jin Ping Mei* is a poetic fiction.

Just as free association of words, names, and places constitutes a writing principle for synchronic and linear plot development, so binary antithesis serves as a complementary principle for diachronic and vertical extension of plot details. *The two principles of free association and binary antithesis are the two golden needles that pull the warp and woof of the creative impulse into a woven fabric of signifiers.* It is these two principles that endow the text with an open hermeneutic space. They provide the logic that organizes disparate materials into a unity in the way described by Barthes: "The logic regulating the Text is not comprehensive . . . but metonymic; the activity of associations, contiguities, carryings-over coincides with a liberation of symbolic energy."[69] They are also that which enables the reader to approach a writing as a text with multiple meanings, as a signifying process of dissemination, as described by Barthes:

> The Text is plural. Which is not simply to say that it has several meanings, but that it accomplishes the very plural of meaning: an *irreducible* (and not merely an acceptable) plural. The Text is not a co-existence of meanings but a passage, an overcrossing; thus it answers not to an interpretation, even a liberal one, but to an explosion, a dissemination. The plural of the Text depends, that is, not on the ambiguity of its contents but on what might be called the *stereographic plurality* of its weave of signifiers (italics in the original).[70]

The plurality of the novel does not come merely from the author's deliberate making; it often emanates from a cooperative reading that employs the signifying principles I have discussed above. Take the principle of binary opposition, for example. Premodern scholars had used it without proclaiming it. We know that the *Jin Ping Mei* has been regarded by some as a hidden attack on Yan Song 嚴嵩 (1481–1568) and Yan Shifan 嚴世藩 (1513–65), the wicked father and son who dominated Ming court politics for a period. According to this view, Yan Shifan had the childhood name Qing'er 慶兒 and the style name Donglou 東樓 (Eastern Tower). By reverse association, the name Donglou gave rise to the name Ximen (Western Gate). Together with Qing'er, the antihero of the novel, Ximen Qing, was subjected to a hidden attack. In the novel, Ximen's servant Laibao goes to the capital to deliver some birthday gifts. When he announces his master's name, the gatekeeper reprimands him: "How dare you announce your Dongmen master and Ximen master here!" Zhang

Zhupo dismisses such attempts to read the *Jin Ping Mei* as a roman à clef,[71] but he attaches a special value to the associations of names, as we have seen. For example, he argues that the narrative detail of Chunmei's being married to Zhou Xiu and dying of sexual indulgence with Zhou Yi has a hidden message. In his opinion,

> *Zhou* means "boat." Zhou Xiu means "smell in the boat." He leaves a stink behind because of Chunmei. Zhou Ren means "people in the boat." Zhou Zhong means "being in the boat." Only Zhou Yi stands for "a free ferry" onto which everybody can get and which can stay wherever it may be. His name alludes to Chunmei's outrageous promiscuity which leads to her demise.[72]

Zhang Zhupo certainly offers an interesting reading, but it is obviously his own idiosyncratic reading. I cannot understand how the allegorical meaning of a free ferryboat ride relates to Chunmei's sexual licentiousness and her demise. In any case, it is Chunmei, not Zhou Yi, who is licentious. Here I wish to offer a different reading. "Zhou" puns with *zhou* 謅, which means "fabricate 編造." In the larger context of the author's creative intention, it may signify the fictitious nature of the novel. In the light of each character with the surname Zhou, it may mean "false" or "fictitious." The account of Zhou Xiu's heroic deeds and eventual death for the country is a made-up story of heroism and loyalty. Similarly, Zhou Ren puns on "false benevolence," Zhou Zhong on "false loyalty," and Zhou Yi on "false righteousness." Zhou Yi is indeed a person of false righteousness, for it is most improper for him to engage in an illicit affair with his master's wife. My reading of *zhou* as "fabricate" not only coincides with the Western view of fiction as "fabrication" but also fits the Chinese conception of pure fiction. The *Jin Ping Mei* is a novel of pure fiction par excellence. Its poetics of pure fiction is at bottom a poetics of fabrication.

A NOVEL OF MULTIPLE DIMENSIONS

A poetics of weaving entails the suturing together of multiple dimensions. The multiple vision and the location of different and conflicting readings suggest that the *Jin Ping Mei* is not only a pure fiction but also a novel of multiple dimensions. Its multiplicity comes from two different categories of making. One category is the conscious weaving of different strands of meanings into a convergent point of ambiguity; the other is the conscious use of language in the naming of characters, places, objects, and situations. Ximen's first son, Guange 官哥, belongs to the first category. The author makes deliberate moves to relate him to a number of characters. It is virtually impossible to tell who his natural father is: Ximen Qing, Hua Zixu, Jiang Zhushan, or as Zhang Zhupo claims, a ghost? The true source for the novel's multifacetedness, however, is the second category. As a text, the novel is quite like language; it is structured but off-center and is without closure. To continue to use the analogy of verbal embroidery, it is comparable to a tapestry woven with different-colored threads and different patterns. A viewer may follow one or more threads and find one or more patterns: a square, a circle, a triangle, a trapezoid, a quadrangle, and so on. So long as one has the patience to search, one will find new patterns.

This new conception and new way of fiction making—a weave of signifiers orchestrated into a multidimensional discourse by the two interrelated weaving principles of association and selection—have endowed the *Jin Ping Mei* with a marvelously self-adjusting quality. If one wants to regard it as having a Confucian vision, it will display a Confucian vision; if one wants to view it as a Buddhist didactic book, it will assume a Buddhist worldview; if one wants to read it as a Daoist book, it will radiate Daoist ideas. If one wants to call it an obscene book, it will reveal obscenities. If one wishes to call it a highly moral book, it will serve as a book to stop licentiousness. Wen Long makes an apt summary of this open condition: "It is all right to call it a book of obscenity; it is also all right to call it a book of moral goodness; it poses no problem if one calls it a book of wonder."[73] Artistically, if one wants to regard it as a great work, it will provide plenty of evidence to support the argument. If one wants to deem it an inferior work, it will also supply ammunition to its detractors. All in all, the novel is so constructed that one can interpret it in a multitude of different ways. As a pioneering effort at conscious pure fiction making, the *Jin Ping Mei* made an innovative contribution to the Chinese theory of the novel, without which later writers of fiction would have groped in the dark.

The Art of the *Hongloumeng*: Poetic Fiction and Open Fiction

The *Hongloumeng* (*A Dream of Red Mansions*) is the apotheosis of the creative drive in Chinese fictional development that aspires to the condition of verbal art. It exemplifies the conception of pure fiction, poetic fiction, total fiction, metafiction, and, above all, open fiction that I have explored in the previous chapters. I have claimed that even though Cao Xueqin never wrote a treatise on theory of fiction, his novel contains conceptual insights that could be utilized to formulate a theory of fiction. I have already discussed some of his insights concerning fiction's genesis and condition on a number of occasions. In this chapter, I will further tap the theoretical insights in the novel and attempt to work out a poetics of fictional writing that underlies the novel's conception through analysis of its thematic concerns and narrative strategies. The formulation of a poetics will contribute to a Chinese system of fiction theory that I will construct in the next chapter.

There are literally cartloads of studies of the novel, but not many are concerned with its condition as a verbal art, and still fewer with its contributions to the Chinese theory of fiction. In Anthony C. Yu's recent study, he breaks new ground in both areas. He unequivocally treats the novel as a verbal art and correctly locates its source of artistry: "[T]he narrative's merit as verbal art lies in its reflexive and innovative insistence, made through myriad occasions and devices."[1] In critical analysis, he makes a radical shift in focus from what the author writes to how he presents what he writes, and Yu places enormous weight on the novel's extraordinary use of language, which he identifies as a sure sign of verbal art. Through a fascinating reading of the vicissitudes of the "stone," he reveals the novel's artistry as sustained on the inherent relationship between the function of the protagonist and the author's conception of language, text, story, and narrative strategies.[2] He also uncovers a number of connections between the novel's motifs and literary theory. After a detailed reading of the stone in terms of Buddhist philosophy, he suggests an "intimated parallel between Buddhist tenets and literary theory."[3] Following the authorial hint at readerly reception in the novel's opening, he explores "how the process of religious enlightenment may parallel aesthetic discovery and act as a trope of literary effect."[4]

I would like to continue where he leaves off. I venture to suggest that there are not just parallels between the novel's motifs and literary theory; I believe the novel as a whole was conceived, constructed, and composed on the author's self-conscious awareness of the reciprocity between the making of the novel and the conception of a fiction theory. By this I mean that while engaged in writing the novel, Cao Xueqin was at the same time pondering on a poetics of fiction to be concretized in practice. From what the opening chapter informs us—"Cao Xueqin in his Nostalgia Studio worked on it for ten years, in the course of which he rewrote it no less than five times"[5]—we may infer that his practice kept altering his theory and his theory kept influencing his practice. The alternation between theory and practice was repeated so many times that there is no way of telling which ultimately influenced which. Because of this evolutionary genesis, Cao Xueqin was able to write a novel that, as Lu Xun rightly points out, shattered all traditional ideas and modes of writing,[6] and became a metafiction.

Because of the intense preoccupation with fiction's rationale, Cao Xueqin turned his novel into a literary text filled with theoretical insights. The *Hongloumeng* displays a remarkable vision of openness, which comes close to the creative vision that scholars of English literature have discovered in James Joyce's two masterpieces, *Ulysses* and *Finnegans Wake*. The making of the novel involves three modes of representation: mimesis, semiosis, and simulation. This tripartite mode of representation enables the novel to become a text that attains the conditions of pure fiction and yields a poetics of open fiction. In following sections, I will explore how the three modes of representation interact and work out Cao Xueqin's ideas about the ontology, epistemology, conceptual vision, and writing model in fictional representation.

THE ONTOLOGY OF REPRESENTATION

Cao Xueqin presents his idea about the ontology of representation through an imaginative creation of the *Daguanyuan* (Total Vision Garden) and the Land of Illusion. In the *Hongloumeng*, both places are artistic topoi. A casual reading suggests that while the former represents a real world, the latter represents an unreal world. The representation, however, is complicated by another world: the social world that exists outside the *Daguanyuan*. In an influential study, Ying-shih Yu argues that the Land of Illusion and the *Daguanyuan* should be considered as one world, because while the former is a heavenly model, the latter is its earthly replica. They represent imaginary worlds, utopian in nature, in contrast to the social world.[7] His thesis has since been reworked by many scholars with variations.[8] In a study of the novel, I have argued against viewing the Land of Illusion and the Total Vision Garden as a utopia. Through detailed analysis, I have demonstrated that the Land of Illusion (and, to a lesser extent, the *Daguanyuan*) is a multivalent topos, which may stand variously for the imperial harem, a courtesan's house, heaven, hell, a boudoir, a nunnery, and even a prison.[9] The contradictory connotations of these places deconstructs the binary opposition between the Land of Illusion and the *Daguanyuan* as utopia and the outside world as dystopia. In its place, I would like to put forward a paradoxical claim that it can represent all these places because it does not refer to any of them except itself. This paradox leads to the question: why does the author create the double worlds of the Land of Illusion and the *Daguanyuan* apart from mimetically presenting the social world?

My answer is that this paradox underlies the author's notion concerning the ontology of representation. His ontology is one of pure fiction predicated on the unity of social reflection, artistic simulation, and self-referentiality. The creation of the two worlds may not be aimed at contrasting the ideal world with the world of reality, but at advancing his aesthetic ideas in fiction writing. In narrative aesthetics, the author's creation of a multivalent topos seems to be aimed at writing a pluralistic novel and advancing a poetics of open fiction. And his conception of such a novel and its poetics of making is based on a philosophical view of the binary opposition between the real and the false and its dissolution. On Baoyu's dream visit to the Land of Illusion, he sees a couplet inscribed on either side of the stone arch at the entrance: "Truth becomes fiction when the fiction's true; / Real becomes not-real when the unreal's real." Then, in chapter 17, Baoyu accompanies his father to tour the newly built *Daguanyuan*. He also sees a stone arch. It is indicated by the author that it is the same marble arch: "The sight of this building and its arch had inspired a strange and unac-countable stir of emotion in Bao-yu which on reflection he interpreted as a sign that he must have known a building somewhat like this before—though where or when he could not for the life of him remember."[10] Since the Land of Illu-sion appears in Baoyu's dream, it should be considered as a false world. After all, people often say, "This is not true, because it is only a dream." Then, the *Daguanyuan*, the counterpart, stands for the real world. This seems to indicate that the Land of Illusion and the *Daguanyuan* form a contrast between the real and the false. But this opposition deconstructs itself by the fact that the stone arch Baoyu sees is in both his dream world and the real world. Ostensibly, the author seems to be saying: the Land of Illusion is false and the *Daguanyuan* is real. But as mimetic representations of facets of the social world, both seem real; or in contrast to the social world, neither is real. Characters in the novel take the artifical and hence false (the *Daguanyuan*) as real; by contrast, the actual and hence real (social world) seems unreal to them. This understanding cor-responds exactly with the inscriptions on the stone arch.

I have mentioned the scholarly consensus that the *Daguanyuan* is a rep-lica of the Land of Illusion, or a projection of the Land of Illusion onto the human world. When we examine this claim more closely, the matter takes a new twist. In terms of the accepted view, the relationship between the Land of Illusion and the *Daguanyuan* is not one of contrast but one of mimesis. According to the theory of mimesis, representation involves a model and a copy. Representation occurs when a copy is made after the model. The model always comes before the copy. Otherwise there would appear the fallacy of "putting the cart before the horse." In artistic representation, normally, it is art that imitates reality. Before postmodern times rarely do we find cases of reversal. In the *Hongloumeng*, however, we do have such a reversal. The Land of Illusion is the model, while the *Daguanyuan* is the copy. But the former appears in a dream, hence it is an illusion, while the latter appears in the narrated events, hence it is a narrated reality. If we accept the *Daguanyuan* as a projection of the Land of Illusion, we would have a case in which reality is modeled after an illusion.

What complicates the matter further is that, as I have pointed out already, the Land of Illusion has no earthly model at all. It is a representation of neither the imperial harem, nor the boudoir, nor a courtesan's house, nor a nunnery, since it can be viewed as representing all of them. It simply has no conceivable unitary model. Evidently, the creation of the Land of Illusion is not a matter of imitation, reduplication, or even of parody. In thus structuring the setting of his marvelous tale, Cao Xueqin's creative vision comes close to the postmodern, because it conceives of a creative act comparable to the post-modern idea of "simulation."

To explain the idea of simulation, John Baudrillard cites the Borges tale that is an allegory of simulation. In the tale, the cartographers of an empire draw up a map of the empire. The empire is depicted in such detail that it completely fills the map. As the empire declines, the map becomes more and more worn and finally only a few shreds are still discernible in the deserts. The ruined map simulates a ruined abstraction, thus bearing witness to an imperial pride rotting like a carcass. In the postmodern era, Baudrillard argues, "simulation is no longer that of a territory, a referential being or a substance. It is the generation by models of a real without origin or reality: a hyperreal. The territory no longer precedes the map, nor survives it. Henceforth, it is the map that precedes the territory—precession of simulacra—it is the map that engenders the territory and if we were to revive the fable today, it would be the territory whose shreds are slowly rotting across the map."[11] The relationship between the Land of Illusion and the *Daguanyuan* is exactly such a case of simulation. Scholars agree that Baoyu's first visit to the Land of Illusion is a thematic guideline for the whole novel. The Land of Illusion precedes the building of the *Daguanyuan*, and the registers foretell the fates of the girls on the registers. When the garden deteriorates, the Land of Illusion also becomes desolate, as if the conditions of the latter were the consequences of the former. In terms of simulation, Cao Xueqin's creative act is not designed to show the power of the black magic of reduplication but "an operation to deter every real process by its operational double, a metastable, programmatic, perfect descriptive machine which provides all the signs of the real and short-circuits all its vicissitudes."[12] In the contrast between the Land of Illusion and the social world outside the *Daguanyuan*, the former, resulting from the act of simulation, becomes a third-order "simulacrum" that no longer allows the code to take priority over or precede the model. The distinction between model and copy, object and representation, is no longer valid. In their place appears an unfamiliar new world constructed out of models or simulacra that have no referent or ground in any reality except their own.

Architecturally, the *Daguanyuan* is also a simulacrum because it is, in Gilles Deleuze's definition, both similar to and different from its possible model(s).[13] Despite its resemblance to the imperial palace (as Wu Hung has argued),[14] it only partially resembles the latter. For quite some time, scholars have been engaged in a debate over where the real model of the garden was located. Some believe its model was located in Nanjing, where the Cao family had a garden; some believe it was located in Beijing, where the Cao family had another garden; still others believe it is a composite place modeled after the gardens in both Nanjing and Beijing.[15] From 1961 to 1963, scholars in China even conducted an earnest search for the locales of the model. The fallacious nature of the view and the futility of the search have been convincingly exposed by some scholars who argue that the garden is but a fictional place. I agree with the latter view in principle, but wish to add that this fictional space is the outcome of superb imagination. One of Yuanchun's poetic lines says, "Earth's fairest prospects all are here installed." Indeed, even if we assemble all the gardens in China, perhaps we would not be able to find its replica. The *Daguanyuan*, as Andrew Plaks rightly point out, is "a summing up, a composite picture of the entire range of Chinese garden art."[16] As a crystallization of Chinese garden art,[17] it is a configurated garden that has no real referential model. Hence, I have good reason to call it a simulacrum in the same way that Disneyland is cited by Baudrillard as a typical specimen of a simulacrum.[18] The *Daguanyuan* resembles Disneyland in that it is an imaginary world that assembles in one place not only all possible garden designs and views but also all possible human types and domestic dramas the author could imagine. It is not for nothing that the author should designate it the "Total Vision Garden."

But Cao Xueqin was not solely engaged in creating a pure fiction, for a simulation differs from pure fiction in that "it not only presents an absence as presence, the imaginary as the real, it also undermines any contrast to the real, absorbing the real within itself."[19] His creative purpose may be similar to the function of simulation. "Simulation," Baudrillard says, "threatens the difference between 'true' and 'false,' between 'real' and 'imaginary.'"[20] On many occasions, Cao Xueqin makes diegetic moves to threaten or disrupt the boundary between fiction and reality. Baoyu's first tour of the *Daguanyuan* in the company of his father and others clearly hints at the lack of distinction between real and unreal. At the sight of the stone arch with its inscription, he sinks into reverie and wonders which is real: the Land of Illusion of his dream visit or the *Daguanyuan* of this real visit. Baoyu's uncertainty testifies to the author's impulse to create a series of simulacra endowed with phantasmagoric power. His uncertainty in turn accentuates the author's lofty claim for his fictive art.

THE EPISTEMOLOGY OF REPRESENTATION

Cao Xueqin's notion about the epistemology of representation is the mainstream in Chinese fiction's long-term development. This epistemology addresses the metaphysical complexity of the relationship between the real world and the imagined world. In the novel, it is artistically simulated through the two story-frame characters, Zhen Shiyin and Jia Yucun, and Jia Baoyu and Zhen Baoyu, who are doubles. In the case of the literary double, the simulation is chiefly achieved through semiosis, the interaction of the sign. The simulation is predicated on the word play of *zhen* (real) and *jia* (false). The wordplay, so obvious in the novel, has attracted the attention of scholars in the field for a long time. Its ingenuity and complexity, when spelled out, anticipate the postmodern idea of deconstruction. Both Jia (false) Baoyu and Zhen (real) Baoyu start with the same temperament, odd ways of behavior, and defiance of conventional morality. But they develop in different directions toward the end of the novel. The "false" Baoyu abandons his family and rejects the world of Red Dust while the "real" Baoyu stays in the world of Red Dust and accepts his social role as a Confucian conformist. But if we take into consideration the wordplay on "false" and "real," we come to an entirely opposite conclusion: only the false (Jia) Baoyu rejects the world of Red Dust; the real (Zhen) Baoyu accepts it. This conclusion, however, is completely reversed if we take note of the pun on Zhen Baoyu's father's name, Zhen Yingjia 甄應嘉 (The real should be false). The implication is that his son is not the real Baoyu but the false Baoyu. According to this, the false Baoyu stays in the world of Red Dust, while the real Baoyu rejects it. Just as we rejoice at having sorted out the complex relationship, there appears another twist. The author declared at the opening that this novel is about "false words retained" and "truth concealed." This declaration throws the reader into total confusion beyond any hope of coming to a clear understanding of who is the real Baoyu and who is the false Baoyu. The author made all these twists and turns not to confuse us but to impart his creative vision—the blurring of the boundary between fiction and reality and the interpenetration between the real and the unreal. As Anthony Yu aptly points out, "[W]ith a technique worthy of the modern Borges or Philip Roth, the Chinese author proceeds to present the dazzling transfer or exchange of attributes between the Zhen and the Jia Bao-yu, so that their words and mutual discovery of the other become virtually a living embodiment of the truth inherent in a dream, a mirror image, or a fiction: that there is the real in the false, and the false in the real."[21]

A parallel case is another pair of characters: Zhen Shiyin 甄士隱 and Jia Yucun 賈雨村. These two characters are almost as important as Jia Baoyu and Zhen Baoyu in conveying the author's creative vision. Structurally, the former pair provides the background while the latter pair acts out the main drama in the foreground. Thematically, both pairs serve to advance the author's epistemology of representation, but the pair of Zhen Shiyin and Jia Yucun goes contrary to the pair of Jia Baoyu and Zhen Baoyu. I have mentioned that Jia (false) Baoyu deserts the world of Red Dust, while Zhen (real) Baoyu remains behind. In the other pair, Zhen Shiyin (truth concealed) rejects the world of Red Dust, while Jia Yucun (falsity retained) prospers in it. If Zhen Shiyin represents the truth concealed, then, his departure means that what is retained in the novel is falsity. It follows from this that what is narrated in the novel should not be taken as literal truth. Jia Yucun's name conveys exactly the same message. Jia Yucun is meant to embody falsity. That he remains in the world of Red Dust and prospers may be understood to mean that the novel is full of falsehood. But according to the last chapter, it is Jia Yucun who instructs Vanitas to seek out Cao Xueqin and ask him to transmit the story. When we view the message conveyed by this pair in relation to the pair of "real" Baoyu and "false" Baoyu, the already complicated message becomes even more convoluted. In a word, the opposition between the real and false is reversed several times. If the author had any message to convey, it is impossible to tell what his intended message could be. If one insists on seeking a message, Anthony Yu suggests one: it is "the emptiness of fiction": "Just as the real world is considered empty and unreal in the Buddhist vision, so the invented world of story is 'baseless' (*huangtang*), 'absurd' (*dahuang*), 'unverifiable' (*wuji*), and 'undatable' (*wu chaodai nianji*)."[22]

People may say that Cao Xueqin's vision is one of nihilism, a negative term that is often used to describe Buddhism. Anthony Yu's comparison of Cao Xueqin's vision to the Buddhist vision[23] seems to corroborate this evaluation. In my opinion, Cao's vision concerning the opposition between the real and unreal is largely a Daoist one,[24] or to use a postmodern term, a deconstructive one. Cao Xueqin's deconstructive vision might have come from his intimate knowledge of Laozi's and Zhuangzi's Daoist philosophy, which finds so many echoes in and exerts so much influence on the novel. Zhuangzi's dream of the butterfly, for example, contributes considerably to Cao's creative vision. Zhuangzi dreams of becoming a butterfly. On awakening, he is not sure whether it is he who dreams of becoming a butterfly or it is the butterfly who dreams of becoming Zhuangzi.[25] The "butterfly" motif is vividly dramatized in Baoyu's dream. In chapter 56, Baoyu dreams of visiting a garden full of girls like the *Daguanyuan* and meeting with a teenager who has the same name, same appearance, and same temperament as he. What is most fascinating is that in the dream, Baoyu A (for the sake of distinction) hears Baoyu B saying that he has just had a dream in which he had the same experience as Baoyu A. When the two Baoyus finally meet each other in the dream, they cannot help but wonder whether they are in a dream. Scholars in both China and the West have already noticed the parallel between Zhuangzi's "butter-fly dream" and Baoyu's dream.[26] But the full implications of the parallel are still open to discussion. Angelina Yee is of the opinion that the reference to the "butterfly dream" represents the author's questioning "not just the illusory nature of his fictional character, Baoyu, but through him, his own self-iden-tity." She even thinks the questioning applies to both the author's and reader's self-identity.[27] Her view is certainly an interesting one, but unfortunately she does not elaborate on it. I cannot figure out how the illusory nature of the characters comes to affect the author's and the reader's perception of their self-identity. Shuen-fu Lin's analysis of Zhuangzi's dream is perhaps more to the point in the context of the novel: "By indicating his inability to deter-mine whether the dreamer dreams the butterfly or the butterfly the dreamer, Chuang Tzu sets forth an argument for the reversibility of subject and object and blurs the distinction between dream and reality."[28]

Having recapitulated the parallel between Zhuangzi's butterfly dream and Baoyu's dream, I hasten to add that by simply pointing out the paral-lel, one cannot do full justice to the originality of Cao's vision. The butterfly dream has certainly influenced his vision, but the profundity and originality of the novel goes far beyond vivid and extended dramatizations of similar motifs and reaches into the deep recess of dreamwork and representation. A closer look at the dramatized parallel reveals Cao's insight into the unreliabil-ity of language and openness of signification and representation. The confu-sion centering around Zhen Baoyu's and Jia Baoyu's names is but the effect or consequence of language. And the "reality" presented in the novel comes into being as a result of signification and representation. As I have demon-strated, its fixed meaning is constantly questioned by the narrative, itself a linguistic composition. Ostensibly, the illusion is generated by the dream; but in essence, it is caused by the confusion with the name Baoyu and the homo-phones, *zhen* and *jia*. Cao Xueqin might have come under the influence of Zhuangzi's linguistic relativism: "A speaker has words, but what he says can not be determinate by any particular means." Zhuangzi attributed the inde-terminacy of words to the slippage of meaning in language representation and to different subjective positions in representation and understanding:

> There is no object which is not "that"; nor is there any object which is not
> "this." From the position of "that," the position of "this" will not show itself.
> But from the position of "this," the speaker knows it is "this." Hence it is said
> that "that" grows out of "this"; "this" also depends on "that." . . . "This" is also
> "that." "That" is also "This."[29]

There is no knowing whether Cao Xueqin was influenced by Zhuangzi's idea, and it is not necessary to know. What is of interest to us is that in Cao Xueqin's representation, he deliberately devised a setting in which this and that, subject and object, self and other, and truth and falsity become revers-ible categories indistinguishable not only to other characters in the novel but also to readers of the novel. From a rigorous psycholinguistic perspective, we may have a better understanding of the interplay between *zhen* and *jia* in terms of Emile Benveniste's observation on the usage of the pronouns "you" and "I" in conversation:

> There is no concept "I" that incorporates all the *I*'s that are uttered at every moment in the mouths of all speakers, in the sense that there is a concept "tree" to which all the individual uses of *tree* refer. . . . Then, what does *I* refer to? To something very peculiar which is exclusively linguistic: *I* refers to the act of individual discourse in which it is pronounced, and by this it designates the speaker.[30]

While Zhuangzi viewed "this" and "that" as reversible categories because of subjective positions, Benveniste describes the pronounced "I" and "you" as signifiers, which are only able to signify their meanings in concrete discursive situations. Except for the different usage of pronouns, both Zhuangzi and Benveniste arrived at the same understanding: these pronouns always imply a speaker and a listener in dialogue. The roles of the speaker and listener are as endlessly reversible as the pronouns that depend upon them. The speaker acts as a speaker at one moment and will become a listener at another moment. The pronouns possess only a periodic meaning and have no standardized and permanent significance. Notwithstanding Zhuangzi's idea, we cannot but admire Cao Xueqin's profound insight into the slippery nature of language, signification, and representation and his artistic rendering of his insight into a fascinating episode that hints at one of his aims in writing the novel. Zhen Baoyu and Jia Baoyu are not just representations of abstract concepts like "this" and "that," "you" and "I," "self" and "other," "truth" and "falsehood"; as two human beings caught in the personal, familial, and social networks of relations, they are a vivid embodiment of the profound idea that anything human is relative and subject to what may be called a deconstructive questioning. In his comment on the *Hongloumeng*, Wang Xilian 王希廉 rightly pointed out this message: "The most important key words in the *Hongloumeng* are *zhen* (real) and *jia* (false). The reader ought to know that the real is false; the false is the real; there is the false in the real; there is the real in the false; the real is not real; the false is not false."[31]

The episode of the dream encounter is perhaps another instance with which the author covertly cautions the reader that the novel is but a fiction and the reality created by it is also a fiction. The moral seems to be: "Don't take what is false as real nor take what is real as false." It goes well with the moral of the "Mirror for the Romantic." The moral of the mirror has been identified and emphasized by previous scholars. They, however, offer a reading based on the surface meaning of the mirror. Few realize that the surface meaning is eroded by wordplay several times. In chapter 12, Jia Rui is lying on his death bed. A Daoist priest comes to rescue him with a magic mirror. Jia Rui is advised to look at the back of the mirror only, and warned against looking at its front. But the back figures a skeleton that frightens him. So he looks at the front side, which figures the beautiful object of his sexual desire—Xi-feng. He goes into the mirror and has sexual intercourse with her until he ejaculates. After doing so a few times, he dies.

What merits our attention in this episode is the reversal of connotations in the mirror. In conventional understanding, the front side 正面 is associated with positive qualities like light, virtue, righteousness, and correct moral behavior, while the back side 反面 is associated with negative qualities like darkness, vice, injustice, and devious behavior. Ostensibly, the images figuring on both sides of the mirror correspond with this understanding: a beautiful woman on the front and an ugly skeleton on the back side. But the functions of the two images reverse their respective face values: the beautiful woman is a curse, while the ugly skeleton is a cure. Jia Rui dies simply because he takes each side at its face value. The moral of this mirror, then, does not seem to reside in the mirror but in the way one uses the mirror: one should not take things at their face value. The retort of the Daoist confirms this moral, "Who told him to look in the front? It is you who are to blame, for confusing the unreal with the real!"[32] The message of this moral is deconstructive indeed. It is as though the author were admonishing the reader not to take anything at its face value: whether it is the "reality" created in the novel or the reality of society. Then the author gives the episode another spin. Jia Rui's name means "false omen." If the author's warning serves as an omen, it is a false one. This twist heightens a sense of skepticism in the novel and produces an equally strong skepticism in the reader.

This skepticism is charged with the great subversive potential inherent in simulacra. "[T]he simulacrum is not simply a false copy," says Deleuze, "it places in question the very notations of copy and model."[33] In fact, when this skepticism is viewed in relation to the couplet on the stone arch, the subversive connotation is even stronger. The novel as fiction is false, and so is the reality created by it. If one takes the fiction as real, then the real reality becomes unreal. This connotation is charged with a subversive potential greater than any real transgression against morality and law. As Baudrillard puts it: "Transgression and violence are less serious, for they only contest the distribution of the real. Simulation is infinitely more dangerous since it always suggests, over and above its object, that law and order themselves might really be nothing more than a simulation."[34] It is worthwhile to consider again the couplet inscribed on the stone arch in the Land of Illusion: "Truth becomes fiction when the fiction's true; / Real becomes not-real when the unreal's real." The insight revealed in the couplet has a similar profundity to that of a saying Baudrillard attributes to Ecclesiastes: "The simulacrum is never that which conceals the truth—it is the truth which conceals that there is none. The simulacrum is true."[35] It is even more interesting to compare it with another couplet in the novel. Toward the end, Baoyu has another spiritual visit to the Land of Illusion. This time, all the prophecies are fulfilled. Even the insight about truth and falsehood is confirmed in another couplet inscribed on the stone arch: "When Fiction departs and Truth appears, / Truth prevails; / Though Not-real was once Real, the Real / is never unreal. 假去真來真勝假，無原有處有非無." This couplet effectively produces another reversal, for it implies that what is narrated in the novel is real, but it was once clouded by the unreal. I cannot but sigh and wonder (the reader may sigh and wonder, too) which is truth and which is falsity. It seems that the vision is a deconstructive one confirmed in the so-called "Hao-liao Song," the message of which is explained by the lame Daoist, "[F]or in all affairs of this world what is fortunate is unfortunate, and what is unfortunate is fortunate; if one is not unfortunate, then he is not fortunate; if he wants to be fortunate, he must be unfortunate."[36]

Having said that Cao Xueqin's vision of truth and falsity is a Daoist and deconstructive one, I must qualify it by saying: it is in the final analysis an artistic vision comparable to Philip Sidney's notion of truth and lie in poetry. In his "An Apology for Poetry," Sidney argues that the poet affirms nothing, and therefore he tells no lies.[37] In Cao Xuqin's case, it could be said that his mode of writing affirms nothing, and hence it can affirm anything. Wang Meng, an eminent Chinese writer who recently completed a commentary on the novel, arrives at a similar understanding. He writes in the preface to the commentary: "The *Hongloumeng* in fact does not tell you anything. You will forever argue about it and forever feel miserable about it. You cannot explain why it was like this but not like that."[38] This understanding coincides with the message that Vanitas wishes to impart to the world at the end of the novel: "I had better copy the story of the stone once again and find someone in the world who has leisure on his hands to publish it and transmit the message so that people may know that the extraordinary is ordinary; the vulgar is not vulgar; the real is unreal; the false is not false."[39] For this reason, I wish to suggest that *a possible message of the author may be that he was writing an open fiction that is about "the openness of fiction."*

CREATIVE VISION: OPENNESS OF FICTION

In a talk with a friend, James Joyce said, "The important thing is not what we write, but how we write."[40] This remark may help us better understand Cao Xueqin's creative vision. According to the opening of the novel, Cao Xueqin spent ten years writing and rewriting this novel five times. His poetic lines, "Every word and sentence are soaked with blood; / Ten years of labor is no ordinary thing," suggest that like Joyce, he was engrossed in how to write and in what to write. The hunting for authorial intention in a writing had been the dominant mode of reading until contemporary literary theories proved it to be problematic. Cao Xueqin's mode of narration, as I have demonstrated, seems to be saying: "My message is open. It is whatever the reader wishes it to mean." It is a concrete way of stating the abstract modern theory about the text, "[A] text is not a line of words releasing a single 'theological' meaning (the 'message' of the Author-God) but a multi-dimensional space in which a variety of writings, none of them original, blend and clash."[41] His mode of narration may not only serve as a critique of the so-called intentional fallacy but also suggests an open mode of reading. This is perhaps one of the "real" messages he wants to convey, at least a footnote to his self-professed claim about how the novel came to be written: "Pages full of idle words / Penned with hot and bitter tears; / All men call the author fool; / None his flavors savors."

That the *Hongloumeng* is an open novel for open readings is, of course, determined by the author's creative vision. In this respect, Cao Xueqin always reminds me of the French novelist Gide, whose most ambitious book is a novel about the writing of a novel, or of Joyce, who seemed obsessed with the reduction of experience to expression for the sake of expression. In the final analysis, *the creative vision (what he writes) of Cao Xueqin is perhaps his vision about creativity (how he writes, how fiction is made, and how it is read). When his creative vision turns into vision of creativity, it is not just that style turns into meaning, and form becomes content; on a higher level, writing becomes theory, and fiction turns into metafiction.* The discussion about how to write fiction at the novel's opening and end attests to the metafictional nature of the novel. The self-conscious reference to the author is a scarcely concealed attempt at metafiction. In the novel, the author is not referred to as its author, but as its editor, who pulls together already existent materials and gives them a better shape. This may, of course, be viewed as an ironic jab at Confucius, who claimed that he "only transmits but does not create." This reference, however, may well be construed as the author's (un)conscious awareness of the conditions of writing, aptly conveyed in Barthes's words: "[A] text is made of multiple writings, drawn from many cultures and entering into mutual relations of dialogue, parody, contestation, but there is one place where this multiplicity is focused and that place is the reader, not, as was hitherto said, the author."[42] Curiously, Cao Xueqin considers himself as the novel's editor, not its author. Zhiyanzhai regarded this detail as the author's ploy to fool the reader.[43] Could it be a sign of the author's deliberate attempt to distance himself from his creation so that he could view the novel from fresh perspectives and perfect the process of creation? In other words, he wants to put himself in the position of a special reader. Vanitas is another special reader who participates actively in the novel's creation. I even tend to regard the editor and Vanitas as two facets of the author's creative consciousness engaged in a dialogue on ways of writing and reading. Cao's ridicule of Vanitas may be read as an allegorical critique of the intentional fallacy and a call for an open reading: "No need for some self-important being to commend it or publish it. You in your insistence on ferreting out facts are like the man who dropped his sword in the water and thought to find it again by making a mark on the side of his boat; you are like a man playing a zither with the tuning-pegs glued fast."[44]

The sword seeker may be regarded as a conventional reader, the dropped sword the original intention of the author, the water of the flowing river the sea of writing, and the carving of a mark on the boat the act of reading. Just as the dropped sword cannot be recovered by means of the mark, the author's intention cannot be rediscovered through reading. Unlike the man playing the zither with the tuning-pegs glued fast, a reader should try to play whatever tunes his zither (the act of reading) allows. The enlightenment Vanitas comes to may also be understood as comparable to the modern understanding of the relations among the author, text, and reader: "Author, copyist and reader were alike in the dark! Just a game of brush and ink splashing for fun, a diversion to stimulate sentiment and satisfy inclination!" "Brush and ink" in Chinese are metonyms for words and writing. The reference to the novel as no more than a game in words and writing should not be construed as a sign of cynicism, a negative assessment sometimes attributed to the reference. For the game in words is meant for the betterment of human culture.

The admission that he was engaged in a "game of brush and ink splashing for fun" reveals the author's conscious act of making fiction for open representation. Fiction as a form of literature is to entertain the mind. The *Hongloumeng* is no exception. As Cao himself says, "It would be a pleasure to share this [account] with a few like-minded friends, to help the wine down after a meal or to while away the solitude of a rainy evening by a lamplit window."[45] The mind hates boredom. A fictional work with a single theme or message, however profound, would eventually lead to boredom. By contrast, a work with multiple themes and open hermeneutic space will entertain its readers for generations to come with no danger of boredom.

The admission may serve as a key to many puzzling details in the novel. For example, the ending of chapter 5 is baffling to both the characters inside the novel and to readers who read the novel. At the end of Baoyu's dream visit to the Land of Illusion, he was being dragged down into the Ford of Error by monsters and demons. Scared out of his wits, Baoyu burst out crying for help. His uttered words, "Save me, Keqing!" surprised Qinshi, who said to herself, "Ke-qing was the name they called me back at home when I was a little girl. Nobody here knows it. I wonder how he could have found it out?"[46] The author does not provide a clue anywhere in the novel. We readers feel greatly puzzled, too. It is truly a case in which the character, reader, and author are all in the dark. The mystery, however, gives the reader much food for thought. One widely known explanation is Yu Pingbo's: that it is an oblique revelation of Baoyu's secret liaison with Qinshi. Another possible explanation is that since Baoyu is an intimate friend of Qinshi's younger brother, Qin Zhong, he might have gotten to know Qinshi's childhood name from her brother. Still another explanation is that it was a case of extrasensory perception. A fourth explanation is that *keqing* is a homophone for "sweetheart." Since Baoyu is married to Keqing at the order of Disenchantment in the dream, it would be natural for him to shout Keqing's name for help at a time of terror. With a little imagination, we as readers could come up with some other explanations. All of them are possible, but none of them is verifiable in the context of the novel. The mystery will never be solved, but it succeeds in forcing the reader to make conjectures, thus effecting a cooperative relationship between the author and the reader. It does not matter what conjectures one may make; the authorial intention seems to have been to leave the solution open to the reader. Many other puzzles in the novel seem to have been intended in the same vein: the metamorphosis of the stone, the disappearance and reappearance of the jade, the story of the magic mirror, and so on.

The opening section and the ending section taken together may show the author's self-conscious vision of literary creation. The vision comes close to the poststructuralist conception of literature as writing, "[W]riting is the destruction of every voice, of every point of origin. Writing is that neutral, composite, oblique space where our subject slips away, the negative where all identity is lost, starting with the very identity of the body writing."[47] The opening section starts with the origin of the novel, continues with a confession about its major theme—"dreams" and "fantasies"—and ends with an advance account of the stone's story. It proclaims to have concealed the truth in the narration. Then, the idea of "truth concealed"(*zhen shi yin qu*) gives rise to the character Zhen Shiyin, who has a dream in his studio about the stone. Through the law of binary opposition, the idea of "truth concealed" leads to its opposite, "falsehood retained," thereby ushering in another character, Jia Yucun. Only after the appearance of both Zhen Shiyin and Jia Yucun does the novel proper begin to develop. Even then, the whole story of the stone is still contained within the structure of binary opposition between Zhen (truth) and Jia (falsehood) to the very end.

With this kind of structure, one wonders: was the author concerned with the opposition between truth and fiction or with the story of the stone? If he was concerned with both, then, what about the claim that the novel is a biography of several dozen extraordinary girls? If the novel centers on the stories of girls, Jia Baoyu or the stone represents but another structural scheme like that of Zhen Shiyin and Jia Yucun. Indeed, the stone and its incarnate human character Baoyu are designated as the carrier of the stories within the superstory. But the stone and Baoyu have their own stories, which are interwoven with the stories of the girls, myths, legends, history, religion, family life, and human relationships. As Anthony Yu points out, Jia Baoyu is meant to be "the incarnate text, story, and stone."[48] Thus, the author seems to have set his mind on making his novel represent the totality of Chinese culture in all its possible aspects. Any reader can dip into the novel, seize upon an aspect or aspects, and declare that it centers around a certain theme. The numerous themes came into existence largely as a result of this appropriation. This totalizing approach serves effectively to convey Cao Xueqin's vision about creativity: the OPENNESS OF FICTION. Because of its open vision, the *Hongloumeng* is destined to be an open novel subject to different and differing interpretations. All the hitherto existent readings support this view, and the diametrically opposed and mutually exclusive interpretations support this view even more.

My study has been focused on some facets of the novel to show that the *Hongloumeng* is an open fiction that escapes the polarized conception of the real and false, male and female, purity and impurity, realistic world and idealistic world, and other binary oppositions. The author's superb vision has endowed the novel with a configuration that enables the reader to deconstruct any attempt to pin down its central theme(s). It is not that previous scholars have not noticed this deconstructive potential. Ying-shih Yu, for one, in his study of the novel as a work constructed on a binary opposition between the ideal world and the world of reality, has touched upon a deconstructive tendency in the novel's structure.[49] He, however, believes that the deconstructive tendency emanates from the interpenetration of the two worlds and especially from the fact that the ideal world is built on the world of reality. What differentiates my view from his is that the deconstructive tendency may not be the outcome of the unity of contradictions in dialectics but may result from the combination of signification, representation, and simulation.

The interactions of signs enabled Cao Xueqin to configurate a hermeneutic space where different codes at different levels act and interact upon each other to produce a theoretically unlimited gamut of themes which may illuminate, complement, or contradict each other. The *Hongloumeng* relies on a signifying practice that Barthes discusses in his conception of a writerly text: it is a segmentation of the text into contiguous fragments (lexias), through which the five codes (semic, hermeneutic, proairetic, symbolic, and cultural) are manipulated to bounce back and forth and against each other to produce unlimited fresh meanings.[50] However, Barthes's segmentation, as far as I understand it, is more about ways of reading than about ways of writing. As one scholar puts it, "The writerly text comes into existence as an archaeological dig at the site of a classic text. It exhumes the cultural voices or codes responsible for the latter's enunciation, and in the process it discovers multiplicity instead of consistency, and signifying flux instead of stable meaning."[51] When I borrow Barthes's "writerly text" to describe the novel, I am not simply referring to ways of reading the novel. I also mean to allow it to embrace ways of writing the novel. I believe that Cao Xueqin is perhaps the first Chinese novelist who was *fully* conscious of the deconstructive potential of language and the infinite possibilities of discourse. He is certainly the first Chinese writer who recognized the all-encompassing capacity of the novel as a literary genre. The *Hongloumeng* is a novel composed with a full awareness of, and sensitivity to, the characteristic features of language and signification. The versatile use of language in its composition is comparable to that of modernist writers. In a conversation with one of his friends, Joyce boasted that he had woven into *Ulysses* so many hidden designs that it would take professors of English a hundred years to unravel them all. The same boast can certainly apply to the novel. In fact, two hundred years have already elapsed, but scholars of the novel are still arguing about what the themes of the novel could possibly be.

The different and conflicting views on the novel are not simply the result of different readings. In the final analysis, the multidimensionality of the novel comes from the complicated networks of signification and representation woven with the author's creative vision and practice. I have demonstrated that the novel is not written as a text that organizes its materials on the principle of mimesis only. It is more than anything else written as a text that constructs the mimetic materials on the principle of semiosis. Semiosis, in Peirce's conception, is an action of the sign.[52] It is interactions of signs in the novel that are largely responsible for the novel as a writerly text that denies the possibility of closure and promotes an infinite play of signification. In addition to mimesis and semiosis, the novel constitutes a congeries of simulacra generated, as we have said, on simulation.[53] Cao Xueqin is well-known to have been fond of word games. His use of wordplay, as Anthony Yu points out,[54] is not just confined to the names of characters and places, which are fairly obvious. Embedded on all levels and in all the nooks and crannies of the novel, they often serve as switchboards that channel our readings in different, opposite, and multiple directions. Placed at strategic junctions of the plot development, they embody the author's diegetic vision.

It is, therefore, the working of language from mimesis through semiosis to simulation in the verbalizations of reality, fantasy, dreams, myths, biography, and history that permits diverse readings and may warrant unlimited interpretations in the future. One insight of structuralism and poststructuralism—from Saussure through Levi-Strauss to Foucault and Derrida—is that language is the one agency that "contains" the author, reader, text, and world in the only form available to us, as a result or effect of discursive practices. The *Hongloumeng* may be cited as an eloquent proof of such an insight. Indeed, in the novel, the author, narrator, reader, characters, and narrative are all woven into a generative entity by the unfolding discourse. But the discursive totality does not impose the "prison house of language" on its components. Through adroit use of discourse, the author, narrator, reader, and characters frequently exchange their roles and enter and exit the discursive entity so unobtrusively that one scarcely notices the changes. Cao Xueqin is the author of the novel, but he also assumes the role of an editor and transmitter. Zhen Shiyin and Jia Yucun are characters, but they also become partial narrators and represent a message of the novel. Vanitas is a reader of the stone's story, but he also becomes a literary agent who gets it transmitted.

It is unnecessary to mention again the multiple roles of the stone as the origin, carrier, and structural frame of the story, the inorganic rock meant for repairing heaven, and the incarnated Baoyu. Rather than inhabiting the "prison house of language," it inhabits a hall of mirrors, a place where a congeries of structures/themes acquires a self-generating power through the power of language. Cao Xueqin does not seem to have been merely interested in setting up some objects to be reflected and re-reflected in the hall of mirrors. One of his interests seems to have been the construction of the hall of mirrors itself, and in setting up the mirrors in such a way that the objects to be reflected are bounced back and forth until one cannot tell what the original objects were. (By no mere accident, the novel features a number of mirrors that play important narrative roles.) Previously, some scholars have focused too much on the objects to the neglect of the hall of mirrors. At most, they have paid attention to individual mirrors as reflecting a single object, whether it be myth, history, biography, Confucianism, Daoism, Buddhism, nihilism, or fatalism. They seem to have forgotten that the novel is not the result of mere mimetic representation. It is also the outcome of simulation, which does not have real referents because it emanates from imaginative construction. Precisely because external referents are often deliberately abolished, facets of the novel can be construed to represent many objects, situations, and conditions. My study elsewhere has linked the Land of Illusion to the imperial palace, the imperial harem, a courtesan's house, a fairyland, heaven, hell, a boudoir, a nunnery, and a prison. One could also construe it to be related to a school (where Baoyu is taught the art of sexual love), a sanatorium (where Baoyu recuperates from his sickness and attains "enlightenment"), a lunatic asylum (Baoyu's distraught experience on his last visit to the place suggests this association), and even a concentration camp (where girls are kept until they are taken out to be metaphorically shot: married to men they do not love; in Yingchun's case, it is almost a literal execution—she is abused by her husband and persecuted to death).

DREAMS AND THE MAKING OF POETIC FICTION

The *Hongloumeng* has always been lauded as an extraordinary triumph of realism or critical realism. This praise is correct only to a certain extent. "Realism" and "critical realism" are two terms that grew out of studies of the eighteenth- and nineteenth-century European novel. A casual comparison of the novel with novels by Henry Fielding, Samuel Richardson, Jane Austen, Charles Dickens, W. M. Thackeray, Gustave Flaubert, and Honoré de Balzac, however, will reveal that neither "realism" nor "critical realism" is an appropriate term to describe the novel as a whole. It does not simply feature some unrealistic elements; in fact, the novel is wholly structured on a magic, fantastic, and phantasmagoric design much like the mechanism of dreams. We may call the novel a superdream that contains many interlocking dreams. In addition to the definitive title, "A Dream of Red Mansions," the novel has a number of alternative titles: "The Story of the Stone," "Records of a Passionate Monk," "The Precious Mirror of Wind and Moon," and "The Twelve Golden Hairpins of Jinling." It is not for nothing that the definitive title, "A Dream of Red Mansions," was chosen. Other titles would not do full justice to the total and totalized themes of the novel. Indeed, in the opening section, the author took the trouble to state: "Moreover, I inserted into the narrated account such words as 'dreams' and 'fantasies,' which constitute the main theme of this book and also serve the purpose of warning the reader [of its content.]"[55] Thus, the novel's relation to dreams is not to be doubted. What has often escaped the reader's attention is the oneiric nature of the writing mode. According to an introduction to chapter 1 by the author's younger brother, "The frequent use of dream imagery in this novel, . . . is due to the fact that the glittering, luxurious world of his youth which the author was attempting to recall in it had vanished so utterly by the time he came to write it that it now seemed more like a dream or mirage than something he had experienced in reality."[56] This seems to suggest that the *Hongloumeng* is, like Marcel Proust's *Remembrance of Things Past*, an attempt on the part of the author to recapture his youthful days that had elapsed like a dream. All this is certainly true, but in re-presenting things past, the author created a superdream not only in content but also in form. In other words, the novel is a literary dream that absorbed a great deal of the signifying mechanisms of dream work.

In the remaining sections, I will explore in depth the relationship between dreams and the *Hongloumeng*. An obvious reason is the abundance of dreams in the novel. A more important reason is that the *Hongloumeng* is a poetic fiction, and much of its poetry comes from the author's ingenious representation of dreams. Since the novel contains so many episodes that are vivid narratives of dream events, it would not be far wrong to suggest that Cao Xueqin must have been a good dreamer (in the daytime and at night). He must have also had an avid interest in the study of dreams, because his presentation of dreams, upon close examination in relation to modern studies of dreams, reveals his remarkable understanding of dream work. No one would dispute that the dreams presented in the novel are literary dreams, the presentation of which is controlled by a conscious literary vision. What is most fascinating is that he consciously employed his insight into the signifying mechanism of dream work to advance strategies of narration that may be called magic realism or oneiric poetics.

It has been a critical consensus among scholars of premodern Chinese fiction that the *Hongloumeng* is heavily indebted to the *Jin Ping Mei*. Not a few scholars have reiterated that without the *Jin Ping Mei*, the *Hongloumeng* could not have appeared. As far as subject matter and narrative skills are concerned, Cao Xueqin certainly learned a lot from the *Jin Ping Mei*. But as far as creative vision and conception of the novel are concerned, Cao Xueqin had another master: his own oneiric experience. Cao Xueqin's poetics of fiction is predicated, among other things, on his profound insight into the mechanism of dream work. Dreams taught Cao Xueqin what to present: fantastic motifs and enigmatic details in the plot, and the unconscious desires and subconscious fears of the characters. This aspect has been explored by C. T. Hsia,[57] Shuenfu Lin,[58] and others in the West, and by Li Yuanzhen,[59] Chen Bingliang[60] and others in China. While these studies have contributed significantly to our understanding of the relationship between dreams and the *Hongloumeng*, they are without exception content oriented and concerned with the dreams themselves. The content approach is very useful and has produced some fascinating studies, but it has its limitations. A major limitation is found in the critical practice of some scholars who have turned to Freud and psychoanalysis for inspirations. In their appropriation of Freud's dream interpretation, previous scholars have mostly adopted a content-oriented approach, indulging in discovering repressed unconscious desires and symbolic meanings. This approach pays almost no attention to the formal representation and processes of signification. It has given Freud's dream psychology a bad reputation from which it still suffers. As a result, there is a complete misunderstanding by the public of the significance of Freud's dream interpretation; his theory is treated as only supplying some fixed keys, and the linguistically oriented techniques are totally ignored. Freud expressed a warning against this misunderstanding in many of his writings. On one occasion, he cautioned: "My procedure is not so convenient as the popular decoding method which translates any given piece of a dream's content by a fixed key. I, on the contrary, am prepared to find that the same piece of content may conceal a different meaning when it occurs in various people or in various contexts."[61] The linguistically oriented approach of his theory can be illustrated with an example directly related to the Chinese language. On one occasion, Freud viewed the signifying mechanism of dream representation as similar to that of Chinese writing: "They [the dream symbols] frequently have more than one or even several meanings, and, as with Chinese script, the correct interpretation can only be arrived at on each occasion from the context."[62]

This is not the right place to discuss Freud's dream theory at length. My brief remarks are meant as an effort to dispel the popular misunderstanding as well as a step to what I am going to do in this section. Cao Xueqin's profound understanding of dreams is significant not only for our understanding of the content of his literary dreams presented in the novel but more importantly for throwing light on his creative vision, conception of the novel, and narrative strategies. Dreams did not simply supply him with source materials for the subject matter; more interestingly, they provided him with inspiration for modes of writing. Dreams taught him how to represent his ideas, how to organize the disparate materials into an open hermeneutic space, and how to make formal elements convey multiple creative visions. In a word, dreams contributed to the formation of his conception of novel making—a poetics of overdetermination.

When congratulated by his contemporaries on his discovery of the unconscious, Freud modestly replied that it was not he who first discovered the unconscious; rather, it was literary writers like Shakespeare and Dostoevsky. His achievement lay, he said, only in a systematic research into its psychological mechanism. Had Freud had the chance to read the *Hongloumeng*, he would have included Cao Xueqin in the ranks of writers who had discovered the unconscious. Indeed, had Freud had the chance to study the dream episodes in the *Hongloumeng*, he would probably have admitted that long before him, Cao Xueqin had already made some important discoveries concerning the signifying mechanism of the psyche which he was able to make only after long and meticulous analysis of real dreams. Let us consider Baoyu's first dream visit to the Land of Illusion. It is a well-known episode that has been analyzed over and again by scholars for different purposes. Toward the end of the dream visit, Baoyu is led into a dainty bedroom where he encounters a surprise: "To his intense surprise there was a fairy girl sitting in the middle of it. Her rose-fresh beauty reminded him strongly of Bao-chai, but there was also something about her of Dai-yu's delicate charm."[63] These few lines have often been taken to mean that Baoyu loves both Daiyu and Baochai and the two kinds of beauty they represent. This is certainly correct. My interest in these lines does not lie in what they may imply, however, but in the way the two girls are turned into a composite image. The composite image is made possible through a technique called "condensation," one of the most important signifying techniques dream work employs in producing pictographic images in dream content.

Basing himself on his findings of dream analyses, Freud describes "condensation" as "an inclination to form fresh unities out of elements which in our waking thoughts we should certainly have kept separate. As a consequence of this, a single element of the manifest dream often stands for a whole number of latent dream-thoughts, as though it were a combined allusion to all of them."[64] A comparison of Baoyu's dream image with Freud's theory is enlightening. I am simply amazed by the insight of Cao Xueqin's literary rendering. In Baoyu's waking thoughts, he knows that he loves both Daiyu and Baochai, for he is attracted to them by the two different kinds of beauty they represent. He also knows that it is impossible for him to have both of them. He, therefore, secretly nurses his love for Baochai while openly professing his love for Daiyu. But in the deepest recess of his mind, he cherishes the fond hope of having both of them. In his waking thoughts, he would most of the time suppress this desire, but in his dream, while the dream censor slackens its guard because of sleep, the unconscious desire evades the daytime repression and almost literally "compresses" the two beauties into one composite image, thereby fulfilling Baoyu's secret wish. Disenchantment's remark further reveals self-conscious effort at condensation: "I have a little sister. Her childhood name is Jianmei (composite beauty) and her style name is Keqing. I am going to give her to you as your bride."[65] The childhood name Jianmei reveals the author's conscious awareness of dream work's condensation, because such a name is an obvious coinage by the author for a special purpose. In Disenchantment's remark, an act of further condensation is done. Now the composite image is born not out of two persons but out of three persons: Daiyu, Baochai, and Qinshi. Cao Xueqin's compressed reference to the two female protagonists is a concrete illustration of the technique of condensation employed by dream work for representations of human figures as described by Freud: "There is another way in which a 'collective figure' can be produced for purpose of dream-condensation, namely by uniting the actual features of two or more people into a single dream-image."[66]

From the perspective of the composite image, we may say that the allusion to Qinshi results from an act of condensation. But from another perspective, we may also say that the mention of Keqing is an act of displacement, another important signifying technique at the command of dream work. "Displacement," according to Freud, is "a transference and displacement of psychic intensities"[67] onto an element in the dream so that a textual difference between dream content and thought content occurs. In the course of displacement, "psychical intensity, significance or affective potentiality of the thoughts is . . . transformed into sensory vividness."[68] In Baoyu's dream, since he was having his dream in Qinshi's bedroom, it is natural for his dream work to transfer his sexual desire onto a woman of her image, because his contact with Qinshi is part of the day's residue before the dream.

I could go on to analyze more dream episodes in the novel, but this dream should suffice for our purposes here. The comparison of the novel with Freud's psychological theory is not simply to show how close Cao Xueqin's insight comes to modern psychological theories. My major aim is to show that *his vision of creativity and techniques of open representation may have been derived from his profound understanding of dreams.* In the study of dreams, one must take note of the distinction made by Freud between dream contents and dream thoughts. Dream contents are simply shifting scenes of pictographic images one sees in sleep. Dream thoughts refer to the process of thinking that lies behind dream content: "Their dominant element is the repressed impulse, which has obtained some kind of expression, toned down and disguised though it may be, by associating itself with stimuli which happen to be there by tucking itself in the residue of the day before."[69] Dream content is manifest while dream thought is latent. Their relationship is like that between a translation and its original: "The dream-thoughts and the dream-content are presented to us like two versions of the same subject-matter in two different languages. Or, more properly, the dream-content seems like a transcript of the dream-thoughts into another mode of expression, whose characters and syntactic laws it is our business to discover by comparing the original and the translation."[70] The dream content and dream thoughts are thus intimately related. But they differ enormously not only in their form but also in the magnitude of space: "Dreams are brief, meagre and laconic in comparison with the range and wealth of the dream-thoughts. If a dream is written out it may perhaps fill half a page. The analysis setting out the dream-thoughts underlying it may occupy six, eight or a dozen times as much space."[71] This means that the dream content is the compressed form of copious dream thoughts.

Similarly, all great literature is a compressed form of writing. This is especially true of poetry. I have claimed in previous chapters that the *Hongloumeng* is a poetic fiction and have provided a number of reasons. A new reason is that like a poem, it is a compressed form of writing. The primary technique for compression is condensation. The other technique is displacement. Condensation and displacement work together to bring about the overdetermination of dream content.[72] And overdetermination is the primary source of multiple interpretation: "[E]ach element in the content of a dream is 'overdetermined' by material in the dream thoughts; it is not derived from a *single* element in the dream thoughts, but may be traced back to a whole number. These elements need not necessarily be closely related to each other in the dream thoughts themselves; they may belong to the most widely separated regions of the fabric of those thoughts. A dream element is, in the strictest sense of the word, the 'representative' of all this disparate material in the content of the dream."[73] Though the dreams in the novel are literary dreams imaginatively represented, the rationale of representation is quite similar.

My discussion of the relationship between dreams and the *Hongloumen* has paved the way for an inquiry into the poetic unconscious responsible for the poetic nature of the novel. "The interpretation of dreams," as Freud's famous saying goes, "is the royal road to a knowledge of the unconscious activities of the mind."[74] Creative writers, thinkers, and critics alike see an intrinsic relationship among dreams, poetry, and the unconscious. Jacques Lacan, who has conducted rigorous analysis of the kinship of poetry, dream, and the unconscious, confirms that poetry is a kind of dream through which the poet accesses his unconscious desires.[75] Since I am exploring Cao Xueqin's poetics of writing, the process goes in the opposite direction. In the next section, I will further explore the mechanisms of the literary dreams and attempt to delve into the poetic unconscious of the author, uncover poetic qualities of the novel, and locate its deeper source of openness.

THE POETIC UNCONSCIOUS AND POETICS OF OPENNESS

In chapter 4, I coined the term "lyric unconscious" to facilitate my study of the oft-neglected movement in Chinese fictional development. In that chapter, I mostly discussed its topographical function in mapping the macropicture of fiction's historical development. I left out its conceptual dimension, which should be more appropriately covered by another term, the "poetic unconscious." I described the latter term in my study of Chinese hermeneutics. In that study, I conceived of the poetic unconscious as an agency in the creative mind that operates in the way poetic language works. Consciously or unconsciously, it compresses different strands of desires into a poem through the linguistic economy of poetic language and endows it with a capacious hermeneutic space.[76] This concept will help us better understand how Cao Xueqin's creative mind works, where we can locate poetic qualities, and why his novel is a poetic fiction as well as an open fiction. I venture to argue that the poetry of the novel and its open poetics were based on a compressing operation by the poetic unconscious. The poetry of the novel is constructed out of the whole mass of Cao Xueqin's life experience. Each of the poetic elements might have been determined many times over in relation to his changing perception of life. The simulated overdetermination through the operations of language is, in my opinion, the major source of the novel's multivalence and polysemy.

Cao Xueqin spent most of his adult life writing and rewriting his masterpiece. In repeated rewriting and editing, he did not seem to simply add new materials to old materials, for if he had done so, his novel would have been several times its present length, and he would not have died leaving it unfinished. It is reasonable to suggest that "add" is not really the right word to describe his way of rewriting. The proper word should be "compression" or "condensation." Each time he rewrote, he compressed the added information and the existing discourse. The resultant mode of representation is not one of addition in the sense that A plus B and C yields ABC, but one in which the outcome features the qualities of A, B, and C but looks like none of them. The signifying mechanism of such rewriting is similar to Derrida's concept of "supplementality." The signifying logic of Derrida's idea is a complicated one. Barbara Johnson's summing up may serve as a convenient explanation: "The logic of the supplement wrenches apart the neatness of the metaphysical binary oppositions. Instead of 'A is opposed to B' we have 'B is both added to A and replaces A.' A and B are no longer opposed, nor are they equivalent. Indeed, they are no longer even equivalent to themselves. They are their own *différance* from themselves."[77] The polymorphous role of Jia Baoyu affords a complicated and ingenious example. Through the joint interplay of "condensation" and "displacement," he is, in addition to being a male child born into the Jia family and a social being in late Qing society, Nü-wa's inorganic stone, the Luminiscent Stone-in-waiting, the stone that has a life, the stone that carries the story, the precious jade which is his soul, but at the same time he is none of them, because he is the totality of them all.

I have stated that the novel is a superdream. There are several reasons for saying so. The primary reason has to do with the structural principle for the organization of the novel's materials. The novel may be divided into two parts that interconnect with and penetrate each other, like the dream content and dream thoughts. Baoyu's visit to the Land of Illusion is like the dream content, while the rest of the novel resembles dream thoughts. One may characterize the dream content and the dream thoughts behind the dream respectively as the tip of an iceberg that floats on the surface and the bulk of the iceberg that remains submerged in water. I think the iceberg metaphor would be appropriate for describing the relationship between the Land of Illusion and the rest of the novel. The cryptic dream visit to the Land of Illusion was meant to be related to the bulk of the novel. One may claim that the Land of Illusion is the key to understanding the novel, but it would be equally valid to claim the converse: the rest of the novel is the key to understanding the dream visit. Both serve to illuminate each other. The relationship between the dream visit and the bulk of the novel is truly like the one between the dream content and dream thoughts: "two versions of the same subject-matter in two different languages." The dream visit is written in cryptic codes, while the bulk of the novel is in discursive language. To put it in another way, the dream visit is like a transcript of the novel's narrative proper into another mode of expression. Just as a real dream interpretation requires a correlation between the dream content and dream thoughts, so we can uncover the meanings of chapter 5 of his novel and the ways of representation only by comparing the dream visit and the bulk of the novel.

Structurally, the novel as a whole may be seen as being organized on the model of a dream. A dream has a core element called the "nodal point," which is a point of contact "upon which a great number of the dream thoughts converge."[78] It functions like a switchboard, a term I have employed in the previous section. In the *Hongloumeng*, the nodal point is itself a dream that is Baoyu's dream visit to the Land of Illusion. To this "nodal point" or switchboard are connected many subnodal points. They are either clues to the fates of the major characters, or hints at the development of the plot, or multivalent words that suggest different perspectives to look at an event, an episode, a place, or a person. In the *Hongloumeng*, the nodal points and subnodal points are programmed like compressed computer documents. They may look simple and easy to understand, but beneath their surface meaning, we may find layer upon layer of hidden meanings. This may be why the Land of Illusion can be construed to represent so many places and institutions, as previous scholars and I myself have pointed out.

One could speculate on how the multivalence came about. Cao Xueqin might have first conceived of the Land of Illusion as a pure and clean place: a female kingdom, a utopia, and a fairyland, but as he rewrote the novel in relation to his changing perception of life and society, he may have realized that purity and cleanliness could not possibly be divorced from impurity and sordidness. Therefore the pure and clean place began to take on negative features of impure and unclean places: brothel, hell, and prison. While a female kingdom, a utopia, and a fairyland represent one pole, a brothel, hell, and a prison represent the opposite pole. In between the two poles there are borderline places: the imperial harem, a rich man's boudoir, or the nunneries. Of course, the actual order of appearance might be different, but the procedure of overdetermination is valid.

Cao Xueqin's insight into the nature of female places is fascinating, but his mode of representing his insight is even more so. That he could make one place represent so many polarized places is a marvelous feat few writers could achieve. What enabled him to accomplish his representation is the technique of condensation through the operation of language codes. His successful use of condensation is seen at its clearest when he handles key words and names. Some of them function like nodal points in a dream or like switchboards. Since I have already elaborated on this, here, I only want to briefly discuss the name "Jianmei" again. David Hawkes translates it as "Two-in-one," which represents an accepted understanding of the word. I venture to argue that "Two-in-one" is adequate from one perspective, but fails to capture the multivalence of the word from other perspectives. In addition to Daiyu and Baochai, the name alludes to Qinshi. The word *mei* itself is a multivalent word. It may refer to the quality of beauty, but it may also refer to beautiful women. In the context of the novel, the epithet may serve as a hint at Baoyu's attraction to all beautiful girls whom he meets and loves. Therefore, "composite beauty" may be a better translation.

The two basic techniques in dream formation, "condensation" and "displacement" are essentially the two wheels that drive the vehicle of discourse. This idea may be able to explain the drastic narrative shifts in the *Hongloumeng*, especially the enigmatic vicissitudes of the stone. The transformation of the stone from Nü-wa's inorganic rock to the Luminiscent Stone-in-waiting, from the stone that laments over its inability to repair the broken heaven to the stone that carries the male protagonist's story, from a huge block of real stone to a jade small enough to be carried in a newborn's mouth, from a tangible material object to an immaterial spirit, and from its disappearance to reappearance—all these miraculous narrative twists and turns cannot be rationally explained unless we treat them as similar in nature to the incredible changes of scenes in dreams. Cao Xueqin's conception of the mythical structural frame for the novel might not have been entirely indebted to his interest in Chinese myths and legends, but might have evolved from his study of dreams. Having said this, I hasten to add that after all, myths and dreams organize their materials on a similar structuring principle and share a similar tendency to invite multiple interpretations. The full implications of the stone's fantastic transformations in the context of the novel remain to be explored.

Having argued that Cao Xueqin's creative vision was considerably influenced by his insight into dream work, I must emphasize that he was not just creating his novel in imitation of dreams. He was writing his novel in simulation of dreams. The difference between imitation and simulation of dreams is that in imitation an author only gives his represented material a dreamlike façade; there is no attempt to reproduce the signifying techniques of dream work. In simulation there is true insight into dream work, and one tries to present ideas, experiences, and perceptions in a dreamlike way so that the signifying techniques of dream work can advance various overt and covert agendas. In the former, what is represented is very important, but in the latter, how the material is presented is even more important. Just as simulation blurs the distinction between reality and fantasy, so dream simulation makes it impossible to tell whether the author has transcribed a real dream or has presented a literary dream. I believe that all the dream episodes in the novel have the literalness of real dreams and the imaginativeness of literary dreams. They look nonsensical but are really meaningful.

Simulation of dreams is based on a profound understanding of dream work and reveals the author's conscious awareness that a dream is a form of writing and writing is a form of dream; both dream and writing are effects and affects produced by language and signs. In his monumental work, Freud has proved the close relationship between literature and dreams. Freud (or anyone who has paid some attention to his or her dreams) has noticed that the dream content often takes the form of a picture puzzle or a rebus: it may depict a house with a boat on its roof, a single letter of the alphabet, the figure of a running man who is bigger than the house but has no head, and so on. In our waking thoughts, we would say this sort of depiction is utterly nonsensical. But if we find a way to decode the images and to relate them in a meaningful manner, we may be surprised to find that the depiction is no longer nonsensical but "may form a poetical phrase of the greatest beauty and significance."[79] Many of the dream details in the *Hongloumeng* are picture puzzles of this kind. Previous scholars have made extensive research into their implications in the context of the novel.[80] It is unnecessary to repeat any part of their research. Here I only want to point out that the picture puzzles or rebuses in the novel were created with the same compositional techniques as dream formation. For example, the juxtaposition of "a bunch of fresh flowers" and "a worn-out mat" produces a combination of sounds: *hua-xi*, alluding to Hua Xiren, Baoyu's maid. Similarly, the picture of "two dead trees with a jade belt hanging in their branches" alludes to Lin Daiyu (her name, through sound association, means "trees with a jade belt hanging in their branches"); and the picture of "a golden hairpin lying half-buried in snow" hints at the name of Xue Baochai (the sound of her name is similar to "snow embraces a golden hairpin). The compositional techniques for these picture puzzles are sound association and visual association, two major techniques employed by dream work for pictographic representation.

If one compares the existent scholarly findings concerning the twelve beauties in the picture puzzles of chapter 5 of the novel with Freud's techniques of dream formation, he will be amazed by the extent to which Cao Xueqin's simulated dream vision resembles real dream formation. Of course, since the dream episodes were simulated, they are not re-presentations of dreams that Cao Xueqin might have had; they are dream simulacra that impart his perceptions, remembrances, visions, views, and messages. What merits our special attention is that Cao Xueqin employed the techniques of dream work for deliberate openness. For example, the word puzzle concerning Wang Xifeng's fate has this line: "yi cong er ling san ren mu 一從二令三人木," which literally means "one/follow/two/command/ three/person/wood." So far there have been nearly ten interpretations.[81] In the context of the novel, all the existent interpretations are plausible, but the search for a "correct" interpretation is still going on. No one in the search seems to have realized that this word game, like a dream puzzle, is deliberately devised to give as many interpretations as readers care to use their imagination.

In reading his novel, we ought to approach the *Hongloumeng* in the way one interprets a dream. In the past, scholars have generally taken the word "dream" in the title of the novel figuratively and metaphorically, but we should not overlook its literality. After all, dreams are constructed like a form of writing, and my study of the novel shows that the open significations correspond pretty well to the techniques of dream work. My advocacy for treating the literality of the dreams in the novel seriously entails a shift in ways of reading. In his discussion of dream interpretation and psychic writing, Derrida points out the limitations of a content approach:

> The dreamer invents his own grammar. No meaningful material or prerequisite text exists which he might simply use, even if he never deprives himself of them. Such, despite their interest, is the limitation of the *Chiffriermethode* [decoding method] and the *Traumbuch* [dream book]. As much as it is a function of the generality and the rigidity of the code, this limitation is a function of an excessive preoccupation with content, and an insufficient concern for relations, locations, processes, and differences.[82]

The limitations of a content approach to psychic writing should alert us to the limitations of such an approach to literary writing. We need to make a drastic shift from what is presented to how it is presented and pay attention to how form, style, and ways of writing convey subtle meanings. Cao Xueqin is an ingenious dreamer who invented his own writing strategies, and we have so far uncovered only a small portion of them. Freud shows that "the elements of the dream are constructed out of the whole mass of dream-thoughts and each one of those elements is shown to have been determined many times over in relation to the dream-thoughts."[83] Generally, one tends to underestimate the amount of compression that has gone into the making of dreams. When further efforts at interpretation are carried out, one is likely to find more thoughts concealed behind a given dream. For this reason, Freud cautions that "it is in fact never possible to be sure that a dream has been completely interpreted. Even if the solution seems satisfactory and without gaps, the possibility always remains that the dream may have yet another meaning. Strictly speaking, then, it is impossible to determine the amount of condensation."[84] The *Hongloumeng* is still a book full of enigmatic details, events, and episodes. These enigmas are overdetermined like dream elements. We have not yet completely cracked their cryptic "codes." For example: What are the multiple implications of the stone? What was meant by the author in endowing the stone with the ability to transform itself? Why is the stone capable of warding off evil spirits and curing sickness? What is the relationship between Nü-wa's stone and the Luminiscent Stone-in-waiting? Still less have we exhausted their connotations. Even if we come to the stage at which all the encoded "messages" have been decoded and all the intended open elements ferreted out, the textual openness of the novel will remain an inexhaustible source.

A WRITING MODEL OF OPEN FICTION

The *Hongloumeng* has some characteristics that remind us of "fabulation" and "metafiction" in American fiction, the "new novel" in France, and "magic realism" in Latin American fiction. In this respect, it anticipates the modern writing tendency that rejects the critical apparatus associated with realism in favor of open form and denies narrative closure and its attendant certainties about meaning. Commenting on the nature of modern narrative, one fiction theorist points out, "[I]t becomes a text, an opaque collection of words that do not refer to any other world, real or imaginary. Such is the 'writable' [writerly] text described by Barthes, as opposed to the 'readable' [readerly] narratives of the past."[85] The *Hongloumeng* is certainly a writerly text. In the conceptual shift from the readerly text to the writerly text, there is a shift from language regarded as "representation" to a language regarded as "signification," language as being no more than a "sign" in a differential system of signs for which there is no real origin or any origin but an arbitrary authority.

Cao Xueqin certainly did not formulate a postmodern poetics of fiction writing, but his creative practice and his ideas about fiction writing put into the mouth of his characters are indicative of comparable insights. He was not exclusively engaged in writing a realistic novel that represents a reality he either observed or imagined, but he was engaged in writing a narrative that employs a language that he conceived of as "signification" and "simulation." There is not only that which is mimetically represented, but also that which signifies, simulates, and generates an endless series of connotations. With the various writing strategies that he used, Cao Xueqin did not mean to write his novel as a closed work, nor does the interaction of signs consign it to be one. We, therefore, ought to approach the novel as an open system while paying enough attention to signifying relations and simulated forms in addition to mimetic representations. Although Cao Xueqin did not write a theoretical treatise on fiction creation, there are sufficient theoretical insights in his novel for us to construct a theoretical paradigm. This is an open paradigm of fiction making, which attempts not so much to represent a slice of life, real or imaginary, as to create a verbal art. It rests on three basic insights that we have teased out of the novel: (1) the novel is a fictional work whose signifying and hermeneutic space results from the interaction of language codes as well as cultural codes; (2) the author made deliberate efforts to leave the hermeneutic space of the novel open; (3) the novel was meant not merely as a mimetic representation but also as an imaginative simulation. The three pillars supporting the paradigm are mimesis, semiosis, and simulation. Mimesis is one pole, while simulation is the other. Semiosis is the mediating factor that connects, opposes, and combines the two poles. This paradigm aims at pure fiction, results in open fiction, and aspires to be poetic fiction. Theoretically, this paradigm founded on the infinite possibilities of language represents the highest contribution that any traditional Chinese novel has made to the Chinese theory of fiction.

Theory of Fiction: A Chinese System

My macro-study of Chinese fiction and micro-study of the chosen master-pieces in relation to contemporary literary theories and Western fiction have come to a close. What has gone before has paved the way for making some claims and a conceptual synthesis. It has put me in a position to claim that the great fictional works of China should be treated as monuments in the development of not only Chinese fiction but also of world fiction. Although my study has devoted some space to historical and critical analysis, my real objective has been to offer a new view of Chinese fiction by reconceptualizing its historical development from a new perspective, and critical analysis has been used as the basis for deriving a poetics for each of the monumental works. In this final part of the book, I would like to make a conceptual leap by constructing a system of fiction theory in the Chinese tradition based on the conceptual insights of reading and writing that have been teased out of the chosen analytic data. I also wish to explore the conceptual foundations of the derived poetics and engage in a dialogue between the individual poetics of the chosen Chinese works and contemporary Western fiction theory. In so doing, I hope to contribute to the internationalization of Chinese fiction and to a transcultural theory of fiction that may bridge the gap between Chinese and Western fictional theories. Consistent with the methodology of this book, this chapter is theory driven but practice oriented. Its ultimate aim is to provide insights and inspiration to writers and readers of fiction in their efforts to create and interpret fictional works and to scholars of fiction who conduct conceptual inquiries into fiction

A SYNTHETIC OVERVIEW

In the introduction, I pointed out that fiction as a discourse in contradistinction to history and reality arose very early in both Chinese and Western traditions, but fiction as a literary genre in the modern sense of the short story, novella, and novel arose rather late in both traditions. Consequently, theory of fiction in each tradition arose relatively late in contrast to the rise of poetic and dramatic theories. In the European tradition, even after the firm establishment of the novel as a popular genre in literary writings in the eighteenth century, writings on the theory of fiction were sporadic, and critical discourse on literary theory continued to focus on poetry and drama well into the nineteenth century.[1] In the Chinese tradition, a similar situation existed. Prose fiction, though popular among the reading public, continued to be viewed as a low form of literature, on a par with drama, but not on an equal footing with poetry. Major literary theorists and critics continued to concentrate on poetry and classical prose and refused to engage in serious discussions of fiction. Only scholars on the margins of the literary establishment conducted studies of fiction. Because their major interest focused on critical comments of fictional works, they turned out a large quantity of commentarial work under the rubric of *xiaoshuo pingdian* (fiction commentaries). This kind of critical discourse is mainly concerned with practical techniques of fiction writing, and only in a secondary manner did it engage in conceptual inquires into the nature, conception, function, ontology, and epistemology of fiction. With few exceptions, there was no interest in constructing systems of fiction theories.

Although Chinese scholars of fiction may not have shown a great interest in conceptual inquires, Chinese fiction writers tackled practically all the major conceptual categories in their creative writings and arrived at an implicit system of fiction theory. This system of fiction theory shares with the European tradition major ideas of fiction and differs from its counterpart in some significant areas. While the similarities in the Chinese theory of fiction prompt me to claim that the history of Chinese fiction has moved steadily toward the internationalization of fiction, its differences may be regarded as contributions made by Chinese fiction to the world system of fiction theory. In the bulk of this concluding chapter, I will attempt to bring out a Chinese system of fiction theory complemented by a poetics of practical criticism.

A Chinese system of fiction theory should be predicated on seven conceptual pillars: (1) genesis: *fa fen zhu shu* 發憤著書 (lyrical and psychological rise); (2) ontology: *wu zhong sheng you* 無中生有 (being in nonbeing, or real in unreal); (3) epistemology: *yi jia wei zhen* 以假為真 (make-believe, or taking the unreal as real); (4) creative conception: *duo yuan gong cun* 多元共存 (many-in-one totality, or to unify multiple themes into a grand narrative); (5) model of writing: *xugu huwen* 訓古互文 (linguistic dissemination); (6) modes of representation: *jian shou bing xu* 兼收並蓄 (kaleidoscopic narration, or multiple narrative modes); and (7) theory of reading: *quan shi kai fang* 詮釋開放 (open hermeneutics, or multiple interpretations). Metaphysically, the totality of the system conceives of fiction as a network of narrative whose self-generative mechanism of meanings is equivalent to that of the Dao or Taiji, the supreme principle in Chinese thought. Aesthetically, it sets for fiction the artistic ideal of pure fiction, metafiction, or poetic fiction 詩化小說. Hermeneutically, it encourages fictional works to strive for the same artistic condition for the highest order of lyric poetry: surplus signification or endless meanings. It is evident that this system differs from its Western counterpart in some essential aspects. In the following, I will elucidate each of the pillars in detail and explore their metaphysical and aesthetic conditions in contradistinction to Western theories of fiction.

GENESIS: LYRICAL AND PSYCHOLOGICAL RISE

About the origins of Chinese fiction, there are three accepted views: (1) it arose from mythology; (2) it originated from collections of gossip and street talk by feudal lords' petty officials; (3) it evolved from historiography. While this scholarly consensus provides an adequate historical (extrinsic) view of fiction's genesis, it fails to account for the conceptual (intrinsic) rise of fiction as a literary genre; still less is it able to distinguish it from other forms of writing and describe the internal tensions between *xiaoshuo* (fiction) and historiography. While taking note of the mythological origin, street-talk origin, and historical origin, there are intrinsic reasons for the rise of fiction, especially the creative impulse to seek entertainment and to reduce psychological tension. But the genesis of individual works of fiction is quite different from that of a genre. The main difference lies in the fact that while the former is largely a conscious act on the part of an individual writer, the latter is a large-scale aesthetic movement driven by many factors, including political, economic, social, and cultural ones. A synthetic view on the genesis of Chinese fiction should not lose sight of the intrinsic aspects of its rise so as to give it some universal significance. In the Chinese tradition, lyric poetry and poetic criticism have exerted a profound influence on Chinese fiction. This impact determined the dual nature of Chinese fiction's genesis: it is spontaneous, expressionist, and therapeutic, on the one hand, and mimetic and social on the other hand. The social rise of fiction has been elaborated extensively in existent scholarship, so I will focus on the lyrical and psychological aspects of fiction's genesis.

In consciously created fictional works, therapeutic and expressive factors play such a significant role in the genesis that we may designate a lyrical and psychological origin of Chinese fiction. The therapeutic and expressionist view of genesis may be traced to Sima Qian's famous idea of *fafen zhushu* 發憤著書: a creative writer writes in order to give vent to his pent-up emotions. But it was fictional practice and criticism that formed the basis of this view. In his commentary on the *Shuihu zhuan* (Water Margin), Li Zhi 李贄 (1527–1602) states:

> The Grand Historian said: "*Shuinan* and *Gufen* are the works by virtuous sages who gave vent to their pent-up feelings." In view of this statement, virtuous sages of ancient times would not compose if they did not have the desire to vent their pent-up emotions. If one wrote without the impulsive desire to vent his feelings, he would be like a person who shivers without

feeling cold, or a person who groans without falling sick. Even though such a person writes, what is there worth reading in his writings? The *Shuihu zhuan* is a fictional work that resulted from giving vent to pent-up emotions.[2]

Sima Qian's idea of genesis refers to artistic and cultural creativity in general. Li Zhi is one of the critics who voiced the idea that fiction also arises from the same kinds of creative impulses as poetry, prose, and other aesthetic activities. In another well-known comment on creativity, he took therapeutic expressionism as the genesis of literature:

> Among those in the world who are really capable of writing, none of them had at first the intention to write. They had so many indescribable but strange things in their hearts, so much in their throats that they wanted to spit out but dared not, so much in their mouth that they wanted to speak out but they could not tell. These accumulated to the full for a long time and gathered a momentum difficult to curb. Once such men saw a scene, they were filled with emotions, and when something touched their eyes, they began to sigh. They seized someone else's wine cup to wash away their own pent-up emotions, gave vent to the grievances in the heart, and sighed sentimentally over their misfortunes against the background of thousand years. No sooner had they stopped than jade and pearls gushed out, the Milky Way brightened the night, and colorful patterns appeared in the sky. They then became arrogant, yelled frenziedly, wept with tears falling down, and could not control themselves.[3]

What Li Zhi describes is not just the situation at the inception of Chinese literature; it presents a moment when the creative urge becomes so strong that it cannot find a way out until a literary work is successfully completed. One might call this creative urge a source of negative healing. In chapter 2, I also discussed the desire to create fictional works for pleasure. The creative urge for entertainment is the other side of the therapeutic genesis. It is the positive form of therapeutic expressionism. The positive and negative aspects constitute a complete picture of fiction's genesis, which is both Chinese and universal. The therapeutic expressionism is spontaneous and poetic. Li Zhi is but one of the traditional scholars who were able to penetrate the deep structure of fiction's genesis and view fiction as having a poetic, expressive origin. This view of fiction's genesis confirms from a different perspective J. S. Mill's view: "[M]any of the finest poems are in the form of novels, and in almost all good novels there is true poetry."[4]

An expressive view is concerned with the genesis of pure fiction and poetic fiction. In contradistinction with historical fiction, whose genesis follows a second-order imitation (historical novels grow out of imitation of official and unofficial histories), the expressive genesis dovetails with a common Chinese expression, *wu zhong sheng you* (to create something out of nothing). In the popular discourse, this saying refers to the act of making up gossip, rumors, and tales out of thin air. It not only relates fiction to its earliest origin in street talk and gossip and explains why it was for a long time despised but also connects it to the metaphysical principles of *you* (being) and *wu* (nonbeing) in Chinese thought. In a conceptual examination of fiction's origin, this idea centers on a dialectics between *wu* (nothing or non-being) and *you* (something or being). It obviously came under the influence of the Chinese philosophical—especially the Daoist—conception of the world as evolving from nothing or nonbeing: "All things under heaven grow out of something; something grows out of nothing 天下萬物生于有，有生于無."[5] In the Chinese tradition, this idea is not only expounded in fiction criticism, but also implicitly and explicitly expressed in some fictional works. In Cao Xueqin's *Hongloumeng*, we can find a concentrated expression of this idea. Cao Xueqin never wrote a treatise on fiction, but like some early fiction writers in the European tradition, he voiced his ideas of fiction in his creative work. As I have already discussed in previous chapters on the *Hongloumeng*, his fictional work is not only a masterpiece of fiction but also contains a theory of fiction. In his implicit system of theory, there is an explicit view of fiction's genesis. The novel opens with a question about the origin of the novel and then goes on to tell the reader how it comes about. Scholars of the novel have discussed extensively the mythical origin of the novel. Some view it as providing an enthralling beginning to the tale and a structural framework for the novel's diverse materials; some view it as offering a thematic reference to the deep structure of Chinese culture, and still others view it as a mode of writing that blends realism with myths and legends. I am inclined to think that the opening coupled with the ending offers a theory of fiction. In this theory of fiction, fiction is conceived of as something that grows out of nothing.

As is characteristic of a creative writer, Cao Xueqin expresses his theory of fiction in the manner of telling a story. In the opening, the author tells us that the genesis of the novel is related to a Chinese myth. Long, long ago, the goddess Nü-wa was entrusted with the stupendous task of repairing the broken sky. She melted down a great quantity of rock, and on the Incredible Crags of the Great Fable Mountain, she molded the melted rock into 36,501 large building blocks. She used all of them except one. In the long aeons of time, this unused block acquired magic power and assumed a life of its own. It bemoans its unworthiness and oblivion. Then, one day, a Buddhist monk and a Daoist priest came by and saw it engrossed in its lamentations. The monk inscribed some words on it and offered to take it to a wonderful place where it could enjoy itself. Having received its agreement, the monk slipped it into his pocket and set off to the human world. Again, many aeons passed. A Daoist priest caught sight of the stone and read the inscriptions on it. He then carried out a conversation with the stone and inquired about the inscribed stories. Convinced by the stone that the inscribed stories were worth publication, the Daoist priest copied everything on it and looked for a publisher. This is how the novel came into being.[6]

This fablelike genesis of the novel, when analyzed critically and conceptually, reveals an implicit idea of fiction. Unlike the Western conception of fiction as an imitation of the natural and human world, it views fiction as a result of expression. Cao Xueqin the author figures in the opening and closing of the novel, but he is presented not as the author but as the editor of the novel. The real author is supposedly the incarnated stone. The source of creation is its being relegated to a useless fate, and the story is based on its vicissitudes in the human world. Because of its dissatisfaction with its unworthy fate, it embarks on a trip to the human world at the invitation of the monk and thus accumulates experiences that are worth retelling in print. Thus, the opening posits a theory of fiction that is expressive in nature. That the stone's unhappiness at its fate should give rise to an extended novel is an imaginative way to propose a theory of fiction's origin that conforms to the expressive genesis of literary creation adequately expounded by Sima Qian and Li Zhe. The original source of the nove, then, is not the imitation of life, but the stirring of human desire for creative activity. In terms of Sima Qian's theory of artistic creation as an expression of frustration and indignation at one's ill fate, Cao Xueqin's multilayered description of the stone's genesis and reincarnation is a symbolic expression of the ontological condition of the novel in particular and of fiction in general. The stone's fate of being rejected for the task of repairing the broken heaven symbolizes the ill fate of numerous traditional Chinese literati who were not chosen by the social establishment, and its experience in the human world as the reincarnated protagonist who has a story to tell symbolizes the rejected literati's re-channeling of their creative energy into literary creation. Anthony C. Yu's brilliant analysis of the opening of the novel supports my conceived genesis for Chinese fiction. After critically examining the origin of the stone in relation to the novel's genesis, he concludes:

> The stone's fecund potency may thus be regarded as part of its original stirring of desire, the process described by the clerics previously as "the fated change of 'extreme repose giving rise to movement, of nothing begetting something (*wu zhong sheng you*).'" The last clause, of course, is a direct inversion of the famed declaration by Laozi (chap. 40) that "something is begotten of nothing (*you sheng yu wu*)." Whereas that philosopher's statement in context seems to assert some kind of cosmogonic process, the clerics' verdict on Stone's longing to enter the human world refers sardonically to the foolish potency of desire. Now an entrenched idiom of modern vernacular, the expression *wu zhong sheng you* signifies a kind of absurd or baseless reasoning, fixing itself as a metaphor in the perpetual denigration of fiction. In terms of the novel, however, desire is double-edged: it impels the stone to seek remedy for a supposed lack in its own existence, but for this experience to generate the plot of an entire work of fiction also presupposes a prior need of a writer to create something out of nothing.[7]

Thus, the novel came into being as a result of the notion of being in nonbeing. The mythic framework, which refers to Nü-wa, the goddess responsible for the creation of humanity in Chinese mythology, endows the novel's genesis with a universal nature applicable to the origins of all pure fictions, and indeed all art. As Yu rightly points out, "Instead of being one of the progenitors of humans, as her mythic role purportedly suggests, her work in the narrative becomes the genesis of fictive origins. And, instead of joining her in the fertile enterprise of cosmic restitution, the rejected stone engages in a different kind of productive labor. Both of their actions, in turn, also mirror the 'life-giving' and 'form-endowing' activities of the artist."[8] The *Hongloumeng* is the peak of Chinese fiction. The theory of genesis it posits is a most sophisticated one in the Chinese tradition. By turning the conventional and often derogative view of "creating something out of nothing" into a legitimate cause for the rise of fiction, it completely rejects the second-order imitation, the core of historical romances, thus dethroning the dominance of history in the making of fiction. It established the legitimacy of pure fiction pioneered by the *Jin Ping Mei* and affirms the blending of first-order imitation and expression.

ONTOLOGY:
BEING IN NONBEING OR REAL IN UNREAL

The expressive view of fiction's genesis obviously has to do with the dominance of lyric poetry, whose genesis has been conceived in the Chinese tradition as a result of natural growth from pent-up emotions. The expressive theory of fiction entails an ontology of fiction distinctly different from that in Western fiction theory, which is dominated by the idea of imitation. Since Aristotle, the essence of fiction has been viewed as imitation of aspects of life in the West. In most recent Western theories, however, some scholars challenge the commonly accepted view that fictional works imitate life. Dolezel, Cohn, Pavel, and others have argued against the reduction of fiction to imitation of life alone and tried to reconceptualize the cardinal concept of mimesis.[9]

In my conceptualization of fiction's genesis, I mentioned the Chinese expression *wu zhong sheng you* 無中生有 ("to create something out of nothing"; to create a fictional account out of imagination). It is a near equivalent to the Western concept of fictionality. I view a variation on the expression, *you sheng yu wu* 有生于無 (something grows out of nothing, or being in nonbeing), as nearly expressing the ontology of Chinese fiction. By no mere accident, this expression is also a metaphysical idea from the Daoist metaphysics, which conceives of everything in the universe as growing out of nothing. This Daoist idea has exerted a powerful influence on the Chinese conception of literature. In traditional poetics, Lu Ji 陸機 (261–303) may be the first literary theorist who viewed literature as a result of something growing out of nothing. In his *Wenfu* (*Rhyme-Prose on Literature*), he states: "It is Being, created by tasking the Great Void, / And it is sound rung out of Profound Silence. / In a sheet of paper is contained the Infinite, / And, evolved from an inch-sized heart, an endless panorama."[10] In contradistinction to the Western view of literature as arising from imitations of aspects of life, it posits an expressive view of literature's genesis as well as its being.

The Chinese notion of fiction, "something out of nothing, or being in nonbeing," implies a rejection of imitation as the sole source of fiction, and this rejection is deeply embedded in the Chinese tradition's perception and conception of fiction's reality and in the actual practice of fiction writing. Daoist metaphysics maintains that the Dao is the emptiness or nothingness that gives birth to all things. In Laozi's *Daode jing* 道德經, "nothing" is the ontology of the Dao, while "something" is its function.[11] The Daoist idea may give us the inspiration to reconceptualize the ontology of fiction. Scholars of fiction theory have been wrestling with the paradoxical condition of fiction: it imitates life, yet it is not a copy of life; it resembles life, yet it is not life. In my opinion, we cannot find a better way to conceptualize the paradoxical condition of fiction than the Chinese conception of the universe. Fiction is being, while the infinity of life is nonbeing. Just as fiction is a reflection or refraction of life, so we may conceive it as the being in nonbeing.

In the discussion of fiction, ancient Chinese scholars and writers did not use the metaphysical concepts of *wu* (nonbeing) and *you* (being). Since they recognized that fiction is a form of imitation of life, they employed some binary terms that are more closely related to life: *zhen* (real) and *jia* (unreal), *shi* (substance) and *xu* (emptiness), *qi* (extraordinary) and *chang* (ordinary). Accordingly, they viewed fiction as something both real and unreal, neither real nor unreal, or simply beyond real and unreal. Through elaborate analysis of the making of some great novels, a number of traditional fiction theorists in the Chinese tradition considered the idea of "creating something out of nothing" as the fundamental concept in Chinese fiction theory. Ye Zhou (fl. 1594–1625), who made pioneering contributions to Chinese theories of fiction, viewed the creation of something out of nothing as the essence of fiction. In his general comment on the *Water Margin*, he categorically declared that the novel is based on "pure invention out of the blue 劈空捏造" and that the characters were created to show typical persons under typical circumstances.[12] In a further comment on the novel, he said, "Writings under heaven should place priority over literary interest. Since literary interest is the ultimate aim, why must a writing be based on real events and real persons?"[13]

Huang Yue 黃越, another traditional fiction theorist, expressed a notion of fiction that also affirms something-out-of-nothingness as the ontology of fiction. He also used incredibly modern metaphors to describe the ontological conditions of fiction:

When it comes to the writing of fictional works, men of letters, equipped with a heart of brocade and embroidery and a pen of winds and thunder, hold heaven and earth in their palms and unfold creation with their fingers. When there is nothing [in real life], they create something out of nothing; when there is something [in real life], they transform it into nothing. Not only is there no need for a prior event to exist, but there is also no need for the model of a character to exist. What they have created is a castle in the air, or the three fairy mountains in the ocean, which appear or disappear in the twinkling of an eye and make the reader startled at the changing condition of winds and clouds. How can a writer be circumscribed by the existence or nonexistence [of prior models] when he begins to wield his pen and dispenses his words![14]

The language in this view of fiction is, on the one hand, reminiscent of the Daoist dialectics of *you* (being) and *wu* (non-being); on the other hand, it also shows a visible influence of the Buddhist ontology of the world and existence. In the Buddhist conception, reality is illusory; all existence is impermanent, and so is one's selfhood. Everything that exists is transitory and codependent on other things. In the popular version of Buddhism, life is simply like a dream. This conception is eloquently imparted in one Buddhist sutra: "[T]he world has no self-nature and has never been born; it is like a cloud, a ring produced by a firebrand, and castle of the Gandharvas, a vision, a mirage, the moon as reflected in the ocean, and a dream."[15] A comparison of the Buddhist view of life and Huang Yue's view of fiction shows a similar use of language. While the former describes the nature of existence, the latter depicts the ontology of fiction. The expressions like castle in the air, mountains beyond the sea, wind and cloud in the sky, moon in the water, and mirage—all point to the paradoxical nature of the world presented in fiction: both real and unreal or neither real nor unreal. In his study of the *Honglou-meng*, A. C. Yu reveals a parallel between Buddhist ontology and fiction: the mirror image and the dream encounter between Jia (false) Bao-yu and Zhen (real) Bao-yu are "a living embodiment of the truth inherent in a dream, a mirror image, or a fiction: that there is the real in the false, and the false in the real (*jia zhong you zhen; zhen zhong you jia*). The Buddhist ontology of the world has now become in a sense the transformed analogue to the ontology of narrative art."[16]

The Chinese view of the ontology of fiction finally evolved into a dialectical view that conceives of fiction as a linguistic entity having its ontology in the interplay between reality and fantasy, the real and unreal. Because of the dominant influence of history, the dialectical view was for some time a mixture of truth and falsehood. Xie Zhaozhi 謝肇制 (fl. 1603), for example, recognized fictionality as the essence of fictional works but was still uncertain about how to approach historical reality and fictional reality in imitation: "Whoever composes fictional works and dramatic works must blend half truth with half falsity. Only in this way can his writing be counted as having achieved playful artistry. Furthermore, feelings and scenes should not stop until they reach the ultimate. It is not necessary to ask whether they are real or unreal."[17] The blending of half truth with half falsity is but another way of viewing fiction as something between reality and fictionality. Thus, the conception of the real in the false and the false in the real becomes the ontology of fiction.

I have emphasized an expressive conception of fiction's genesis in the Chinese tradition. This view of fiction, however, does not rule out the notion of fiction as a result of imitation of the natural and human world, as in the Western theory of fiction. The paradoxical notion of the real in the false implies an ontological condition of fiction that is both expressive and mimetic, realistic and romantic. This again is imaginatively expressed in the *Hongloumeng*. The opening line of the novel states that the author experienced a dream and therefore wanted to write the novel. This seems to suggest that the novel grows from a nonrealistic experience. But it goes on to tell us that the subject matter of the novel concerns the lives of a group of girls whom he had encountered in his life. This obviously refers to something real. Thus, the notion of fiction is both expressive and mimetic. While the expressive part is responsible for the nonrealistic details of the novel, or the poetic qualities, the mimetic part addresses the realistic details of social life. Whereas nonrealistic details form the nonbeing of the novel, the realistic details constitute the being of the novel. While nonbeing is the inspirational source of the novel, being constitutes the narrative body of the novel. The being (representational in nature) and nonbeing (expressive in nature) of the novel constitute two opposite qualities like the *yin* and *yang*. They penetrate and interact with each other, and operate in a way similar to the operations of the Dao or Taiji. *Wu* or nonbeing is the ontology of the Dao; *you* or being is its function. Throughout, the novel is constructed on the interaction of *you* (being) and *wu* (nonbeing), which is found in the interplay between the two key concepts *jia* (false) and *zhen* (real), whose implications are found in the family names of major characters, in the structure of the novel, and in the general themes of the narrative.

The ontological interaction between being and nonbeing thus turns into a paradoxical interplay between the real (*zhen*) and unreal (*jia*) in fiction's representation of narrative details. It finds a most fascinating expression in the two couplets that inform of the thematics as well as the structural principle of the *Hongloumeng*. The first couplet "Truth becomes fiction when the fiction's true;/ Real becomes not-real when the unreal's real 假作真時真亦假，無為有處有還無" seems to affirm fiction's nonbeing in being. The second couplet "When Fiction departs and Truth appears, / Truth prevails; / Though Not-real was once Real, the Real / is never unreal 假去真來真勝假，無原有處有非無" seems to emphasize its being in nonbeing. I have already discussed the profound implications of the interplay between real and unreal for the novel on the local level of criticism. On the general and conceptual level of fictional theory, the two couplets may be viewed as the expression of a conceptual concern with the ontology of fiction. From the viewpoint of narrative theory, Cao Xueqin seems to suggest, literary fiction is a paradox of being and nonbeing. On the ontological level, it is nonbeing because it deals with something that is "untrue or unreal"; but on the functional level, it is being because it imitates and represents reality and claims to be true by the principle of verisimilitude. Vanitas, the supposed first reader of the stone's story, offers a final assessment of the novel, which may be taken to be the ontological status of the *Honglou-meng* in particular and of all pure fiction in general:

Uncanny and not uncanny (*qi er bu qi*);
Vulgar and not vulgar (*su er bu su*);
Real and not real (*zhen er bu zhen*);
False and not false (*jia er bu jia*).[18]

Ontologically, pure fiction writers in the Chinese tradition view fiction as a creative transcendence of the representation of multiple worlds, both real and imagined. Cao Xueqin's *Hongloumeng* is essentially a book-length, imaginative definition of what fiction is. By narrating a lengthy tale of how multiple worlds interpenetrate each other and are transcended in the process of narration, he arrives at an unstated definition of fiction: fiction is an artistic discourse that is both true and false and neither true nor false. In terms of the interplay and interpenetration of and alternation between truth and falsehood in the *Hongloumeng*, an ontological definition of fiction would be that fiction is a truthful account of nonexistent reality, or a presentation of truthful falsehood, or simply false truth. This conception of fiction coincides with Genette's view that fiction is "beyond truth and falsehood"[19] in the sense that it leaves aside the question of the referential values and ontological status of the representations it induces.[20]

EPISTEMOLOGY:
MAKE-BELIEVE OR TAKING THE UNREAL AS REAL

If fiction, as Cao Xueqin suggests, is beyond truth and falsehood, how should the author and reader approach it? To understand the ontological condition of fiction, we must examine its epistemology. In Chinese pure fiction, make-believe or to take what is false as true is the epistemology of fiction. The series of paradoxes between being and nonbeing, real and unreal, truth and falsehood, vulgar and not vulgar, uncanny and not uncanny, and so on are not difficult to understand if we approach them in relation to Western epistemological inquiries into the nature of fiction. In John Searle's "The Logical Status of Fictional Discourse," we can find an epistemological definition of fiction as "shared pretense."[21] This notion of fiction arose very early in Chinese fictional works. As early as in Tang fiction, the claim to a true account of life in an imaginative story signifies the notion of fiction as shared pretense. Although the narrated stories are patently untrue in terms of social reality or historicity, the author would end the story by stating that so-and-so witnessed such-and-such a thing or had heard someone who witnessed it. I have pointed out in chapter 2 various reasons for this odd narratological intrusion. Here I will add one more. The claim to truth while there is no truth to claim is evidently a pretense, a ploy to coax the reader into believing the story. This pretense is like children's game of homemaking. Two children, a boy and a girl, may pretend to get married, set up a house, and enact a series of daily routines that a married couple usually engages in. They know clearly that their married life is not true, yet they act it out so earnestly that they derive a lot of fun from it. For them to enjoy the game of homemaking, the precondition is that they must take it to be true and psychologically believe it. The same is true of fiction. Fiction cannot give pleasure unless the reader willingly suspends his disbelief while reading the tale. By declaring a narrated account to be true at the end of the story, the author was in fact implying that what has been narrated is not true, but if a reader wants to enjoy a good story, he ought to pretend to take it as true. With this move, the author is trying to make the reader believe in his narrated tale in a hypothetical way. Thus, a fictional work not only becomes a shared pretense on the part of the reader as well as the author but also produces a space for make-believe. This Chinese notion of shared pretense contains an implication that can be adequately understood with S. T. Coleridge's famous notion of "willing suspension of disbelief." In its epistemological dimension, fiction is predicated on a willing suspension of disbelief, without which fiction in its ontological sense of the word cannot exist. Ye Zhou 葉晝 correctly pointed out the epistemology of fiction in his comment on the *Water Margin*: "Events in the *Shuihu zhuan* are all fictitious, but they are narrated as though they were real. This is why its artistry is brilliant."[22]

Ye Zhou's contemporary, Feng Menglong 馮夢龍 (1574–1645), expressed a view about the epistemology of fiction that displays an admirable insight into the dialectical relationship between truth and falsehood in fiction. He was of the opinion that the value of fiction does not lie in the truthfulness or falsity of imitated persons and actions but lies in whether what a fictional work represents is true to life:

> Must historical fiction be all true? I reply: not necessarily so. Must it all be false? I reply: not necessarily so. Then, should one rid the false and keep the real? I reply: not necessarily so. . . . In fiction writing, a character may not necessarily have a real model in life, and the described events may not necessarily serve to beautify a person in real life. . . . If an event described is real, its rationale must not be false. In other words, even if an event is fictitious, its rationale should be real.[23]

Clearly, the Chinese fiction theorist was already concerned with some basic issues of imitation widely explored in contemporary fiction studies: Do all literary characters have actual prototypes? Should the author and reader distinguish between characters who are based on actual prototypes and those who are made up? Should events be mere incarnations of abstract properties? His observation anticipates Auerbach's famous notion that the novel should be viewed as "the representation of an entire human existence which has no issues."[24]

In the Chinese tradition, the idea of shared pretense surpasses its Western counterpart in intensity. The extent to which a fiction writer makes the reader take what is not true as true completely defies the law of probability.

In numerous Chinese fictional works, characters are foxes, snakes, fish, dragons, ghosts, or goddesses in human form, and they interact with human characters in human ways and do things that observe the law of probability. It is not that in Western fiction, no such phenomena exist. In Greek mythology and epics, human characters and divine characters both enter the arena. In George Orwell's *Animal Farm*, animals talk and lead a humanlike lives. In *Alice's Adventure in Wonderland*, Alice goes through a series of miraculous adventures with the White Rabbit, the Cheshire Cat, The Mock Turtle, and other strange characters. In ghost stories, the living and the dead fall in love with each other. And in science fiction, human characters interact with extraterrestrial beings. But Greek mythology and epics were collectively created and are not fictional works in the modern sense of the word. Orwell's tale is a political allegory. Ghost stories are later literary creations than the Chinese tales of the strange. Moreover, most of the fictional works with fantastic details are allegories or fairy tales.

By contrast, in generally accepted realistic novels like the *Jin Ping Mei* and *Hongloumeng*, there are numerous instances of miraculous and fantastic happenings that simply violate realistic principles in literary creation and the laws of probability. Simen Qin's reincarnation in the *Jin Ping Mei*, and the stone's reincarnation in the *Hongloumeng* are not created as allegorical details, but are meant as an unconventional manner of representation, the implications of which remind us of those of the fantastic. Todorov defines the fantastic thus: "[T]he fantastic is based essentially on a hesitation of the reader—a reader who identifies with the chief character—as to the nature of an uncanny event. This hesitation may be resolved so that the event is acknowledged as reality, or so that the event is identified as the fruit of imagination or the result of an illusion."[25] But in the Chinese tradition, the fantastic elements cannot be adequately explained in terms of a hesitation on the part of the reader; nor can they be resolved as the results of imagination or illusion. In the Chinese novels like the *Shuihu zhuan*, the *Jin Ping Mei*, and the *Hongloumeng*, the fantastic happenings are neither the result of the reader's hesitation nor characters' illusion but are part and parcel of the plot development. They are so prevalent that one may call them instances of "magic realism," because they both have magically realistic features: "the mingling and juxtaposition of the realistic and the fantastic or bizarre, skilful time shifts, convoluted and even labyrinthine narratives and plots, miscellaneous use of dreams, myths and fairy stories, expressionistic and even surrealistic description, arcane erudition, the element of surprise or abrupt shock, the horrific and the inexplicable."[26]

But even magic realism is not adequate in explaining the fantastic in the Chinese tradition. In most fictional works of magic realism, fantastic details, despite their relations to myths, legends, and fairy tales, are largely the effects of the transformations of reality by the subconscious or unconscious mind. In Chinese fiction, fantastic details are treated as though they were realistic details. Moreover, they are woven into mythic or supernatural frameworks that may be taken from mythology, legends, or folklore, or simply be invented by the fiction writer. A typical example is the use of stone lore in the three great classical Chinese novels: the excavation of an enigmatic stone tablet that releases 108 stars of heavenly spirits and earthly fiends who are reincarnated as the major protagonists in the *Water Margin*, the miraculous birth of a monkey out of a stone who become the hero in the *Journey to the West*, and the reincarnation of a mythic stone whose vicissitudes become the subject matter and plot of *A Dream of Red Mansions*. The magic representation of the stone in the last novel is especially unusual. It is a creation by Nü-wa, the legendary progenitor of human beings in Chinese mythology; it reincarnates into the male protagonist; it can change in size freely; it can be a gigantic block and yet it can become as small as a sparrow's egg and be carried in a baby's mouth at birth. Its appearance and disappearance coincide with the male protagonist's ups and downs in life. It launches the protagonist into life and eventually brings him back to its mythic origin. These kinds of miraculous happenings do not simply constitute intriguing details; they form hidden structures that control the unfolding of the plot, the characterization, and the imparting of hidden themes. They cannot be explained away by realism; nor can they be understood by recourse to surrealism, magic realism, and simulation. Miraculous happenings in Chinese fiction were not entirely meant as intriguing details to cater to the popular taste, but intended as ways to understand life and reality beyond the surface meaning, and their manner of presentation suspends the normal faculty of consciousness and logical reasoning. The aim is to express subconscious and unconscious ideas and feelings and to reveal the true nature and substance of history, society, life, and the human soul. Thus, it is no exaggeration to say that the epistemology of Chinese fiction anticipated the rise of surrealism and magical realism in modern times. As it differs fundamentally from Western surrealism and magic realism, it may be called "mythical realism" or "supernatural realism."

Why does traditional Chinese fiction set great store by unrealistic representation? Xie Zhaozhi (fl. 1603), a scholar in the Ming dynasty, rightly pointed out the reason why Chinese fiction writers were so fond of presenting unrealistic subject matter in their fictional works: "Fictional writings and vulgar vernacular books are not recorded by the petty officials of the court. Though their contents are so extremely unreal and absurd as to violate propriety, they contain in themselves some supreme principles."[27] He cited the *Journey to the West* as an illustration. In his view, despite its dazzling complexity and absurdity, the novel presents an allegory of the human mind with the monkey as a representation of the human spirit and the pig as a representation of human desires. Profound principles of life are beyond ordinary human perception and conception and therefore require extraordinary means of representation in fictional art. Yuan Yuling 袁于令 (1592–1674), Xie's contemporary, examined the issue more closely and uncovered more profound insight into unrealistic representation. He not only saw a dialectical dynamism between the real and unreal and the rational and irrational for the representation of reality but moreover suggested that the unreal and irrational in fictional writings may reveal the most profound truth and offer insights into the deep recess of the human mind:

> If a fictional work is not unreal, then it is not belletristic; if its untruth is not extreme, then it is not unreal. This makes us realize that [in fictional works] the most unreal things under heaven are precisely the most real things; the most irrational rationale is the most truthful reason. Therefore, to write about the real is not as good as writing about the unreal, and to talk about a Buddha is not as good as talking about a monster. The monster is none other than one's self.[28]

CREATIVE CONCEPTION: MANY-IN-ONE TOTALITY

The Chinese conception of fiction is quite different from that of the Western tradition, at least before the rise of modernist fiction in the West. The core difference is that Chinese fiction is conceived of as an open system of representation with multiple visions, multiple thematics, multiple forms, and multiple messages for open interpretations. By multiple vision I mean a sense of openness in the ideological conception of fictional works. This is especially clear in the monumental works that I have studied in this book. The ideological vision in the *Jin Ping Mei* is neither Confucian, Buddhist, Daoist, nor populist. In the *Hongloumeng*, the ostensible stand against Confucianism and preference for Buddhist and Daoist ideologies are frequently undercut in the sense that each ideological position is invariably turned against itself and toward its opposite. In other fictional works, the author's clearly stated sympathy for a certain ideological position is frequently bent toward its opposite or different positions. By multiple thematics, I mean that the themes of a fictional work are multiple, multidimensional, and multivalent. I have listed different readings of the themes of some chosen works, and my purpose was not to display my knowledge of existent scholarship, but to show the openness in the creative vision and thematics of Chinese fiction. To varying degrees, the fictional works studied have evinced a tendency toward openness. Mostly they are conceived with an open vision in general; and the *Hongloumeng*, in particular, is a veritable example of the notion that fiction is an open system of representation.

The multiple conception of fiction did not come out of the blue. It had aesthetic and metaphysical foundations. First and foremost, it was influenced by aesthetic suggestiveness in Chinese poetics. In traditional Chinese poetics, there may be said to have been an open conception of poetry. I have explored it extensively elsewhere.[29] Here I will only cite a few famous expressions that posit an open conception of literary works: *yi zai yanwai* (what is intended should go beyond words), *yanwai zhi yi* (a text should convey meanings beyond the expressed words), and *wen you jin er yi you yu* (The text may come to an end but the implications are more than plenty).[27] Admittedly, poetry is different from fiction, but as fictional works in the Chinese tradition strive to emulate and compete with lyric poetry, the open position advocated in poetics is transformed into an open conception of fiction. Indeed, the chosen fictional works examined in this book all show indebtedness to the open conception in poetics, especially the idea of aesthetic suggestiveness.

Metaphysically, the views of fiction as being arising from nonbeing, as an entity beyond truth and falsehood, and as make-believe inevitably give rise to a creative conception of fiction as a unity of multiplicities. This total conception is, of course, influenced by philosophical Daoism and the dialectics of *you* (being) and *wu* (nonbeing). Plaks conducts an excellent study of this metaphysical influence in his conceptual inquiry into Chinese narrative theory. Here, it suffices to quote his conclusion: "[T]he Chinese narrative stance imputes greater validity to neither the balanced overview nor the emotional response of the individual human perspective, preferring instead to include both of these aspects within a larger complementary vision. . . . As a result, the possibility of meaning in the Chinese narrative texts is simply the sense that the sum total of human experience is intelligible, that it is 'meaningful' even when it leads to no propositional conclusion."[31]

While Plaks emphasizes the impact of what he calls "complementary bipolarity" and "multiple periodicity" in Chinese philosophy, I would like to trace the many-in-one conception of fiction to the metaphysical idea of *wu* (ontological nonbeing). In contemporary literary thought, literary openness is predicated on the ontological conception of a literary text as an empty structure constructed of words, which are empty signifiers. In contemporary literary theory, some contemporary theorists have employed the analogies of an "empty basket" and "empty shelf" to characterize the openness of a text. These are, of course, the Western ways of representing the ontological basis of literary openness. In traditional Chinese literary thought, the openness of a text is given a philosophical basis of ontological void similar to the empty Dao or Taiji (the Great Ultimate) or Wuji (the Non-Ultimate). The essence of this ontological void is *wu* (nothingness or nonbeing).

Wu is the ontology of the Dao, the first philosophical principle in the Chinese tradition. Philosophical Daoism holds that the Dao is the emptiness or nothingness that gives birth to all things. In the *Daode jing* 道德經 the unnamable and indescribable Dao is compared to an "empty bowl." In Laozi's conception, "nothing" is the ontology of the Dao while "something" is its function.[32] Wang Bi, the exegete of Laozi's *Daode jing*, considers *wu* 無 (nothing) to be the origin of the universe: "Myriads of things and shapes share their home in One. Through what do they lead to One? Through *Wu* (nothing)."[33] Although Chinese thinkers gave the first principle of the universe a variety of names: the *Yi* (Changes), the Nonultimate, the Great Ultimate, or the Dao, the origin and foundation of the universe are believed to be *wu*, a concept that covers a gamut of meanings including "nothingness," "nonbeing," "absence," "emptiness," and "unperceived presence." In philosophical Daoism, *wu* (nothing or nonbeing) is inseparably bound with its opposite, *you* (something or being). Though both "nothing" and "something" are the two aspects of binary opposition in the Dao, "nothing" gives rise to "something." Laozi states in the *Daode jing*, "The myriad creatures in the world are born from Something, and Something from Nothing."[34] Similarly, Zhuangzi views "nothing" as the origin of "something": "In the great beginning, there was non-being. It had neither being nor name. The One originates from it; it has oneness but not yet physical form."[35]

The Daoist conception of *wu* has exerted a profound impact on the open conception of fiction. Cao Xueqin's idea of open fiction is clearly influenced by the interplay between *you* or being and *wu* or nonbeing. There are clear indications of this. First, the novel displays a predilection for Daoist ideas, and it is a Daoist priest who copied the inscribed account and sought a publisher. Second, the novel states through the mouth of another Daoist priest a conception about the novel that is close to the Daoist vision of the world. As A. C. Yu describes the nature of the novel's world using epithets from the novel, "[T]he invented world of story is 'baseless' (*huangtang*), 'absurd' (*dahuang*), 'unverifiable' (*wuji*), and 'undatable' (*wu chaodai nianji*)."[36] We need to note that most of these epithets are taken from Zhuangzi's philosophical writings. Third, as I have analyzed in detail in previous chapters, the novel is essentially structured on the interplay between truth and falsity, which is another way of stating the interplay between being and nonbeing. We may recall the couplet inscribed on either side of the stone arch at the entrance of the Land of Illusion: "Truth becomes fiction when the fiction's true;/ Real becomes not-real when the unreal's real." In the context of the novel, it hints at an understanding of the general theme. In the larger context of fiction theory, it represents the notion of pure fiction that I have labored to expound. In the opening, there is another passage: "Vanitas, starting off in the Void (which is Truth) came to the contemplation of Form (which is Illusion); and from Form engendered Passion; and by communicating Passion, entered again into Form; and from Form awoke to the Void (which is Truth)."[37] The interplay between Void and Form, truth and illusion suggests that the novel (fiction as a broad term) is a paradoxical concept like the Dao. Laozi characterized the Dao thus: "The Dao is empty, yet use will not drain it."[38] The Dao is empty, yet it is full, and moreover it gives rise to everything in the world. In my detailed analysis of the *Hongloumeng* and the *Jin Ping Mei*, I have pointed out the various open features of the two novels. In retrospect, I am of the opinion that they are typical examples of open fiction. They are not about a particular subject matter, because a good variety of implied themes and meanings coexist in them and none of them dominate the others.

Compared with the Chinese tradition, the idea of open conception of fiction arose rather late in the West. In 1924, Bakhtin wrote a treatise on fiction entitled "Epic and Novel." In it he addresses a tendency in fictional creation that he calls the novelization of other genres. He describes this phenomenon as having these salient features: "They become more free and flexible, their language renews itself by incorporating extraliterary heteroglossia and the 'novelistic' layers of literary languages, they become dialogized, permeated with laughter, irony, humor, elements of self-parody and finally—this is the most important thing—the novel inserts into these other genres an indeterminacy, a certain semantic open-endedness, a living contact with unfinished, still-evolving contemporary reality (the open-ended present)."[39] Bakhtin identified openness as a salient feature in modern fiction. But it was not until the 1960s that a conscious conception of open fiction came into being. Umberto Eco, after studying Joyce and Kafka, formulated his poetics of openness.[40] Interestingly, in his theorizing on open work, Eco mentions the Chinese tradition: "Yet this does not mean that the existence of 'open' work and of 'work in movement' adds absolutely nothing to our experience because everything in the world is already implied and subsumed by everything else, from the beginning of time, in the same way that it now appears that every discovery has already been made by the Chinese."[41] I quote this passage from Eco not so much because it confirms my view that open conception of fiction existed in China long ago, but because Eco expresses a philosophical idea that is the metaphysical basis of open work and that coincides pretty well with the Chinese metaphysical idea that everything is related to everything else.

MODEL OF WRITING: LINGUISTIC DISSEMINATION

In the development of Chinese fiction, there is a series of turns that have constituted a transition of fiction from a derivative form of history and philosophy to an independent genre of verbal art. Accompanying the transition is a gradual change in the function of fiction's language from a perception based on the denotations of the symbol to one based on the connotations of the sign. This change resulted in a fundamental change in the conceptual model for fiction creation. As the final outcome is a turn to fiction as verbal art, the definitive model for fiction writing is linguistic in nature. Predicated on the shift from the perception of language as a vehicle to a conception of fictional language as both the means and source of narrative materials, the definitive model is one of linguistic conception. This model finds its concentrated manifestations in the composition of the *Jin Ping Mei* and the *Hongloumeng*. Having demonstrated how the model operates in those two fictional masterpieces, I will synthesize the insights derived from the critical analysis and further explore its origin, rationale, and impact on fictional creation from a conceptual standpoint.

The model, I believe, originates from Chinese poetic theories, especially from the foundational treatise of Chinese poetics, *Shi daxu* 詩大序 (the Great Preface to the *Book of Songs*). In my study of China's first theoretical treatise on literature, I argued against a commonly accepted critical opinion that it is loosely constructed. I suggested that it is conceived on a unique philological principle of composition, and its way of presentation in relation to its content contains an implicit statement of a paradigm of reading and writing that I call "intertextual dissemination." I further argued that this paradigm not only set the pattern of reading the *Book of Songs* but also influenced the hermeneutic development of the Chinese tradition.[42] Here I would like to suggest that the disseminative pattern of reading and writing has influenced the writing of Chinese fiction as well. This is not difficult to understand. The Great Preface has been recognized as the first and probably the most important treatise on Chinese poetry. It was part of the repertoire of readings for an educated Chinese in traditional China. Its impact on the composition of poetry has been adequately recognized, but its influence on the writing of fiction has not yet been touched upon. The writing principle implicitly developed in that treatise, I believe, serves as a model of composition not only for poetry but also for fiction. Indeed, many Chinese fictional works, both short and extended, have implicitly adopted that model of writing, and derived a significant part of their fictional art from it.

That model is based on the time-honored branch of Chinese scholarship *xungu* 訓詁, a complex philological approach to ancient Chinese texts. *Xungu* was originally a way of exegesis, but the writer of the Great Preface turned it into a way of composition. In Chinese philology, there are some fundamental principles of exegesis. Here are two of them: "to seek meaning through the shape of a word 以形索義" and "to seek meanings through the sound of a word 以聲索義."[43] In my study of *Zhouyi* hermeneutics and *Shijing* hermeneutics, I have demonstrated that these two principles of philological scholarship helped generate a great deal of the *Zhouyi* and *Shijing* scholarship. In the composition of the Great Preface, the author, whoever he might have been in history, turned the two fundamental principles into the warp and woof that are used to weave the text of the treatise, thereby creating a unique writing principle that shares some affinity with the modernist and postmodern notion of the materiality of the sign.

The common ground between the writing model in the Great Preface and the definitive model of fictional writing is the poststructuralist idea of textuality, which refers to the written condition of a literary text—that is, the material aspects that have gone into the making of discourse. The poststructuralist idea of textuality suggests that a text is a material entity made of words (semiotic signs) rather than abstract concepts. Language is conceived of not to produce a simple reference to a reality outside language but to weave a text with a multiplicity of potentially conflicting meanings. Since a text is, as Roland Barthes describes, a "network" or "woven fabric of signifiers" that practices the infinite deferment of the signified, the definitive model is one of the semiotic sign.[44] A fictional work composed on this model can be approached, experienced, and appreciated in reaction to the signifying practice of the sign. So much attention has been paid to the sound, shape, and sense of some words and terms in the fictional works explicitly or implicitly adopting the linguistic model of writing that the philological principles of Chinese *xungu* became a principle of composition as well as a source of compositional materials.

In this book, I have argued that in fictional works that aspire to be pure fiction and can be appreciated as verbal art, the writing model is not based on the model of historiography but on the model of the disseminative sign. I have tried to demonstrate this clearly in the case of the art of the *Jin Ping Mei* and *Hongloumeng*. In both masterpieces, the model of the semiotic sign not only shapes the structure and emplotment, but also determines narrative details such as characters, setting, and events. In the *Jin Ping Mei*, the extended narrative is woven out of the naming of persons, places, and things with *leng* (cold) and *re* (hot) and their derivatives like "life" and "death," "rise" and "fall," and "in favor" and "out of favor" as the warp and woof. In the *Hongloumeng*, the main narrative thread is centered on the interplay and intertextuality of the stone/jade—its mythic origin, its life in human form, its appearance and disappearance, and its interrelations to its material sources in Chinese history, culture, and literature—with *zhen* (real) and *jia* (false) as its structural principle. Jing Wang's brilliant study of the intertextuality of the Chinese stone lore and the stone symbolism in the *Water Margin*, the *Journey to the West*, and the *Dream of the Red Chamber* lends strong support to my argument for the definitive model of fictional writing based on the function of the semiotic sign.[45] This model of writing, predicated on the multiplicity of the sign and the intertextual relations of narrated materials, encourages the creation of fictional works that aspire to be pure fiction, poetic fiction, metafiction, and open fiction.

A DEFINITION OF OPEN FICTION

I have tried to show that in spite of the fact that traditional Chinese fiction developed separately from the Western tradition, its theory gradually became merged with that of the Western tradition. The convergence of fictional theory leads us to the realization that fiction is a kind of open work with open visions, open conceptions, open themes, open forms, and open messages for open interpretations. Openness may serve as a bridge across the divide between Chinese and Western fiction, fiction theory, and literary theory in general. Here I would like to make a conceptual move to theorize on openness in the making of fiction and attempt at a definition.

Although Eco and other theorists have theorized extensively on open work and poetics of openness, none of them has ever formulated a hard-and-fast definition of openness, perhaps because of the difficulty it involves and the controversy it may arouse. The closest to a definition is found in Eco's *The Role of the Reader*: "[A]n open text is a paramount instance of a syntactic-semantico-pragmatic device whose foreseen interpretation is a part of its generative process."[46] This definition is characteristic of Eco's conception and exploration of openness. It takes into account the role of the reader in the creation of openness, but that openness is largely pre-programmed by the author. In this sense, it may be regarded as a narrow definition. Incorporating the reader-oriented views of openness by other radical theorists, I venture to formulate a broader definition: Openness refers to the textual conditions created by perceived writing strategies that consciously or unconsciously endow a text with the capacity to allow readers to adopt different subject positions and reading strategies in a cooperative process of reading, with the result that the text becomes multivalent, polysemous, and amenable to different and even conflicting interpretations. To further explicate this definition, it is necessary to distinguish three kinds of openness:

1. *Textual or natural openness.* The reason I call this openness "natural openness" is that it is a kind of openness that is common to all works of art. As Eco puts it, "[A] work of art is never really 'closed,' because even the most definitive exterior always encloses an infinity of possible 'readings.'"[47] But this kind of openness most often results from semiosis, which is unlimited, and the changing perspectives and multiple readings by the reader, whose life experiences and emotive conditions are constantly changing. It has little to do with the author's artistic designs.

2. *Conscious or intentional openness.* It is a kind of openness that derives its status from the author's deliberate use of language, narrative techniques, and structural arrangements to leave the text open. This kind of openness has become a favored literary quality as a result of its advocacy by modernist and postmodern art movements.

3. *Unconscious or unintentional openness.* This kind of openness also emanates from the author, but it is not known to the author's conscious mind. Rather it finds its way into a text through some psychological mechanism, which leaves traces of the author's previous life experience in the text without the author consciously knowing them. For example, some readers find in Eco's *The Name of the Rose* some themes that he was not aware of until he came across relevant critical readings.[48]

Although theoretically we can distinguish the three kinds of openness, in critical practice it is difficult to separate one from another. For the purpose of opening up a literary work to new possibilities of interpretation, the distinction makes little difference, but for those who are creative writers, a knowledge of intentional openness will prove immensely useful to their creative work. This book has suggested that fictional openness is predicated on open ways of writing and reading fiction. The three kinds of openness are all related to the act of reading and writing. Or to put it in another way, they emanate from three kinds of making: the author's making, the reader's making, and the text's making. Conscious openness results from the author's intentional use of language, style, tone, and technique to convey an enriched representation. Unconscious openness results from the reader's act of relating the text to its author and to the reader's own experience. Textual openness results from textual semiosis.

MODES OF REPRESENTATION: KALEIDOSCOPIC NARRATION

In the West before the rise of modernism, the dominant form of prose fiction was realism and its variations. The conceptual foundation of realism is the Aristotelian theory of mimesis. Based on the imitation of the natural and human worlds, the central tenet of realism is that a fictional work must be true to life. This tenet was strictly observed in fictional works by writers in the European tradition: Daniel Defoe, Samuel Richardson, Henry Fielding, Jane Austen, the Brontë sisters, Charles Dickens, W. M. Thackeray, George Eliot, Arnold Bennett, Thomas Hardy, Henry James, and others in the English tradition, and Miguel Cervantes, Gustave Flaubert, Victor Hugo, Emile Zola, Guy de Maupassant, Leo Tolstoy, Fyodor Dostoevsky, and others on the European continent. Whether these writers created their fictional works in the realistic, critically realistic, or naturalistic modes, they all wrote having in mind the tenet of being true to life. This tenet was so predominant that I have referred to it as the "tyranny of realism." The few fictional works that violated this tenet are relegated to minor positions or rationalized in terms of characters' delusion and narrative ambiguity. This situation remained intact even after the rise of modernism, when innovative fictional works by Joyce, Lawrence, Kafka, Proust, Woolf, Faulkner, and others challenged the tyranny of realism. By contrast, in the Chinese tradition fictional works like the *Shuihu zhuan*, the *Xiyou ji*, the *Jin Ping Mei*, and the *Hongloumeng* were regarded as masterpieces of fiction, even though they clearly violated the tenet of realism. One may claim that one of the greatest contributions of Chinese fiction to the international theory of fiction is its rejection of the dominance of realism in imitation and the mixture of different representational modes.

In his *Anatomy of Criticism*, Northrop Frye posits an influential theory of historical criticism in terms of fictional modes underlying the development of the Western literary tradition. His theory conceptualizes European fiction into five modes: (1) myth; (2) romance; (3) the high mimetic mode; (4) the low mimetic mode; and (5) the ironic mode. Although Frye predicates his theory on "the hero's relative power of action," the attributive modifying the hero's power—"which may be greater than ours, less, or roughly the same"[49]—suggests that his theory is essentially a modification of Aristotle's mimetic view of characters in the *Poetics*. By applying the reconceptualized mimetic theory to the historical development of Western fiction, Frye arrives at his five fictional modes. In my article on Frye's theory of fictional modes in relation to the Chinese tradition, I argued that his theory is quite applicable to the historical development of Chinese literature.[50] In this book, however, I would like to mention some radical differences. Frye's five fictional modes are derived from the entire history of European fiction in its poetic, dramatic, and prose fictional forms. He clearly states that in the last fifteen centuries, European fiction has steadily gone through the five modes and that one mode usually dominates a given period of fictional work, or at least a literary genre. This domination by one fictional mode to the exclusion of other modes is not to be found in the Chinese tradition. Quite early in the development of Chinese fiction, the five modes posited by Frye already coexisted or intermixed in a fictional work as though they belonged to the same family.

The *Hongloumeng* is such a specimen. It is structured on a time-honored myth in the Chinese tradition: the repairing of the broken heaven and the creation of humanity by the goddess Nü-wa. The protagonist is one of the unused stones in the heaven-repairing project, reincarnated in human form. The novel's plot is a romantic tale. It follows the romantic vicissitudes of the reincarnated stone in the human world and its return to its origin. Like the hero in Frye's conception of the romantic mode, the Chinese protagonist is often "superior in degree to other men and to his environment" as he is born into a wealthy aristocratic family, pampered by his elders, and frequently aided by superhuman beings. The characterization of Baoyu also employs the high mimetic mode, for he is "superior in degree to other men but not to his natural environment." In Frye's conception, such a hero "is a leader." Baoyu is also a leader, but ironically, he is not the leader of an army of robust men but a leader of a group of beautiful maidens in a gigantic garden. Naturally, "what he does is subject to social criticism and to the order of nature." He may have his way with his grandmother, mother, relatives, and all the servants, but he is at the beck and call of the Confucian world order and its champion, his father. In many episodes, Baoyu is depicted as a low mimetic figure, because he is "superior neither to other men nor to his environment." He is one of the earthly human beings, like those around him, having all the human desires and committing different kinds of human follies. In other episodes, Baoyu is characterized as a person belonging to the ironic mode, because he is "inferior in power or intelligence to ourselves." That he is often at his wit's end and subject to physical, emotional, and spiritual frustration is indeed capable of giving the reader a "sense of looking down on a scene of bondage, frustration, or absurdity."[51]

The intermixture of different forms of representation in a Chinese fictional work may cover ways of mimesis, themes and motifs, narrative techniques, generic forms, language registers, points of view, and tones and styles. It is so multifarious that it may be described as kaleidoscopic in nature. Indeed, the fictional form of the masterpieces like the *Jin Ping Mie* and *Hongloumeng* resembles the spectacular view in a kaleidoscope. Because of its kaleidoscopic nature and the interlocking of content and form, the multiplicity of forms escapes easy categorization. Nevertheless, I may classify them into these categories: (1) multiple mimetic modes (in terms of Aristotle's theory of imitation): realistic, surrealistic, naturalistic, magic realism, romantic realism, simulation, the fantastic, and so on; (2) multiple thematic modes (in terms of Northrop Frye's theory of fictional modes): mythic mode, romantic mode, high mimetic mode, low mimetic mode, and the ironic mode;[52] (3) multiple narrative modes: history, unofficial history, biography, autobiography, myths, legends, folklore, allegory, fable, popular storytelling, street gossip, and so on; (4) multiple generic forms: pseudoepic, family saga, lyric poetry, dramatic dialogue, prose essay, satire, parody, pastiche, and so on; (5) multiple use of language registers: literary language, archaic classicism, vernacular, the language of the illiterate, and so on; (6) multiple use of points of view: first person, third person, omniscient, character as narrator, authorial intrusion, dramatic asides, and the intermingling of the writer, reader, commentator, editor, and characters (as in the *Hongloumeng*); (7) multiple use of tones and styles: serious and bantering, detached and intimate, casual and pompous, satirical and ironic, and so on.

What accounts for the kaleidoscopic nature of multiple narrative forms in traditional Chinese fiction? There are perhaps two reasons for it: one is metaphysical and the other is formal. The metaphysical reason for the Chinese multiplicity of formal presentation is the philosophical idea of the equality of things in the world. In his "Qiwu lun" (Equality of Things) chapter, Zhuangzi views myriad things under heaven, be they big or small, beautiful or ugly, normal or abnormal, self or other, life or death, and so on, as being unified by the Dao, which is also called the One:

> Let us take, for instance a large beam and a small beam, or an ugly woman and Hsi-shih (famous beauty in ancient China), or generosity, strangeness, deceit, and abnormality. The Tao identifies them all as one. What is division [to some] is production [to others], and what is production [to others] is destruction [to some]. Whether things are produced or destroyed, [Tao] again identifies them all as one.[53]

This conception of the myriad things in the universe may have accounted for the employment of multiple narrative modes in representation, with men and women, gods and fairies, ghosts and demons, animal and plant spirits, and so on, all participating in the complex and multifaceted drama of human life.

The formal reason is the interpenetration of content and form, style and tone. Because of the open conception of fiction in the chosen fictional works, there is a tendency to blur the boundaries between content and form. As I have demonstrated in a study of the *Jin Ping Mei*, there is a clear indication that form and content interpenetrate each other to such an extent that content may serve as form and form may serve as content.[54] This phenomenon warrants us to claim that in the Chinese theory of fiction, there is a form of content and a content of form. The intermixture of form and content (or the content in form and form in content) is the textual basis of multiple forms on the discursive and narrative level. The stylistic basis of the multiple forms is the mixture of discourse styles. Traditional Chinese fiction employs different registers of language and different forms of style. The narrative style may be plainly descriptive, expository, argumentative, or heavily ornate and expansive, with tones ranging from commendatory, sympathetic, and empathetic to sarcastic, satirical, and ironic.

The mixture of forms, styles, and tones gives some fictional works the ability to parody and satirize other genres as well as their own various styles—a feature of fictional representation that is postmodern in nature. For example, the *Jin Ping Mei* takes an episode from the *Shuihu zhuan* and uses it as an ironic narrative frame for the whole novel. In using the borrowed materials from the *Shuihu zhuan*, the novel not only parodies the heroic thematics of its model but also caricatures various characters taken from the original novel. In the *Shuihu zhuan*, Wu Song is a hero who successfully kills his brother's murderers, but in the *Jin Ping Mei*, Wu Song fails pathetically in his attempt to avenge his brother. Not only that, but he entraps himself in a criminal case and gets exiled. He does not return to reattempt his revenge until the latter half of the novel. And instead of going about his revenge in a heroic or manly manner, he pretends to offer to marry his brother's murderess and dupes her. He finally kills Jinlian, the comurderer of his brother, but Simen Qin, the archperpetrator of the murder, is already dead, forever beyond Wu Song's attempt at revenge. Wu Song does complete his task of revenge, but his heroic stature in the *Shuihu zhuan* is significantly diminished. With this change in diminished heroism, Wu Song drops from the thematic level of romance in Frye's theory through the high mimetic and low mimetic levels to the ironic level. By characterizing the hero thus, the author certainly intended to parody the original model, but he may not have entirely aimed at poking fun at the imitated model and the reading public who admire heroes and heroism. He might have been consciously engaged in creating a new novel, inventing a new representational mode, and enlarging the novel's hermeneutic space.

THEORY OF READING: OPEN HERMENEUTICS

Throughout this book, I have tried to pay special attention to the multifarious nature of fiction and fictional theory. Multiplicity of creative vision and open form entail an open poetics of practical criticism. When we base ourselves on the multiple visions, conceptions, and interpretations in the study of the chosen works, we have every reason to advance a poetics of multiplicity in fiction reading. This poetics shares some common techniques with the poetics of openness advanced by Umberto Eco and other Western literary theorists, such as ambiguity, paradox, irony, aporia, multivalence, polysemy, polyphony of unmerged voices, the author's deliberate attempt to leave a work incomplete, the decision to leave some key elements open to the reader or chance, and so on. Because of the differences in language medium, there is no denying that some characteristic features of multiplicity in this study are distinctly Chinese, and emanate from the conscious use of the Chinese language's signifying mechanisms. For example, the principle of juxtaposition is a privileged technique sanctioned by classical Chinese. The special representational features of classical Chinese facilitates the juxtaposition of discourse components that range from as small an element as the coinage of a word to as large an element as the arrangement of a novel's plot. Nevertheless, the open poetics of the Chinese tradition shares with the Western tradition some creative principles of multiplicity. One of them is suggestive representation. In an attempt to achieve multiple visions, the chosen Chinese fictional works have displayed a conscious effort at making crucial junctures of a text suggestive. The blocks of discourse rendered suggestive range from local elements to overall structure:

an image, a personal name, a place-name, a phrase, a sentence, an episode, plot arrangement, characterization, and subject matter.

In the introduction, one of the objectives that I set myself was to locate some practical principles of fiction that might prove useful for writing and reading. In the process of this book, I have tried to work out quite a few strategies of multiplicity, which are scattered in the discussions of individual texts. Here I will attempt to summarize the insights teased out in the preceding chapters, including those present in other Chinese fictional works, but untouched by this study:

1. *Networks of multiple-directional signification.* The networks of signification in Chinese fiction share much common ground with Joyce's scheme of composition manifested in *Finnegans Wake*, which is, in Eco's apt summary, "a labyrinth of 'colored ribbons' in which space and time are confusedly woven into a flowering maze of cyclical connection."[55] While Joyce's scheme of composition relies heavily on newly coined words, phrases, personal names, place-names, and other paronomastic devices, the Chinese mode of multiplicity takes full advantage of the iconic, monosyllabic, and homophonic features of the Chinese character. The advantage of the iconic nature of the Chinese character for expression and representation does not lie in its etymological link with the signified, but in the "firstness" of the word as icon. In terms of Peirce's notion of firstness, the Chinese character, standing in and of itself, may be viewed as a sort of less-mediated sign (than that of alphabetic languages), because literary Chinese imposes few rigorous morphological elements such as tense, voice, case, number, gender, or verbal conjugation. As less-mediated signs (programmed with few morphological constraints), they are conducive to the production of multiplicity, because they can be combined quite freely like picture puzzles to form discourses, which not only signify horizontally on the syntagmatic axis but may also manifest possibilities of surplus signification vertically on the paradigmatic axis, and even diagonally and reversely. The picture puzzles and word puzzles that hint at the fate of the twelve female characters in the *Hongloumeng* are typical. They not only play a structuring role for the whole novel but also constitute a network of multifarious signification and representation.

2. *The poetics of paronomasia.* In terms of formal logic, literary Chinese comes very close to natural language, which has no formal logic but is ruled by a rhetoric, a logic of substitutions. Literary Chinese mostly consists of monosyllabic words, many of which are homophones and near homophones. These characteristics of literary Chinese make it much easier for writers to use paronomasia in their writings. Until the advent of modernism, paronomasia or wordplay was generally dismissed by serious writers, Chinese and Western, as a mere "word game" that cannot impart serious intentions of the author and his writings. In the 1980s, avant-gardist writings like Joyce's *Ulysses* and *Finnegans Wake* were criticized in China for having no great literary merit. They were thought to be just a dazzling display of word games. This criticism,

however, apparently forgot that ancient Chinese writers, including Confucius and others, were inordinately fond of using paronomasia. Chinese authors in all periods have made a point of utilizing paronomasia to give their works multiple implications with a complex network of cultural associations. Through paronomasia, a literary text is able to generate a variety of paths of association by phonic and/or semantic affinity. In many cases, an instance of paronomasia, by phonetic and semantic similarity, can become a nodal point composed of chains of lexemes for a series of associations, each of which has the potential of becoming another nodal point of other associative chains. In this respect, the *Jin Ping Mei, Hongloumeng*, and some of Lu Xun's fictional works have worked on a writing principle of paronomasia strikingly similar to the "poetics of pun," a composing technique that Eco has found to be a major structural principle of Joyce's *Finnegans Wake*.

3. *Linguistic suture.* In the making of multiplicity, juxtaposition is a widely used technique that eventually develops into what I wish to call "linguistic suture." In this book, I have tried to identify the weaving metaphors constantly used by Chinese fiction commentators in describing the structure and form of Chinese works. The iconic nature of Chinese characters as less-mediated signs facilitates the creation of linguistic suture, which comes close to the cinematic model of suture. Theorists of cinematic suture concur that films are made by means of interlocking shots, and the juxtaposition of disparate images produces montage effects, which result in a large potential space for the viewer to exercise his or her imagination. In filmmaking shot relations can be viewed as the equivalent of syntactic ones in language discourse, as the agency whereby meaning emerges and a subject position is constructed for the viewer. In the making of a fictional work, linguistic suture is achieved through the juxtaposition of language codes standing for images, and subject positions are implied for the reader through relations among discourse blocks. Linguistic suture in a literary work displays a greater violence in the joining together of disparate images than cinematic suture, so much so that it often gives an impression of being unrealistic, incredible, inconsistent, and conflicting. (This could be said, for example, of the juxtaposition of improbable images in Lu Xun's stories, the disparate modes of narration in narrative works like the *Jin Ping Mei*, and the metamorphosis of the stone in the *Hongloumeng*.) Linguistic suture gives rise to simulacra. The apotheosis of a simulacrum may be compared to the artistic representation of the Chinese dragon. There is no such animal as the dragon in reality. The artistic image of a dragon is the suturing together of various parts of existent animals commonly seen in Chinese culture: a snake's body, a horse's head, a deer's horns, an eagle's claws, a fish's scales, and so on. The disparate parts are adroitly joined together and the resultant whole forms a simulated *Gestalt*, which is realistically nonexistent, anatomically harmonious, aesthetically pleasing, and symbolically polysemous. The dragon born of imagistic suture has a life of its own, always generating new cultural implications, and a fictional work that

consciously exploits such linguistic suture is also endowed with a life of its own, constantly producing new meanings. In this respect, the making of a fictional work truly exemplifies the Chinese saying for literary creation: *wu zhong sheng you* (to fictionalize something out of nothing).

4. *The open field of possibilities in composition.* The multiplicity of a text comes from the limitless sets of possible relations in the combinations of words. The diverse ways in which words interact with each other are neither inhibited by an external necessity that would prescribe the organization, nor determined by the internal necessity that is the claim of organic form. Instead, they are overdetermined by a shifting combination of sign relations like serial form. In this respect, fictional multiplicity comes close to the scientific term "field effect," and the making of multiplicity is like constructing an open field both in the process of writing and that of reading. Following the dissolution of hierarchical orders, contemporary science has proposed the notion of "field" in physics, which, as Eco observes, "implies a revised vision of the classic relationship posited between cause and effect as a rigid, one-directional system."[56] The abandonment by science of a unidirectional system of causation for a multidirectional field of possibilities has given rise to a corresponding shift in the arts from closed to open forms. The removal of rigid causality has affected literary and artistic composition. Eco cites the composer Henri Pousseur as his example of the influence of such a scientific concept on artistic composition. In literature, Charles Olson remarks in "Projective Verse" that "any poet who departs from closed form . . . ventures into FIELD COMPOSITION—puts himself in the open."[57] An open text, then, is not just an open space of signification; it is an open field of possibilities in which words become energized in the way iron chippings become magnetized under the force of a magnet. In the *Hongloumeng*, we may say that the novelist constructed such a magnetic field in which the denotation of a word changes and turns into a series of connotations. This point is particularly clear in the interplay between *zhen* (real) and *jia* (false) in the novel. Because of the open field effect, the two words no longer retain their conventional meanings but go through a series of deconstructive mutations as the narrative unfolds.

5. *The open field of interpretation.* The construction of an open field is not just the task of the writer; it is also the task of the reader. With what Barthes calls the death of the author and what Eco calls the "discarding of a static, syllogistic view of order, and a corresponding devolution of intellectual authority to personal decision, choice, and social context," the reader is entitled to construct various new signifying fields for a given text. But how is one to construct an open signifying field? Well, a reader can make full use of the indeterminacy warranted by a given text and by the signifying mechanisms of the sign. In addition to taking note of the representational quality of the sign, he or she may pay attention to the sign itself—its sound, shape, and sense—and try to see its materiality as carrying other than surface implications in the fluid signifying process and in the context of the text. Such efforts to construct an

open field constitute a practical way of reading: one first chooses a few apo-
rias or undecidable words, names, phrases, events, episodes, and so on; ponders
on their sound, shape, sense, and all possible associations these chosen items
may evoke; situates the possible associations within the context of the text;
and finally weaves the associations into a meaningful network of signification
and representation. Since the context of a text consists of numerous details,
scenes, and episodes, each facet of the context is capable of putting the woven
network into a new situation, thereby making it possible to yield fresh and
different implications of which the author may or may not be conscious at the
time of composition.

Toward a Transcultural Theory of Fiction

Nowadays when scholars talk about fiction theory, they usually refer to European or Western fiction theory. In studies of other time-honored literary traditions, discussions of fiction theory are always based on the Western system of fictional concepts such as imitation, realism, naturalism, modernism, and postmodernism. Chinese fiction has been treated in the same way. In the worldwide context, the rise of Chinese fiction was not late. European fiction can trace its origins to medieval romance in the twelfth century and short stories in prose that did not appear until the fourteenth century,[1] while mature Chinese fiction written in prose dates to the Tang (seventh to tenth centuries). Short tales appeared as early as the Wei, Jin, Northern and Southern dynasties (third—sixth century). With the exception of the Japanese novel the *Tale of Genji* (c. 1010), the first novel to appear in history was a Chinese one. But despite the large amount of theoretical data on fiction, the Chinese tradition lags behind its Western counterpart in conceptual inquiries into the conditions of fiction and in formulating systems of fictional theories.

In his efforts to promote non-Western literature, Fredric Jameson argues against the conventional way of assessing the literary achievements of non-Western literary works in terms of the Western yardstick. He says this way of promotion is self-defeating: "[I]t borrows the weapons of the adversary: the strategy of trying to prove that these texts are as 'great' as those of the canon itself." "What is more damaging than that," he continues, "perhaps, is its tendency to remind us of outmoded stages of our own first-world cultural development and to cause us to conclude that 'they are still writing novels like Dreiser or Sherwood Anderson.'"[2] By this he means that the third-world writings would not be highly regarded if the third-world writers are still viewed as writing in the outmoded modes of realism or critical realism. But what if the third-world writers were employing modes and techniques of writing that predated those of Western modernism and postmodernism?

Traditional Chinese fiction theory lags behind its Western counterpart in conceptual inquiries, but the fiction theory explicitly or implicitly expressed in the practice of Chinese fiction does not fall behind. In fact, many Chinese fictional principles anticipated similar or exact ideas in modernist and even postmodern fiction in the West. Some principles may be considered uniquely Chinese and should be regarded as contributions made by Chinese fiction to the transcultural study of fiction. Previously, some scholars have nursed the view that except for a few masterpieces, traditional Chinese fiction has some drawbacks that disqualify it from ranking among the greatest fiction in the world: episodic structure, lack of interest in psychological exploration, mixture of mimetic modes, authorial intrusion, and so on. Seldom did they stop to ponder what has given rise to these idiosyncrasies. Still less did they realize that the idiosyncrasies are signs of artistry and anticipated the characteristic features of modernist and postmodernist fiction.

This book has tried to show that, despite the idiosyncratic features, traditional Chinese fiction more or less went through a similar process of development to that of Western fiction, though not necessarily in the same chronological order as that of the West. It embraces practically all the major forms of modern fiction. In some areas, however, it made some unique contributions to the internationalization of fiction, and traversed a road of development quite different from that of European fiction. While the latter developed from epic and romance, through realistic, naturalistic, and critically realistic fiction, to modernist and postmodernist fiction, Chinese fiction followed no such discernable pattern of development. In representative Chinese fictional works, we can find an overlapping and integration of all these modes. The total effect of such an integration is what may be termed metafiction, metanarrative, and open fiction in contemporary fiction criticism, or grand fiction, total fiction, and kaleidoscopic fiction, as I have called them. In this concluding part, I would like to examine the conceptual reasons for the sameness and difference, the so-called limitations and idiosyncrasies, and explore possible conceptual grounds for a transcultural theory of fiction.

CONCEPTUAL ROOTS OF
SAMENESS AND DIFFERENCE

In the course of this inquiry, I have compared and contrasted Chinese fiction with its Western counterpart and found that in historical development, Chinese and Western theories of fiction share basically similar concerns. Ontologically, both Chinese and Western fictional works are concerned with representations of life, reality, and the world. Epistemologically, both traditions explore fiction's relation to history, philosophy, poetry, drama, and other literary genres. In the origins of fiction, both traditions saw the social and psychological rise of fiction. In reading and writing, both traditions witnessed a trend to openness in fictional creation and interpretation.

The common concern in Chinese and Western fiction is determined by the basic sameness in human needs for producing and consuming fiction. Despite the salient features of the Chinese language, some major ideas of Chinese fiction have cross-cultural significance. *These shared, common, and similar ideas have a universal value, because they are grounded in the sameness of the human psyche and the sameness of a literary text as a verbal construct.* Take fictional openness, for example. The ideas of openness are based on the common signifying mechanisms of fictional language and similar needs that a human subject may have for creating and reading fiction. In contemporary theories, the human subject is a complex entity, of which the conscious mind is only a small part, like the tip of an iceberg. Since one cannot know the possibly unlimited unconscious processes that shape one's conscious thought, this view of the subject has replaced the pre-Lacanian view that one's conscious wishes and feelings originate within a unified self. Conscious thought must be seen as the "overdetermined" manifestation of a multiplicity of structures that intersect to produce the unstable (or deceptively stable) constellation conventionally called the "self." These structures encompass not only unconscious desires, fears, needs, and phobias, but also a host of conflicting social, political, ideological, and material factors of which we are equally unaware. They constitute the theoretical basis for the kaleidoscopic ways of representation and multiple ways of interpretations of fiction in Chinese and Western traditions.

The differences mainly lie in ways of representation. The most striking contrast between Chinese and Western fiction is that whereas in the Western tradition the dominant mode of representation is realism and its variations, in the Chinese tradition the most eye-catching mode of representation is the fantastic and its variations. The fantastic is one of the defining features of traditional Chinese fiction. This is clear in the epithets that define the various fictional genres in the evolution of Chinese *xiaoshuo*: *shenhua* (tales of gods), *zhiguai* (records of the strange), *zhiren* (records of extraordinary persons), and *chuanqi* (transmissions of the strange). The fantastic informs almost all major Chinese fictional works, even novels that are widely believed to be masterpieces of realism. Of the six great Chinese novels, the *Xiyouji* is patently a novel of fantasies; fantastic episodes appear in the *Sanguo yanyi*; and the fantastic provides a structural frame for the narratives of the *Shuihu zhuan*, the *Jin Ping Mei*, and the *Hongloumeng*. The only exception is the *Rulin waishi*; it is devoid of fantastic details, but it still features extraordinary persons and events.

The artistic differences arose from the differences in cultural conditions, especially the differences in metaphysical thought. At the risk of oversimplification, I will briefly contrast Chinese and Western worldviews and discuss their impact on Chinese and Western conceptions of fiction. Ontologically, the Western worldview, colorful as it is, has been dominated since Plato by what has been described as the "metaphysics of presence"—the notion of the world as constituted by some properties or essence enduringly present in things. By contrast, the Chinese worldview may be characterized as the "metaphysics of absence." It views the world as consisting not so much in substances as in the nonsubstance that gives rise to being. The metaphysical idea, *you shen yu wu* 有

生于無 (nothing gives rise to something), as I have discussed in the previous chapter, was transformed into the Chinese equivalent to Western fictionality, *wu zhong shen you* 無中生有 (something grows out of nothing). Epistemologically, Western metaphysics has since Aristotle divided the world into two separate realms: the subjective world and the objective world. This is exemplified in René Descartes's paradigmatic dualism between *res extensa* and *res cogitans*, a dualism that may be recast as a division between the human being as the thinking subject who observes and the world as observed objects.[3] By contrast, Chinese metaphysics conceives of the world as a totality of interconnections, interpenetrations, and transformations between the human and the natural realms. This is typified in the Confucian notion of *tianren heyi* 天人合一 (unity of heaven and man) and the Daoist notion that *wanwu yu wo weiyi* 萬物與我為一 (myriad things and I are one). David Hall and Roger Ames suggest that when Zhuangzi recommends that we become "one with all things," "this is not a Vedanta-like call to surrender one's particularity and dissolve into a unitary and perfect whole. Rather, it is a recognition that each and every unique phenomenon is continuous with every other phenomenon within one's field of experience."[4]

The Western ontology of presence and epistemology of dualistic division have not only promoted the zeal for scientific discoveries but may also have aided the development of realism and its variations like naturalism, critical realism, and psychological realism. All of them seem to have grown out of the creative impulses to observe, describe, and inquire into life, society, and the human mind. By contrast, the Chinese ontology of nonbeing and epistemology of totality may have helped bring about persistent authorial intrusions, simulated narrator-reader interactions, the mixture of narrative modes, the intercommunication between the human and non-human realms, and the kaleidoscopic nature of Chinese fiction. It is unthinkable that the Western metaphysics of presence and subject-object differentiation could have helped bring about magic realism and fantastic modes of narration before modernism; it is equally unthinkable that the Chinese ontology of non-being and epistemology of totality could have helped develop the coolheaded narration by Jane Austen, quasi-clinical observations by Emile Zola, and single-minded descriptions of the flow of consciousness by James Joyce.

MIMETIC DOGMA AND CHINESE DISSENT

In the preceding chapters, I have refuted some scholarly opinions that regarded characteristic features of Chinese fiction as "limitations." The so-called faults not only are Chinese fiction's forte but also reveal some profound insights that anticipated contemporary fictional theories. Take authorial intrusion for example. It has been viewed as a drawback in fiction in the Western tradition since the eighteenth century, but in traditional Chinese fiction it has never been viewed as a problem. Thematically and ideologically, we may regard authorial intrusion as a result of the moral concerns of fiction writers with didacticism. But philosophically it comes from a different worldview—a different way of perceiving and experiencing the world and a different mode of conceptualizing and representing the world. In the Chinese philosophical system, there are categories like the perceiving subject and the perceived object, but the subject and object are not cognitively separated, because it is the belief that everything under heaven is connected with everything else and there is no way to separate the subjective and objective worlds totally and absolutely. As Zhuangzi (369–286 BC), a founder of philosophical Daoism, points out:

> The universe and I exist together, and all things and I are one. Since all things are one, what room is there for speech? But since I have already said that all things are one, how can speech not exist? Speech and the one then make two. These two (separately) and the one (the two together) make three. Going from this even the best mathematician cannot reach [the final number]. How much less can ordinary people![5]

Here, Zhuangzi offered a mode of perception totally different from the analytic one that started with Descartes, who divided the universe into mutually exclusive (albeit interacting) thinking subject and perceived object. In Zhuangzi's mode of perception, there is no absolute demarcation between the perceiving self and perceived other; they are unified through the all-pervasive Dao. This all-in-one idea anticipated Heidegger's existentialist view of the to-be-in-the-worldness of the subject. Fiction creates a world of its own. It is in turn created by the author. The author and his creation are distinguishable, but unlike God in the West, who is distinctively separable from and transcendent above his creation, a fiction writer in the Chinese tradition is not perceived as a being separable from his created world. He is inextricably caught in the web of his own creation through his personal history, self-identity, ideological position, modes of observation, and artistic techniques. This may allow us to understand more deeply why, in the *Hongloumeng*, the author, narrator, editor, reader, and characters are woven into a grand narrative.

The Chinese epistemology of totality may have given rise to the Chinese belief in the text as a medium that inscribes the author's totality. This belief anticipated Edward Said's alternative to Foucault's conception of the author as a discursive function. Said suggests that we should view an author's career as a course "whose record is his work and whose goal is the integral text that adequately represents the efforts expended on its behalf," and that "A text is the source and the aim of a man's desire to be an author, it is the form of his attempts, it contains the elements of his coherence, and in a whole range of complex and differing ways it incarnates the pressures upon the writer of his psychology, his time, his society."[6] It is unnecessary to elaborate on this idea in the Chinese tradition. Suffice it to quote Mencius's famous notion of *zhiren lunshi* (to know a person through his time) and his rhetorical question. "Is it acceptable to chant a person's poetry and read his books without knowing about this person?"[7] Chinese fiction writers seem to have arrived at this understanding long before similar ideas appeared in the West. One sign of this realization is the existence of the above-mentioned "limitations" or idiosyncrasies in Chinese fiction. Another sign is a lack of dogmatic attitudes toward mimesis, realism, objectivism, and authorial presence.

By contrast, adherence to these issues in the West evolved into some dogmatic tenets that gained wide acceptance for a long time before they were exposed to be false. Those tenets include: "all fiction must imitate life and be true to life," "true fictional works must be realistic," "fictional authors should be objective," "fiction writers should stay out of fictional works as much as possible," "good fictional works should not engage in preaching to the reader,"[8] and so on. Traditional Chinese fiction deviates radically from these tenets and, by the yardstick of these tenets, seems to be an art manqué. But my study has proven that these deviations anticipated many insights uncovered by modern fiction studies. In the 1960s, Wayne Booth launched the first assault on these dearly cherished tenets. In *The Rhetoric of Fiction* (1961) he challenges exactly such critical tenets.[9] Postmodern theories have further desanctified them. In a way, I may claim that fictional theory and practice in the Chinese tradition have challenged these dogmas for hundreds of years.

Chinese fiction theory is predicated on the ontological and epistemological view of fiction as a multiplicity of worlds that are not necessarily the result of an imitation of the real world. Western fiction theory, however, has centered on mimesis, which has given rise to a series of debates over the nature of fiction. In the debates, there are basically three positions: "the full rejection of the mimetic character of fiction, the recognition of the partial role imitation plays in fiction, and the firm assertion that human imagination and therefore fiction are essentially mimetic."[10] After critiquing the positions for and against mimesis, Thomas Pavel, a literary theorist, argues: "[W]hile it is right to see mimesis as essential for understanding what fiction is, it is nevertheless wrong to see mimesis as adequate for understanding what fiction does. It is even more wrong to take the act of assessing imitation as our main task when reading fiction."[11] China has never observed the dogma of mimesis, because it has conceived of fiction as multiple worlds—some real, some unreal, still some purely imagined out of the creative mind. Here the Chinese notion of fiction merges with a position in most recent fiction theory, which "consists in abandoning ontological physicalism and positing a multiplicity of worlds, most of them nonexisting. This option sees fictional worlds as alternative worlds, and fictional statements as referring to states of affairs that occur in such alternative worlds."[12]

This position was held in traditional Chinese fiction for centuries, but has been practically abandoned in modern and present-day Chinese fiction. But I believe only such a notion of fiction can enable us to fully understand the rise of fictional works of surrealism, magic realism, the fantastic, romantic realism, and the tales of the strange in the Chinese tradition. As Pavel rightly points out: "We like to recognize our world in the works of imagination, but we also appreciate fiction for its ability to make us less dependent not just on actual stimuli but on actuality as such. In other words, we also appreciate it for its power to create alternative sets of situations, thereby putting the actual world into perspective, challenging its supremacy."[13] Pavel believes all fictional works have this power, but two forms of prose fiction are especially effective in wielding this power. One is the idealist novel, which started with the Greek romance, and was continued by nineteenth and twentieth-century popular fiction; and the other is the antirealist narrative prose exemplified by Rabelais, Sterne, the surrealists, and the magic realists. Had he known of Chinese fiction, he would include Chinese tales of the strange and traditional novels of manners with mythic frames and supernatural elements.

Thus, the Chinese deviation from the mimetic and realistic dogmas is deeply embedded in the Chinese worldview, especially the philosophical view of the interconnectedness of the subject and object, the observer and the observed. So, while the fictional modes predicated on the dominant realistic tradition have their philosophical foundation in Western metaphysics, which posits a separation between the subject and object, the observer and the observed, the Chinese fictional modes of kaleidoscopic totality find their philosophical basis in the metaphysical view of oneness and equality of things.

CONCEPTUAL BASIS FOR
A TRANSCULTURAL FICTION THEORY

After British gunboats blasted open China's closed door to the outside world, Chinese fiction increasingly converged with Western fiction. Nowadays, it is virtually impossible to distinguish Chinese and Western fictional works without the difference in language media. A regrettable consequence of the coming of Western fictional theories turns out to be that the precious legacies of traditional Chinese fiction theory have been consigned to oblivion. Present-day Chinese fiction theory is practically a branch of Western fiction theory. There is not just a divide between Chinese and Western fiction but also a divide between traditional and modern Chinese fiction. Even more ironical is that traditional Chinese fiction studies have increasingly become a subject on the margins of general fiction studies in the worldwide context of globalization. How can we address and redress the regrettable situation?

In my view, the dual divide in the field of Chinese and comparative literature is a consequence arising from an almost total abandonment of the Chinese system of fiction theory and an unconditional surrender to and acceptance of the Western system of literary theory. To redress the situation, I think we should tackle the foundational issues, especially the conceptual basis for bridging the dual divide in an international context. The convergence of Chinese and Western metaphysics has made it easier than ever before to undertake this task. Martin Heidegger's metaphysical theory of human existence would give much assistance to our assignment. Heidegger critiques Western empiricism that divides the world into "subjects" whose principal task is to perceive and "objects" whose character is to be perceived, and advocates a return to early Greek thinking about being as an emerging-into-presence. His conception of "Nothing" as the ontology of metaphysics and such ideas as the *Dasein*'s unitary phenomenon of being-in-the-world, human beings' embeddedness in concrete situations of action, and the need to capture the totality of human existence through a "phenomenology of everydayness"[14] are in total harmony with Chinese metaphysical thinking about human existence, especially with the Daoist system of metaphysics. Heidegger's theory about being, language, and literature should be brought into dialogue with Chinese metaphysics to try to locate a common theoretical ground for bridging the divide between Chinese and Western fiction theories.

The Chinese conception of fiction is ontologically and epistemologically embedded in the first philosophical concept in the Chinese tradition: the Dao or Taiji. Chinese fiction in its multiplicity of representation of life and kaleidoscopic forms is an artistic form of the Dao/Taiji. So one may conceptualize fiction as a system of signs constructed on the metaphysical principle of the Dao or Taiji. Although most traditional Chinese literary theorists consciously conceived of fiction as external manifestations of the Dao or Taiji, fiction writers and commentators explicitly and implicitly conceived fiction itself as a minor Dao or Taiji. In extended Chinese fictional works, we may locate the sources of numerous characteristic features in the philosophical conception of the Dao or Taiji. In Chinese fiction commentaries, to view an extended fictional work as a narrative constructed on the principles of the Taiji is not uncommon. Zhang Xinzhi 張新之 (fl. 1828–1850), a Qing commentator, believed that major Chinese novels were organized on the yin-yang principles of the *Yijing* (Book of Changes).[14] We must remember that in Laozi's and Zhuangzi's conception, yin and yang are precisely the constitutive principles of the Dao. The *Book of Changes* describes the Dao: "One *yin* and one *yang* are called the Dao" (一陰一陽之謂道).[16] Laozi's *Daode jing* (The Way and Its Virtue) describes the Dao as a generative principle:[17] "The way [Dao] begets one; one begets two; two begets three; three begets the myriad creatures."[18] According to the accepted interpretation of this passage, "one" refers to the totality of the Taiji, "two" stands for the dyad of yin and yang, "three" refers to the trinity of heaven, earth, and man.[19] Since both the *Yijing* and *Daode jing* belong to the repertoire of books an educated person in traditional China must read, Chinese fiction writers and commentators may have obtained their ideas about the conditions of fiction from the metaphysical conception of the Dao. Indeed, if a fictional work is perceived to be organized on yin and yang, it implies that it is conceived as a Dao-like entity. Zhang himself appears to have employed the hermeneutic practice of the yin-yang symbolism to comment on the *Hongloumeng*, the *Jing Ping Mei*, and other fictional works. In his extended commentary, he states explicitly that the novel "uses the examples of the *I Ching* 易經 [Book of Changes] to portray the waxing and waning of fortunes."[20]

In modern times, a number of scholars have taken heed of the traditional commentaries and provided fascinating insights into the relationship between the metaphysical conception of the Taiji and the conception of fictional works. Recent scholarship in the West has shed more light on how extended fictional works are organized and generate meanings through some symbolic structures based on the yin-yang principles. In his study of the *Hongloumeng*, for example, Andrew Plaks demonstrates that the novel is intrinsically structured on the philosophical principle of yin-yang bipolarity and five-agent periodicity. He traces a number of Chinese narrative features to the philosophical roots in Chinese thought, and argues that "complementary bipolarity and multiple periodicity are, among other possible patterns, abiding aesthetic forms that lend consistency and continuity to the system of Chinese literature."[21] Maram Epstein, in her study of late imperial Chinese fiction, has uncovered an even broader and deeper impact of the yin-yang theory on the structure and meaning of Chinese fiction. She points out, "[T]he manipulation of *yinyang* symbolism in fictional texts is a central node where formalism and orthodoxy intersect," and "curiously, even as philosophical interest in *yinyang* metaphysics was declining during the late imperial period, the use of *yinyang* symbolism in fiction composition and interpretation became increasingly important."[22] The scholarship by Chinese and Western scholars is just one step short of declaring that some fictional works were conceived of as a form of the Dao or Taiji. Basing myself on the conceptual insights in both traditional fiction theory and modern studies of the conditions of fictional works, I may draw the conclusion that a Chinese fictional work is explicitly and implicitly conceived of as a minor Dao or Taiji.

FICTION AS A LINGUISTIC REPRESENTATION OF THE ONE

If fiction is a form of the Dao, as I maintain, it may have considerable conceptual significance for a transcultural theory of fiction. However, one needs to reconceptualize it as the "One," a unifying first principle in Chinese, Western, and other traditions. In his "Qiwu lun" (Equality of Things) chapter, Zhuangzi views myriad things under heaven as being unified by the Dao, which is also called the One: "Nothing escapes from Tao [Dao]. Such is perfect Tao [Dao], and so is great speech. The three, Complete, Entire, and All, differ in name but are the same in actuality. They all designate (*chih*, mark) the One."[23] In so saying, Zhuangzi was talking about the Dao as an all-encompassing entity. By no mere coincidence, the first principle in the West, the Logos, is also called "one." In my conceptual inquiry into the possibilities of locating a common conceptual basis for Chinese and Western studies, I have argued that by no mere accident, the Dao and Logos are called the "One" in both traditions and have been conceived of as a unifying principle.[24] In Western philosophical thought, Heraclitus remarked on the Logos: "Listening not to me but to the Logos[;] it is wise to agree that all things are one."[25] Heidegger explains what the Logos says simply as: "All is One."[26] Just as the Dao and Logos find a conceptual common ground in the One, so Chinese and Western fictions may find a common basis in the One. This One-to-One basis may facilitate our efforts in constructing a transcultural system of fiction theory.

The One is not just a unifying principle; it is also a structuring and life-giving force.[27] Laozi said, "Heaven in virtue of the One is limpid; Earth in virtue of the One is settled; Gods in virtue of the One have their potencies; The valley in virtue of the One is full; The myriad creatures in virtue of the One are alive; Lords and princes in virtue of the One become leaders in the empire. It is the One that makes these what they are."[28] I may add that an extended fictional work in virtue of the One is able to get its myriad characters, details, scenes, episodes, and narrative threads organized, structured, and emplotted. In analytic terms, we may call the One "theme," "central thesis," "controlling idea," "intrinsic structure," or "intrinsic pattern." But, artistically, it is a kind of mysterious, ethereal pneuma, a creative force of totality like the indescribable and unnamable Dao that gives a fictional work its being and distinguishes a masterpiece from a mediocre work.

I have already pointed out that Chinese fiction writers conceived of fiction as a form of writing that could be reasonably compared to the all-encompassing power of the self-generative Dao/One. A fictional work generates multiplicity of meanings or openness precisely in the way the Dao/One generates myriad things in the universe through the interaction of yin and yang. Although no theorist in the Western tradition has conceived of fiction as a form of the self-generative One or Logos, similar conceptualizations are implied. D. H. Lawrence, who viewed the novel as "a bright book of life," declared it to be a growing literary form that escapes any conceptual attempts to pin it down.[29] Joyce's *Ullysses* exemplifies the self-generating notion of the novel. Though it only narrates a day in the life of the protagonists, scholars have claimed that Joyce meant to use it to encompass the whole of Western civilization, from Homer's *Odyssey* through Western mythology, the theology of the church, the history of paganism, European history, Irish legends, Jewish history, and so on; or as some critics believe, it was meant to cover everything under the sun. In a similar fashion, and long before Joyce, Cao Xueqin created the *Hongloumeng*, a totalizing novel that encompasses Chinese mythology, philosophy, history, arts, architecture, family sagas, human relationships, topical politics, self, identity, and society.

In the final analysis, the Chinese conception of fiction is an artistic conception of the Dao. The various conceptual ideas that I have identified—being out of nonbeing, real in the unreal, beyond truth and falsity, make-believe, man-in-one totality, kaleidoscopic representation, and multiple interpretations—constitute a complete system of fiction theory predicated on the metaphysics of the Dao. Equipped with its sweeping and totalizing power to represent life and the world, fiction may be viewed as a miniature Taiji, another name for the Dao or the One. From a comparative perspective, fiction in the West may also be viewed as the One, another name for the Logos or Idea. Fiction in both Chinese and Western traditions organizes myriad characters, scenes, events, and actions into one unified and coherent entity in the same way the Dao or the Logos unifies myriad things of the universe into the One. Based on Chinese and Western theories of fiction, I venture to suggest that fiction as a miniature version of the all embracing Dao or Logos is a linguistic form of the One. Like the Dao/One, it is self-generative and can represent and account for everything under heaven and on earth. The art of Chinese fiction, and indeed, fiction of any tradition, is essentially an artistic way of coming to terms with the first principle, the Logos or Idea in the West, the Dao or Taiji in China. Just as the Dao and Logos find a conceptual common ground in the One, so Chinese and Western fiction may find a common basis in the One. This One-to-One correspondence may serve as the conceptual basis for constructing a transcultural system of fiction theory.

My conceptualization of fiction may seem to blur the boundaries between fiction and metaphysics. But this vision about the interrelation between metaphysics and literature is sanctioned by both metaphysical thinking and literary practice. In his metaphysical thinking about Being, Heidegger turned to poetry, especially the poetry of Hölderlin, for the roots of being. In his later writings, the poet holds as much authority as the philosopher.[30] "[A] great Poet," said S. T. Coleridge, "must be, implicitè if not explicitè, a profound Metaphysician."[31] Fiction and philosophy used to be one in both Chinese and Western traditions. What connects them is the metaphysical conception of poetry as the establisher of being: "Poetry," Heidegger writes in an essay on Hölderlin, "is the establishment of Being by means of the word."[32] The intrinsic relationship between poetry and Being, on the one hand, and poetry and philosophy, on the other, is the philosophical reason why I devoted a whole chapter to explore the poetic nature of Chinese fiction. Chinese *xiaoshuo* used to lead a symbiotic existence with history and philosophy. What unified the three separate categories in later classifications is poetry, the core and roots of Being.

D. H. Lawrence once lamented the split between philosophy and fiction and wished that the two could come together again in the novel.[33] In his fictional practice, he struggled hard to fuse thinking and fiction and produced a series of novels to exemplify his creative vision. Among his fictional works, *Women in Love* is widely acknowledged as his best work. It is a tour de force that rolls history, philosophy, and poetry into one. Conceptually, its success is derived from his notion of a balance between passion and thought, body and spirit, the male and female, and the creative and destructive forces in human existence. His view of life's opposites unified by the poetry of lived experience corresponds pretty well with Chinese yin-yang theory that conceives of the Dao as the unifying One. The conceptual convergence on the One may provide a common conceptual basis and a vision for constructing a transcultural theory of fiction. Recent theoretical research has problematized the time-honored view of fiction as a mimetic representation of life, reality, and the world.

Chinese fictional works with fantastic and magic realistic narratives have further problematized the mimetic view from another cultural perspective. Since fiction is a verbal art that concerns itself with language and its relation to perceived realities, we cannot find a more abstract and comprehensive idea than the unifying principle of the universal One in our reconception of fiction. Thus, in a metaphysical spirit, I may close this book by proposing a general conception of fiction: Prose fiction is a linguistic representation of the One, the Being that unifies poetry, history, and philosophy.

Notes

PREFACE

1. Kermode, *Art of Telling*, 7.

INTRODUCTION.
THEORY OF FICTION

1. Eagleton, *After Theory*, 88.

2. J. Hillis Miller, "Narrative," in Lentricchia and McLaughlin, *Critical Terms for Literary Study*, 66.

3. Barthes, *Image-Music-Text*, 79.

4. See Hanan, "Early Chinese Short Story: A Critical Theory in Outline," 299–338; Hanan, *Chinese Short Story*; Hanan, *Chinese Vernacular Story*; Plaks, *Chinese Narrative*; Ye Lang, *Zhongguo xiaoshuo meixue*; Wu Gongzheng, *Xiaoshuo meixue*; Rolston, ed., *How to Read the Chinese Novel*; Wang Rumei and Zhang Yu, *Zhongguo xiaoshuo lilun shi*; and Meng Zhaolian and Ning Zongyi, *Zhongguo xiaoshuo yishu shi*.

5. The only exception is Andrew Plaks's study. He has conducted conceptual inquiries into Chinese narrative and published a few articles. His focus, however, is a broad one on "narrative." See his "Conceptual Models in Chinese Narrative Theory," 25–47; "Towards A Critical Theory of Chinese Narrative," *Chinese Narrative*, 309–52; and "Full-length *Hsiao-shuo* and the Western Novel: A Generic Reappraisal," 163–76.

6. I have thumbed through the current fiction scholarship and found that histories of fiction number in the triple digits. A major research project on Chinese fiction sponsored by the Chinese State Commission of Education has turned out eighteen book-length studies of Chinese fiction, which include *Han Wei Liuchao xioashuo shi* 漢魏六朝小說史, *Sui Tang Wudai xiaoshuo shi* 隋唐五代小說史, *Song Yuan xiaoshuo shi* 宋元小說史, *Mingdai xiaoshuo shi* 明代小說史, *Qingdai xiaoshuo shi* 清代小說史, *Wan Qing xiaoshuo shi* 晚清小說史, *Biji xiaoshuo shi* 筆記小說史, *Chuanqi xiaoshuo shi* 傳奇小說史, *Huaben xiaoshuo shi* 話本小說史, *Zhanghui xiaoshuo shi* 章回小說史, *Lishi xiaoshuo shi* 曆史小說史, *Shenguai xiaoshuo shi* 神怪小說史, *Shiqing xiaoshuo shi* 世情小說史, *Xiayi gong'an xiaoshuo shi* 俠義公案小說史, *Zhongguo xiaoshuo lilun shi* 中國小說理論史, *Zhongguo xiaoshuo yishu shi* 中國小說藝術史, *Zhongguo xiaoshuo wenhua shi*

223

中國小說文化史, and *Zhongguo xiaoshuo yanjiu shi* 中國小說研究史. The titles of them inform us that all of these are histories of fiction, which deal with either a historical period or a fictional genre.

7. See Bishop, "Some Limitations of Chinese Fiction," 237–47.

8. Zheng Zhenduo, "*Shuihu zhuan* de yanhua" 112–13.

9. Irwin, *The Evolution of a Chinese Novel*, 5, 23.

10. Birch, foreword, xi.

11. M. D. Gu, "Is Mimetic Theory in Literature and Art Universal?" 459–99, and Gu, "Mimetic Theory in Chinese Literary Thought," 403–24.

12. Dolezel, *Heterocosmica*; Cohn, *Distinction of Fiction*.

13. Wang Rumei and Zhang Yu, *Zhongguo xiaoshuo lilun shi*, 13.

14. Rolston, *Reading and Writing between the Lines*, 131.

15. Wang Rumei and Zhang Yu, *Zhongguo xiaoshuo lilun shi*, 1.

16. Mill, "What Is Poetry?" 537.

17. See the concluding chapter of Freedman's *Lyrical Novel*, 271–83.

18. See "The Inspiration," in Lau et al., *Modern Chinese Stories and Novellas*, 419.

19. Wang Rumei and Zhang Yu, *Zhongguo xiaoshuo lilun shi*, 14.

20. J. J. Y. Liu, *Chinese Theories of Literature*, 1.

21. Eco, *Aesthetics of Chaosmos*, 1.

22. Ibid.

23. Schorer, "Technique as Discovery," 102.

24. Fowler, *Linguistics and the Novel*, 3.

CHAPTER 1.
CHINESE NOTIONS OF FICTION

1. Reed, *Exemplary History of the Novel*, 24, 22, 56.

2. Martin, *Recent Theories of Narrative*, 28.

3. Plaks, "Conceptual Models in Chinese Narrative Theory," 27.

4. The earliest appearance of the term *xiaoshuo* is found in the fourth century BC, while *xushi* (narration) did not appear until the Tang.

5. Plaks, ed., *Chinese Narrative*, 309.

6. Scholes and Kellogg, *Nature of Narrative*, 8.

7. Ibid., 3.

8. Bakhtin, "Epic and Novel," 61.

9. Lawrence, *Phoenix*, 528.

10. Patrick Hanan, "The Early Chinese Short Story," 300.

11. Mair, "Narrative Revolution in Chinese Literature," 21–22.

12. J. A. Cuddon, *A Dictionary of Literary Terms and Literary Theory*, 343.

13. Plato from a negative perspective and Aristotle from a positive perspective viewed poetry, which includes lyrics, epics, and drama, as fiction, because poetry denotes a thing made, having a status of falsehood, feigning, and even lying. In his study of fiction, Frye adopts a similar position in his study of fictional modes. See *Anatomy of Criticism*, 33–67.

14. Y. W. Ma, "Fiction," 31.

15. S. Lu, *From Historicity to Fictionality*, 51.

16. Modified from Watson's translation, in Zhuangzi, *Complete Works of Chuang Tzu*, 296

17. See Xunzi, *Xunzi yizhu* 荀子譯注, 491.

18. Wilhelm, "Notes on Chou Fiction," 252.

19. Ban Gu, "Yiwen zhi," *juan* 30, p. 30a. The English version is from Lu Xun, *A Brief History of Chinese Fiction*, 3.

20. Dewoskin, "On Narrative Revolution," 38.

21. Liu Zhiji, *Shitong*, 273.

22. Wang Rumei and Zhang Yu, *Zhongguo xiaoshuo lilun shi*, 55–58.

23. Ibid., 56.

24. Ban Gu, "Yiwen zhi," *juan* 30, 30a.

25. Hu Yinglin, *Shaoshi shanfang bicong*, 886:304

26. Ibid., 886:305.

27. Ji Yun, "Xiaoshuojia lei," 282.

28. Adapted from the English translation of Lu Xun's *Brief History of Chinese Fiction*, 374.

29. Zhang Xuecheng, *Wenshi tongyi*, *juan* 5, p. 36a.

30. Wilhelm "Notes on Chou Fiction," 251.

31. Ibid.

32. See *Ciyuan* 辭源 (Beijing: Shangwu yinshuguan, 1995), 1326.

33. Many scholars, ancient and modern, Chinese and Western, have identified it as a literary text. I will further discuss this point.

34. Li Shan's notes to "Xinlun" in Xiao Tang, *Wenxuan*, 439.

35. Liu Zhiji, *Shitong* 史通, 275.

36. Lu Xun, *Zhongguo xiaoshuo shilüe*, p. 3.

37. See Ban Gu, *Qian Hanshu*, *juan* 30, p. 29b.

38. English version from Vincent Shih's translation in Liu Hsieh, *The Literary Mind and the Carving of Dragons*, 113.

39. Zhang Xuecheng *Wenshi tongyi*, *juan* 5, pp. 35b–36a.

40. The English translations are taken from Waley, *Analects of Confucius*, 88, 99, 127.

41. Wen Yiduo, *Shenhua yu shi* 201–6. English translation is from Mair, "Narrative Revolution in Chinese Literature," 4.

42. Plaks, *Chinese Narrative*, 314.

43. Ji Yun, *Siku quanshu zongmu*, 1205. For Nienhauser's view, see *Indiana Companion*, 632.

44. Porter, *From Deluge to Discourse*, 105–6.

45. Lu Ji, *Wenfu*, 224–25.

46. Luo Fu Jushi 羅浮居士, "*Shenlou zhi* xiaoshuo xu 蜃樓志小說敘," in Yuling Laoren, *Shenlow zhi quanzhuan*, iii.

47. Wu Gongzheng, *Xiaoshuo meixue*, 24.

48. Ibid.

49. Ibid.

50. Yuan Zhen, *Yuanshi Changqin ji, juan* 10, p. 4a.

51. Lu Xun, *Lu Xun quanji*, 9:309.

52. Lu Xun, *Zhongguo xiaoshuo shilüe*, 54.

53. Meng Zhaolian and Ning Zongyi, *Zhongguo xiaoshuo yishu shi*, 34, 88.

54. Lu Xun, *Lu Xun quanji*, 6:321.

55. Hu Yinglin, *Shaoshi shanfang bicong*, 886:387.

56. Li Xiusheng and Zhao Yishan, *Zhongguo fenti wenxue shi-xiaoshuo juan*, 39.

57. Gan Bao, *Soushen ji*, p. 2.

58. Ibid.

59. Lu Xun, "Zhongguo xiaoshuo de lishi de bianqian," in *Lu Xun quanji*, 9:311.

60. Dewoskin, "Six Dynasties *Chih-Kuai* and the Birth of Fiction," 51.

61. Ibid., 49.

62. See Tao Qian, *Tao Yuanming ji jiaojian*, 402–3.

63. I translated this tale into English myself.

64. Paul De Man, "Resistance to Theory," 11.

65. See Shen and Xia, eds., *Han Wei Liuchao xiaoshuo xuan*, 188–90.

66. Meng Zhaolian and Ning Zongyi, *Zhongguo xiaoshuo yishu shi*, 8.

67. Ibid., 101–8.

68. Ibid., 102.

CHAPTER 2.
THE NATURE OF (CHINESE) FICTION

1. All the mentioned scholars have made a similar claim with varying degrees of emphasis. Wen Yiduo's opinion is representative: "If it had not been for that little bit of fresh stimulus brought in by religious forces and the fact that our own songs had been sung to such a degree that they could not be sung again, we might have gone on producing stories such as the two chapters of didactic anecdotes in Han Fei tzu or 'Tan the Prince of Ye' 燕丹子 and embryonic song-and-dance dramas such as 'The Nine Songs' 九歌 but we definitely never would have had Yuan drama and chaptered novels." Quoted in Mair, "Narrative Revolution in Chinese Literature," 4.

2. Mair, "The Narrative Revolution in Chinese Litterature," 22.

3. Dewoskin, "On Narrative Revolution," 32.

4. Ibid., 44.

5. Collingwood, *Idea of History*, 231–82.

6. Frye, *Anatomy of Criticism*, 82–83; Frye, *Fables of Identity*, 53–54.

7. Dewoskin, "On Narrative Revolution," 36.

8. Nienhauser, "Origins of Chinese Fiction," 191.

9. Liu Zhiji, *Shitong*, 275–76.

10. Dewoskin, "The Six Dynasties *Chih-kuai* and The Birth of Fiction," 23.

11. Ibid., 27.

12. Rolston, *Reading and Writing between the Lines*, 131.

13. See S. Lu, *From Historicity to Fictionality*.

14. Aristotle, *Poetics*, 53.

15. Martin, *Recent Theories of Narrative*, 182.

16. Lu Xun, "Zhongguo xiaoshuo de lishi de bianqian," *Lu Xun quanji*, 9:323.

17. Zhang Xuecheng, *Zhangshi yishu, juan* 14, p. 25a. English translation from S. Lu's *From Historicity to Fictionality*, 77.

18. Dolezel, *Heterocosmica*; Cohn, *Distinction of Fiction*.

19. Scholes, "Language, Narrative, and Anti-Narrative," 206.

20. Ibid., 207.

21. Ibid.

22. Ibid.

23. Young, "Conjectures on Original Composition," 339.

24. Ibid., 341.

25. Ian Watt stresses the sociological reasons for the rise of extended fiction in *The Rise of the Novel* (1957), 35–59. For the Chinese side, see Li Xiusheng and Zhao Yishan, *Zhongguo fenti wenxue shi*, 122–26; Chen Meilin et al., *Zhanghui xiaoshuo shi*, 32–38.

26. Plaks, "Full-length *Hsiao-shuo* and the Western Novel," 166.

27. Ibid., 176.

28. Meng Zhaolian and Ning Zongyi, *Zhongguo xioashuo yishu shi*, 165–70.

29. Průšek, "Urban Centers: The Cradle of Popular Fiction," 259.

30. Edward Seidensticker situates the novel's genesis within the context of mid-Heian literature, and speculates that because Japan was relatively free from the harem politics that so beset other Oriental countries, talented ladies of the court channeled their energies into writing. See his introduction to Murasaki, *Tale of Genji*, viii. According to Murasaki's own diary-memoir, her novel was read by others in the court and even read to the emperor. See Waley's introduction to his translation in Waley, *Tale of Genji*, xiii.

31. Lu Ji, *Wenfu*, 224.

32. Sima Qian, *Shiji, juan* 130, 10:3300.

33. Ibid.

34. Lu Xun, "Zhongguo xiaoshuo de lishi de bianqian," 9:302.

35. Requoted from Cai et al., *Zhongguo wenxue lilun shi*, 3:327.

36. Ibid.

37. Li Zongwei, *Tangren chuanqi*, 11.

38. Freud, *Freud Reader*, 439.

39. Robert, *Origins of The Novel*, 21–40.

40. Yu Ji, "Xieyunxuan ji," *juan* 38, p. 11a–b.

41. See Pu Songling, *Liaozhai zhiyi*, 181–83.

42. Zhang Wencheng, *You xianku*, edited with a preface by Lu Xun, dated 1927.

43. S. Lu, *From Historicity to Fictionality*, 105.

44. Freud, *Freud Reader*, 442.

45. Ibid., 443.

46. The English translation is quoted from S. Lu, *From Historicity to Fictionality*, 51–52.

47. S. Lu, *From Historicity to Fictionality*, 52.

48. Holland, *Dynamics of Literary Response*, 30.

49. Chen Meilin et al., *Zhanghui xiaoshuo shi*, 95.

50. See Hegel, *Novel in Seventeenth-Century China*.

51. Lu Xun, *Lu Xun quanji*, vol. 1.

52. This passage is translated after consulting the English version in Rolston, *How to Read the Chinese Novel*, p.195.

53. Cai Yuanfang, "*Dong Zhou lieguo zhi* dufa," 1a.

54. Chen Yinke, *Yuan Bai shijian zhenggao*, 111–12.

55. See *Beijing Qingnian Bao* 北京青年報, November 5, 2002.

56. Jin Shengtan, *Du Diwu caizishu* fa 讀第五才子書法, "Comment on Chapter 13." Adapted from Rolston, *How to Read the Chinese Novel*, p.133. I added one sentence that is found in the Chinese version.

57. Adapted from Rolston, *How to Read the Chinese Novel*, 132.

58. Requoted from Cai et al., *Zhongguo wenxue lilun shi*, 4:331.

59. Hu Shi, "*Sanguo zhi yanyi* xu," 389.

60. Zheng Zhengduo, *Chatuben Zhongguo wenxue shi*, 721.

61. Requoted from Wang and Zhang, *Zhongguo xiaoshuo lilun shi*, 45.

62. Bell. "Aesthetic Hypothesis," 15, 17.

63. Li Zhehou, *Mei de licheng*, 22.

64. Bell. "Aesthetic Hypothesis," 17.

65. See Richard Anderson's excerpt from *Calliope's Sisters* in Korsmeyer, *Aesthetics*, 29.

66. Kant, *Critique of Judgment*, 386.

67. Ma and Lau, *Traditional Chinese Stories and Novellas*, 197, 202.

68. Freud, *Complete Psychological Works*, 9:153.

69. Ibid., 153.

CHAPTER 3.
THE AESTHETIC TURN IN CHINESE FICTION

1. Plaks, *Four Masterworks of the Ming Novel*, 3.

2. Ibid., 16.

3. Ibid., 47.

4. Wilhelm, "Notes on Chou Fiction," 251.

5. Ibid., 262–63.

6. See Li Xiusheng and Zhao Yishan, *Zhongguo fenti wenxue shi*, 3–37; J. C. Y. Wang, "Early Chinese Narrative," 3.

7. Hu Yinglin. *Shaoshi shanfang bicong*, 886:305b .

8. Robert Scholes, "Language, Narrative, and Anti-Narrative," 206.

9. Martin, *Recent Theories of Narrative*, 182.

10. This is Wallace Martin's summary of Smith's view. See *Recent Theories of Narrative*, 183.

11. Barbara H. Smith, *On the Margins of Discourse*, 29.

12. Aristotle, *Poetics*, 51.

13. Robert Scholes, "Language, Narrative, and Anti-Narrative," 205.

14. Y. W. Ma, "Fiction," 31.

15. Shi Yuliang 石育良, in Li and Zhao, *Zhongguo fenti wenxue shi*, 10.

16. See relevant descriptions accompanying the subtitles of the chapters in Cervantes, *Don Quixote*.

17. Hanan, "Nature of Ling Meng-ch'u's Fiction," 87.

18. Ibid.

19. Riffaterre, *Fictional Truth*, 29–30.

20. Zhang Xuecheng, *Zhangshi yishu, juan* 14, p. 23b.

21. Eagleton, *After Theory*, 90.

22. Roland Barthes in Lane, *Introduction to Structuralism*, 154.

23. Deleuze, "The Simulacrum and Ancient Philosophy," 256.

24. Baudrillard, *Selected Writings*, 166.

25. Cao and Gao, *Story of the Stone*, 1:130.

26. Marthe Robert, *Origins of the Novel*, 21–40.

27. Freud, *Sexual Enlightenment of Children*, 41–45.

28. Freud, *Introductory Lectures on Psychoanalysis*, 332–35.

29. Plaks, *Chinese Narrative*, 348.

30. Cohn, *Distinction of Fiction*, 23.

31. English translation from Ma and Lau, *Traditional Chinese Stories and Novellas*, 142.

32. See McKillop, *Samuel Richardson*, 16–42.

33. Ma and Lau, *Traditional Chinese Stories and Novellas*, 143.

34. Forster, *Aspects of the Novel*, 81.

35. See Eco, *Aesthetics of Chaosmos*.

36. Smith, "Narrative Versions, Narrative Theories," in Mitchell, *On Narrative*, 217–18.

37. The English translation of Hu's remark is from Sheldon Lu's *From Historicity to Fictionality*, 50–51.

38. Lawrence, *Phoenix*, 535.

39. Lawrence, *Phoenix II*, 416.

40. Peirce, *Philosophical Writings of Peirce*, 282.

41. Scholes, "Language, Narrative, and Anti-Narrative," 206.

42. Rolston, *How to Read the Chinese Novel*, 193.

43. A. C. Yu, *Rereading the Stone*, 257–8.

44. Zhang Xuecheng, *Zhangshi yishu, juan* 3, p. 53a–b.

45. Hu Shi, "*Sanguo zhi yanyi* xu," 389–391.

46. Ibid., 390.

47. Li and Zhao, *Zhongguo fenti wenxueshi-xiaoshuo juan*, 250.

48. See Cao Jiping et al., *Da Song Xuanhe yishi* 大宋宣和遺事.

49. Zhang Xuecheng, *Zangshi yishu, juan* 3, p. 53a–b.

50. Quoted from Rolston, *How to Read the Chinese Novel*, 132–3.

51. Kristeva, *Kristeva Reader*, 63.

52. Requoted from ibid., 62–63.

53. Saussure, *Course in General Linguistics*, 68.

54. Kristeva, *Kristeva Reader*, 64.

55. Mao Zonggang in Rolston, *How to Read the Chinese Novel*, 152–95.

56. Kristeva, *Kristeva Reader*, 64–65.

57. Porter, *From Deluge to Discourse*, 59

58. Ibid., 111,

59. Ibid., 149.

60. Kristeva, *Kristeva Reader*, 70.

61. Ibid., 70–71. Italics in the original.

62. Ibid., 64.

63. Ibid., 72. Italics in the original.

64. Ibid., 63–73.

65. Barthes, *Elements of Semiology*, 89–90.

66. Ibid., 90.

67. Ibid., 114.

68. See *Wenyuange Siku quanshu*, 849:863

69. See Barthes, *S/Z: An Essay* (1974); Lacan, *Ecrits*, 30–113; Foucault, *Order of Things*; Derrida, *Writing and Difference*; Kristeva, *Desire in Language*; Kristeva, *Revolution in Poetic Language*; de Man, *Blindness and Insight*; de Man, *Allegories of Reading*; and Culler, *On Deconstruction*.

70. Pu Songling, in Guo, *Zhongguo lidai wenlun xuan*, 3:331.

71. Zeitlin, *Historian of the Strange*.

72. See his letter to Felice, January 16, 1913.

CHAPTER 4.
THE POETIC NATURE OF CHINESE FICTION

1. Plaks, *Four Masterworks of the Ming Novel*, 22–50.

2. Yu-kung Kao, "Lyric Vision In Chinese Narrative Tradition," 227–43.

3. Wong Kam-ming, *Chinese Narrative*, 225.

4. Freud, *Complete Psychological Works*, 23:159.

5. Freud, *Ego and the Id*, 3–10.

6. Ibid., 30–33.

7. Patrick Hanan, "The Early Chinese Short Story," in Birch, *Studies of Literary Genres*, 320–21.

8. Ibid., 322.

9. See Rolston, *Reading and Writing between the Lines*, 237–42.

10. See Chen Qinghao, *Xinbian Shitou ji Zhiyan zhai pingyu jijiao*, 25–26.

11. Jakobson, and Morris Halle, *Fundamentals of Language*, 78.

12. Plaks, *Chinese Narrative*, 311.

13. Yu-kung Kao, "Lyric Vision In Chinese Narrative Tradition," 236–43.

14. For a brief idea of how language in general and literature in particular became the unconscious of psychoanalysis, see Françoise Meltzer, "Unconscious," in Lentricchia and McLaughlin, *Critical Terms for Literary Study*, 147–62.

15. Hoffman and Murphy, *Essentials of the Theory of Fiction*, 5.

16. Freedman, *Lyrical Novel*.

17. Cao and Gao, *Story of the Stone*, 1:49–50.

18. Ibid., 1:50

19. Ibid., 201–2.

20. Ibid., 201.

21. The English translation is adapted from Owen, *Readings in Chinese Literary Thought*, 130.

22. Gérard Gennett adequately sums up this restriction: "Plato deliberately leaves out all nonrepresentational poetry—and thus, above all, what we call lyric poetry—and a fortiori all other forms of literature. . . . Plato obviously was not unaware of lyric poetry, but he excludes it here with a deliberately restrictive definition . . . a restriction that, via Aristotle, will become—and for centuries will remain—the basic tenet of classical poetics." Gennett, *Archtext*, 9–10.

23. Bakhtin, "Epic and Novel," 67.

24. Mill, "What Is Poetry?" 537.

25. Ibid., 538.

26. Wordsworth, "Preface to the Second Edition of *Lyrical Ballads*," 441.

27. English translation is quoted from James Liu, *Chinese Theories of Literature*, 69.

28. Hou and Wang, *Jin Ping Mei ziliao huibian*, 214.

29. Cao and Gao, *Story of the Stone*, 1:20–21.

30. Lu Hsun, *Selected Stories*, 65.

31. Woolf, "Mr. Bennett and Mrs. Brown," 35.

32. Ibid., 39.

33. Coleridge, "Biographia Literaria," 471.

34. Joyce's letter to Miss Weaver, December 17, 1931. See Ellmann, *James Joyce*, 615.

35. Freedman, *Lyrical Novel*, 271.

36. See Chen Yinke, *Yuan Bai shijian zhenggao*, 108; and Ch'en Shou-yi, *Chinese Literature*, 308.

37. David Hawkes, in Cao and Gao, *Story of the Stone*, 1:21.

38. Plaks, "Conceptual Models in Chinese Narrative Theory," 33.

39. Andrew Plaks in Plaks, *Chinese Narrative*, 334.

40. Ibid., 335.

41. Plaks, "Conceptual Models in Chinese Narrative Theory," 34.

42. Freedman, *Lyrical Novel*, 271.

43. For a view of how the story is structured, see Gu, "Lu Xun, Jameson, and Multiple Polysemia," 434–57.

44. All the mentioned stories are found in Lu Hsun, *Selected Stories of Lu Hsun* (1977).

45. Su Shi, in Guo, *Zhongguo lidai wenlun xuan*, 2:310

46. Jakobson and Halle, *Fundamentals of Language*, 81–82.

47. Kao, "Lyric Vision in Chinese Narrative Tradition," 237–38.

48. Ibid.

49. Lu Ji, *Wenfu*, 224.

50. Cudden, *A Dictionary of Literary Terms and Literary Theory*, 522.

51. Freedman, *Lyrical Novel*, p. 21.

52. Quoted in ibid., 22.

53. S. T. Coleridge, "Biographia Literaria," 471.

54. Cudden, *Dictionary of Literary Terms and Literary Theory*, 562.

55. Barthes, *Mythologies*, 116.

56. Liangyan Ge, *Out of the Margins*.

57. See Gu, "Paradox of Vision and Vision of Paradox," 175–203.

58. Zhong Rong, *Shipin*, 1:3.

59. Satyendra, "Metaphors of the Body," 85–97, explores how the physical body was carefully contrived to symbolize the changing conditions of the male protagonist, the state, and the novel as a whole.

CHAPTER 5.
THE ART OF THE *JIN PING MEI*

1. *Zhongguo fenti wenxue shi—xiaoshuo juan*, 250–51.

2. Allen, *English Novel*, xxi.

3. Hanan, "The Early Chinese Story," 314–15.

4. I have gleaned these major views of the novel's themes from current scholarship on the *Jin Ping Mei*. The list is by no means exhaustive. The reader may refer to relevant information in studies by Wu Han, Zhou Juntao, Wang Rumei, Du Weimo, Liu Hui, Hou Zhongyi, Hu Fagui, Hu Wenbing, Zhang Qingshan, Lu Ge, Ma Zhen, Lü Hong, Sun Xun, Wei Ziyun, Xu Shuofang, Ye Guitong, Zhu Yixuan, and others, all listed in the bibliography.

5. See Ma Zheng 馬征, *Jin Ping Mei zhong de xuan'an*, 33.

6. The alternation between praise and denigration has dogged the novel since its appearance. Yuan Zhongdao 袁中道 (1578–1624), a contemporary of the author, praised it as "exceedingly well written." Shen Defu 沈德符 (1578–1642), another contemporary, attributed it to the hand of a great scholar. See Hou and Wang, *Jin Ping Mei ziliao huibian*, 84, 85. But adverse criticism attributed its authorship to an anonymous village schoolmaster. C. T. Hsia characterizes it as a book with "low culture and ordinary mentality" (*Classic Chinese Novel*, 168).

7. See Roy in Nienhauser, *The Indiana Companion*, 287.

8. Ning and Luo, *Jin Ping Mei dui xiaoshuo meixue de gongxian*, 1.

9. See Rolston, *How to Read the Chinese Novel*, 133.

10. Hou and Wang, *Jin Ping Mei ziliao huibian*, 225.

11. Zhang Zhupo, in Hou and Wang, *Jin Ping Mei ziliao huibian*, 31.

12. Many commentators employed the analogy of architectural construction to explain the conception of fiction writing and to explore how to organize narrative elements into a textual edifice. The "theory of structure" of Li Yu 李漁 (1611–80), for example, is based on the architectural metaphor. See Li, *Li Liweng quhua*, 7.

13. Hou and Wang, *Jin Ping Mei ziliao huibian*, 56.

14. Plaks, *Mingdai xiaoshuo sida qishu*, 1.

15. Plaks, *Four Masterworks of the Ming Novel*, xi.

16. Roy, "Chang Chu-p'o's Commentary on the *Chin P'ing Mei*," 115–23.

17. Ibid., 122.

18. Ye Lang, *Zhongguo xiaoshuo meixue*, 154–99.

19. See relevant sections in Hou and Wang, *Jin Ping Mei ziliao huibian*.

20. Hou and Wang, *Jin Ping Mei ziliao huibian*, 214.

21. Watt, *Rise of the Novel*, 54.

22. See Robert, *Origins of the Novel*.

23. Ibid., 21–40.

24. Ibid., 25.

25. Holland, *Dynamics of Literary Response*, 45.

26. Bloom states: "What make a scene Primal? A scene is a setting as seen by a viewer, a place where action, whether real or fictitious, occurs or is staged. Every Primal Scene is necessarily a stage performance of fantastic fiction" (*Map of Misreading*, 47).

27. M. D. Gu, "Genesis and Evolution of Literary Forms," 457, 465.

28. Tanner, *Adultery in the Novel*, 11.

29. Ibid., 3.

30. Eagleton, *Literary Theory*, 158.

31. See Zhang Hongxun, "Shi tan *Jin Ping Mei* de zuozhe, shidai, qucai," 83–93; and Hanan, "Sources of the *Chin P'ing Mei*," 23–67.

32. Hsia, *Classic Chinese Novel*, 178.

33. Ibid., 169–70

34. Hou and Wang, *Jin Ping Mei ziliao huibian*, 170.

35. Xu Shuofang, *Lun Jin Ping Mei de chengshu ji qita*, 47–48.

36. See Wang Rumei, *Lun Jin Ping Mei*, 321.

37. See Barthes, *Pleasure of the Text*, 64.

38. See Derrida, *Positions*.

39. Hou and Wang, *Jin Ping Mei zhiliao huibian*, 13.

40. Yuan Zhongdao, "You ju fei lu," 220.

41. Ibid., 13.

42. Zhang Zhupo, in Hou and Wang, *Jin Ping Mei zhiliao huibian*, 188.

43. Ibid., 13.

44. Ibid., 188.

45. Ibid.

46. Zhang Zhupo, in Hou and Wang, *Jin Ping Mei zhiliao huibian*, 17.

47. Plaks, *Four Masterworks of the Ming Novel*, 101–103.

48. Zhang Zhupo, in Hou and Wang, *Jin Ping Mei zhiliao huibian*, 103.

49. See Proust, *A la recherche du temps perdu*.

50. Zhang Zhupo, in Hou and Wang, *Jin Ping Mei zilaio huibian*, 171.

51. Wen Long, *Wen Long piping Jin Ping Mei*, 274.

52. Ibid., 191.

53. Zhang Zhupo, in Hou and Wang, *Jin Ping Mei zhiliao huiban*, 193.

54. See Lu Ge and Ma Zheng, *Jin Ping Mei Renwu daquan*, 438–39, 521–22.

55. Ibid., 199–200.

56. *Jin Ping Mei dufa*, Section 40, in *Jin Ping Mei ziliao huibian*, 35,

57. Zhang Zhupo, in Hou and Wang, *Jin Ping Mei ziliao huibian*, 31.

58. Ibid., 11.

59. Ibid., 11.

60. The English translation is from David Roy, "Chang Chu-po's Commentary on the *Chin P'ing Mei*," 118.

61. Zhang Zhupo, in Hou and Wang, *Jin Ping Mei ziliao huibian*, 48.

62. Ibid., 107.

63. Barthes, *S/Z*, 160.

64. Quoted from Rolston, *How to Read the Chinese Novel*, 224.

65. See Roy, "Chang Chu-po's Commentary on the *Chin P'ing Mei*," 119.

66. Zhang Zhupo, in Hou and Wang, *Jin Ping Mei ziliao huibian*, 12.

67. Plaks, *Four Masterworks of the Ming Novel*, 81–85.

68. Zhang Zhupo, in Hou and Wang, *Jin Ping Mei ziliao huibian*, 47.

69. Barthes, *Image-Music-Text*, 158.

70. Ibid., 159.

71. Zhang Zhupo, in Hou and Wang, *Jin Ping Mei ziliao huibian*, 34.

72. Ibid., 193.

73. Wen Long, *Wen Long piping Jin Ping Mei*, 275.

CHAPTER 6.
THE ART OF THE *HONGLOUMENG*

1. A. C. Yu, *Rereading the Stone*, xi.

2. Ibid., 151–71.

3. Ibid., 169.

4. Ibid.

5. Requoted from Cao and Gao, *Story of the Stone*, 1:51.

6. Lu Xun, *Lu Xun quanji*, 8:350.

7. Ying-shih Yu, "The Two Worlds of *Hunglou meng*," 5–8.

8. For a succinct summary of scholars' various views, see Gu, "*Hongloumeng* as an Open Novel," 255–58. But for detailed information of how the variations on the same thesis are argued, the reader should consult articles by Ding Gan, Jiang Chao, Jiang Wenqing, Liang Zuo and Li Tong, Song Haoqing, Stephen Soong, Tao Bai, Wang Xiangdong, Wang Xiangfeng, Angelina Yee, Haiyan Lee, Zhang Zhi, and Zhu Mei-shu. See also the relevant pages in Yu Pingbo, *Yu Pingbo lun Hongloumeng*, 635–36, 651–52; Ying-shih Yu, *Hongloumeng de liange shijie*, 1–16; Plaks, *Archetype and Allegory*, 200–201; and Wai-yee Li, *Enchantment and Disenchantment*, 156.

9. See M. D. Gu, "*Hongloumeng* as an Open Novel," 253–82.

10. Cao and Gao, *Story of the Stone*, 1:343.

11. Baudrillard, *Selected Writings*, 166.

12. Ibid., 167.

13. Deleuze, "Simulacrum and Ancient Philosophy," 261–62.

14. Wu, "Beyond Stereotypes," 311–18.

15. The Qing scholar Yuan Mei thought that the *Daguanyuan* was a real garden in Nanjing. He even believed that his own garden was its prototype. Modern scholars like Gu Jiegang and Yu Pingbo vigorously dispute his opinion and maintain that the original model was a garden in Beijing. See Yu Pinbo, *Hongloumeng bian*, chap. 9.

16. Plaks, *Archetype and Allegory*, 187.

17. It is believed by some scholars that if one could master the architectural designs of the *Daguanyuan*, one would no longer need to do any course work in traditional Chinese gardens.

18. Baudrillard, *Selected Writings*, 171–72.

19. Mark Poster, in Baudrillard, *Selected Writings*, 6.

20. Baudrillard, *Selected Writings*, 168.

21. A. C. Yu, *Rereading the Stone*, 149.

22. Ibid., 168.

23. Of course, Anthony Yu does not stop at the Buddhist vision. See his discussion after ibid., 168.

24. Some scholars argue against the accepted interpretation of the ending: namely, that after rejecting the world of Red Dust, Baoyu becomes a Buddhist monk. Instead, he is described as a "naked babe," an existence he aspires to on several occasions in the novel. That he is bareheaded and barefoot, and wears a scarlet-red cape symbolizes the condition of a naked babe fresh from the womb. See Zhu Meishu, "Jia Baoyu sixiang chulun," 28–31

25. See Zhuangzi, *Complete Works of Chuang Tzu*, 49.

26. See Jiang Chao, "Cao Xueqin he Zhuang fuzi," 209–10; Shuen-fu Lin, "Chia Po-yu's First Visit to the Land of Illusion," 81; and Angelina C. Yee, "Self, Sexuality, and Writing in *Hongloumeng*," 380–81.

27. Yee, "Self, Sexuality, and Writing in *Hongloumeng*," 381.

28. Lin, "Chia Po-yu's First Visit to the Land of Illusion," 81.

29. Zhuangzi, *Zhuangzi*, 23–24.

30. Benveniste, *Problems in General Linguistics*, 226.

31. Wang Xilian, "Hongloumeng ping 紅樓夢評," in Zhu Yixuan, ed., *Hongloumeng ziliao huibian* (1985).

32. Cao and Gao, *Story of the Stone*, 1:253.

33. Deleuze, "Simulacrum and Ancient Philosophy," 256.

34. Baudrillard, *Selected Writings*, 177.

35. Requoted from Baudrillard, *Selected Writings*, 166. The saying is nowhere to be found in the Bible.

36. I have translated the "Hao-liao song" into a version that takes into account the message in Zhen Shiyin's commentary: the indeterminacy of one's fortune and misfortune.

37. Philip Sidney, in Adams, *Critical Theory since Plato*, 168.

38. See Wang Meng, "*Hongloumeng* pingdian xu," 3.

39. Cao and Gao, *Story of the Stone*, 5:374.

40. Power, *Conversations with James Joyce*, 95.

41. Barthes, *Image-Music-Text*, 146.

42. Ibid., 148.

43. Yu Pingbo, *Zhiyanzhai Hongloumeng jiping*, chap. 1, p. 40.

44. Cao and Gao, *Story of the Stone*, 5:375.

45. Ibid.

46. Ibid., 1:148.

47. Barthes, *Image-Music-Text*, 142.

48. A. C. Yu, *Rereading the Stone*, 171.

49. Ying-shih Yu, "Two Worlds of *Hunglou meng*," *Renditions* 2 (1974) 21.

50. Barthes, *S/Z*, 13–15, 18–23.

51. Silverman, *Subject of Semiotics*, 246.

52. Semiosis, in Peirce's conception, is an action of the sign, an irreducibly triadic process comprising a relation among a sign, its object, and its actual or potential interpretant. It is particularly concerned with how the interpretant is produced.

53. Baudrillard, *Selected Writings*, 166–184.

54. A. C. Yu points out, "That *Hongloumeng* exploits to the utmost both the semantic nuances and cultural overtones of its language . . . is a marvel acknowledged by all. One factor that adds to both fascination and vexation incurred in its reading lies . . . in the author's penchant for paronomastic games and riddles. . . . [H]e managed to structure a continuously suggested and suggestive polysemy in numerous proper names, place names, terms, and phrases of his composition" (*Rereading the Stone*, 54).

55. This remark is quoted from the Yadong Library edition of Cao and Gao, *Hongloumeng*, with prefaces by Gao E, Cheng Weiyuan, Hu Shi, and Chen Duxiu (reprint, Haikou: Sanhuan chubanshe, 1990), 1.

56. The quotation is from Hawkes's introduction to Cao and Gao, *Story of the Stone*, 20.

57. C. T. Hsia, *Classic Chinese Novel*, 275–78.

58. See Lin, "Chia Po-yu's First Visit to the Land of Illusion," 77–106.

59. See Li Yuanzhen, "*Hongloumeng* li de meng 紅樓夢裏的夢," 192–99.

60. See Chen Bingliang, "*Hongloumeng* zhong de shenhua he xinli," 185–200.

61. Freud, *Complete Psychological Works*, 4:105.

62. Ibid., 5:353.

63. Cao and Gao, *Story of the Stone*, 1:145.

64. Freud, *An Outline of Psychoanalysis*, ch. 5.

65. The English version is my own translation.

66. Freud, *Interpretation of Dreams*, 327.

67. Ibid., 343.

68. Freud, *On Dreams*, 52–53.

69. Requoted from Fodor and Gagnor, *Dictionary of Psychoanalysis*, 52.

70. Freud, *Interpretation of Dreams*, 311–12.

71. Ibid., 313.

72. Freud, *On Dreams*, 58.

73. Ibid., 48.

74. Freud, *Interpretation of Dreams*, 647.

75. See Jacques Lacan's detailed analysis of the relations among dreams, language, and the unconscious in *Ecrit*, 147–61.

76. Gu, *Chinese Theories of Reading and Writing*, 245–49.

77. Barbara Johnson, "Translator's Introduction," in Derrida's *Dissemination*, xiii.

78. Freud, *Interpretation of Dreams*, 317.

79. Ibid., 312.

80. For a fairly systematic summary, one may turn to David Hawkes's appendix to Cao and Gao, *The Story of the Stone*, 1:527–34.

81. For a summary of the existent interpretations, refer to *Hongloumeng xuekan* 2 (1982): 225–30.

82. Derrida, *Writing and Difference*, 209.

83. Freud, *Interpretation of Dreams*, 318.

84. Ibid., 313.

85. Martin, *Recent Theories of Narrative*, 83.

CHAPTER 7.
THEORY OF FICTION

1. Hoffman and Murphy, *Essentials of the Theory of Fiction*, 5.

2. Li Zhi, in Guo, *Zhongguo lidai wenlun xuan*, 3:124.

3. Ibid., 3:121.

4. Mill, "What Is Poetry?" 537.

5. Laozi, *Daode jing*, 24.

6. Cao and Gao, *Story of the Stone*, 1:1–3.

7. A. C. Yu, *Rereading the Stone*, 120.

8. Ibid., 121.

9. See Dolezel, *Heterocosmica*; Cohn, *Distinction of Fiction*; Pavel, "Fiction and Imitation," 521–41.

10. Lu Ji, *Wenfu*, 225. English translation by Shih-hsiang Chen is from Birch, *Anthology of Chinese Literature*, 207.

11. See D. C. Lau's translation of Lao Tzu, *Tao Te Ching*, 57

12. See Ye Zhou, in *Zhongguo meixueshi ziliao xuanbian*, 2:183.

13. Ibid.

14. Requoted from Ye Lang *Zhongguo meixueshi dagang*, 377.

15. Suzuki, *Lankavatara Sutra*, 37–38.

16. A. C. Yu, *Rereading the Stone*, 149.

17. Xie Zhaozhi, "Wu zazu 五雜俎," *juan* 15, in Wang and Zhang, *Zhongguo xiaoshuo lilunshi*, 47.

18. The Chinese in parentheses are from Cao and Gao, *Hongloumeng* (1982), 3:1646. The English translation is from A. C. Yu, *Rereading the Stone*, 267.

19. Gennett, *Fiction et diction*, 20.

20. Schaeffer, *Pourquoi la fiction?* 210–11.

21. Searle, "Logical Status of Fictional Discourse," 319–32.

22. *Ming Rongyutang ke Shuihu zhuan*, comment at the end of chap. 1.

23. Feng Menglong, Preface to *Jingshi tongyan*, p. 1a.

24. Auerbach, *Mimesis*, 488.

25. Todorov, *Fantastic*, 156.

26. Cudden, *Dictionary of Literary Terms and Literary Theory*, 522.

27. Xie Zhaozhi, in Cai et al., *Zhongguo wenxue lilun shi*, 3:331.

28. Yuan Yuling, in Cai et al., *Zhongguo wenxue lilun shi*, 3:333–4.

29. M. D. Gu, "Suggestiveness in Chinese Literary Thought," 490–513.

30. Zhong Rong, *Shipin*, 1:3

31. Plaks, "Conceptual Models in Chinese Narrative Theory," 43.

32. See D. C. Lau's translation of Lao Tzu, *Tao Te Ching*, 57

33. Wang Bi, *Wang Bi ji jiaoshi*, 117.

34. Lao Tzu, *Tao Te Ching*, 101.

35. Zhuangzi, *Zhuangzhi*, annotated by Guo Xiang, 141. The English translation is from Chan, *Source Book*, 202.

36. Anthony C. Yu, *Rereading The Stone*, 168.

37. Cao and Gao, *Story of the Stone*, 1:51

38. Laozi, *The Laozi*, annotated by Wang Bi, 2.

39. Bakhtin, "Epic and Novel," 52–53.

40. See Eco, *Open Work*.

41. Ibid., 22.

42. M. D. Gu, *Chinese Theories of Reading and Writing*, 196–206.

43. For a detailed discussion of these two principles, see Lu Zongda and Wang Ning, *Xungu yu xunguxue*, 56–134.

44. Barthes, in *Image-Music-Text*, 158–59.

45. See Wang, *Story of Stone*.

46. Eco, *Role of the Reader*, 3.

47. Eco, *Open Work*, 24.

48. Eco et al., *Interpretation and Overinterpretation*, 67–68.

49. Frye, *Anatomy of Criticism*, 33.

50. M. D. Gu, "Universal Significance of Frye's Theory of Fictional Modes," 162–76.

51. All the quotations are from Frye, *Anatomy of Criticism*, 33–34.

52. Frye, *Anatomy of Criticism*, 33–35.

53. From Chan, *Source Book*, 184.

54. See M. D. Gu, "Paradox of Vision and Vision of Paradox," 175–203.

55. Eco, *Aesthetics of Chaosmos*, 69.

56. Eco, *Open Work*, 14.

57. Olson, *Human Universe*, 52.

CONCLUSION.
TOWARD A TRANSCULTURAL THEORY OF FICTION

1. For historical dates of fictional development, see Cudden's *A Dictionary of Literary Terms and Literary Theory* (Oxford: Blackwell, 1991), 802.

2. Jameson, "Third-World Literature in the Era of Multinational Capitalism," 65.

3. For a succinct account of Cartesian dualism, see Audi, *Cambridge Dictionary of Philosophy*, 195–96.

4. Hall and Ames, *Thinking from the Han*, 248.

5. Chan, *Source Book*, 186.

6. Said, *Beginnings*, 196.

7. Meng Zi, *Menzi zhushu*, in Ruan Yuan, *Shisanjing zhushu*, 2:2746.

8. In his classic of fiction study, *The Rhetoric of Fiction*, Wayne Booth makes a list of these generally accepted rules before his time. A glance at the table of contents is sufficient.

9. Booth, *Rhetoric of Fiction*, part 1, 3–168.

10. Pavel, "Fiction and Imitation," 521.

11. Ibid., 521–22.

12. Ibid., 528.

13. Ibid., 529.

14. See Heidegger, *Basic Writings*, 37–138, 343–449; and Heidegger, *Early Greek Thinking*. For a succinct account of his main ideas, see Passmore, *Hundred Years of Philosophy*, 476–87.

15. Rolston, *How to Read the Chinese Novel*, 323–40.

16. *Zhouyi zhengyi* 周易正義, *juan* 7, p. 66, in Ruan Yuan, ed., *Shisanjing zhushu*, 1:78.

17. Laozi, *Laozi*, annotated by Wang Bi, p. 25.

18. The English translation is that of D. C. Lau, in Lao Tzu, *Tao Te Ching*, 103.

19. Han Yongxian, *Zhouyi tanyuan*, 31.

20. The English translation is from Rolston, *How to Read the Chinese Novel*, 324.

21. Plaks, *Archetype and Allegory*, 53; Plaks, *Chinese Narrative*, 335.

22. Epstein, *Competing Discourses*, 7, 11.

23. Quoted from Chan, *Source Book in Chinese Philosophy*, 203. The Chinese source material is from Zhuangzi, *Zhuangzi*, annotated by Guo Xiang, 239.

24. M. D. Gu, "Universal 'One,'" 86–105. For a different version in Chinese, see Gu, "Zheng Xi zhi 'Yi,'" 65–75. .

25. Kirk et al., *Presocratic Philosophers*, 187.

26. Heidegger, *Early Greek Thinking*, 59.

27. Laozi, *Laozi*, annotated by Wang Bi, 23.

28. The English translation is that of D.C. Lau, in Lao Tzu, *Tao Te Ching*, 100.

29. Lawrence, *Phoenix*, 528.

30. Heidegger, *Poetry, Language, Thought*, 89–142.

31. Samuel Taylor Coleridge wrote these words to William Sotheby on July 15, 1802.

32. Requoted from Passmore, *Hundred Years of Philosophy*, 485.

33. Lawrence stated in an article on the novel: "It seems to me it was the greatest pity in the world, when philosophy and fiction got split. They used to be one, right from the days of myth. Then they went and parted, like a nagging married couple, with Aristotle and Thomas Aquinas and that beastly Kant. So the novel went sloppy, and philosophy went abstract-dry. The two should come together—in the novel" (*Phoenix*, p. 520).

Selected Bibliography

WORKS IN CHINESE AND JAPANESE

Ban Gu. "Yiwen zhi 藝文志." In *Qian Hanshu* 前漢書. Shanghai: Tongwen shuju, 1894.

Beida Zhongwen xi 北大中文系. *Zhongguo xiaoshuo shi* 中國小說史. Beijing: renmin wenxue chubanshe, 1978.

Cai Yuanfang 蔡元放. "*Dong Zhou lieguo zhi* dufa 東周列國志讀法." In *Dong Zhou lieguo zhi* 東周列國志. Shanghai: Zhusu shuwu, 1894.

Cai Zhongxiang et al. 蔡鍾翔等. *Zhongguo wenxue lilun shi* 中國文學理論史. 5 vols. Beijing: Beijing chubanshe, 1987.

Cao Jiping et al. 曹濟平等, eds. *Da Song Xuanhe yishi* 大宋宣和遺事. Nanjing: Jiangsu guji chubanshe, 1993.

Cao Xueqin and Gao E 曹雪芹, 高鶚. *Hongloumeng* 紅樓夢. 3 vols. Beijing: Renmin wenxue, 1982.

———. *Hongloumeng* 紅樓夢. Haikou: Sanhuan chubanshe, 1990. Reprint of *Qianlong renzi ben* 乾隆壬子本 (1792).

———. *Qianlong Jiaxuben Zhiyanzhai chongping Shitouji* 乾隆甲戌本脂燕齋重評石頭記. Taipei: Hu Shi jiniangguan, 1961.

Cao Yibing 曹亦兵. *Xiayi gong'an xiaoshuo shi* 俠義公案小說史. Hangzhou : Zhejiang guji chubanshe, 1998.

Chen Bingliang 陳炳良. "*Hongloumeng* zhong de shenhua he xinli 紅樓夢中的神話和心理." *Hongloumeng xuekan* 5 (1980): 185–200.

Chen Meilin et al. 陳美林等. *Zhanghui xiaoshuo shi* 章回小說史. Hangzhou: Zhejiang guji chubanshe, 1998.

Chen Qinghao 陳慶浩, ed. *Xinbian Shitou ji Zhiyan zhai pingyu jijiao* 新編石頭記脂硯齋評語輯校. Rev. ed. Beijing: Zhongguo youyi, 1987.

Chen Xizhong et al. 陳曦鍾等. *Shuihu zhuan huiping ben* 水滸傳會評本. Beijing: Beijing daxue chubanshe, 1981.

Chen Yinke 陳寅恪. *Yuan Bai shijian zhenggao* 元白詩箋證稿. Shanghai: Shanghai gudian wenxue chubanshe, 1958.

Ciyuan 辭源. Beijing: Shangwu yinshuguan, 1995.

Ding Gan 丁淦. "Taixu huanjing de xianshi yiyun 太虛幻境的現實意蘊," in *Hongloumeng xuekan* 4 (1982): 163–76.

Dong Jieyuan 董解元. *Xixiangji zhugongdiao* 西廂記諸宮調. Jinan: Qilu shushe, 1984.

Du Weimo 杜維沫 and Liu Hui 劉輝, eds. *Jin Ping Mei yanjiu ji* 金瓶梅研究集. Jinan: Qilu shushe, 1988.

Fang Xuanling 房玄齡 et al. *Jinshu* 晉書. Beijing: Zhonghua shuju, 1974.

Feng Menglong 馮夢龍. Preface to *Jingshi tongyan* 警世通言. Taipei: Dingwen shuju, 1974.

Gan Bao 干寶. *Soushen ji* 搜神記. Beijing: Zhonghua shuju, 1979.

Gu Mingdong 顧明棟. "Zhong Xi zhi 'Yi': Zuowei Zhong Xi yanjiu zhi gongtong lilun jichu de Dao yu Luogesi 中西之'一'：作為中西研究之共同理論基礎的道與邏格斯." *Wenyi yanjiu* 文藝研究 1 (2001): 65–75.

Guo Shaoyu 郭紹虞, ed. *Zhongguo lidai wenlun xuan* 中國曆代文論選. 4 vols. Shanghai: Shanghai guji chubanshe, 1979.

Han Yongxian 韓永賢. *Zhouyi tanyuan* 周易探源. Beijing: Huaqiao chuban gongsi, 1990.

He Wenhuan 何文煥, ed. *Lidai shihua* 曆代詩話. 2 vols. Taipei: Muduo chubanshe, 1982.

Hou Zhongyi 候忠義, *Sui Tang Wudai xiaoshuo shi* 隋唐五代小說史. Hangzhou: Zhejiang guji chubanshe, 1997.

———. *Zhongguo wenyan xiaoshuo shigao* 中國文言小說史稿. Beijing: Beijing daxue chubanshe, 1990.

Hongloumeng xuekan 紅樓夢學刊. Vols. 1–22. Tianjin: Baihua wenyi. Vols. 23–68. Beijing: Wenhua yishu chubanshe, 1978–1997.

Hou Zhongyi 候忠義 and Wang Rumei 王汝梅, comps. *Jin Ping Mei ziliao huibian* 金瓶梅資料彙編. Beijing: Beida chubanshe, 1985.

Hu Fagui 胡發貴. "Lanlin Xiaoxiao sheng de shijie he rensheng 蘭陵笑笑生的世界和人生." *Ming Qing xiaoshuo yanjiu* 明清小說研究, 5:199–205. Beijing: Wenlian, 1987.

Huili 慧立 and Yanzong 彥宗. *Da Tang Ci'ensi Sanzang fashi zhuan* 大唐慈恩寺三藏法師傳. Taibei: Guangwen shuju, 1963.

Hu Shi 胡適. "*Sanguo zhi yanyi* xu 三國志演義敘." In *Zhongguo zhanghui xiaoshuo kaozheng* 中國章回小說考證. Shanghai: Shanghai shudian, 1980.

Hu Wenbin 胡文彬 and Zhang Qingshan 張慶善, comps. *Lun Jin Ping Mei* 論金瓶梅. Beijing: Wenhua yishu chubanshe, 1984.

Hu Yinglin, *Shaoshi shanfang bicong* 少室山房筆從. In *Wenyuange Siku quanshu*, 886:302–10.

Jiang Chao 姜超. "Cao Xueqin he Zhuang fuzi 曹雪芹和莊夫子." *Hongloumeng xuekan* 紅樓夢學刊 1 (1989): 203–18.

Jiang Wenqin 蔣文欽. "'Nüer shijie' de liang ge cengci 女兒世界的兩個層次." *Wenzhou shizhuan xuebao* 溫州師專學報 1 (1985): 15–24.

Jin Ping Mei yanjiu 金瓶梅研究. 4 vols. Nanjing: Jiangsu guji chubanshe, 1990–1993.

Ji Yun 紀昀. *Siku quanshu zongmu* 四庫全書總目. Reprint. Beijing: Zhonghua shuju, 1965.

Jin Shengtan 金聖歎. *Diwu caizi shu Shi Nai-an Shuihu Zhuan* 第五才子書施乃庵水滸傳. Reprint. Beijing: Zhonghua shuju, 1975.

Jin Shengtan 金聖歎. "Du *Diwu caizishu* fa 讀第五才子書法." Chen Xizhong et al. *Shuihu zhuan huiping ben*, 1:15–22.

Kong Zi 孔子. *Lunyu zhushu* 論語注疏. In Ruan Yuan, *Shisanjing zhushu* 十三經注疏.

Laozi 老子. *Daode jing* 道德經. Annotated by Wang Bi. Shanghai: Shanghai guji chubanshe, 1995.

Liang, Zuo 梁左 and Li Tong 李彤. "Cao Xueqin de wutuobang huanxiang zhiyi 曹雪芹 的烏托邦幻想質疑." In *Hongloumeng xuekan*, 1 (1982): 178–93.

Li Hanqiu 李漢秋, ed. *Rulin waishi yanjiu ziliao* 儒林外史研究資料. Shanghai: Shanghai guji chubanshe, 1984.

Lin Chen 林辰. *Shenguai xiaoshuo shi* 神怪小說史. Hangzhou: Zhejiang guji chubanshe, 1998.

Li Rihua 李日華. *Nan Xixiangji* 南西廂記. Beijing: Zhonghua shuju, 2000.

Li Shiren 李時人 and Cai Jinghao 蔡鏡浩, eds. *Da Tang Sanzang qujing shihua* 大唐三藏取經詩話. Beijing : Zhonghua shuju, 1997.

Liu Hui 劉輝, comp. *Jin Ping Mei chengshu yu banben yanjiu* 金瓶梅成書與版本研究. Shenyang: Liaoning renmin chubanshe, 1986.

Liu Xie 劉勰. *Wenxin diaolong* 文心雕龍. Annotated by Lu Kanru 陸侃如 and Mu Shijin 牟時金. Jinan: Qilu shushe, 1995.

Liu Yiqing 劉義慶. *Youming lu* 幽明錄. Shanghai: Shangwu yinshuguan, 1927.

Liu Yuchen 劉毓忱, ed. *Xiyou ji zilaio huibian* 西遊記資料彙編. Zhengzhou: Zhongzhou shuhuashe, 1983.

Li Xiusheng 李修生 and Zhao Yishan 趙義山, eds. *Zhongguo fenti wenxue sh-xiaoshuo juan* 中國分體文學史-小說卷. Shanghai: Guji chubanshe, 2001.

Li Yu 李漁. *Li Liweng quhua* 李笠翁曲話. Changsha: Hunan renmin chubanshe, 1980.

Li Yuanzhen 李元貞. "*Hongloumeng* li de meng 紅樓夢裏的夢." *Xiandai wenxue* 現代文學 47 (1971): 192–99.

Li Zehou 李澤厚. *Mei de lichen* 美的曆程. Beijing: Zhongguo shehui kexue chubanshe, 1984.

Li Zhuowu ping zhongyi Shuihu quanzhuan 李卓吾評忠義水滸全傳. Suzhou: Yuan Wuya, 1612.

Li Zongwei 李宗為. *Tangren chuanqi* 唐人傳奇. Beijing: Zhonghua shuju, 1985.

Liu Zhiji 劉知幾. *Shitong* 史通. In *Sibu congkan danxingben* 四部叢刊單行本. Shanghai: Zhonghua shuju, n.d.

Lu Ge 魯歌 and Ma Zhen 馬征. *Jin Ping Mei Renwu daquan* 金瓶梅人物大全. Changchun: Jilin wenshi chubanshe, 1991.

Lu Ji 陸機. *Wenfu* 文賦. In Xiao, *Wenxuan* 文選, 224–28.

Lu Zongda 陸宗达 and Wang Ning 王寧. *Xungu yu xungu xue* 訓詁與訓詁學. Taiyuan: Shanxi jiaoyu chubanshe, 1994.

Lu Xun 魯迅. *Lu Xun lun wenxue yu yishu* 魯迅論文學與藝術. 2 vols. Beijing: Renmin wenxue chubanshe, 1980.

———. *Lu Xun quanji* 魯迅全集. 16 vols. Beijing: Renmin wenxue chubanshe, 1981.

———. "Zhongguo xiaoshuo de lishi de bianqian 中國小說的歷史的變遷." In vol. 9 of *Lu Xun quanji* 魯迅全集. Beijing: Renmin wenxue, 1981.

———. *Zhongguo xiaoshuo shilüe* 中國小說史略. Beijing: Renmin wenxue, 1973.

Lü Hong 呂紅. "*Jin Ping Mei* de tupu yu shiluo 金瓶梅的突破與失落." In *Jing Ping Mei yanjiu* 金瓶梅研究, 4:149–163. Nanjing: Jiangsu guji chubanshe, 1993.

Luo Guanzhong 羅貫中. *Can Tang Wudai yanyi zhuan*, 殘唐五代演義傳. Shanghai: Shanghai guji chubanshe, 1990.

———. *Sanguo yanyi* 三國演義. Shanghai: Shanghai guji chubanshe, 1989.

———. *Sansui pingyao zhuan*, 三遂平妖傳. Beijing : Beijing daxue chubanshe, 1983.

———. *Sui Tang liangchao shizhuan* 隋唐兩朝史傳. Shanghai: Shanghai guji, 1990.

Ma Zheng 馬征. *Jin Ping Mei zhong de xuan'an* 金瓶梅中的懸案. Chengdu: Sichuan renmin chubanshe, 1994.

Meng Zhaolian 孟昭連 and Ning Zongyi 寧宗一. *Zhongguo xiaoshuo yishu shi* 中國小說藝術史. Hangzhou: Zhejiang guji chubanshe, 2003.

Meng Zi 孟子. *Mengzi zhushu* 孟子注疏. In Ruan Yuan, *Shisanjing zhushu* 十三經注疏.

Miao Zhuang 苗壯. *Biji xiaoshuo shi* 筆記小說史. Hangzhou: Zhejiang guji chubanshe, 1998.

Min Ze 敏澤. *Zhongguo wenxue lilun piping shi* 中國文學理論批評史. 2 vols. Beijing: Renmin wenxue chubanshe, 1981.

Ming Rongyutang ke Shuihu zhuan 明容與堂刻水滸傳. Shanghai: Shanghai renmin, 1975.

Ning Zongyi 寧宗一. *Shuobujin de Jin Ping Mei* 說不盡的金瓶梅. In *Ning Zongyi xiaoshuo xiju yanjiu zixuanji* 寧宗一小說戲劇研究自選集. Tianjin: Tianjin guji chubanshe, 1994.

Ning Zongyi 寧宗一 and Luo Derong 羅德榮, eds. *Jin Ping Mei dui xiaoshuo meixue de gongxian* 金瓶梅對小說美學的貢獻. Tianjin: Shehui kexueyuan chubanshe, 1992.

Ouyang Jian 歐陽建. *Lishi xiaoshuo shi* 歷史小說史. Hangzhou: Zhejiang guji chubanshe, 2003.

Plaks, Andrew. *Mingdai xiaoshuo sida qishu* 明代小說四大奇書. Beijing: Heping chubanshe, 1993.

Pu Songling 蒲松齡. *Liaozhai zhiyi* 聊齋志異. Shanghai: Guji chubanshe, 1979.

———. *Liaozhai zhiyi: quanjiao huizhu jiping* 聊齋志異：全校會注集評. Jinan : Qilu shushe; 2000

Qian Hanshu 前漢書. In *Ershisi shi* 二十四史. Shanghai: Tongwen shuju, 1894.

Ruan Yuan 阮元, ed. *Shisanjing zhushu* 十三經注疏. 2 vols. Beijing: Zhonghua shuju, 1980.

Shi Changyu 石昌渝. *Zhongguo xiaoshuo yuanliu lun* 中國小說源流論. Beijing: Sanlian shudian, 1994.

Sima Qian 司馬遷. *Shiji* 史記. 10 vols. Beijing: Zhonghua shuju, 1959.

Shen Weifang 沈偉方 and Xia Qiliang 夏啓良, eds. *Han Wei Liuchao xiaoshuo xuan* 漢魏六朝小說選. Henan: Zhongzhou shuhua she, 1982.

Song Haoqin 宋浩慶. "Daguanyuan lide beihuan lihe 大觀園裏的悲歡離合." *Hongloumeng xuekan* 3 (1991): 73–86.

Soong, Stephen C. 宋淇. "Lun Taguanyuan 論大觀園." *Mingbao yuekan* 明報月刊. (Hong Kong) 81 (September 1972): 4.

Tao Bai 陶白. "Cao Xueqin he Zhuangzi 曹雪芹和莊子." *Hongloumeng xuekan* 2 (1981): 79–102.

Tao Yuanming 陶淵明. *Soushen houji* 搜神後記. Shanghai: Shanghai guji chubanshe, 1998.

———. *Tao Yuanming ji jiaojian* 陶淵明集校箋. Shanghai: Shanghai guji chubanshe, 1996.

Wang Bi 王弼. *Wang Bi ji jiaoshi* 王弼集校釋. Beijing: Zhonghua shuju, 1980.

Wang Meng 王蒙. "*Hongloumeng* pingdian xu 紅樓夢評點序." *Hongloumeng xuekan* 2 (1995): 1–3.

Wang Rumei 王汝梅. *Lun Jin Ping Mei* 論金瓶梅. Beijing: Wenhua yishu chubanshe, 1984.

———, ed. *Zhang Zhupo piping diyi qishu Jin Ping Mei* 張竹坡批評第一奇書金瓶梅. 2 vols. Jinan: Qilu shushe, 1988.

Wang Rumei 王汝梅 and Zhang Yu 張羽. *Zhongguo xiaoshuo lilun shi* 中國小說理論史. Hangzhou: Zhejiang guji chubanshe, 2001.

Wang Shifu 王實甫. *Xixiangji* 西廂記. Nanjing: Jiangsu guji chubanshe, 1986.

Wang Xiangdong 王向東. "Qinggan yu lizhi de chongtu—Xi Daguanyuan lixiang de jianli he pumi 情感與理智的沖突－析大觀園理想的建立和破滅." *Hongloumeng xuekan* 2 (1995): 95–108.

Wang, Xiangfeng 王向峰. "Cao Xueqin de wutuobang huanxiang 曹雪芹的烏托邦幻想." *Hongloumeng xuekan* 1 (1979): 25–40.

Wei Ziyun 魏子雲. *Jin Ping Mei tanyuan* 金瓶梅探源. Taipei: Juliu tushu gongsi, 1979.

Wen Long 文龍. *Wen Long piping Jin Ping Mei* 文龍批評金瓶梅. In Liu Hui. *Jin Ping Mei chengshu yu banben yanjiu*, 184–276.

Wenyuange Siku quanshu 文淵閣四庫全書. Reprint. Taipei: Shangwu yinshuguan, 1983–86.

Wen Yiduo 聞一多. *Shenhua yu shi* 神話與詩. Beijing: Guji chubanshe, 1956.

Wu Cheng'en 吳承恩. *Xiyou ji* 西遊記. Beijing: Zuojia chubanshe, 1954.

Wu Gongzheng 吳功正. *Xiaoshuo meixue* 小說美學. Nanjing: Jiangsu renmin chubanshe, 1985.

Wu Han 吳晗. "Jin Ping Mei de zhuzuo shidai jiqi shehui beijing" 金瓶梅的著作時代及其社會背景. In *Dushi zhaji* 讀史札記, 1–38. Beijing: Sanlian shudian, 1957.

Wu Jingzi 吳敬梓. *Rulin waishi* 儒林外史. Beijing: Renmin wenxue chubanshe, 1975.

Xiang Kai 向楷. *Shiqing xiaoshuo shi* 世情小說史. Hangzhou: Zhejiang guji chubanshe, 1998.

Xiao Tong 蕭統, comp. *Wenxuan* 文選. Taipei: Qiming shuju, 1950.

Xiao Xiangkai 蕭相愷. *Song Yuan xiaoshuo shi* 宋元小說史. Hangzhou: Zhejiang guji chubanshe, 1997.

Xiao Xinqiao 蕭欣橋 and Liu Fuyuan 劉福元. *Huaben xiaoshuo shi* 話本小說史. Hangzhou: Zhejiang guji chubanshe, 2003.

Xue Hongji 薛洪績. *Chuanqi xiaoshuo shi* 傳奇小說史. Hangzhou: Zhejiang guji chubanshe, 1998.

Xiaoxiao Sheng 笑笑生. *Jin Ping Mei cihua* 金瓶梅詞話. 5 vols. Facsimile repreint, Tokyo: Daian, 1963.

———. *Xinke xiuxiang piping Jin Ping Mei* 新刻繡像批評金瓶梅. 2 vols. Jinan: Qilu shushe, 1989.

Xu Shuofang 徐朔方. *Lun Jin Ping Mei de chengshu ji qita* 論金瓶梅的成書及其他. Jinan: Qilu shushe, 1988.

Xuanzang 玄奘 and Bianji 辨機. *Ta Tang xiyue ji* 大唐西域記. Beijing: Wenxue guji kanxing she, 1955.

Xunzi 荀子. *Xunzi yizhu* 荀子譯注. Shanghai: Shanghai guji chubanshe, 1995.

Ye Guitong 葉桂桐 et al., eds. *Jin Ping Mei zuozhe zhimi* 金瓶梅作者之迷. Yinchuan: Ninxia renmin chubanshe, 1988.

Ye Lang 葉朗. *Zhongguo meixueshi dagang* 中國美學史大綱. Shanghai: Shanghai renmin, 1985.

———. *Zhongguo xiaoshuo meixue* 中國小說美學. Beijing: Beijing Daxue chubanshe, 1982.

Yuan Zhen 元稹. *Yuanshi Changqin ji* 元氏長慶集. Shanghai: Zhonghua shuju, n. d.

Yuan Zhongdao 袁中道. "You ju fei lu 遊居柿錄." In Hou and Wang, *Jin Ping Mei zhiliao huibian*, 220.

Yu Ji 虞集. "Xieyunxuan ji 寫韻軒記." In *Taoyuan xuegu lu* 道園學古錄, *juan* 38. Shanghai: Shangwu yinshuguan, 1929.

Yuling Laoren 瘦嶺老人. *Shenlou zhi quanzhuan* 蜃樓志全傳. Tianjin: Baihua wenyi chubanshe, 1987.

Yu Pingbo 俞平伯. *Hongloumeng bian* 紅樓夢辯. Shanghai: Yadong, 1929.

———. *Yu Pingbo lun Hongloumeng* 俞平伯論紅樓夢. Shanghai: Guji chubanshe, 1988.

———, comp. *Zhiyanzhai Hongloumeng jiping* 脂硯齋紅樓夢輯評. Shanghai: Wenyi lianhe chubanshe, 1954.

Yu Yingshi 余英時. *Hongloumeng de liange shijie* 紅樓夢的兩個世界. Tapei: Liangjing, 1978.

Zhang Hongxun 張鴻勳. "Shi tan *Jin Ping Mei* de zuozhe, shidai, qucai 試談金瓶梅的作者，時代，取材." In Hu and Zhang, comps., *Lu Jin Ping Mei*. 83–93. .

Zhang Jun 張俊. *Qingdai xiaoshuo shi* 清代小說史. Hangzhou: Zhejiang guji chubanshe, 1997.

Zhang Xuecheng 張學誠. *Wenshi tongyi* 文史通義. Shanghai: Zhonghua shuju, n.d.

———. *Zhangshi yishu* 章氏遺書. N.P.: *Jiaye tang kanben* 嘉業堂刊本, 1922.

Zhang Zhi 張之. "Shitan Cao Xueqin dui zongjiao de taidu 試談曹雪芹對宗教的態度." *Hongloumeng xuekan* 3 (1981): 277–302.

Zhang Zhupo 張竹坡. *Zhang Zhupo pingdian Jin Ping Mei* 張竹坡評點金瓶梅. In Hou and Wang, *Jin Ping Mei ziliao huibian*, 1–194.

Zheng Zhenduo 鄭振鐸. *Chatuben Zhongguo wenxue shi* 插圖本中國文學史. Vol. 4. Hong Kong: Shangwu yinshuguan, 1961.

———. "*Shuihu zhuan* de yanhua 水滸傳的演化." In vol. 1 of *Zhongguo wenxue yanjiu* 中國文學研究. Hong Kong: Guwen shuju, 1961.

Zhongguo meixueshi ziliao xuanbian 中國美學史資料選編. Compiled by the Philosophy Department of Beijing University. 2 vols. Beijing: Zhonghua shuju, 1985.

Zhong Rong 鍾嶸. *Shipin* 詩品. In He, ed. *Lidai shihua*. Taipei: Muduo chubanshe, 1982.

Zhou Juntao 周鈞韜. *Jin Ping Mei sucai laiyuan* 金瓶梅素材來源. Zhengzhou: Zhongzhou guji chubanshe, 1991.

Zhou Ruchang 周汝昌. *Cao Xueqin xiaozhuan* 曹雪琴小傳. Tianjin: Baihua wenyi, n.d.

Zhu Meishu 朱眉叔. "Jia Baoyu sixiang chulun 賈寶玉思想初論," *Hongloumeng xuekan* 2 (1979): 3–38.

Zhu Yixuan 朱一玄, ed. *Hongloumeng ziliao huibian* 紅樓夢資料彙編. Tianjin: Nankai daxue chubanshe, 1985.

———. *Jin Ping Mei ziliao huibian* 金瓶梅資料彙編. Tianjin: Nankai daxue chubanshe, 1985.

Zhu Yixuan 朱一玄 and Liu Yuzhen 劉毓忱, eds. *Sanguo yanyi ziliao huibian* 三國演義資料彙編. Tianjin: Baihua wenyi chubanshe, 1983.

———. *Shuihu zhuan ziliao huibian* 水滸傳資料彙編. Tianjin: Baihua wenyi chubanshe, 1983.

———. *Xiyouji ziliao huibian* 西遊記資料彙編. Tianjin: Baihua wenyi chubanshe, 1983.

Zhuangzi 莊子. *Zhuangzi* 莊子. Annotated by Guo Xiang. Shanghai: Shanghai guji chaubanshe, 1995.

Zhuangzi 莊子. *Zhuangzi yigu* 莊子譯詁. Annotated by Yang Liuqiao 楊柳橋. Shanghai: Guji chubanshe, 1991.

WORKS IN WESTERN LANGUAGES

Adams, Hazard, ed. *Critical Theory since Plato*. San Diego, CA: Harcourt Brace, 1971.

Allen, Walter. *The English Novel: A Short Critical History*. New York: E. P. Dutton, 1954.

Aristotle. *Poetics*. In Adams, *Critical Theory since Plato*, 47–66.

Audi, Robert, ed. *The Cambridge Dictionary of Philosophy*. Cambridge: Cambridge University Press, 1995.

Auerbach, Erich. *Mimesis: The Representation of Reality in Western Culture*. Garden City, NY: Doubleday, 1957.

Bakhtin, M. M. *The Dialogic Imagination: Four Essays*. Austin: University of Texas Press, 1981.

———. "Epic and Novel." In Hoffman and Murphy, *Essentials of the Theory of Fiction*, 48–69.

Barnes, Djuna. *Nightwood : The Original Version and Related Drafts*. Normal, IL: Dalkey Archive Press, 1995.

Barthes, Roland. *Elements of Semiology*. New York: Hill and Wang, 1967.

———. *Image-Music-Text*. Translated by Stephen Heath. New York: Hill and Wang, 1977.

———. *Mythologies*. Translated by Annette Lavers. New York: Noonday Press, 1972.

———. *The Pleasure of the Text*. New York: Hill and Wang, 1974.

———. *S/Z: An Essay*. Translated by Richard Miller. New York: Hill and Wang, 1974.

Baudrillard, Jean. *Selected Writings*. Translated by Mark Poster. Stanford, CA: Stanford University Press, 1988.

Bell, Clive. "The Aesthetic Hypothesis." In Feagin and Maynard. *Aesthetics*, 15–22.

Benveniste, Emile. *Problems in General Linguistics*. Coral Gables, FL: University of Miami Press, 1971.

Birch, Cyril, ed. *Anthology of Chinese Literature*. New York: Grove Press, 1966.

———, ed. *Studies in Chinese Literary Genres*. Berkeley and Los Angeles: University of California Press, 1974.

———. Foreword to Plaks, *Chinese Narrative*, ix-xii.

Bishop, John. "Some Limitations of Chinese Fiction." In *Studies in Chinese Literature*, edited by John Bishop, 239–247. Cambridge, MA: Harvard University Press, 1966.

Bloom, Harold. *The Anxiety of Influence: A Theory of Poetry*. New York: Oxford University Press, 1975.

———. *A Map of Misreading*. Oxford: Oxford University Press, 1975.

Boccaccio, Giovanni. *The Decameron*. New York: Norton, 1982.

Booth, Wayne. *The Rhetoric of Fiction*. Chicago: University of Chicago Press, 1983.

Brewitt-Tailor, C. H., trans. *Romance of the Three Kingdoms*. 2 vols. Rutland, VT: Charles E. Tuttle, 1959.

Cao Xueqin and Gao E. *The Story of the Stone*. Translated by David Hawkes and John Minford. 5 vols. Harmondsworth, England: Penguin, 1973–86.

Carroll, Lewis. *Alice's Adventure in Wonderland*. New York: Modern Library, 1925.

Cervantes, Miguel de. *Don Quixote*. London: Folio Society, 1995.

Chan, Wing-tsit, comp. and trans. *A Source Book in Chinese Philosophy*. Princeton, NJ: Princeton University Press, 1963.

Chatman, Seymour. *Story and Discourse: Narrative Structure in Fiction and Film*. Ithaca, NY: Cornell University Press, 1978.

Ch'en, Shou-yi. *Chinese Literature: A Historical Introduction*. New York: Ronald Press, 1961.

Cohan, Steven, and Linda M. Shires. *Telling Stories: A Theoretical Analysis of Narrative Fiction*. New York: Routledge, 1988.

Cohn, Dorrit. *The Distinction of Fiction*. Baltimore, MD: Johns Hopkins University Press, 1999.

Coleridge, S. T. "Biographia Literaria." In Adams, *Critical Theory since Plato*, 468–71.

Collingwood, R. G. *The Idea of History*. Reprint, London: Oxford University Press, 1980.

Cuddon, J. A. *A Dictionary of Literary Terms and Literary Theory*. Oxford: Blackwell, 1991.

Culler, Jonathan. *On Deconstruction: Theory and Criticism after Structuralism*. Ithaca: Cornell University Press, 1982.

De Bary, Wm. Theodore, comp. *Sources of Chinese Tradition*. 2 vols. New York: Columbia University Press, 1960.

Defoe, Daniel. *Robinson Crusoe*. 1719. Reprint. New York: Norton, 1975.

Deleuze, Gilles. "The Simulacrum and Ancient Philosophy." In *The Logic of Sense*. New York: Columbia University Press, 1990.

De Man, Paul. *Allegories of Reading: Figural Language in Rousseau, Nietzsche, and Proust*. New Haven, CT: Yale University Press, 1979.

———. *Blindness and Insight: Essays in the Rhetoric of Contemporary Criticism*. New York: Oxford University Press, 1971.

———. "Resistance to Theory." *Yale French Studies* 63 (1982): 3–20.

Derrida, Jacques. *Dissemination*. Chicago: University of Chicago Press, 1982.

———. *Margins of Philosophy*. Chicago: University of Chicago Press, 1983.

———. *Positions*. Chicago: University of Chicago Press, 1981.

———. *Writing and Difference*. Chicago: University of Chicago Press, 1978.

Dewoskin, Kenneth J. "On Narrative Revolution." *Chinese Literature: Essays, Articles, Reviews* 5 (1983): 29–45.

———. "The Six Dynasties *Chih-Kuai* and the Birth of Fiction." In Plaks, *Chinese Narrative*, 21–52.

Dolezel, Lubomir. *Heterocosmica: Fiction and Possible Worlds*. Baltimore, MD: Johns Hopkins University Press, 1998.

Eagleton, Terry. *After Theory*. New York: Basic Books, 2003.

———. *Literary Theory: An Introduction*. Oxford: Basil and Blackwell, 1983.

Eco, Umberto. *The Aesthetics of Chaosmos: The Middle Ages of James Joyce*. Tulsa, OK: University of Tulsa, 1982.

———. *The Open Work*. Cambridge, MA: Harvard University Press, 1989.

———. *The Role of the Reader: Explorations in the Semiotics of Texts*. Bloomington: Indiana University Press, 1979.

Eco, Umberto, et al. *Interpretation and Overinterpretation*. Cambridge: Cambridge University Press, 1992.

Egerton, Clament, trans. *The Golden Lotus*. 4 vols. London: Routledge and Kegan Paul, 1972.

Ellmann, Richard. *James Joyce*. New York: Oxford University Press, 1982.

Epstein, Maram. *Competing Discourses: Orthodoxy, Authenticity, and Engendered Meanings in Late Imperial Chinese Fiction*. Cambridge, MA: Harvard University Asian Center, 2001.

Feagin, Susan, and Patrick Maynard, eds. *Aesthetics*. Oxford: Oxford University Press, 1997.

Fodor, Nandor, and Frank Gayno. *Freud: Dictionary of Psychoanalysis*. New York: Premier Book, 1965.

Forster, E. M. *Aspects of the Novel*. Harmondsworth, England: Pelican Books, 1976.

Foucault, Michel. *The History of Sexuality*. Vol. 1. New York: Vintage Books, 1978.

———. *The Order of Things: An Archaeology of the Human Sciences*. London: Tavistock, 1970.

Fowler, Roger. *Linguistics and the Novel*. London: Methuen, 1977.

Freedman, Ralph. *The Lyrical Novel: Studies in Hermann Hesse, André Gide, and Virginia Woolf*. Princeton: Princeton University Press, 1963.

Freud, Sigmund. *Beyond the Pleasure Principle*. New York: Norton, 1961.

———. *Complete Psychological Works*. Edited by James Strachey. Standard edition. 24 vols. London: Hogarth Press, 1953–74.

———. *The Ego and the Id*. Translated by James Strachey. New York: Norton, 1960.

———. *The Freud Reader*. Edited by Peter Gay. New York: Norton, 1989.

———. *The Interpretation of Dreams*. New York: Avon Books, 1965.

———. *Introductory Lectures on Psychoanalysis*. Translated by James Strachey. New York: Norton, 1966.

———. *On Dreams*. Translated by James Strachey. New York: Norton, 1950.

———. *An Outline of Psychoanalysis*. New York: Norton, 1970.

———. *The Sexual Enlightenment of Children*. New York: Collier Books, 1963.

Frye, Northrop. *Anatomy of Criticism: Four Essays*. Princeton, NJ: Princeton University Press, 1957.

———. *Fables of Identity: Studies in Poetic Mythology*. New York: Harcourt, Brace, and World, 1963.

Ge, Liangyan. *Out of the Margins: The Rise of Chinese Vernacular Fiction*. Honolulu: University of Hawaii Press, 2001.

Gennett, Gérard. *The Archtext: An Introduction*. Berkeley and Los Angeles: University of California Press, 1992.

———. *Fiction et diction*. Paris: Seuil, 1991.

Gu, Ming Dong. "Brocade of Human Desires: The Poetics of Weaving in the *Jin Ping Mei* and Traditional Commentaries." *Journal of Asian Studies* 63, no. 2 (2004): 333–56.

———. *Chinese Theories of Reading and Writing: A Route to Hermeneutics and Open Poetics*. Albany: State University of New York Press: 2005.

———. "The Genesis and Evolution of Literary Forms: An Inquiry across Cultural Boundaries." *Tamkang Review* 27, no .4 (1997): 443–75.

———. "The *Hongloumeng* as an Open Novel: For a New Paradigm of Redology." *Monumenta Serica: A Journal of Oriental Studies* 51 (2003): 253–282.

———. "Is Mimetic Theory in Literature and Art Universal?" *Poetics Today*, 26 no. 3 (2005): 459–99.

———. "Lu Xun, Jameson, and Multiple Polysemia." *Canadian Review of Comparative Literature* 28, no. 4 (2001): 434–57.

———. "Mimetic Theory in Chinese Literary Thought." *New Literary History* 36, no. 4 (2005): 403–24.

———. "Paradox of Vision and Vision of Paradox: Ideology and Form in the *Jin Ping Mei*." *Journal of Oriental Studies* 37, no. 2 (1991): 175–203.

———. "Suggestiveness in Chinese Literary Thought: Symphony of Metaphysics and Aesthetics." *Philosophy East & West* 53, no. 4 (2003): 490–513.

———. "The Universal 'One': Toward a Common Conceptual Basis for Chinese and Western Studies." *Diacritics: A Review of Contemporary Criticism* 32, no. 2 (2002): 86–105.

———. "The Universal Significance of Frye's Theory of Fictional Modes." In O'Grady and Wang, *Northrop Frye*, 162–76.

Hall, David L., and Roger T. Ames. *Thinking from the Han: Self, Truth, and Transcendence and Western Culture*. Albany: State University of New York Press, 1998.

Hanan, Patrick. *The Chinese Short Story*. Cambridge, MA: Harvard University Press, 1973.

———. *The Chinese Vernacular Story*. Cambridge, MA: Harvard University Press, 1981.

———. "The Early Chinese Short Story: A Critical Theory in Outline." In Birch, *Studies in Chinese Literary Genres*. 299–338..

———. "The Nature of Ling Meng-ch'u's Fiction." In Plaks, *Chinese Narrative*, pp. 85–114.

———. "Sources of the *Chin P'ing Mei*." *Asia Major* 10 (1963): 23–67.

———. "The Text of the *Chin P'ing Mei*." *Asia Major* 9 (1962): 1–57.

Hawkes, David. "The Translator, the Mirror and the Dream—Some Observations on a New Theory," *Renditions* 13 (1980): 5–20.

Hegel, Robert E. *The Novel in Seventeenth-Century China*. New York: Columbia University Press, 1981.

Heidegger, Martin. *Basic Writings*. Edited by David Farrell Krell. Rev. ed. New York: Harper Collins, 1977.

———. *Early Greek Thinking*. New York: Harper and Row, 1975.

———. *Poetry, Language, Thought*. New York: Harper and Row, 1971.

Hoffman, Michael, and Patrick Murphy, eds. *Essentials of the Theory of Fiction*. Durham, NC: Duke University Press, 1988.

Holland, Norman. *The Dynamics of Literary Response*. New York: Oxford University Press, 1968.

Hsia, C. T. *The Classical Chinese Novel: A Critical Introduction*. New York: Columbia University Press, 1968.

Irwin, Richard G. *The Evolution of a Chinese Novel: Shui-hu chuan*. Cambridge, MA: Harvard University Press, 1953.

Jakobson, Roman. "Closing Statement: Linguistics and Poetics." In T. A. Sebeok. Ed. *Style in Language*, edited by T. A. Sebeok. Cambridge, MA: MIT Press, 1960.

———. *Language in Literature*. Cambridge, MA: Harvard University Press, 1987.

Jakobson, Roman, and Morris Halle. 1956. *Fundamentals of Language*. The Hague: Mouton & Co.

Jameson, Fredric. "Third-World Literature in the Era of Multinational Capitalism." *Social Text* 15 (1986): 65–88.

Joyce, James. *Finnegans Wake*. New York: Viking Press, 1939.

———. *Ulysses: The Corrected Text*. New York: Random House, 1986.

Kafka, Franz. *Letters to Felice*. New York: Schocken Books, 1973.

Kant, Immanuel. *Critique of Judgment*. In Adams, *Critical Theory since Plato*. 379–90.

Kao, Yu-kung. "Lyric Vision in Chinese Narrative Tradition: A Reading of *Hung-lou Meng* and *Ju-Lin Wai-Shih*." In Plaks, *Chinese Narrative*, pp. 227–43.

Kermode, Frank. *The Art of Telling: Essays on Fiction*. Cambridge, M.A.: Harvard University Press, 1983.

Kirk, G. S., et al. *The Presocratic Philosophers: A Critical History with a Selection of Texts*. New York: Cambridge University Press, 1963.

Korsmeyer, Carolyn. *Aesthetics: The Big Questions*. Oxford: Blackwell, 1998.

Kristeva, Julia. *Desire in Language*. New York: Columbia University Press, 1980.

———. *The Kristeva Reader*. New York: Columbia University Press.

———. *Revolution in Poetic Language*. New York: Columbia University Press, 1984.

Lacan, Jacques. *Ecrits: A Selection*. London: Tavistock, 1977.

———. *The Four Fundamental Concepts of Psycho-analysis*. London: Tavistock, 1977.

Lane, Michael. Ed. *Introduction to Structuralism*. New York: Basic Books, 1970.

Lao Tzu. *Tao Te Ching*. Translated by D. C. Lau. Harmondsworth: Penguin Books, 1962.

Lau, Joseph S. M., et al., eds. *Modern Chinese Stories and Novellas: 1919–1949*. New York: Columbia University Press, 1981.

Lawrence, D. H. *Phoenix: The Posthumous Papers of D. H. Lawrence*. Edited by Edward D. McDonald. New York: Viking Press, 1968.

Lee, Leo Ou-fan. *Voices from the Iron House: A Study of Lu Xun*. Bloomington: Indiana University Press, 1987.

Lentricchia, Frank and Thomas McLaughlin, eds. *Critical Terms for Literary Study*. Chicago: University of Chicago Press, 1990.

Levi-Strauss, Claude. *Anthropologie structurale*. Paris: Plon, 1958.

Levy, Andre. "About the Date and the First Printed Edition of the *Chin P'ing Mei*." *Chinese Literature: Essays, Articles, Reviews* 1, no. 1 (January 1979): 43–47.

Li, Wai-yee. *Enchantment and Disenchantment: Love and Illusion in Chinese Literature*. Princeton, NJ: Princeton University Press, 1993.

Lin, Shuen-fu. "Chia Po-yu's First Visit to the Land of Illusion: An Analysis of a Literary Dream in an Interdisciplinary Perspective." *Chinese Literature: Essays, Articles, Reviews* 14 (1992): 77–106.

Liu, James J. Y. *The Art of Chinese Poetry*. Chicago: University of Chicago Press, 1962.

———. *Chinese Theories of Literature*. Chicago: University of Chicago Press, 1975.

Liu Hsieh. *The Literary Mind and the Carving of Dragons*. Translated by Vincent Yu-chung Shih. Taipei: Chung Hwa Book Co., 1975.

Lu, Sheldon. *From Historicity to Fictionality: The Poetics of Chinese Narrative*. Stanford, CA: Stanford University Press, 1994.

Lu Xun [Hsun]. *A Brief History of Chinese Fiction*. Translated by Hsien-yi Yang and Glalys Yang. Peking: Foreign Languages Press, 1976.

———. *The Complete Stories of Lu Xun*. Translated by Yang Xianyi and Gladys Yang. Peking: Foreign Languages Press, 1964.

———. *Lu Xun: Selected Works*. Translated by Yang Xianyi and Gladys Yang. 4 vols. Peking: Foreign Languages Press, 1956.

———. *Old Tales Retold*. Translated by Yang Xianyi and Gladys Yang. Peking: Foreign Languages Press, 1972.

———. *Selected Stories of Lu Hsun*. New York: Norton, 1977.

Lukács, Georg. *The Theory of the Novel: A Historico-philosophical Essay on the Forms of Great Epic Literature*. Translated by Anna Bostock. Cambridge, MA: MIT Press, 1971.

Ma, Y. W. "Fiction." In Nienhauser, *Indiana Companion to Traditional Chinese Literature*, 31–48.

Ma, Y. W., and Joseph Lau, eds. *Traditional Chinese Stories and Novellas: Themes and Variations*. New York: Columbia University Press, 1978.

The Mahabharata. Rendered in English by Willliam Buck. Berkeley and Los Angeles: Univeristy of California Press, 1973..

Mair, Victor. "The Narrative Revolution in Chinese Literature: Ontological Presuppositions." *Chinese Literature: Essays, Articles, Reviews* 5 (1983): 1–22.

Martin, Wallace. *Recent Theories of Narrative*. Ithaca, NY: Cornell University Press, 1986.

McKillop, Alan Dugald. *Samuel Richardson: Printer and Novelist*. Chapel Hill: University of North Carolina Press, 1960.

Mill, John Stuart. "What Is Poetry?" In Adams, *Critical Theory Since Plato*. 536–543.

Miller, J. Hillis. "Narrative." In Lentricchia and McLaughlin, *Critical Terms for Literary Study*. 66–79.

Mitchell, W. J. T., ed. *On Narrative*. Chicago: University of Chicago Press, 1980.

———. "Representation." In Lentricchia and McLaughlin, *Critical Terms for Literary Study*. 11–22.

More, Thomas. *Utopia: A New Translation, Backgrounds, Criticism*. New York: Norton, 1975.

Murasaki, Shikibu. *The Tale of Genji*. Translated by Edward Seidensticker. New York: Alfred Knopf, 1976.

Nienhauser, William, ed. *The Indiana Companion to Traditional Chinese Literature.* Bloomington: Indiana University Press, 1986.

———. "The Origins of Chinese Fiction." In *Monumenta Serica* 38 (1988–89): 191–217.

O'Grady, Jean, and Wang Ning, eds. *Northrop Frye: Eastern and Western Perspectives.* Toronto: University of Toronto Press, 2003.

Olson, Charles. *Human Universe.* Edited by Donald Allen. New York: Grove Press, 1967.

Orwell, George. *Animal Farm: A Fairy Story.* London: Folio Society, 1988.

Owen, Stephen. *Readings in Chinese Literary Thought.* Cambridge, MA: Harvard University Press, 1992.

Passmore, John. *A Hundred Years of Philosophy.* 2nd ed. Harmondsworth, England: Penguin, 1972.

Pavel, Thomas. "Fiction and Imitation." *Poetics Today* 21, no. 3 (2000): 521–41.

Peirce, Charles Sanders. *Collected Papers.* Ed. Charles Hartshorne and Paul Weis. 8 vols. Cambridge, MA: Harvard University Press, 1931–58.

———. *Peirce on Signs.* Edited by James Hoopes. Chapel Hill: University of North Carolina Press, 1991.

———. *Philosophical Writings of Peirce.* Edited by Justus Buchler. New York: Dover, 1955.

Plaks, Andrew H. *Archetype and Allegory in the "Dream of the Red Chamber."* Princeton, NJ: Princeton University Press, 1976.

———, ed. *Chinese Narrative: Critical and Theoretical Essays.* Princeton, NJ: Princeton University Press, 1977.

———. "The Chongzhen Commentary on the *Jin Ping Mei*: Gems amidst the Dross." *Chinese Literature: Essays, Articles, Reviews* 8, nos. 1 and 2 (July 1986): 19–30.

———. "Conceptual Models in Chinese Narrative Theory." *Journal of Chinese Philosophy* 4, no. 1 (1977): 25–47.

———. *The Four Masterworks of the Ming Novel.* Princeton, NJ: Princeton University Press, 1987.

———. "Full-length *Hsiao-shuo* and the Western Novel: A Generic Reappraisal." In *China and the West: Comparative Literary Studies*, edited by William Tay et al., 163–76. Hong Kong: Chinese University Press, 1980.

Plato. *The Republic.* Cambridge: Cambridge University Press, 1963.

Porter, Deborah L. *From Deluge to Discourse: Myth, History, and the Generation of Chinese Fiction.* Albany: State University of New York Press, 1996.

Power, Arthur. *Conversations with James Joyce.* London: Millington, 1974.

Preminger, Alex, et al., eds. *The Princeton Encyclopedia of Poetry and Poetics.* Princeton, NJ: Princeton University Press, 1993.

Proust, Marcel. *A la recherche du temps perdu.* 3 vols. Paris: Gallimard, 1954.

———. *Remembrance of Things Past.* New York: Vintage Books, 1982.

Průšek, Jaroslav. "Urban Centers: The Cradle of Popular Fiction." In Cyril Birch, ed., *Studies in Chinese Literary Genres*, 259–98.

Ramayana [*King Rama's Way*]. Rendered into English by William Buck. Berkeley and Los Angeles: University of California Press, 1976.

Reed, Walter. *An Exemplary History of the Novel: The Quixotic versus the Picaresque*. Chicago: University of Chicago Press, 1981.

Richardson, Samuel. *Clarissa: or, The History of a Young Lady*. London: Folio Society, 1991.

———. *Pamela, or Virtue Rewarded*. New York: E. P. Dutton, [1955–57].

Riffaterre, Michael. *Fictional Truth*. Baltimore, MD: Johns Hopkins University Press, 1990.

Robert, Marthe. *Origins of the Novel*. Bloomington: Indiana University Press, 1980.

Rolston, David, L., ed. *How to Read the Chinese Novel*. Princeton, NJ: Princeton University Press, 1990.

———. *Reading and Writing between the Lines: Traditional Chinese Fiction Commentary and Premodern Chinese Fiction*. Stanford, CA: Stanford University Press, 1997.

Roy, David T. "The Case for T'ang Hsien-tsu's Authorship of the *Jin Ping Mei*." *Chinese Literature: Essays, Articles, Reviews* 8, nos. 1 and 2 (July 1986): 31–62.

———. "Chang Chu-p'o's Commentary on the *Chin P'ing Mei*." In Plaks, *Chinese Narrative*, 115–23.

———, trans. *The Plum in the Golden Vase*. Vols. 1 and 2. Princeton, NJ: Princeton University Press, 1993–2001.

Said, Edward. *Beginnings: Intention and Method*. New York: Basic Books, 1975.

Satyendra, Indira. "The Metaphors of the Body: The Sexual Economy in the *Chin P'ing Mei tz'u-hua*." In *Chinese Litereature: Essays, Articles, Reviews* 15 (1993): 85–97.

Saussure, Ferdinand de. *Course in General Linguistics*. London: Peter Owen, 1960.

Schaeffer, Jean-Marie. *Pourquoi la fiction?* Paris: Seuil, 1999.

Scholes, Robert. *Elements of Fiction*. Oxford: Oxford University Press, 1968.

———. "Language, Narrative, and Anti-Narrative." In Mitchell, ed., *On Narrative*. 200–8.

Scholes, Robert, and Robert Kellogg. *The Nature of Narrative*. New York: Oxford University Press, 1966.

Schorer, Mark. "Technique as Discovery." In Hoffman and Murphy, *Essentials of the Theory of Fiction*, Durham, 101–114.

Searle, John. "The Logical Status of Fictional Discourse." *New Literary History* 6 (1975): 319–32.

Sebeok, Thomas A. *A Sign Is Just a Sign*. Bloomington: Indiana University Press, 1991.

Silverman, Kaja. *The Subject of Semiotics*. New York: Oxford University Press, 1983.

Smith, Barbara H. *On the Margins of Discourse: The Relation of Literature to Language*. Chicago: University of Chicago Press, 1979.

———. "Narrative Versions, Narrative Theories." In Mitchell, *On Narrative*. 209–32.

Sterne, Lawrence. *The Life and Opinions of Tristram Shandy*. Oxford: Clarendon Press, 1983.

Suzuki, D. T., trans. *The Lankavatara Sutra, A Mahayana Text*. London: Routledge, 1932.

Tanner, Tony. *Adultery in the Novel: Contract and Transgression*. Baltimore, MD: Johns Hopkins University Press, 1979.

Todorov, Tzvetan. *The Fantastic: A Structural Approach to a Literary Genre*. Ithaca, NY: Cornell University Press, 1975.

———. *Genres in Discourse*. Cambridge: Cambridge University Press, 1990.

———. *The Poetics of Prose*. Ithaca, NY: Cornell University Press, 1977.

Waley, Arthur, trans. *The Analects of Confucius*. New York: Vintage Books, 1938.

———, trans. *The Tale of Genji*. By Lady Murasaki. New York: Modern Library, 1960.

Wang, Jing. *The Story of Stone: Intertexuality, Ancient Chinese Stone Lore and the Stone Symbolism in "Dream of the Red Chamber," "Water Margin," and the "Journey to the West."* Durham, NC: Duke University Press, 1992.

Wang, John C. Y. "Early Chinese Narrative: The *Tso-chuan* as Example." In Plaks, *Chinese Narrative*, 3–22.

Watt, Ian. *The Rise of The Novel: Studies in Defoe, Richardson and Fielding*. Berkeley and Los Angeles: University of California Press, 1960.

Widmer, Ellen and Kang-i Sung Chang, eds. *Writing Women in Late Imperial China*. Stanford, CA: Stanford University Press, 1997.

Wilhelm, Hellmut. "Notes on Chou Fiction." In *Transition and Permanence: Chinese History and Culture*. Edited by D. C. Buxbaum and F. W. Mote, 251–63. Hong Kong: Cathay Press, 1972.

Wong, Kam-ming, "Point of View, Norms, and Structure: *Hung-lou meng* and Lyrical Fiction." In Plaks, *Chinese Narrative*, 203–26.

Woolf, Virginia. "Mr. Bennett and Mrs. Brown." In Hoffman and Murphy, *Essentials of the Theory of Fiction*, 24–39.

———. *The Waves*. London: Hogarth Press, 1980.

Wordsworth, William. "Preface to the Second Edition of *Lyrical Ballads*." In Adams, *Critical Theory since Plato*. 432–43.

Wu, Hung. "Beyond Stereotypes: The Twelve Beauties in Qing Court Art and the 'Dream of the Red Chamber.'" In Widmer and Chang, *Writing Women in Late Imperial China*, 311–18.

Yang, Hsien-yi, and Gladys Yang, trans. *The Scholars*. Beijing: Foreign Language Press, 1957.

Yee, Angelina C. "Self, Sexuality, and Writing in *Hongloumeng*," *Harvard Journal of Asiatic Studies* 55, no. 2 (1995): 373–407.

Young, Edward. "Conjectures on Original Composition." In *Critical Theory since Plato*, 337–47.

Yu, Anthony C. "History, Fiction and the Reading of Chinese Narrative." *Chinese Literature: Essays, Articles, Reviews* 10 (1988): 1–19.

————, trans. *Journey to the West*. 4 vols. Chicago: University of Chicago Press, 1977–83.

————. *Rereading the Stone: Desire and the Making of Fiction in "Dream of the Red Chamber."* Princeton, NJ: Princeton University Press, 1997.

Yu, Ying-shih. "The Two Worlds of *Hunglou meng*." *Renditions*, no. 2 (1974): 5–21.

Zeitlin, Judith T. *Historian of the Strange: Pu Songling and the Chinese Classical Tale*. Stanford, CA: Stanford University Press, 1993.

Zhuangzi. *Complete Works of Chuang Tzu*. Translated by Burton Watson. New York: Columbia University Press, 1968.

Index